House of Commons

Science and Technology Committee

Forensic Science on Trial

Seventh Report of Session 2004–05

Volume II

Oral *dence*

Ordere to be

HC 96-II
Published on 29 March 2005
by authority of the House of Commons
London: The Stationery Office Limited

The Science and Technology Committee

The Science and Technology Committee is appointed by the House of Commons to examine the expenditure, administration and policy of the Office of Science and Technology and its associated public bodies.

Current membership

Dr Ian Gibson MP (*Labour, Norwich North*) (Chairman)
Paul Farrelly MP (*Labour, Newcastle-under-Lyme*)
Dr Evan Harris MP (*Liberal Democrat, Oxford West & Abingdon*)
Kate Hoey MP (*Labour, Vauxhall*)
Dr Brian Iddon MP (*Labour, Bolton South East*)
Mr Robert Key MP (*Conservative, Salisbury*)
Mr Tony McWalter MP (*Labour, Hemel Hempstead*)
Dr Andrew Murrison MP (*Conservative, Westbury*)
Geraldine Smith MP (*Labour, Morecambe and Lunesdale*)
Bob Spink MP (*Conservative, Castle Point*)
Dr Desmond Turner MP (*Labour, Brighton Kemptown*)

Powers

The Committee is one of the departmental Select Committees, the powers of which are set out in House of Commons Standing Orders, principally in SO No.152. These are available on the Internet via www.parliament.uk

Publications

The Reports and evidence of the Committee are published by The Stationery Office by Order of the House. All publications of the Committee (including press notices) are on the Internet at www.parliament.uk/s&tcom
A list of Reports from the Committee in the present Parliament is included at the back of this volume.

Committee staff

The current staff of the Committee are: Chris Shaw (Clerk); Emily Commander (Second Clerk); Alun Roberts (Committee Specialist); Hayaatun Sillem (Committee Specialist); Ana Ferreira (Committee Assistant); Robert Long (Senior Office Clerk); and Christine McGrane (Committee Secretary).

Contacts

All correspondence should be addressed to the Clerk of the Science and Technology Committee, Committee Office, 7 Millbank, London SW1P 3JA. The telephone number for general inquiries is: 020 7219 2793; the Committee's e-mail address is: scitechcom@parliament.uk

Witnesses

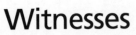

Written Memoranda

Oral evidence

Taken before the Science and Technology Committee

on Wednesday 15 December 2004

Members present:

Dr Ian Gibson, in the Chair

Dr Evan Harris
Dr Brian Iddon
Mr Robert Key

Mr Tony McWalter
Bob Spink
Dr Desmond Turner

Witnesses: **Mr Stephen Rimmer**, Director of Policing Policy, **Mr Tim Wilson**, Head of Science Policy Unit, and **Mr Mike Silverman**, Forensic Pathology, Science Policy Unit, Home Office, examined.

Q1 Chairman: Thank you very much for waiting. I am sorry, it is the end of the year and there are lots of arguments going on about various other inquiries that we are involved in. It is another day and another inquiry and you are the first, and thank you very much. It is nice to see lots of suits but no white lab coats, but I am sure some of the people here get bedecked in them now and again and are very interested in this forensic science inquiry of ours. I will let you, Tim, introduce your team first, but thank you very much for coming and my penetrating Committee will be asking you some questions which I am sure you will enjoy.
Mr Rimmer: I am Stephen Rimmer. I am director of policing policy in the Home Office. I have got responsibility for all police issues within the Home Office, including its relationships with key partners such as the Forensic Science Service.
Mr Wilson: I am Tim Wilson, the head of the Science Policy Unit, responsible for work on the transition of the FSS but also for the DNA expansion programme and forensic science and forensic pathology in general.
Mr Silverman: I am Mike Silverman. I work with Tim in the Science Policy Unit. I have in the past been an operational forensic scientist for some twelve years for the Metropolitan Police and have been a purchaser of forensic science as a scientific support manager with Kent and I have worked for a while with the Forensic Science Service in their national accounts department.

Q2 Chairman: Great. Is one of you going to answer? If you want to have three of you answering something just indicate, but we have a lot of questions and since you are first up to bat the bowling gets fast.
Mr Rimmer: I will normally kick off but my colleagues may then add to that, if that is okay.

Q3 Chairman: Okay, Stephen. Thank you. Your memorandum refers to systemic weaknesses. Are there? Is it in a bad state? Is it in a mess? Is it a shambles, or what? Give us the picture, please.
Mr Rimmer: The picture as ministers see it is that the Forensic Science Service has been a very successful trading fund.

Q4 Chairman: Who says so?
Mr Rimmer: Ministers.

Q5 Chairman: How many?
Mr Rimmer: Well, the current Home Secretary is firmly of that view.

Q6 Chairman: That is David Blunkett, who thinks you are a success. Okay.
Mr Rimmer: He thinks the Forensic Science Service is a success, yes, and that it has delivered high quality services to the Criminal Justice system over a number of years as a trading fund. However, they also are very clear that the FSS has reached its limits in terms of capability while operating as a trading fund and that there is a number of significant factors which are now starting to militate against optimum performance for the organisation. We have set those out in the evidence, but just briefly to summarise those, if I may, first of all increasingly the forensic science market is a highly competitive one and the competition is increasing year by year its market share. Secondly, as this Committee will be well aware, the technological changes are fast and evolving around issues such as DNA miniaturisation and the need to respond rapidly to those changes is not one that ministers believe the trading fund status will deliver. Thirdly, the procurement environment for the principal customer at the moment of Forensic Science Service (ie the police service and indeed the Criminal Justice system more generally) is becoming increasingly driven by requirements around best value and efficiency, notably after the Gershon Review, which has highlighted procurement as one of the key areas of requirements around efficiency in the public sector and that is entailing a huge culture change within the police service about how it views, how it deals with and contracts with major services such as forensics. Fourthly, the FSS itself, so far as ministers are concerned, badly needs a level of investment in private sector capital and expertise that trading fund status simply cannot provide and under our accounting rules will not in the foreseeable future be able to provide to liberate the Forensic Science Service to compete in that rapidly changing commercial environment, which is essential so far as

ministers are concerned. Fifthly, it would be fair to say in some areas of performance while ministers are very clear that the FSS is a success, not a failure, there are concerns around issues, notably timeliness, which is something that (as this Committee knows) has been picked up by both the NAO and the PAC and the general requirement on the system as a whole to improve the numbers of offences brought to justice reinforces in ministers' minds the need to fully equip the Forensic Science Service to deliver the best possible performance. Being a success story as an organisation clearly is not incompatible with changing over time to meet new factors and new environments.

Q7 Chairman: Are you happy with the management structure within your forensics because some people, even yourselves, have indicated and you have said so too that really there are some weaknesses there that need addressing. You are a slow, tepid bunch of people who do not get a move on with things and operate in the 21st Century, allegedly.
Mr Rimmer: That is absolutely not the Home Office's position.

Q8 Chairman: Of course you would say that, but some people think that. How are you going to allay that fear?
Mr Rimmer: Well, there is no doubt that part of the challenge about moving to a Government Owned Company in the next few months is to determine the capabilities of the current management. That is clearly part of the process and that will be done rigorously.

Q9 Chairman: Tell me more about that. I mean, everybody says that but nothing happens. That is our experience. What are you doing? Are you appointing new people, are you sacking people?
Mr Rimmer: Okay. I will ask Tim in a moment to add to this. The most important thing we have done in the last few months—and I am conscious of him sitting there so I will try not to embarrass him—is that the ministers have selected a new non-executive chairman of the FSS about six months ago, something like that, Bill Griffiths, with a strong track record both in private and public sector operations and he has huge confidence from ministers to lead the organisation through major change. Now, it clearly is not only a judgment for him and his non-executives but we will be one of the elements of that process. I will ask Tim to broaden it out, but one of the key elements of that process that you focused on from our perspective is the judgments of the non-executives in how far and how significant the changes are that need to be made within the executive team. That is clearly a key role for the non-executives and for the chairman in particular, but there are other dimensions that Tim might want to add to.
Mr Wilson: We are working with the Shareholder Executive, which is taking a role in respect of Government owned entities across many departments, looking at the corporate governance structure of the FSS, moving from an accounting

officer led body to a body which functions under the leadership of a corporate board and works in a more commercially focused way in terms of its strategic and business planning and the professionalisation of its functions.

Q10 Chairman: Have you got business people on that board?
Mr Wilson: The FSS already has a main board member who is not a forensic scientist and this is one of the issues for the coming months working with Bill Griffiths and the shareholder executive to look at the competences of main board members against the new structure.

Q11 Mr Key: So that is a no? Let us be clear, that is no, he does not have industrial experience?
Mr Wilson: There is no one with industrial experience on the main board, no, amongst the executive directors.
Dr Turner: I am the proud owner of several tee shirts which say, "I told you so." One of them relates to air traffic control and you may remember the saga of the air traffic control partial privatisation (or PPP as Government likes to call it).
Mr Key: You mean "Our air is not for sale"?

Q12 Dr Turner: "Our air is not for sale," yes, that is the one, except that you guys would have sold it completely! But I do seem to remember that it immediately ran into trouble and had to be bailed out by the Government because the private investment just did not materialise. Now, how confident are you that any partial privatisation of the FSS would not run into similar difficulties?
Mr Rimmer: There is a number of dimensions to that. First of all—

Q13 Chairman: You can start by saying yes or no! Just say no and then try and defend it.
Mr Rimmer: How confident are we? We are confident. I mean, I have to make it clear the Government does not use the term "partial privatisation", they deliberately use the term public private partnership because the Government will continue to have a significant stake in the future of the FSS and I hope that is clear in the evidence and it is important to emphasise that. As far as the investment profile is looking at the moment—and Tim may wish to add to this—our business advisers and ourselves have been already in significant discussions through the shareholder executive and other sources with a wide range of investors and there is no doubt that there is very significant interest in a wide range of the business community about the capabilities and the opportunities facing this organisation. Generally it seems to us out there that there is a general belief amongst potential investors in the intellectual capital on which the FSS is built, the fact that it has a very significant share of a growing market.

Q14 Chairman: Is that the City of London or is it the Hull City Council, or what?

Mr Rimmer: No, it includes significant investment bodies. We cannot go into details because this is all commercially confidential discussion at the moment.

Q15 Chairman: Well, that did not take long. The first five minutes and we are into commercial secrets. Right. Okay.

Mr Rimmer: Well, that is the position we are in. The level of interest in the FSS is significant. As I say, the recognition about their role in an expanding market is significant and of course there are going to be risks in moving towards a public private partnership but I would say at this stage the level of interest is, if anything, greater than we had anticipated, but Tim may wish to add to that.

Q16 Dr Turner: Are you then saying that commercial investors can see a good return on this, i.e. a profit?

Mr Rimmer: Well, of course that is one of their criteria.

Q17 Dr Turner: So how do you think this is going to reflect on the prices that police forces are going to have to pay for their investigations?

Mr Rimmer: One of the critical issues about the Government remaining a significant player in the future of the FSS—and bear in mind, as I am sure you know, we are not going straight into a public private partnership, we are going to be testing out how, as a Government Owned Company the FSS operates when that milestone is reached sometime next year. But in terms of the Government's role one of its absolutely critical responsibilities is to sort out an effective contractual framework to enable police forces, who at the moment basically do not operate on a contractual basis with the FSS, which leads to all sorts of issues and inefficiencies—that that framework is appropriate for all the interested parties, which includes the Government and ultimately the criminal justice system.

Mr Wilson: If I could also pick up one of the previous questions as well, please, NATS raised issues, and I hope that Government has learned from the lessons of NATS, particularly the risks involved and the kind of processes that we have put in place now to assess the risk before we proceed to a stage to take into account the criticisms of transactions like that made particularly by the PAC. In the case of interest in the FSS, there will be no move to the market unless we are sure there is a substantial interest in the market. Also, in taking forward this project we are looking at value for money in two senses; value for money from the potential proceeds from selling a stake in the FSS but also the overriding value for money in terms of the purchase of forensic science services by the police. We know that market and the services the police need will need investment. It requires equity to support that investment. That costs money[1] and it is a question of getting the right balance so that we obtain value for money with the police getting

modern technology which enables detections to increase and to use police manpower more efficiently.

Q18 Mr McWalter: Your outline business case says that the FSS as it is currently structured is vulnerable to a loss of business for a number of reasons and a crucial element of that is it is a labour-intensive business and it has got as a result very high fixed costs. That is a very negative way of putting what you have just put positively as the FSS has got a substantial intellectual capital. I mean, the outline business case actually is pretty clear. That is an encumbrance and they want to get rid of it and smash the thing to pieces because it is too expensive compared with these lean commercial organisations which do not have this incubus.

Mr Rimmer: No, that is not a fair reflection at all of the outline business case. The outline business case is there absolutely to assess a whole range of strengths and weaknesses of the organisation and it highlights a significant number of strengths as well. Ministers are absolutely clear—and they have said this publicly on a number of occasions—that they do not see this process at all as leading to the dismembering, as it were, of the FSS.

Q19 Mr McWalter: In that case why is the outline business case not saying that that is something that is a real problem and you want to get rid of it? Why does it say instead that that is something which it is absolutely vital that it be retained because of the expertise and knowledge that that incorporates? That, by the way, would destroy, as far as I can see, the key argument really in the outline business case.

Mr Wilson: May I come back on that point, please. In some respects the FSS is two businesses. There is a high volume of commoditised analytic business that has been driven very much by the expansion in the use of DNA in recent years and the FSS and its competitors have very successfully commoditised much of that work while maintaining high standards. There is a huge intellectual capital, though, in the business on its professional case work, which is added value case work which requires people capable of taking a very holistic view of the issues that arise in a police investigation. That kind of experience is something which needs to be cherished because we have some of the most capable professional forensic scientists in the world. Most of them are in the FSS; some of them are in another organisation also providing services to the police.

Q20 Mr McWalter: Well, you are either going to sack people or you are not and if you are going to sack people to make this organisation leaner and more competitive then you should come clean and say so with the consequences that that would involve; or you are going to leave the people in place, in which case the case for this radical change, I think, seems to be very poorly made.

Mr Rimmer: I am sorry, that seems to me to be based on a false premise that the FSS is locked in some sort of time warp where people are not going to have to—

---

[1] *Note by the witness:* This point should have been more accurately expressed: "In both the public and private sectors there has to be an adequate return on equity."

Q21 Mr McWalter: No, not at all.

Mr Rimmer: Well, it is because the FSS has already had to make major restructuring, major reductions as a result of the competitive pressures they are already under and the whole purpose—and this is why ministers are pushing forward on this, it is not on any sort of basis of ideology—is to enable the FSS to compete more effectively in the future so that people working within it can have a fulfilling and rewarding career rather than get slowly over time dismantled because the commercial environment within which police forces are operating is going to look for business elsewhere.

Mr McWalter: In an environment where police budgets are constantly under pressure the FSS has suffered enormously from the 1990 changes. That is the reality, is it not?

Q22 Mr Key: Mr Rimmer, you told us in your written evidence that the Forensic Science Service is seeing highly trained staff now leaving the FSS to join competitors. Why are they leaving?

Mr Rimmer: Well, I do not know the exact numbers and I think you may wish to speak to the FSS itself. We are not here to micro manage the FSS. There are relatively small numbers in recent months who have left the FSS and there is always a turnover of staff. It is an issue which within the Home Office we are going to keep a very close eye on because it could obviously indicate a degree of organisational resilience or lack of it depending on what that level of turnover is, but I would not want to say that at the moment there is any strong evidence that there is a great drift of people leaving the FSS.

Q23 Mr Key: I am sorry, but the strong evidence is in the evidence from the FSS. Surely if you are managing this project in the Home Office you cannot say, "Well, it's nothing to do with me, Guv, it's only the FSS who are saying this," because surely they are the very people who have told us, "Highly trained staff are now leaving the FSS to join competitors," and the Home Office argument is therefore, "We've got to join the competitors." Is the answer not just to make conditions better for your existing highly trained staff?

Mr Rimmer: No. The issues around turnover are always going to be there in a competitive environment. I am not sure whether it is in the evidence, but I know that the FSS also are able to get people coming back from the commercial environment as well as losing them out. I do not see why that at the moment is an issue of major concern about the transformation process. I am not saying it is nothing to do with us. What I am saying is we need to keep an eye on that in general terms but we are not going to be panicked into individual cases of people moving on which may or may not have something to do with terms and conditions around the FSS or competitors.

Q24 Mr Key: We are told, too, that the Home Office's new headquarters under construction will not be able to accommodate all the staff as originally planned. What will happen to the FSS staff? Will they manage to be fitted in to the new headquarters or will there not be room for them?

Mr Wilson: It has never been intended that the FSS staff should be located in the Home Office. Their premises are entirely separate from 2 Marsham Street. Could I just comment on the previous question. There is an issue about the rigidity of pay and conditions of service as a trading fund because it is inherently part of Civil Service terms and conditions, which reduces the flexibility in a competitive market for seriously required professional staff and I am sure that Dr Werrett and his colleagues will say something about that. They have conducted exiting views by staff leaving. I do not think that pay and conditions is the sole issue from what I understand, but they will no doubt correct me if I am wrong. Some of the uncertainty about the future direction of the organisation is another issue and clearly with expanding markets people may see opportunities by changing organisations that they see as a challenge which they want to rise to.

Q25 Mr Key: What would be the net cost of developing the PPP? In other words, any organisation which is being developed to take account of the new technology is going to cost more even if it were to stay within the Home Office under the existing arrangements?

Mr Wilson: Yes.

Q26 Mr Key: But what is the difference between that cost and the projected cost of the new PPP?

Mr Wilson: The new PPP in terms of transaction costs is currently estimated to be about £3 or £4 million. That partly depends on how the transaction is managed, the number of stages in the transaction, the timetable for the transaction and market conditions at the time of any change.

Q27 Chairman: Where are these figures available, this perspective?

Mr Wilson: This is a kind of figure that I mentioned when I toured the seven FSS lab laboratory sites and was asked the same question by members of staff.

Q28 Dr Turner: So that is the amount of money that you expect to receive for the transaction?

Mr Wilson: No, that is a transaction cost.

Q29 Dr Turner: Can we be clear what the £3 or £4 million means.

Mr Wilson: The transaction cost of employing advisers specifically for—

Q30 Dr Turner: Just the consultancy services?

Mr Wilson: The consultancy services, yes, and our own internal management costs of that process.

Q31 Mr Key: Please could you explain a little more about the nature of this market that is developing and which you are having to compete with. Who are the competitors?

Mr Wilson: There are two organisations that have a significant share in the market, Forensic Alliance, who undertake professional case work and with an associate company undertake DNA analysis and other analytical services. They have about 8% of market share compared with about 83% of the contested market held by the FSS. There is also LGC Limited. That was previously the laboratory of the Government chemist. They have extensive experience in analytical work and are prominent in DNA analysis. I think Mr Silverman would add something more from direct experience of people active in the market.

Mr Silverman: I would also include the police themselves, I think, because they have the greater proportion of the forensic market at the moment. They do most of their own fingerprinting, they do screening within forces and I would suspect that if the market was appropriate and better value could be obtained they would see that they would do more forensic science.

Q32 Mr Key: Is the competition all Government owned, in the public sector, or are they PPPs or purely private companies?

Mr Wilson: They are two private companies which are backed by venture capitalists.

Q33 Dr Iddon: Could I just intervene, Chairman? I have worked with the Greater Manchester Police for thirty days on the police parliamentary scheme and I have visited Bradford Park, which is an amazing establishment, quite frankly. If you go ahead with this PPP and the police are forced to buy from the PPP at a higher price, as Des Turner pointed out, would you not drive more and more of the work in the direction of the police because it would be in their best interests to do it cheaply in-house?

Mr Wilson: Best value legislation requires that the police have to critically examine whether to make or buy a function and I do not think anyone would underestimate, following the Gershon Report, the drive within the police on this to achieve economies. The Home Office is supporting the police service in the creation of a centre for procurement excellence as part of an agenda which requires them to achieve 3% savings over the next three years, 1.5% of which are cashable. So that combined with the best value legislation creates a tremendous pressure on the police to ensure that they are achieving best value. As far as forensic services undertaken in-house and what they buy from external providers, the police need to look collectively at the most sensible way forward in terms of how they source their services in order to get the most competitive prices while maintaining integrity on which evidential standards rely and quality assurance so that the forensic intelligence that they are making use of for the purpose of detection is actually up to the mark.

Mr Rimmer: As well as those pressures on the police, the Government is clearly anticipating that the commercial environment will become increasingly competitive. Those proportions that Tim has outlined are very fast-growing. The FSS has lost about 10% of the market share in the last three years.

As long as there are parameters around how that competitive environment operates (which is why I go back to the contractual framework of the FSS because that is one of the key leaders to ensure that happens) then the Government welcomes that, not least because it will dovetail with the police's own requirements to manage price in a cost-efficient way. So those two elements, the pressures on the police to deliver best value and the growing commercial competitive environment from the Government's perspective, should dovetail.

Q34 Bob Spink: Given that this is the only country in the world that is going this route of PPP for its forensic science service, there are two little areas I want to explore. First of all, how do you maintain public confidence, particularly the confidence of juries, given that forensic science is taking a massively increasing importance in the criminal justice system?

Mr Rimmer: Tim will add to this. That is an absolutely central objective for ministers to maintain and build on that public confidence and of course already juries are looking at evidence which has had the involvement of those commercial providers. What matters is obviously the quality threshold of what is being provided through the criminal justice system and how that impacts on the evidence that is presented to juries and courts. There is nothing in the process of me being the FSS to PPP that from a Government perspective is incompatible with maintaining that focus on the delivery of quality services to juries and courts. Tim may want to elaborate on how we are going to do that.

Mr Wilson: May I please split the question in two. I think that maintaining the integrity of forensic science is critical irrespective of whether the organisation doing the forensic science is, as it were, owned by Government or in private hands. This is a central issue for the police. Whichever way the market develops the police—and they may well be giving evidence themselves later—firmly expect to see adequate arrangements in place to regulate quality and that is part of the new procurement structure that we will be putting in place. For its part the Government is supporting independent quality within forensic science through its support for the Council for the Registration of Forensic Practitioners. Many FSS staff are so registered. Similarly, we have engaged in a major programme of reform and modernisation with forensic pathology where there have been similar issues arising, although many forensic pathologists are from the NHS and universities. So I think this cuts across where they come from. In terms of international comparisons, I am not a forensic scientist but I think that our standards of integrity and quality assurance bear comparison with anywhere in the world and we should be rightly proud of that. I do not think that that will be lost sight of. Where forensic science is expanding most rapidly in terms of government funding, the United States, they are very much following a mixed economy approach and this is something we have seen in this country because of the tremendous growth of e-forensics (in which I am not directly involved) that would not have happened without the capability of working with private ITC companies in order to interrogate computers and the like, particularly in cases of child abuse. So the US is very much going forward on a mixed economy. I discovered the other month that this is also the pattern for Lander in Germany, where there is a process in some of the federal states there of putting their DNA analytical work out to tender to either privately or publicly, or academically managed laboratories. The practice varies apparently from area to area. Sometimes it is only the state laboratories who are working at capacity. But as forensic science changes, particularly as e-forensics become more significant and as demand for forensic science grows as we can see the impact forensic science can have on detections, it seems inconceivable that we can go forward without some kind of mixed economy. I think the issue is for the police as customers and users of forensic science to remain very firmly in control, to operate in a very unified manner and to ensure that they are getting the standards that they require.

Q35 Bob Spink: Tim has just said that it is essential that we move forward with some kind of mixed economy, so I come to my second part of this question. Given the growing importance of forensics and given that we are the only country to adopt this model, do you have a plan B if this model does not work?
Mr Rimmer: Can we be clear about this. The Government has set out a direction of travel where the presumption is that we will move to a public private partnership.

Q36 Chairman: It has not got through Parliament yet. Will it need changes? You are saying it is irrevocable. I do not believe that. Convince me it is.
Mr Wilson: The legislative change is an Order to wind up the trading fund.
Mr Rimmer: Of course there will be parliamentary scrutiny throughout this process. Part of that process, though, is to test out very rigorously what will happen in terms of a transition to a Government Owned Company and the Home Secretary has, I think, already made it clear to MPs that he wants to test that model, as it were, out very rigorously. The analysis that we have had to date, both from the independent McFarland Review and the subsequent work done through the business place suggests strongly that there are greater advantages to have in maximising the flexibilities that PPP would offer. But the Home Secretary is very clear that he will only reach that point when the Government Owned Company model (for want of a better term) has been fully tested and that is the sort of step by step, if you like, evidence based approach he is taking. He is not saying, "I'm doing this whatever else happens," and in a sense therefore there is not any plan B because each step of the process will be based on an assessment about what is in the best interests both of the FSS as an organisation but obviously the wider criminal justice system. In particular, there will be some very rigorous tests, terms and conditions

precedent, around which any move to PPP ultimately will not be agreed by Government because that is the basis on which there will be transparency about moving it forward.

Q37 Dr Turner: I want to ask about the interim stage that is hypothesised, the publicly owned company or GovCo. How long do you anticipate that that particular stage would take? How long would it have to operate as a Government Owned Company, a publicly owned company, before you consider that it was time to move on to PPP? What would happen, for instance, if the FSS as a publicly owned company was operating very happily, competing very nicely, thank you, and there was actually no particular reason to involve the private sector?
Mr Rimmer: Well, Tim will wish to answer this. The Home Secretary is shortly going to be writing to MPs following a very useful meeting he had last month to set out his expectations at this time and there will be alongside that a parliamentary statement to set out his expectations about timescales moving into a Government Owned Company and to respond precisely to your point about his expectations around the minimum length of time it will be likely to operate before final decisions around a PPP are taken. I genuinely cannot give you the precise time yet because he is still looking at the paperwork literally as we speak, although he is still keen to get something out before the recess on that. But he is very clear that the GovCo status needs to work through in sufficient time to demonstrate whether at this stage the analysis around the flexibilities that GovCo does not appear to provide, around things such as procurement—he wants the time to be sufficient to test out whether (a) that analysis is correct (ie that those flexibilities really are not there under GovCo status), and (b) if they are not there whether that materially affects the performance of the FSS.

Q38 Dr Turner: This seems to be starting from the assumption that a GovCo will not provide everything that is needed.
Mr Rimmer: Yes.

Q39 Dr Turner: So that is setting up the GovCo to fail, is it not?
Mr Rimmer: No, it is absolutely not setting out to fail. He is quite clear that he wants it tested out in its own terms but he is responding to the independent report from Robert McFarland which, as far as he is concerned, no one has yet given conclusive evidence why this would not be the case, that the flexibilities that will enable the FSS to optimise its performance in a commercial environment would be much more workable through a PPP model than a GovCo, or indeed any other model.

Q40 Dr Turner: But surely the only things that matter are its management and its capacity to invest?
Mr Rimmer: Yes, and—

Q41 Dr Turner: Is there a reason why a GovCo cannot do that just as well as a PPP?

Mr Rimmer: Yes. There are significant issues around investment.

Q42 Dr Turner: Well, I think you will have to justify it. I think that is the point.

Mr Rimmer: Yes. Tim may want to add to that.

Mr Wilson: It is not the case that the GovCo would be established to fail because the Government would not envisage putting a failed organisation out to the market as a PPP. The policy is very much based on recognition that trading fund status, as the FSS is now, is inadequate in order to face the changing competition that it faces. There are going to be very clear objectives for GovCo which will result in a transformation in the management and strategic direction of the business. There remains an issue beyond the changes that one can achieve in GovCo about access to investment because as a Government Owned Company it will still be subject to investment via the Home Office within the Home Office departmental expenditure limits and competing with resources from that set pool rather than being able to access money commercially. If there are potential alternatives to that which emerge in the meantime that is something that the Government may want to consider—

Chairman: We are really running out of time so we are going to have to be really short and sharp with our questions and our answers. Bob, are you finished, because I want to get Evan and Brian in? They have got questions on some other aspects. We want to try and get as much evidence from you as we can in this session.

Q43 Dr Harris: Do you see the need for a regulator to oversee the development of the forensic services market and what form might such a regulator take and what powers would it have? I know that is a big question but if you could, as the Chairman says, be as succinct as you can.

Mr Wilson: Yes, and we have a model in the custodian of the DNA database, which is explained in our memorandum, but we can give you supplementary evidence if you wish.

Chairman: Please do, yes.

Q44 Dr Harris: That is a model within the service, but are you saying that that would be able to guarantee adherence to technical standards in the private sector across the whole range of forensic services?

Mr Wilson: Yes, and using the leverage of the police as customers and CPS and people like Customs & Excise as customers for setting the quality standards that providers need to work to, and other issues such as sharing forensic intelligence that individual providers acquire which needs to be shared across police force boundaries.

Q45 Dr Harris: That would include laboratory accreditation?

Mr Wilson: Yes.

Q46 Dr Harris: So are you saying that is an alternative and therefore there is no role for an expanded Council for the Registration of Forensic Practitioners who are already doing the regulation, as you know, of individual practitioners. Do you see them as having any expanded role in this structure?

Mr Wilson: I see advantage in the Council sticking to its existing remit, which is independently validating the professional competency of individuals, irrespective of for whom they work, whereas that may be an issue which could be taken into account in the procurement framework, which may require providers to have a certain percentage of people, for example, who are registered or going through the process of applying for registration. There needs to be a raft about quality of accreditation, about the processes followed in the laboratories and the integrity with which the laboratories are managed.

Q47 Dr Harris: You could set that percentage, whatever it was at the moment, on average. So what you are saying is you are not moving towards a system where it would be a requirement that all those people doing the sort of work we are talking about would either have or be moving under supervision towards that accreditation?

Mr Wilson: That is a long-term ambition, I think, of the Council and the Government to see registration. The issue has been how we can encourage accreditation of individuals without severely paralysing the criminal justice system, because I think at the moment about a third of potential individuals are qualified for accreditation (I will check my facts and come back if there is wrong)[2] and there is pressure on the Council to accredit people in quite different fields, in civil law, domestic law as well as criminal justice.

Q48 Dr Harris: In respect of regulation of prices, would you just leave prices to the open market or would you consider putting a cap on prices for core services, given the pressures the police say they are under and are under?

Mr Wilson: I think this will be more a process of the police acting as an intelligent customer, pooling information about market conditions and seeking to ensure—particularly through more consolidated purchasing, increasingly perhaps on a regional rather than a force by force basis—better control over the market and better management of the market.

Q49 Dr Harris: What about this question of the Forensic Science Service being a provider of last resource and forcing it to do that? How do you envisage that playing in the market and how would you compensate them? Has the thinking been done?

---

[2] *Note by the witness:* The CFRFP have advised the witness that they estimate between 30–40% of experts (the proportion varies for each specialism) are currently accredited.

Mr Wilson: We are beginning to develop our thinking on that. A new group has been established which is tripartite, led by ACPO, APA and the Home Office, which will be grasping that issue. It is very important that the FSS is not disadvantaged economically by the cost of free riders, by people relying on the FSS as a provider of last resort. That has to be properly remunerated in a way which corresponds to value for money.

Q50 Dr Harris: There is a couple of key questions that we have not covered on public confidence because I think this is essential. Firstly, do you envisage international companies being able to compete in the UK market, or indeed—I do not know if you covered this earlier—would you partner in the PPP with a foreign-owned, foreign-run company?
Mr Wilson: Forensic science is already international. Much of the IPR is owned by US companies and there is US investment in the UK forensic science market already.

Q51 Dr Harris: So that is a "No", you do not see a problem?
Mr Wilson: As long as we are regulating entry into the market in terms of quality assurance and integrity standards through ACPO indicating very clearly the conditions for trade, I think that is something which can be managed in a way which does not conflict with international procurement law. The obverse of that coin is the opportunity for the UK, which has a competitive advantage in forensic science, to actually take its services elsewhere.

Q52 Dr Harris: But there are some security issues, are there not, around security clearance?
Mr Wilson: Yes.

Q53 Dr Harris: Do you envisage there being security clearance rolled out into the private sector and do you think that will maintain public confidence, because it only takes one mole to be unveiled and that might be a problem for your political masters?
Mr Wilson: Well, this is an issue which has to be faced in quite a lot of engagement with private sector providers in areas such as e-forensics already and a whole range of Government services where private contractors are undertaking managing sensitive information.

Q54 Dr Harris: Yes. That is why we do not contract out the Anti-Terrorism Squad. There might be a reason not to do it.
Mr Wilson: But the management of the Criminal Records[3]—
Mr Rimmer: I think there is a general point here about the fact that this Government has no intention whatsoever of sort of cutting an umbilical cord between itself and either the FSS as an organisation or in terms of the general impact of forensics on public confidence. Of course ministers are well aware

that ultimately those questions will be for them. We cannot plan for every particular eventuality in that context but we need to ensure we have got a framework that enables ministers not only to take account of public confidence issues but clearly to be able to intervene where necessary. Now, I do not think they envisage needing to intervene in any particular circumstance around the examples you have given because they have confidence that the contractual basis and the security vetting processes will sort that out. But if on that or any other front they thought there were genuine public confidence issues then they are clearly going to regard themselves as having a direct role in resolving any concerns.

Q55 Dr Harris: In an earlier question you claimed that the Government is taking an evidence-based approach, but then you described what was not an evidence-based approach based on research, you described a step by step approach, saying, "We'll take it one step at a time and check." I think those are different things and I would like to ask what research you have done into the development of the FSS as a PPP and as to how that will affect public confidence.
Mr Rimmer: There have been two key processes at work. Firstly, the independent McFarland Review, which I do not know if you have had a chance to look at but it has looked very carefully at the status of the work of the FSS, the roles of other competitors, the market and a whole range of potential models.

Q56 Dr Harris: We have only had access to the executive summary, so that is not published research as I would understand it. It is not research and it is not published.
Mr Rimmer: Well, the summary gives you at least, I hope, a flavour of how rigorous that process was. Since then, of course, with the outline business case in particular we have been looking to extract all the relevant information in a way which is genuinely objective and evidence-based and I do think the step by step approach—of course it can mean different things in respect of research, but it acknowledges the fact that we have got to keep an eye on what is happening to a rapidly evolving commercial environment.

Q57 Dr Harris: My last question. My colleague asked earlier whether you had learned anything from previous PPP experiences and an equivalent essential service might be NATS. Your answer was, and I wrote it down, "Well, we'll learn lessons from NATS." Is the lesson ever, "Don't do it"?
Mr Rimmer: Yes, absolutely, and what the outline business case covers very rigorously, in my view, is a set of issues which are surfaced when you look at cases of successful and unsuccessful or aborted PPPs. We have, I think, something like fifteen or sixteen criteria, as it were, for assessing whether PPP is the right model to deliver high quality forensic services in this context and the conditions precedent, which I referred to earlier, will reflect—and I hope in

---

[3] *Note by the witness:* Bureau involves a public private partnership.

a very transparent way because we think in the New Year we will be able to get a summary of the conditions precedent out in the public domain even before we go into GovCo—we will be setting out clearly what are the criteria against which we will be testing whether PPP is the right model or not.

Q58 Dr Iddon: Assuming that the FSS has some IPR, who will benefit from exploitation of that in the PPP?
Mr Wilson: This is an issue that we are looking at jointly with ACPO and APA in order that the police do not find themselves in the position of paying twice. Some IPR will be held by the FSS but IPR which could have a monopolistic impact, particularly things such as national data reference collection such as the National Database, will be very firmly held within the public sector. That was announced by Hazel Blears back in January.

Q59 Dr Iddon: I am worried about blue sky research which is long-term. What will be the impact of a PPP on that kind of long-term research?
Mr Wilson: I hope that it means we will be able to do more research of that kind in the UK and the IPR will remain in the UK. The other week I saw some face recognition research being undertaken by the University of Sheffield, funded by the American Government, the IPR rights of which will go to America. There is no one in the UK able to fund that research.

Q60 Dr Iddon: In order to stimulate research would the Government be willing to put more money into R&D?
Mr Rimmer: Can I answer that not least by flagging our overall science and technology strategy up. We have limited resources on R&D and obviously the climate for expansion in resource terms is difficult at the moment, but I know ministers will look very seriously at issues around central support on R&D, not least because this strategy, which I hope Members have had a chance to read, is very much an attempt to try and encapsulate futures thinking around research and development needs right across the piece, and that includes the FSS as part of that strategic overview but so too is the general market in forensics. This provides, we hope with increasing

impact, a sense of priorities given the limited resources that we will want to put into it in R&D terms.

Q61 Dr Iddon: How will the Government prevent a single company exploiting something coming out of the PPP? Obviously competition is a way of keeping prices down, but if we have a monopoly supplier then that is going in the opposite direction.
Mr Wilson: I think we have found ourselves in that position already in terms of some of the things the police use. What we need to do—and this is something we are discussing with the police—is move increasingly to output specifications based on clear universal scientific and QA standards which then a range of competitors can provide rather than developing a single solution and then find that police business processes get locked into a single source.

Q62 Dr Iddon: I have one last question. Forensic science is rapidly taking over from pure science in universities. Chemistry departments are closing; forensic science departments are opening. I am not sure that is a good thing but we can debate that with other witnesses. Would you be willing to stimulate (as the EPSRC has) research in the forensic science area in the universities?
Mr Wilson: We are already working with the Council in terms of identifying projects of interest to the Government and we feed into their decisions, hopefully in a positive way.

Q63 Chairman: Thank you very much. It is a bit rushed, I know, but very valuable as a start. Could I ask you, Steve, as a last question when we can expect a statement in this arena now, forensic science?
Mr Rimmer: Hopefully before the recess.

Q64 Chairman: You have got two days.
Mr Rimmer: Early next week, we hope.

Q65 Chairman: So we should be here on Monday to hear it, should we?
Mr Rimmer: It will be a written statement, not an oral statement.

Q66 Chairman: It will not be a leak to the *Guardian*, will it?
Mr Rimmer: I have absolutely no comment on that.
Chairman: Thank you very much indeed and all the best for the holiday season. Thank you for coming.

Witnesses: **Dr Dave Werrett**, Chief Executive, and **Mr Bill Griffiths**, Non-Executive Chairman, Forensic Science Service, examined.

Q67 Chairman: Dr Werrett and Bill Griffiths, thank you very much for coming. I do not know if you heard what was going on in the last session.
Dr Werrett: I was listening intently, Chairman.

Q68 Chairman: I will bet you were. You did not fall asleep. Good. Thank you very much for coming and helping us. You are second up and the questions will be orientated around different things but some of them will be similar. Let me start with the first one

about the Sleepy Hollow effect in the FSS. What have you got to say about that, that you are not commercially orientated enough, and so on. You have heard all that stuff. What are you doing to address it? How is the management structure? How do you feel?
Dr Werrett: If I could start and then I will hand it back to my chairman. I would of course dispute it completely and we are not a Sleepy Hollow. I think I can confidently say in terms of forensic science that

we lead the world in this country and the Forensic Science Service has been instrumental in leading the world. I could give you a history of things that I have done over the 30 years within the Forensic Science Service that I have been there, and that has been through rigorous investment, business cases and very good programme control of projects and delivery.

Q69 Chairman: Why is all this coming up now, Dr Werrett? Why is this suddenly a big issue? Is it just because of the PPP?

Dr Werrett: I do not think it is suddenly a big issue. If you look at the history of this, in 1990–91 the Forensic Science Service started to charge for its services. The basic problem was that more service was required by police forces than the Forensic Science Service could possibly supply and so we decided to let the market decide how big the Forensic Science Service should be. In 1991 we had a turnover of about 20 million; we now have a turnover of 147 million. If I could return to the first part of your question—

Q70 Bob Spink: Just before Dr Werrett does that, he said that we lead the world now. Can he be confident that we will be leading the world in 10 years after this change?

Dr Werrett: I think the development of the marketplace is such that to continue to lead the world we need more commercial freedoms in which to operate. The latest innovation and project that we are carrying out is a multi-national project. It is a huge project involving 10 to 12 companies and it would have been greatly facilitated if we could have acted in a commercial way. The problem with Government procurement rules is that you have to not only run competitive tenders on a compulsory basis but you have to declare to the world what you are about to do through OJEC and companies which are on the verge of breakthroughs and who want to liaise and trade with you do not particularly want you advertising what you want to do next.

Bob Spink: Okay. Thank you.

Q71 Chairman: Carry on. You wanted to briefly finish off.

Dr Werrett: Yes. Before I hand over to Bill, I would just like to say that for the last several years now we have run virtually as a commercial company with accrual accounts. We charge for everything we do. Our governance structure is similar to—well, it is modelled on Higgs. We consulted with the Institute of Directors only yesterday and our governance structure is as it is with Higgs. We have a main board with a majority of non-executives on it, we have a development and remuneration committee, we have audit committees, and so on. We run effectively like a commercial company, but I will leave it to my chairman to make that judgment.

Mr Griffiths: I joined the FSS about 18 months ago, first as a non-executive director before becoming chairman.

Q72 Chairman: Where did you come from?

Mr Griffiths: My background is mostly Unilever, in different parts of the world, and a little bit in ICI and I have got some experience of working in science-based businesses. I have done some work through the University of Manchester (UMIST) and I have got some experience of other Government departments through non-executive positions there. So with that sort of knowledge base and experience base I was remarkably struck, on joining the FSS, as to the quality of the business and that is the quality of the science and innovation but also the quality of the management team and the fact that, as has been said, it is a business which is used to dealing with customers. It is customer-focused, it is used to invoicing, it is used to collecting money in and all the normal commercial business—

Q73 Chairman: Do people pay their invoices, though?

Mr Griffiths: That is also part of the experience of being commercial and obviously dealing with that, and indeed the management structures, the governance structures, are pretty progressive. So that is good. I do not think that therefore the issue is about a snap judgment about whether the FSS is good or bad. I think it is very good. The issue is to what extent it needs to change and what is the transformation agenda for the business to keep it healthy, to keep it leading, and to respond to the inevitable forces out there—market forces, competitive forces, but frankly also what are the demands of the customers. That is the key question.

Q74 Chairman: What do you think of the criticisms that are made of it, from your experience from Unilever, for example?

Mr Griffiths: Well, I think one can always pick an entity which is in the public sector and level criticisms that it might not be as commercial, as agile, as flexible as a best in class private sector business. I think it is a question of degree.

Q75 Chairman: What did you find when you first got there?

Mr Griffiths: I found that on a scale of relative competitiveness and flexibility the FSS scores high. I was very pleasantly surprised at how many things were in place. That is not to say we cannot improve and that is not to say that it is adequate for an increasingly competitive environment, but this is a business which is already thinking commercially. It is highly innovative and that will be a key attribute of any requirement for a healthy business. It has got dedicated staff, who have got clearly a good grasp of the business's vision and what it is there to do. So a lot of the building blocks are in place and that scores very highly from my point of view. I do not think we are talking about a business that is in the doldrums, struggling, and it is a mammoth task to make it—

Chairman: You have made that very clear. Thank you.

Q76 Mr Key: You have obviously got substantial experience in the private sector as well as the private sector. Am I right that the United Kingdom is the only country in the world which is seeking to put its Forensic Science Service into the private sector?

Mr Griffiths: As far as I know it is, but let me just kind of disaggregate this issue. From our point of view, what we want is not a particular status or not *per se*. What we want is the capacity to make the business healthy and healthy includes, where necessary, being cost-effective and where necessary providing innovative unique services for customers. So I think where I come from is a position in which there is a transformation agenda to do that, of which status, and particularly the construction of the company, if you like, the business, the company, is one element. But it has got to be business-led. It is not a status for status sake, privatised or Government Owned Company, or whatever, it is what is fit for the business to flourish and to deliver its plan (a plan which we are formulating for the future years) and which has ultimately got to deliver to the criminal justice system and to the customers.

Q77 Mr Key: I find some difficulty with this concept of having a private sector Forensic Science Service at all. Are you not concerned about the loss of the public sector ethos here?

Mr Griffiths: Well, I think we can have a public service ethos and a customer respect in a business which still has, for the sake of argument, private sector shareholders. The question is how to do it and to what extent that is easily done, but there is no doubt about it, for the health of the business we need to harness the public service ethos (which is there in the staff, the quality of work, and so on) and we have to marry that with a total respect for what the customer requires.

Q78 Mr Key: But will anyone else do business with you? I mean, the Americans will not. Europol will not, will they, if they think you are a private company?

Mr Griffiths: No, I think it is a question of what kind of company we are, what kind of employees and what kind of service we deliver. I do not think the status necessarily should get in the way of the reputation, if you like, in the marketplace and the reputation for science that the business has.

Dr Werrett: Could I just add, within the United States it is very much a mixed economy and involves in fact the injection of many millions of dollars into forensic science. Some of it has been done on the basis that the state laboratories actually used that money to procure services from private sector laboratories and the idea of that was to boost the capacity of forensic science within the United States.

Q79 Dr Turner: Could we come back to the parallel with NATS. When NATS was going to go for a PPP that again, to the best of our knowledge at the time, was the only instance of an air traffic control service going out of public ownership and of course I do not have to remind you of the troubles that that has got into. What gives you the confidence that an FSS PPP

will not run into not necessarily exactly the same kind of difficulties but other difficulties which will trip it up in just the same way and, as my colleague has suggested, lose the confidence that comes with the public ethos?

Mr Griffiths: Well, I think the foundation for any change of status, particularly going to a PPP, is that there is a well-articulated business plan and a clearly defined set of requirements placed upon the business to deliver that plan and the PPP should not be constructed in such a way, in my view, that it would contradict those requirements. So we have got to work forward now in deciding, as we change status and as we move into a more competitive marketplace, which is our plan, what are our intentions for the business to develop it, to make it stronger, to what extent are the demands on the business in terms of performance measures going to change as we embrace the competitive market, and then and only then should a construction be developed for a PPP if that is necessary. I think that sequence will unfold over the next year or two. It will be a business-led, management-led proposition for the business and it needs the full endorsement of the shareholders, whether they are the current shareholders/stakeholders in the business or future ones.

Q80 Dr Turner: But you are still presuming PPP rather than stopping at a GovCo if a GovCo can deliver everything that is needed?

Mr Griffiths: What I would say is that we are presuming we will put forward the FSS's view as to what it needs to do to stay healthy in terms of a business and out of that will come requirements for funding, structures, and all sorts of things, not the other way round; in other words business-led.

Q81 Mr McWalter: You have just talked about the American model, but in America when they make those commitments to investment they make damn sure that the jobs that come from that stay in America and they would be absolutely delighted to have market opportunities here for their companies which they would never vouchsafe to our companies because of the American very strict rules about security clearance. So really are you not in fact just opening the door for some cheapo loss-leading American companies to move into the market here and in doing so actually undermining the very expertise that you have inherited?

Mr Griffiths: I think there is a distinction between a potential competitor from America or anywhere else moving into the UK market. That is clearly possible at the moment and our primary concern is to stay in the forefront, both competitively where necessary and in terms of innovation. Whether a route through an investment would be a threat to us I think very much depends on choices about what structuring the PPP had, what people were allowed to invest and on what conditions they wanted to take a share. Again, I go back to the point that we are trying to formulate a plan which keeps the FSS as a business healthy and the issue of structure and shareholding should be addressed as a function of that rather than us prejudging, if you like, the attitude. We are going to be faced with competition come what may and who knows where the competition will come from. I think our job in the management team is to keep the business as robust and healthy and prepared for that as possible.

Q82 Mr McWalter: But if I am a hard-pressed chief constable I am going to go to somebody who will provide this service cheaply and all of the benefits of the FSS, the innovation, the investment, the sort of long-term strategy, the tradition of very, very rigorous examination, and so on, which is an integral part of that public service ethos that we have talked about, that is all very nice but, quite frankly, if that fancy service is too expensive for me I am going to go to somebody who does not do a lot of that stuff but gives me the service cheaply and works 90% of the time as effectively. I will just cut corners, will I not, and that is the FSS down the plughole?
Mr Griffiths: To some extent the FSS has a business which it clearly has to benchmark against competitive pricing and its aim is to be as competitive as possible, particularly in the so-called commoditised end of the market, and in other areas the FSS is clearly promoting value added services and products and it is our job to convince the customers that those are truly value added and value for money and an enlightened customer can recognise the difference between buying on price and buying on a combination of price, plus service, plus value in use, and I think that is our job.

Q83 Dr Harris: Everything you have just said in answer to the question about why you are going down this path with regard to the public sector could have been said if you were running the police, that you would like to keep the public service ethos, that it is good to have a mixed market, the Americans are doing it. If the Americans invaded Canada that is not a reason why we should do it. Can you see any reason why there are reasons for this step which you would not apply to a PPP for the police or bringing in a mixed economy into the police service itself?
Mr Griffiths: I go back to the answer, which is that we are trying to move the FSS on to deliver services in a more competitive market. What structure we need, whether it is a GovCo which is entirely Government owned but which would just operate in a different way or more likely that we need more flexibility, I think is where we are starting. There are other considerations which have to be judged as to what the appropriate structure might be, which people might be allowed to invest, and so on, but from our point of view we are starting from a business-led proposition not a dogmatic structural end-game which we are trying to get to.

Q84 Dr Harris: Do you think that nationalisation, moving the other way, is still on the agenda and always has been, or would you say there is an element of ideology in where we are moving?

Mr Griffiths: I think the mindset is to give the FSS a chance to be a stronger, more competitive business. That is where we start and I think that is what inspires this project.
Dr Harris: The Home Office said it had no restrictions on who the partner might be. It said that it could be anyone, international companies. Do you have any qualms at all about having your partner being, I do not know, a newspaper magnet or a Russian oil baron, or them selling their share on to something even more dubious than those two noble professions? Is that not an issue?

Q85 Mr McWalter: There could be some forensic inquiries, could there not, which might be a bit compromised by those forms of power?
Mr Griffiths: There is an issue about the difference between a shareholder and somebody who is intrusive and knows about the business. Perhaps newspapers are not a good example in that respect. There is a difference between a shareholder who is a shareholder and one who would know about very sensitive or other commercially valuable things in the organisation.
Chairman: Des, you have got a penetrating question.

Q86 Dr Turner: Well, I hope so. You have mentioned several times the mixed economy of forensic services in the United States. Can you tell us something about the effect this has on standards? For instance, I am told that the turn-around time for burglary investigations in St Louis is one and a half years and a murder DNA sample in California three months. Not very impressive.
Dr Werrett: I think it is singularly unimpressive. There are other examples. New York State, for example, has invested a lot of money and forensic science is providing a very good service, but I think that is precisely why some of the money was tagged to go to the private sector because there was a realisation that the state laboratories could not handle the volume of work that was coming in. So particularly where it was convenient to do so, and that is in the areas of DNA testing, the money was tagged to actually purchase services from the private sector and in that way boost the capacity rather quickly. I think they are going through a period of realisation that we went through probably around 1996–97–98 when we began to realise what a fantastic tool DNA in particular was for forensic science in general and if you look at our history there where we had to expand four or five-fold, our turn-around times were pretty awful at that time. Our turn-around times are an awful lot better now.

Q87 Dr Turner: Can you satisfy us as to how a PPP is going to guarantee the rapid turn-around times that crime solution urgently and desperately needs and that you are not going to fall into excessive delays?
Dr Werrett: I think I would return to the answer my chairman gave, in that rather than look at it as a PPP doing it, I think it is about some of the innovations that we have got currently being developed being turned into excellent service and it is how, as a business, we can do that with the instruments that we

have currently got. Trying to do it in a Government situation, with Government procurement, with no investment (because the Home Office under the current arrangements is our bank and there is very little possibility of us borrowing money to invest from the Home Office), under those situations looking to take what is a relatively expensive innovative programme into a service which I think could revolutionise the speed with which forensic science is delivered without investment would be very difficult and quite slow.

Q88 Dr Turner: No one questions the need for investment but it is perfectly possible for this to be delivered through GovCo.
Dr Werrett: If it could be delivered through GovCo, as my chairman said, I think it is a question of will the business acquire the freedoms to act in a way which will allow it to continue its path of excellent innovation and be business-led.

Q89 Bob Spink: I just want to continue this line on standards but particularly move to quality rather than timing. In this sort of mixed market I was just envisaging that there might be some small group, a small company or a small number of people, who specialise in a particular niche market who have standardised or commoditised a particular service which they can give in an area of forensics and can deliver that because they are small with very, very low fixed costs and therefore offer a very attractive service financially and in terms of speed for the police, and I can see these people giving this service. I want to draw a parallel here with that scenario in the mixed market with what happened in, say, expert evidence where somebody developed a particular niche market. It was in cot deaths and he gave his service and we saw some massive travesties of justice in that area which took perhaps 10 years to discover and are still unfolding now. So how are we going to protect from this? Does this give you concerns? How are we going to regulate this?
Dr Werrett: Anyone in the current climate can call themselves a forensic scientist and stand in the witness box as we are now. So that is an issue which is with us today and it is up to the judge to decide whether he accepts that expert witness or not. So that is a concern. It is a concern I have had throughout my professional life and I have welcomed the introduction of the Council for Registration of Forensic Practitioners, which seeks to actually formalise the competence and demonstrate the competence of forensic scientists, and I welcome that approach. We as an organisation also subscribe to international quality standards and we are externally accredited. So I think that is the kind of hallmark that we would continue to aim for, but yes, it is an issue and it is an issue which faces us today. So if the approach is to have a regulator then that is one way of doing it.

Q90 Dr Harris: Would you be attempted to cherry-pick the most profitable parts of the service if you became a PPP?

Dr Werrett: I think one of our greatest strengths and indeed commercial advantages is that we tend to offer a one-stop-shop service.

Q91 Dr Harris: So I am a shareholder and I want you to give me a return. I do not want you to do this one-stop-shop. Give me a return. Let us do the high throughput, high profit, high value service. Let us concentrate on that.
Dr Werrett: But the strength of the organisation and its commercial success I would hope to be able to justify to you as a shareholder is based on the fact that it does operate the comprehensive service. There was at one time a sort of feeling going around that there were bits of the service that were not profitable and bits of the service that were loss-making. That is simply not true. Under the Treasury's rules and guidelines, as we currently operate, all parts of our service have to provide a contribution to the organisation.

Q92 Dr Harris: So how do you think the Government is going to ensure that it actually maintains the broad range? Is it going to require you, because it cannot require the market by definition, to provide everything that you are currently providing and in the future will need to provide?
Dr Werrett: I cannot really answer for them.

Q93 Dr Harris: But you say that you think you are going to be expected to be a provider of last resort. In your evidence you recognise that, both in the interim and, I would argue, in the developed market as well.
Dr Werrett: Yes. I think the provider of last resort, if I may say so, is a slightly different question to the shareholder question. By "provider of last resort" I presume the current thinking is that there may come a time when a police force which generally tends to use the competition for its services will come to us and say, "We need you for this." It is either too big a job, they cannot do it, they are snowed under with work, or whatever, and the question is should the Forensic Science Service maintain capacity to provide that service as a last resort. I think we can do that, but I think we will do it on a business-led commercial basis. At the moment we publish a universal price list across all the forces. I would expect, as the market develops, for contracts to develop between ourselves and the forces which use us on a regular basis and our price list will be adjusted for those who want to use us on a one-off basis and the price would reflect that.

Q94 Dr Harris: So what you are saying is that it will just be the market that does it? As a member of the public, I want confidence that there is not going to be a part of the service that is no longer there because it is unaffordable in the market and will you not need compensation? These police forces that need to do these rare one-offs are going to have to find the money at very high prices for you to maintain that flexibility. I would not have confidence that that is going to encourage the police to do those sorts of tests.

Dr Werrett: I am not quite sure—

Mr McWalter: It is about, is it not, a competitive disadvantage? That is what Evan is asking. You say you are competitively disadvantaged by your brief and the shareholders are going to be unhappy about it and members of the public are going to be unhappy about the prospects that that recognises.

Q95 Dr Harris: I think what you are saying is that for some services which are at price X because it is inefficient for you to provide them that price will rise significantly within the market even as other prices are falling?

Dr Werrett: No. I am sorry if I have made you think that. That is not what I am saying at all. What I am saying is that as the market contractualises, which it currently is doing—and I think it will continue to contractualise whether or not we become a GovCo—currently the number of contracts between ourselves and police forces are very few. We have operated on basically a customer practice, but increasingly police forces (and I think Tim Wilson mentioned Gershon) are looking to procure services in a competitive way and move to formal contracts between ourselves and themselves. So as the market continues to do that there will be police forces with whom we have agreements, with whom we have regularised pricing structures, and so forth. There may be other forces who choose to use us on a one-off basis for which as a business we will need to make judgments about how much capacity that is likely to use. That will probably be a more expensive way for us of providing a service.

Q96 Dr Harris: But you will provide it? You will absolutely provide it?

Dr Werrett: Yes, we will provide it, and on the basis of providing it in that way it is likely to be more expensive.

Q97 Dr Harris: There will be ebb and flow in demand for some of the services and you welcome being able to be flexible, but you have a high fixed cost with your salaries and you have people in careers in the FSS. How are you going to create the flexibility? Just stick everyone on short-term contracts?

Dr Werrett: No.

Q98 Dr Harris: Is that a guarantee you will not?

Dr Werrett: Well, under TUPE the terms and conditions of moving from the public sector to the private sector have to be comparable.

Dr Harris: I am sorry, you will recruit people on to short-term contracts, that is what I meant.

Q99 Dr Turner: TUPE does not last very long, so any change in commercial circumstances can wipe out TUPE.

Dr Werrett: Well, not any change, but—

Q100 Dr Harris: I am sorry, I did not mean you would move individuals on, I just meant you will start recruiting people who used to have a career on to short-term contracts.

Dr Werrett: Could I just say we actually do that now. We take in agency staff to boost capacity where we need to in emergencies and we let them go again.

Q101 Dr Harris: So it is not your plan to increase the proportion?

Dr Werrett: No, in fact generally our plan is more about securing what the demand is likely to be and then move to a greater proportion of permanent staff because agency staff are more expensive.

Q102 Dr Harris: So we can expect that as a performance indicator, as one of these things that is going to be a measure of how you are doing, what proportion of your staff or salary is in—

Dr Werrett: It is not for me to set my performance measures.

Q103 Dr Harris: But would you have happy if that was a performance measure?

Dr Werrett: I think it would be rather an unusual performance measure.

Q104 Dr Harris: But you just advocated it. You said you hoped to do it. Surely you hope to be measured on things you hope to do? I do.

Dr Werrett: I am advocating it as good business practice, but I think our measures may be slightly different for that.

Q105 Chairman: Prospect and the PCS trade union, said there is currently no regulation of the forensic marketplace in respect of training or the use of new and novel scientific processes. What do you say to that?

Dr Werrett: There is no regulation in that there is no statutory regulation. There is regulation in that all of the providers subscribe to certain elements of forensic science that is provided now and subscribe to that regulation, and I think Tim Wilson mentioned the custodian of the National DNA Database. To provide results to the National DNA Database you have to go through a rigorous proficiency testing regime which continues after you have passed your initial tests during the period that you are supplying results to the National DNA Database, and that is subscribed to by all suppliers. You are not allowed in unless you do that.

Q106 Chairman: Does that mean you disagree with this statement?

Dr Werrett: It means that there is no formal, as we might say, statutory requirement.

Q107 Chairman: Do you think we need it or might need it?

Dr Werrett: This is a very big subject because forensic science itself is a very big subject and that has always been the difficulty. Courts use forensic evidence from all sorts, from lots of different ologies, if I can put it that way, and I think it is quite different to regulate it in that way.

Q108 Chairman: Do you not think the public are advantaged by having a regulator, given some of the high profile cases that forensic scientists and surgeons and others have been involved in in court where they have been ridiculed by the press and therefore the public pick it up? Would a regulator help in that arena?

Dr Werrett: I think if a regulator could help those situations then it would be a worthwhile thing.

Q109 Dr Iddon: I would like to know how much you invest in R&D as a percentage of your revenue income.

Dr Werrett: Currently about 12%.

Mr Griffiths: 12% is quoted, yes.

Q110 Dr Iddon: Is that going up or down, or has it been stable?

Dr Werrett: It has actually gone up by about 1% for last year to this year. It is one of our agency targets to not only encourage that investment but also increase the level of investment we get from outside, not from just our customers. So if, for example, we had grants from the FBI and so forth, unlike the grants that were referred to earlier we keep the IPR for that work that we are doing there.

Q111 Dr Iddon: Do you see much change in a PPP or a GovCo? Do you think there will be pressure to reduce that?

Dr Werrett: We are an organisation whose prosperity is characterised by great innovation and I think it will be a huge commercial mistake not to continue with that innovation.

Q112 Dr Iddon: There is a lot of new developments coming in forensics, of course. What about hand-held devices for the police to do DNA or fingerprints at the roadside and of course drug testing at the roadside? Are you investing heavily in that area or leaving it to the competition?

Dr Werrett: We are investing heavily in that area, although I have a wry smile on this one because six years ago after visiting California and seeing several biotech companies there I came back and confidently predicted that in five years' time we would have a hand-held device. There is no sign of it yet, but what we have done is taken a halfway step. We have certainly miniaturised some of the DNA equipment and I think you will see in the next few months that we are taking another step forward in that area.

Q113 Dr Iddon: Okay, that is one step forward. Where are the new avenues of opportunity in forensics, do you think?

Dr Werrett: For us, I think we need to expand our capability in electronic forensic science. The use of mobile phones and computers is an obvious area where we need to excel.

Q114 Dr Turner: Have you found that your R&D efforts have been unduly constrained by the availability of investment? Have you been able to spend as much as you actually need on R&D or do you find that you cannot do work which you feel is potentially extremely important because you cannot fund it?

Dr Werrett: I think there is one step before that. Actually doing the R&D is quite difficult because of the Government procurement rules. A lot of the R&D that we are doing currently is R&D that involves other companies. Forensic science traditionally has combed the academic world and to some extent the industrial world for advances that we can forensicate and DNA was a prime example of that.

Q115 Chairman: What was that, forensicate?

Dr Werrett: Yes, a new word.

Q116 Chairman: Is that in the Oxford English Dictionary?

Dr Werrett: I have been to America too often. I am sorry.

Q117 Chairman: No wonder you are blushing.

Dr Werrett: I think the problem we have is actually being nimble in placing contracts or striking up those partnerships and then spending the money, but I think even when we did the National DNA Database and we had to invest heavily we did then borrow the money from the Home Office. I foresee times coming where we may want to borrow money again fairly soon.

Q118 Dr Turner: So I think the answer is you have not yet been constrained but you think you might be in the future?

Dr Werrett: We are constrained by the rules with which you can conduct research within Government and that is about procurement.

Q119 Dr Turner: A GovCo would make that easier, would it not?

Dr Werrett: If some of that procurement constraint was lifted.

Q120 Dr Iddon: So why does Government not change the procurement rules if they are inhibiting you?

Dr Werrett: I would welcome a political move to change those procurement rules. They are European procurement rules.

Q121 Dr Iddon: European?

Dr Werrett: Yes.

Q122 Dr Iddon: Okay. You mentioned mobile phones and communication technology in general, but of course the Internet and the Web, e-forensics in general, is that something you are investing in?

Dr Werrett: Certainly we have a contract with the National Crime Squad, which we are particularly proud of, where we provide them with a service from scenes of crime to courtroom and a lot of their work is to do with computers, so the answer is yes.

Q123 Dr Iddon: So you are into that. Do you think the Government needs to stimulate investment in R&D in private sector forensics?
Dr Werrett: I cannot really answer that one.

Q124 Mr Key: Perhaps you could answer mine then. The Forensic Science Service is much admired for its training and I think you delivered about four hundred and fifty training courses last year to over 50 police forces and at the moment that training is cost-neutral. I am not saying it does not cost anything but it is cost-neutral. When you become a PPP you are going to have to start charging police forces and others for that service, are you not, with a profit element, not just cost-neutral?
Dr Werrett: Not necessarily. It depends how we approach it. I think you are probably seeing some of our competitors and perhaps you might like to ask some of our competitors about their approach to training because I think they probably use it in a neutral way at the moment as it is a very good way of educating policemen in the services that you provide.

Q125 Mr Key: The FSS has perhaps unfairly got a reputation for being the best place to train and move on. Are you anticipating that when you are a PPP you will still be able to recruit, to attract sufficient graduates to train as forensic science practitioners? Will it make a difference?
Dr Werrett: I am absolutely convinced that we would be able to attract enough graduates. I am actually concerned at the number of forensic science courses that you see in universities these days because I am not quite sure where all these people are going to work, but what we need to work on are incentives and remuneration packages that retain those people once we have trained them and those are somewhat limited sometimes within the public sector.

Q126 Mr Key: Have you identified any particular specialisms where there are shortages of forensic practitioners and therefore identified niche markets which you might seek to address when you are a PPP?
Dr Werrett: There are some areas which we see as niche markets, yes.

Q127 Mr Key: Such as?
Dr Werrett: I am aware that my biggest competitor is actually in the room at the moment, so I wonder if I could refrain from answering that publicly.

Q128 Chairman: Are you frightened of your competitor? Do you want me to throw him out?
Dr Werrett: It is a her actually!
Chairman: She has every right to be here, yes.

Q129 Mr Key: Well, it is pretty disappointing. Can you give us a general flavour of the sorts of areas which are going to be particularly important over the next few years?

Dr Werrett: Some of the areas we have already referred to within electronic forensic science, so there are some areas there.
Chairman: Dr Werrett, you can write to us secretly.
Mr Key: And we will publish it later!

Q130 Dr Harris: The Chairman will sell it on ebay! I would like to ask you about the views of your staff. Why is there such a divergence of views between staff and management based on the evidence we have seen and what we have read on whether the PPP of the FSS is a good thing, and what steps are you taking to bring them on board, or have you given up?
Dr Werrett: I have certainly not given up, in fact I am right smack bang in the middle of a tour around all the laboratories at the moment. I talk to all staff probably once every four to five months. I do it in sessions where I try to keep them relatively small, 30 to 40 is preferable but in the London laboratory it is much bigger, it tends to swell to one hundred and fifty. It makes it quite an arduous tour but it gives me a very good feel. I explain to them it is Chatham House rules and it gives me a very good feel of the feelings that are out there, and yes, the majority of staff are against PPP. The latest survey has just come in. I have not had time to compile the data yet but from the last survey 75% of staff were against PPP.

Q131 Chairman: Why do you think they are against it?
Dr Werrett: The major issues are uncertainty over pensions, uncertainty over what it actually means because it would be nice for people like me to stand up in front of my staff and say, "A GovCo is dah, de dah, de dah, de dah, and a PPP is"—

Q132 Chairman: What about principle objections about the whole thing?
Dr Werrett: There are objections such as, "I joined a public service and I want to maintain a public service and that's what I want to do, good things with my science." I do not actually see myself that that is incompatible with a commercial company.

Q133 Chairman: What would Government have to do to attain that, keep it as a public service?
Dr Werrett: I think it is a question of us maintaining our ethos and our values as we move through to getting the freedoms that we need, and I think I would return to the point that Bill made, that it is about the freedoms that we need to act in a more commercial way.

Q134 Chairman: Do you feel you are swimming against the tide?
Dr Werrett: No, I do not feel I am swimming against the tide. I would not say either it was an easy period.

Q135 Dr Harris: But you say in your evidence that staff are leaving and when we finally got evidence in your name and not under the auspices of the Home Office you make the point specifically that staff are leaving, "Highly trained staff are now leaving the FSS to join competitors," and reading between the lines, and indeed in the lines, if you are going to go down this path you want to go quicker rather than slower?

Dr Werrett: Absolutely. I think one of the other daunting things for people is the lack of speed of the decision process. I think if you are going to make decisions, obviously you have got to analyse them and be careful about them but you need to make them fairly speedily.

Q136 Dr Harris: But this could be quite damaging, the hostility of staff and the fact that you are being stretched out on a rack during the process. So this could actually undermine the FSS given you have this loss of staff?

Dr Werrett: Yes. I think the loss of staff, as I think Steve has said, is not huge at the moment but the indications are there. We recently lost—

Q137 Dr Harris: This is Steve—
Dr Werrett: Stephen Rimmer.

Q138 Dr Harris: From the Home Office?

Dr Werrett: Yes. We have recently lost seven or eight staff to a laboratory that is being set up in Tamworth. We did exit interviews with people and people left for different reasons, but if there is going to be a competitive marketplace, which is clearly developing now, then we will have to come to terms with the fact that people move from one establishment to another and there will be a market for forensic scientists.

Q139 Dr Turner: Obviously it is essential for the successful investigation that you can have data sharing between different providers where necessary. Is a PPP likely to get in the way of data sharing between a privatised FSS and its other competitors?

Dr Werrett: I would hope not. The databases that Tim referred to, there is a keenness to maintain those in the public arena so that data sharing continues.

Dr Turner: Good. Finally from me, if you do become a PPP can you, as the FSS, guarantee that it will stay in one piece and that perhaps less profitable parts of it might not be hived off, or whatever?

Dr Harris: Privatised.
Chairman: Forensicated twice!

Q140 Dr Turner: Would it remain as a comprehensive service?

Dr Werrett: I do not think I can offer a guarantee in that direction. I mean, that is asking me to predict the future.

Q141 Chairman: Forensic science is a big thing, as you say, in education. All these young people are being seduced by it at the moment and you are wondering about whether there are going to be jobs, and so on, because of tv and all that kind of stuff. Have you been involved in the courses which have been developed in our universities?

Dr Werrett: I have not been involved with many. There is an awful lot. In fact some of the forensic scientists who chose to take early retirement when we reduced in size have gone to lecture to some of those courses. Some courses I have been involved with and some have been established for years and years and years and are good courses, but it does worry me that because of the trendiness at the moment for forensic science so many people may be pinning some hopes on it.

Q142 Chairman: When you look down the line at forensic science what do you think it is going to be like? Forget the PPP stuff. What is it going to be like? Is it going to be full of scientists doing more technologies or is it going to stay just waiting for things to happen? Are you going to provoke things to happen? Are you going to mix with people like Kinetic and companies like that and find out what they are doing, or is it just that you have got too much to do? What is your attitude? What is the feeling working in this?

Dr Werrett: My attitude is the latter and I think it is a very exciting world, and I think we are just about to go through another era of great excitement.

Q143 Mr McWalter: I am just staggered by how naïve really in a way you seem to be about the markets. It feels to me like you are a racehorse, you have got a lot of virtues and you are great of your type, and you are entering into a stock car race where a load of cheapo stuff is going to be—I mean, the reality is that you are going to be subject to intense pressures in the cherry-picked parts of the market and you do not have the capacity to do that back, so you are going to get shafted! I mean, there is a very good reason for your staff feeling unnerved. It does not matter whether it happens quickly or slowly. In the end they are going to be very badly positioned in terms of their continuing employment.

Dr Werrett: I would like to rigorously defend that one because in the commoditisation of the marketplace, particularly in DNA analysis, we have actually led, completely led the automation of DNA analysis worldwide. We have lots of visitors from overseas who have come to see what we have done for DNA analysis, automating it, not only from the mechanical point of view—where we used to have three or four hundred people we now have forty or fifty people churning out probably four or five times as many tests—but also from an expert system point of view where most of the analysis is now done by expert systems. So we have led that commoditisation. We have realised and anticipated that that is going to be cheap and that these people are going to come in. So no, I do not think we are naïve. We have got the business into a position where we understand where to put the added value and where to have the commercial pressures to make things cheaper. But at the same time I would add that cheap does not necessarily mean value and there are areas where we emphasise to our customers that value requires a little more expenditure but gives you much greater outcomes. Where we have worked alongside police forces, particularly in the partnership projects, to address the whole supply chain where they are doing some of the work and we are doing some of the work, the outcomes are so much greater and that is really good value.

Chairman: Okay. Well, Dr Werrett and Bill Griffiths, thank you very much for coming here and helping to set the scene for us in an inquiry which will extend into the New Year. We wish you well in the holiday season and thank you very much for taking time out to bring your expertise and obvious enthusiasm, and doubts, to this meeting. Thank you very much indeed.

Wednesday 12 January 2005

Members present:

Dr Ian Gibson, Chairman

Dr Evan Harris   Mr Tony McWalter
Dr Brian Iddon   Dr Desmond Turner
Mr Robert Key

Witnesses: **Mr Alan Kershaw**, Chief Executive, and **Professor Evelyn Ebsworth**, Chairman, Council for the Registration of Forensic Practitioners, **Professor Jim Fraser**, President, and **Dr Ann Priston**, Vice-President, Forensic Science Society, examined.

Q144 Chairman: May I apologise profusely for being late. There is a report in which there is some dissension in the Committee—we love dissension in this Place, as you know—and, while it is not settled, we took a little longer than we thought we would have to at this stage. Thank you very, very much for coming to help us with this inquiry. I am quite sure you have been catching up with some of the issues we have been picking up on. You can tell that we are very concerned and interested in what is happening to this very worthwhile service, so we are very glad you are here. I do not know how you want to answer, but if only one of you answers it will save a lot of time. There are events happening in the House today, and we have other people to see as well. We will try to be short and sharp and perhaps you could too—that means just saying yes or no! We have had some evidence about a large number of forensic science courses not producing graduates with the skills required by employers in these particular sectors. Is that true or false?

Professor Fraser: It is true. Forensic science is already a very competitive field to get into—it has been for as long as I can recall—and my understanding is that next year there will be something like 2,000 graduates produced with degrees that are notionally in forensic science. It is not employer-driven and the likelihood is that a significant proportion of them will not end up working in forensic science.

Q145 Chairman: What is missing in some of the courses in terms of the basic knowledge of sciences and social science or whatever?

Professor Fraser: On the basis of the SEMTA report which looked at some of the evidence—the only people to have researched it in any way—they vary greatly. Fundamentally, most employers, certainly on the laboratory side of forensic science, require a degree in science subsequently to be built on with professional skills and professional practice. The courses which are being produced vary from 100% "forensic"—and I am not quite sure what that means—to something like 75% science. The courses with 75% science in them might well be perfectly fit for purpose, but for those with the 100% forensic it is very unclear what that person's scientific skills are likely to be.

Q146 Chairman: Do you think colleges and universities are taking this subject area seriously enough as part of their core activity?

Professor Fraser: It looks to me as if it is driven by the HE sector.

Q147 Chairman: Or is it just that a lot of people want to go to university, we have to meet targets, Amanda Burton runs a good script, and so on? What do universities think of it? Do vice-chancellors know what it is, for example?

Professor Fraser: I am not sure I can speak on behalf of every university in the country but certainly from the professional side these courses are not driven by any need.

Professor Ebsworth: I am quite sure that most vice-chancellors know perfectly well what these courses are but my own personal view (nothing to do with my council) is that the forensic courses ought to be built on a first degree in pure science or in some special discipline where the forensic element can be brought out. Using the label "forensic" is not a good way to teach basic science—which people moving into forensic science really ought to need.

Q148 Mr McWalter: Have you not failed people by not trumpeting this? Is it not the case in respect of populist courses of this kind, which pretend to give people skills but which actually do not give them skills, that bodies like yours have a duty to the wider public to unmask these things and stop them at source?

Professor Ebsworth: My council does not deal with courses. This is more a matter for the Forensic Science Society but I certainly feel that this ought to be made clearer. The great problem is that the number of people qualified in and interested in reading pure science is going down fast. It is very important that these subjects do not disappear from the university curricula.

Q149 Chairman: Are they under threat? Are they under threat, like chemistry at Exeter?

Professor Ebsworth: Certainly. Chemistry is a key subject in this matter and that is clearly under threat in some universities.

Q150 Chairman: Have you made a noise about support for chemistry, given that you have a growing subject, I guess?

Professor Ebsworth: I have in a different context, of course, because I am a Fellow of the Royal Society of Chemistry.

Q151 Chairman: There are lots of them around!

Professor Ebsworth: Yes. I noticed!—some very distinguished chemists, indeed. The register is focused on individuals, not on courses. I think the Forensic Science Society is in a very strong position to make these noises and I am sure it can and will and does.

Professor Fraser: If I may come back to Mr McWalter's question, the society now has an accreditation programme which has gone through this. We have somewhere in the region of 20 universities interested. We have 11 who have definitely signed up and the accreditation process will be on the basis of academic practice and general science assessment by a panel of individuals.

Q152 Mr McWalter: Are you going to unmask those who run courses which clearly lack the capacity to be accredited? Are you going to unmask them as effectively fraudulent?

Professor Fraser: I am not sure if we would use the word "fraudulent" but we will make it plain that they cannot be accredited by the Forensic Science Society. The rights of individual HE institutions to put on individual courses is—

Q153 Mr McWalter: Fraud is that it says this on the bottle but it does not have that inside. That is what fraud is.

Professor Fraser: I accept that. There is another issue, that they may well not approach us for accreditation, and we cannot compel people to be accredited. But the serious players in this field, who want in some way to become involved in the development of forensic science, have approached the society to be accredited. Somewhere around 50% of those institutions who are involved in teaching forensic science have approached the society for accreditation.

Q154 Mr McWalter: You may gather that I would like you to be a bit more robust.

Professor Fraser: Absolutely.

Mr Kershaw: I think it is fair to say that the universities who are offering these courses would not claim to be offering them a career in forensic science, but it is very hard for an 18-year old going in not to be beguiled by the word "forensic" and to see the possibility and perhaps to waste their time at university as a result.

Q155 Dr Turner: It would seem to me that forensic science lends itself to the sort of natural training structure of a basic first degree in, say, chemistry, topped off by a vocational post-graduate diploma or master's degree—

Professor Ebsworth: Absolutely.

Q156 Dr Turner: — which would be the qualification which bodies like yours could recognise as qualifying them for registered practice. This would start to get round what seems to be happening today when kids go to university: "Look at chemistry." "Oh, no, boring" or "Too hard. Let's go and do forensic science." It is sexy but it is misleading.

Professor Ebsworth: Yes.

Q157 Dr Turner: It could have the double benefit of getting more people doing basic science and sorting out those who really want to do forensic science and making sure they come with the right scientific background.

Professor Ebsworth: Indeed.

Q158 Dr Turner: That is something you could promulgate, if you agree with it.

Mr Kershaw: Yes. Our council does not have the resources to mount an inspection programme of all these courses. That would be quite beyond us. It is not part of our remit, at least in this early stage. But, if I may offer an example of the kind of thinking that is worth looking at as a model for the future: In Dundee a very distinguished forensic anthropologist, Professor Sue Black, whom you may have seen and certainly you will have heard of, is pioneering a course which is effectively a training in forensic anthropology of some 10 years in total: an initial course teaching anthropology and then going on to a Master's degree and so on and then into actual practice. The 10 years is not all in actual study, but, to make a competent forensic anthropologist, someone whom we would want to register, that is the kind of time scale that is maybe needed until you know someone is distinguished enough to be practising competently and so forth.

Q159 Chairman: In the events of the last few weeks I notice that lots of forensic scientists have gone from this country out there. How many are we taking about?

Professor Fraser: I have no idea. I am sorry. Also, the term "forensic science", when used in the press, is often used very vaguely. It is not very clear.

Q160 Chairman: That is interesting. I get the impression, a mere paper-reader, that forensic science is doing the business and that this is part of the British effort.

Professor Fraser: I think they are, but it is not clear exactly who is doing it and how many are doing it.

Q161 Chairman: Is it worth finding out, so we can use such figures in this inquiry and so on, and show the value of it in times like this?

Professor Fraser: It might well be but the approaches that have been made to the society on this issue have been on the basis of: "How can I help here?" and it has not been clear who is co-ordinating the help effort at this stage.

Q162 Chairman: How do you mean?

Professor Fraser: Well, we were approached after someone had approached the Home Office and the Met Police and various other government departments and agencies and they were saying, "We don't know where to go here. We don't know who is co-ordinating things, we don't know who is organising things" and so on, so it is not very clear at the moment who might provide those figures. It might well be at some later stage that those figures will be available.

Q163 Chairman: It seems very relevant to this debate here.
Professor Fraser: But I accept the point that it might be interesting to know who these people are and whether they are actually what we might consider to be forensic scientists.

Q164 Chairman: It just gets equated with DNA testing and you and I know it is a lot more than that.
Professor Ebsworth: We have started registering forensic anthropologists very much on the basis of the demand for them in dealing with some of the problems in Bosnia and the awful difficulties in identifying bodies from mass graves and so on. This is an impulse that has come through to us and to which we have responded. At least now people can find people on our register who are certified as competent to do this work.

Q165 Chairman: Do you think there will be more of that?
Professor Ebsworth: I think there will be. It is becoming clear that it is vital work and a tremendous lot depends on it now.
Mr Kershaw: Aside from numbers, the very fact that UK forensic scientists are at the centre of this is a measure of the regard in which forensic science from this country is held in the rest of the world.

Q166 Dr Turner: It is equally important that your customers—normally police forces investigating crime—have a sufficient understanding of forensic science itself in order to make intelligent use of your services.
Professor Ebsworth: Yes.

Q167 Dr Turner: There is a lot of variation between the success of police forces in so doing. Who makes sure that police forces understand enough to be intelligent customers of forensic science? Who is covering this angle and educating the police and regulating their use of it?
Professor Ebsworth: We work a lot with police forces. We work a lot with ACPO, who are an essential element in making sure the police are aware of what is on offer. Most police forces now have individuals who are the focus for interest and involvement in this. There are all sorts of resources; they focus their resources in different areas. We have a very mixed take-up for regulation between police forces, but as people move around from one force to another you can see how the interest in and knowledge of what goes on increases. The main vehicles are links through ACPO, and through the standards organisations and through the individual registrants who are associated with our council and the assessors, some of whom are policeman, they become aware of what is going on. In essence, it is a culture change. It is taking time but I am quite pleased with the speed at which it has gone. Remember, CRFP did not exist until June 1998.

There was absolutely nothing. For the first year and a half, the only people doing it were an excellent civil servant called Jill Parry and me, so we have made quite a lot of progress in that time, and I think the extent to which the police are becoming committed to the adherence to the public definition of standards that we represent is encouraging. I am very happy with the support we have had from them.

Q168 Dr Turner: Clearly there does need to be a minimum standard that can be expected.
Professor Ebsworth: Yes.

Q169 Dr Turner: Of all forces. I am sorry, I am asking purely because I genuinely do not have a clue about the answer, but, when the Home Office, for instance, inspects a police force, does their forensic competence form part of their inspection, do you know?
Mr Kershaw: Jim has been in a police force, so he will know better than I, but certainly Her Majesty's Inspector of Constabulary over the last five or six years has focused on this. It is part of their general inspections of forces. There have also been specific thematic inspections of the use of forensic science, and the result has shown that the take up has been patchy. Ways in which we are trying to help include the fact that when a police force is contracting out for a particular service they can know from our register that someone has been checked out in some way and assessed as competent in the field and can be dealt with if it turns out not to be so. But the driving force is probably HMIC rather than anything else. Perhaps Jim has more to say on that.
Professor Fraser: The documented evidence in relation to police knowledge of forensic science, in terms of making the best use of forensic science, is consistently clear, that their knowledge needs to improve and therefore their training needs to improve. In terms of specialist elements of policing, they are generally much better served—so senior investigating officers in homicides and specialists squads are usually much better trained and much better informed—but there is a real difficulty here in how you put on the ground for the average police force the level of sophistication of some of the scientific techniques or the investigative value that is here. I think the trick is probably more about good partnerships and good liaison and good reliable advice to make sure that forensic science is exploited with sound training which obviously needs to be improved.

Q170 Dr Turner: It would be useful for every force to have its own forensic advisor to whom any police officer could turn in an investigation for advice on how to proceed in the investigation with the use of forensics. Does this happen on the ground? If so, does it happen consistently? Is it a way of dealing with the issue?
Professor Fraser: It does not happen consistently. There are a large number of police forces and I think—the point you made right at the outset—that there is a lot of unexplained variation. The exact reasons why that does not happen, I do not think are

particularly clear. There is no model for good practice, as far as I can see, in using forensic science. There is a real need, instead of everyone trying to do it their own particular way, to develop models which can be agreed as useful and good practice and they can then become benchmarks against which you test and improve. Something like that would be of considerable benefit to the effective use of forensic science across the board.

Q171 Dr Turner: Would your organisation be in a position to help in the evolution and monitoring of such a good practice model?
Professor Fraser: I think the Forensic Science Society would be in a position to work with other partners in developing models of good practice—particularly for the smaller suppliers, because the larger organisations would have their own stake in this but the Forensic Science Society in employer terms represents the smaller employers. We could do that and we would be very keen to do that as part of our contribution to safeguards and regulation in this field.

Q172 Dr Turner: Do you think it would be a very important and useful thing to do?
Professor Fraser: I do, yes.
Dr Priston: Could I add—

Q173 Chairman: Yes, Dr Priston, I was going to ask you to say something.
Dr Priston: As far as I am aware, most of the major forces or all the forces should have a link into their laboratory, whichever laboratory it is. When they are carrying out any investigation they will have a close link to an advisor for that investigation, so as far as the science side of it is concerned it should not in theory be too much of a problem.

Q174 Mr Key: Dr Priston, can you confirm that the Forensic Science Society requires all its reporting officers to be registered but that registration is voluntary?
Dr Priston: They desire it. It is voluntary, yes.

Q175 Mr Key: CFRP told us in evidence that in a free society no-one should seek to constrain the courts as to the evidence they can hear, in the context of the fact that you too have a purely voluntary arrangement. Is it not time for it to be compulsory and not voluntary?
Professor Ebsworth: No, I do not think so. I do not think we can ever work on that basis because there are always going to be cases when individuals come with special expertise that will only be used once in a court. I would be very happy if all organisations employing people to give evidence regularly in courts were to insist, as employers, that their people should be registered. What I hope will happen in the fullness of time is that courts will ask if someone like that is registered, and, if they are not, they will ask why not. There may be good reasons, and, if there are, fair enough. I have never seen it as feasible to insist that everyone giving expert evidence in court should be registered, partly because of the certainty

that you will meet the occasional true expert, perhaps from another country, who simply cannot be expected to conform with the pattern. I want to see courts asking questions; I want to see employers insisting that people reaching a certain grade giving evidence will be on our register.

Q176 Mr Key: Does the Forensic Science Society agree with that?
Dr Priston: I am sure it does.
Professor Fraser: Yes.

Q177 Mr Key: Talking of registration, is the rate of practitioners registering speeding up or slowing down?
Mr Kershaw: It is speeding up. We are now at a point where, in the mainstream specialities, where we started, close to 40% of the potential take-up have taken it up already. With the police forces increasingly making it part of management policy that, for certain grades, for recruitment, for training purposes, registration would be part of someone's career progression and expected, it is becoming harder and harder for forensic staff to move between police forces if they do not have registration, so *de facto* it is starting to have an effect. Yes, the take up has been slow, because, as the Chairman commented earlier, it does involve quite a considerable cultural change when a professional group which has never been regulated before suddenly finds that opportunity, and if they do not actually have to then it is very slow to move. It is becoming harder to practice full time in forensic practice without registration, and I think our moves, having tested in the courts towards the end of last year, to encourage the courts to ask the question more fully, will actually drive that forward faster.

Q178 Mr Key: Is it all graduate entry into the profession?
Mr Kershaw: No.
Professor Fraser: Fingerprint experts and scenes of crime officers who could be registered are not necessarily graduates.

Q179 Mr Key: Is recruitment on the increase or decrease? You said registration is increasing. What about recruitment initially?
Mr Kershaw: I cannot give you figures, but I am sure the Home office will be able to help with this. I think the numbers of full-time forensic staff in the police have been increasing, not least because of particular initiatives to increase the DNA database, and that has obviously widened the pool of people from whom we can get an application for registration. In the forensic science service I think the numbers are probably fairly stable. Dr Priston can answer that for us.
Dr Priston: I cannot really answer that. I do not know the answer. I think it probably is on the increase but I do not know.
Professor Fraser: In general terms the whole sector is expanding and has been expanding for the past five years or more—five to 10 years—largely driven by

DNA and largely driven by government funding, but my impression is that that is beginning to slow down now.

Q180 Mr Key: There is not an oversupply. You are not going to find too many people coming into the profession with nothing to do.

Professor Fraser: There have always been, in my experience, too many people who want into forensic science. Because it is a very small sector, typically, for a single job, you will have hundreds of applicants.

Professor Ebsworth: Could I just point out that the specialities to which the register is open are increasing all the time. As we recognise new areas, for example involving digital evidence and computer crime and things of that kind, that immediately widens the pool of people who will come on to the register. I am sure it also widens the opportunities for employment. You can see how important issues connected with computer crime and mobile phones and things of that sort are becoming and how desperately important it is to define standards in these novel areas. The council is much involved in this process and we hope to open our register to some people in this context during the coming calendar year, but that is going to mean that the sector looks bigger than defined in our register anyway.

Q181 Mr Key: Finally, I know that she is a pathologist but how much of this is due to Amanda Burton and *Silent Witness*? We have seen *Time Team* giving a boost to archaeology and *Vets in Practice* to the vets. Is this having the same impact on your profession?

Professor Ebsworth: I think CSI has probably an even bigger one because you see more people doing the job. This is one of the problems: it makes it all romantic and then people without enormous qualifications go off to university and say, "I want to do this" and so the forensic courses that we were talking about earlier have a label that makes them seem—I am reminded of that marvellous remark made by Haig about Lloyd George—"always caught with a bright fly." People will gobble it up.

Q182 Chairman: Do you think that is the problem with chemistry at Exeter?

Professor Ebsworth: Now, I am not making any comments! I knew some excellent chemists in Exeter.

Q183 Dr Harris: Before we leave this issue of registration, how usual is it for an organisation like the Forensic Science Society to be accrediting or seeking to accredit university courses and not the professional regulatory body? If we take doctors, the GMC not only credits the university undergraduate courses but also the pre-registration house officer year. The Royal Colleges/BMA—and perhaps you see yourselves as more like the Royal Colleges—are involved in postgraduate registration. I know you have said that you do individuals not courses, but I think it is a common model for you people to be accrediting the courses rather than you—that is, the registrars rather than the Forensic Science Society.

Professor Fraser: I am not sure how common it is. Certainly in other professional bodies it is often the case that they will accredit individuals and organisations, but my understanding—and no doubt CRFP will comment—is that they are largely responsible for individual competence. We think—that is, ourselves and CRFP—certainly in informal discussions, that there is considerable strength in having the register of competence separate from the representation of the profession and the development of the profession.

Q184 Dr Harris: I agree with that, but I am talking about the accreditation of courses leading to competence. I would like you to give an example of another profession where there is a registration scheme, where the registration people are not doing the accreditation courses that are a part and parcel of though not sufficient perhaps for registration.

Mr Kershaw: There are two particular reasons why the analogy does not stand up fully. First of all, there are no courses which produce a fully fledged forensic practitioner. It is always applied and applied in actual practice. Unlike the GMC, which is registering people at the end of an undergraduate course and then pre-registration training and as a fully fledged doctor with full registration, forensic practice does not work in that way, because it is actual practice which proves your competence in the field. Secondly, we are dealing with a complete spread of professions, and we are, as it were, overlaid on a whole load of other professional arrangements anyway and it would be very easy to fall over each other. If I could carry on with the reasons, because this is starting to sound like—

Q185 Dr Harris: No, you have satisfied me!

Mr Kershaw: The GMC, of course, has statutory responsibilities over medical courses.

Q186 Dr Harris: Understood. As you will one day. I would like to ask you about the issue of expert witnesses, which is very topical. To what extent is the ability of expert witnesses to appreciate the legal process and communicate forensic evidence to courts appropriately, a limitation on the effective use of forensic evidence in court?

Professor Fraser: This is one of the fundamentals of forensic science that distinguishes it from, say, laboratory science or other types. Apart from understanding legal process and the ins and outs of the relevant case law, it is crucial that you can communicate it. I know, certainly from my experience, that, in the training courses which forensic scientists are involved in, they get communication in expert witness skills. I do not know, for example—and I will invite CRFP to comment with the Chairman's permission—the extent to which those expert witness skills are incorporated in the registration process. It is a fundamental aspect of forensic science that you can communicate the strengths and weaknesses of your evidence, not just carry out some kind of laboratory-based evaluation.

Q187 Dr Harris: There is a problem, in that the skills are not there and that is an issue—
Professor Fraser: I think there is a problem if you have a completely unregulated sector, but I think with the convergence of registration and professional status of the Forensic Science Society that will begin to lower the risk. I do not think you can ever completely exclude it, because the legal situation is that the courts have the right to decide who will be an expert witness and it might well be that there will be circumstances where someone will give expert evidence who is not particularly capable of communicating that.

Q188 Dr Harris: So there is a problem but it might be getting better.
Professor Fraser: I believe it will get better and has got consistently better.

Q189 Dr Harris: To what extent are the skills in this area part of the assessment?
Professor Ebsworth: You have to recognise that there are different skills involved here. There is giving oral evidence, giving evidence in person in court, and there is writing reports that become part of evidence. In the civil courts, people rarely appear in person. The assessment of written reports is a very important component of the process of judging competence to go on the register. It is much more difficult to find ways of assessing the presentation of evidence in court in person. We are anxious to develop the processes of assessment for use so as to try to bring those in. But that of course can work both ways. You can find people who are not particularly competent experts who become extremely plausible in court and can persuade people to believe things which do not stand up in detail—so one does not want to over-paint that one. But, going back to your basic question, the writing of reports is a very important component of judging whether someone should be on the register.
Mr Kershaw: The thing that our assessors are looking for is the ability to communicate highly technical matters to a non-technical audience in a way that will help them to assess that as part of their overall judgment of a case.

Q190 Dr Harris: After the registration process, are there schemes in the forensic science community that are working to deal with the questions and criticisms made of the poor quality of evidence or expert evidence given? Is this something that you are trying to deal with proactively?
Professor Fraser: I think this is something that the forensic profession has faced for the past few decades or more. We are continually attempting to train people and respond to what are quite complex legal situations. The training has consistently improved in past years—and, again, without repeating myself too much, with registration and

professional membership, that is likely to continue to improve the circumstances. But I think the situation will always be there.

Q191 Dr Harris: There is one thing I cannot understand. In the miscarriages of justice cases that there have been in respect of alleged sudden infant death versus homicide is there a case that there should have been more focus on why the defence side did not bring its own expert witnesses or that the lawyers were not trained to point out the flaws in the expert evidence or that the judge was not able to direct at an early stage and intervene and say, "Hold on a sec"? Because everyone is blaming the expert witness, who is presumably, arguably, doing an honest job the best they can, and nothing has been said about the job of lawyers and defence experts.
Dr Priston: I think that is absolutely right. I think there is tremendous lacking in training for lawyers at all levels—barristers and judges as well. I think any expert, whether it is a forensic scientist or medical examiner or whoever, is very constrained by the legal system and sometimes it is very difficult for them.

Q192 Chairman: What would happen if that did happen, if they were all trained and up to the mark and they said, "I am not sure that band there is evidence in itself, blah, blah . . ."? Suppose they were too clever by half.
Dr Priston: We would not want them to become their own experts, would we? But we want from them an understanding of what is involved and an appreciation—
Professor Ebsworth: There were quite a lot of experts called in at least one of these cases, I seem to remember. Was it not 33? It was an enormous number. It becomes quite hard to know exactly who is doing what to whom. If I may take a specific point: my vice-chairman Judge Anthony Thorpe has been involved in discussion with people from the forensic community and with people from the law to try to find a satisfactory way of making formal statements about DNA evidence in court that will stand up to the appropriate levels of scrutiny necessary both in the first court and in the Court of Appeal. I think they have made a lot of progress and it is something that I believe the council has catalysed. It is very important to get these statements clear and clearly understood by the legal profession and accepted by the scientific profession.

Q193 Dr Harris: We talk about the legal profession, and there is a particular role, is there not, for judges?
Professor Ebsworth: Yes, indeed.

Q194 Dr Harris: You can talk about judges and juries, but it is very hard to train jurors, and judges can direct. We have been talking about barristers and lawyers, but should there be something for judges and should there be judges with specialisms dealing with these sorts of cases?
Dr Priston: I do not think judges need to have particular specialisms but I do think they should have training, and I think training should be part of a lawyer's training right at the very outset, from

pupil barrister upwards. Because judges are just—and I am not being rude—promoted barristers, if their training is at a fundamental level it will live with them.

Q195 Dr Harris: And are judges saying, "Yes, please, we agree. We recognise the shortcomings"?
Dr Priston: The judges love it. The judges have a very strict timetable and so it is difficult to get the judges, but I have run some courses in London for the circuit judges of all the London courts and some of the judges of the Court of Appeal and of the High Court, one day courses, and it is hard to get them to come but, when they do come, they love it and they all say, "We had no idea of the detail."

Q196 Dr Harris: Should we be recommending that the Department for Constitutional Affairs (as the Lord Chancellor's Department now is) should be ensuring that judges are free to attend?
Dr Priston: Yes.

Q197 Dr Harris: And, indeed, arguably recommending it as far as they can?
Dr Priston: Absolutely. Yes.

Q198 Dr Harris: Do you think the defence is getting a fair hearing in respect of (a) a shortage of good expert witnesses to whom they have access, and (b) a sufficiency of forensic experts who are independent of the Forensic Science Society because of the relatively small non Forensic Science Society sector?
Professor Fraser: I do not think that is the main issue. There is sufficient private sector provision for most areas to cover this. I think the barrier is often ignorance or time pressures or issues around legal aid provision. I think the fundamental barrier is around a lack of knowledge of the importance or significance of the scientific evidence in the first place. There are plenty of people from whom you can get advice.

Q199 Dr Harris: You gave us written evidence on this point.
Professor Ebsworth: We hope our register will make it much easier for anybody involved in the legal process, defence lawyers or whatever, to find people who can do a competent job for them, and I believe the Legal Services Commission is looking very positively at finding financial resources where experts are clearly properly qualified.

Q200 Dr Harris: In your opinion—to quote a question you ask in your evidence—does the defence get as good a service as the prosecution.
Professor Ebsworth: I think it has access to as good a service as the prosecution. I think now experts are able and willing to stand as much for the one side as the other. The determination of how good the service really is will depend on resources and not the ability of defence counsel.

Q201 Dr Harris: Is that a yes or a no?
Professor Ebsworth: The answer is yes, but under certain provisos.

Q202 Dr Harris: You would agree.
Professor Fraser: Yes.
Mr Kershaw: If I may add, the Legal Services Commission have a proposal out for consultation at the moment where legal aid would be paid more readily in the case of a defence case bringing forward a registered expert rather than … They could use someone who is not on the register but they would have more steps to go through in order to demonstrate the case. In other words, they are trying to use the register as a form of quality control, partly to make sure the legal aid budget is effectively spent, but I think the useful spin-off for the defence there is that they will have access to information about people who have at least been tested in some way and who could be complained about and dealt with if things went wrong. This has never existed before.

Q203 Dr Iddon: I want to turn briefly to novel technologies and research and development. In some areas, for example testing chemicals, particularly pharmaceuticals, on animals, there is a long validation process, and there is a body set up, ECVAM, in Ispra, Italy, which takes years to validate those processes. Do you have any similar validation methods for new technologies?
Professor Ebsworth: As far as registration is concerned, which is what we deal with, the answer is yes. Because we are at the moment in the process of setting up the appropriate definitions of standards, which is what I think we are really talking about, for the whole area of digital evidence, which struck us as very important. There is an enormous number of people working in this area. Standards are not defined. We have worked with leading groups there and are in the process of defining these standards. This kind of activity is going to spread to all sorts of other new technologies and I think it is an important role that the council can play.

Q204 Dr Iddon: Who decides and at what stage do you decide that the evidence available from the new technology, following analysis of the results, can be accepted by the courts?
Professor Ebsworth: The courts will of course decide ultimately, but our council will set up working groups with people working from the areas but, so to speak, managed by us, working against the standards which are defined by the council—these are broad standards—and if what emerges from the work of these groups appears to meet the standards to which the council's overall functions are defined then we will run pilot studies and if those are effective then we will move towards opening the register.

Q205 Dr Iddon: Is it made clear in the courts that the evidence to be presented is arising from the new technology with all that that implies?
Professor Ebsworth: I cannot answer for that because I have not been present, but I have seen one or two prosecutions involving computer crime collapse because it is quite clear that the protocols did not quite work out properly. So I think the answer is yes. But it is going to become increasingly

important in a whole range of cases, ranging from child pornography to terrorism, where the significance of mobile phone records, for example, becomes absolutely central to the prosecution, so I think it is desperately important to get on with this.

Dr Priston: May I say that I think new techniques are subjected to the same sort of testing as experts; that is, that they are tested by cross-examination and the defence will produce their own experts and challenge, and that is the way that the techniques are introduced when they are robust enough.

Mr Kershaw: In terms of science more broadly, one at least of the research councils—and I think the society refers to this in its evidence—is showing some interest in the forensic sector. Certainly it is not an area which has attracted a great deal of public funding for research purposes in the past, where the evidence you see almost every day for potential difficulties in the courts is producing pressure which is causing great scrutiny to be given to these things. But it must be a problem for the courts when a novel technique is introduced by someone who sounds plausible: if that is not effectively shot down in cross-examination, then miscarriages could occur.

Q206 Dr Iddon: How can the courts assess the competency of a practitioner who is taking evidence from emerging technology to the courts?

Mr Kershaw: That is difficult. If it is a speciality we are not yet registering because it has not reached a stage of maturity where we want to give it that seal of approval, then I think the court has to draw its own conclusions from that fact and accept it is moving in a new area and, I am afraid, get the best advice it can.

Dr Priston: Quite often the courts will not accept evidence if it is that new that there is no peer challenge. They will not accept it; the judge will rule that that cannot go before the jury.

Professor Fraser: I disagree to some extent with my colleagues. I do not think the provision of new technology should be driven exclusively by the professional sector. I think it is important, given the circumstances we were talking about earlier, where we may have serious miscarriages of justice because of scientific evidence or because of methodology or technology, that people from outside the professional sector need to be engaged. So I would like to see a much broader model that engaged the legal profession and other stakeholders in the decisions in using novel technology. The question facing the legal system is: Do we use this in the interests of justice now? The risk is that some time down the road—five, 10, 15 or 20 years—we will find out that there is a flaw in the technology. I think we need buy into that decision by a very wide range of parties. I do not think that is here at the moment.

Q207 Dr Iddon: My concern is that there may be only one person who is developing emerging technology, they go to court and give evidence for the prosecution, and there is no competent person to give evidence for the defence. How often does that happen?

Dr Priston: I suspect that would not be allowed. In my experience, an expert with no possibility of a challenge who was presented by the prosecution was not accepted by the court.

Q208 Dr Iddon: At what stage will the courts accept this kind of evidence if there are very few people involved in the field? It must have been true of DNA.

Professor Ebsworth: It was, yes. But DNA is not all that old, of course: Alec Jeffreys discovered this about 20 years ago, so that is a very new development. In some areas it is not a problem of a lack of people, it is that there are too many people without defined standards. I think that could well apply in aspects of computer crime nowadays: there are stacks of people working in the area but no-one quite knows what they say means. That is why I think it is extremely important that standards are properly defined. I do not disagree with Jim. I think it has to be looked at by people who are not necessarily involved in the forensic side but in the science of it as well. Things have to be as right as they possibly can. On the other hand, you have to use what is there—as long as you can use it fairly.

Q209 Chairman: Our last question concerns this issue of privatisation, as you might have expected. We read the papers today and we hear all the burbling and so on that is going on. Well, we are hardened politicians and it takes a lot to convince us that things are home and dry, so we are going to go ahead and ask you questions about the PPP and what you think about it and the views of your organisation. We know that the interpretation of forensic evidence is very contextual sensitive—various things come in and it has to fit in with all the other types of evidence and so on—so how would that be affected if part of it was coming from the private sector, however it was formed, and part of it from the way it is now, the public sector? Do you think that would bias it in any way? Do you think that would make it messy?

Professor Fraser: From the perspective of the Forensic Science Society we do not have a position on privatisation. We already have lots of members who work in private forensic science so we do not see any fundamental issue around it. There has not been any great representation from the membership of the society in relation to this issue.

Q210 Chairman: That does not mean they do not care.

Professor Fraser: That does not mean they do not care—that is why I modified the end of that sentence there before I completed it. But, given that there is already a private market there, given that we have growing registration and a growing professional body, our response would be that you need growing registration in the market, growing approved accreditation and on-going vigilance really, to ensure that the courts get the standard of expert they require.

Q211 Chairman: How would your organisations fit into that regulatory process, however it was set up?

Professor Fraser: We would fit in in a number of areas. We would fit in, for example, in the accreditation of university courses, so that we have people coming through with the appropriate education. We provide qualifications; by professional membership, which is on the basis of clear evidence and a fairly rigorous process; by continued professional development; and by probably growing formal links with CRFP in terms of managing or regulating the sector.

Q212 Chairman: What kind of powers would the regulator have to have? Would it be a hands-off, nice little cosy regulator, or would it be sharp and nasty?
Professor Fraser: I think we are talking about a network of registration here rather than an individual regulatory body, so I will maybe hand over to Alan when it comes to the issues about—

Q213 Chairman: I want to hear how complicated it might become.
Professor Fraser: It is difficult to say, to be honest. I do not really know, but certainly you would need to have a pretty robust and fairly clear disciplinary process. The test of the regulation, the test of the quality of the professional body will be in their willingness to cut out the bad wood basically, and we are prepared to do that.
Mr Kershaw: CRFP has no responsibilities in relation to how the service is organised and delivered and therefore we have no comment on the question of privatisation. I think it is fair to say our council will work with whatever organisations are working in the field to ensure that standards are right. The point is that it is the matter of who gives evidence in court, who is competent to do that and how to deal with them if they are not, which is our concern rather than the organisations themselves. It is not the organisations which go to court; it is the individuals who do. That is our concern. I would endorse entirely what Jim ways about network of regulation. This is not something, especially with 50-odd professions working in this field, which a body can come along and do to those professions. It has to work in partnership with the representative and the standard-setting bodies and that is why we are keen to work so closely—

Q214 Chairman: In an area of human activity where you have so many individual regulation processes going on in how to work together, what is your paradigm?
Mr Kershaw: I think we would want to make sure we are not having several bodies trying to discipline the same person.

Q215 Chairman: There is a tendency to have too many of them.
Mr Kershaw: We certainly would not want that. We are a small and not particularly well resourced organisation. We do not want to take on more than we need in order to do the job properly, but, so long as we can regulate individuals but there are systems in place for assessing new technologies and so on,

and provided there are ways of accrediting a university course which is overdue, then I think the system will work well.

Q216 Mr McWalter: But one of the ways in which private companies can sometimes get a very strong hold on the market is by having cheaper people available to them, particularly if they are turning out thousands of people who characterise themselves as graduates in forensic science. If I was going to run one of those rather sharp practice companies, I would start employing them and then arguing belligerently that the old establishment was not tuned to modern ways and that in fact these services could be provided a great deal more cheaply by my forensic science graduates rather than your accredited ones and those people are quite likely to be the only people that many private individuals could afford to represent them in court. We all know, as MPs, that our constituents often do not get justice because they cannot afford justice, so I think there is a market here for a really downgraded forensic science if the private sector gets very sharp about its act. I do think you might need to consider that in addition to that regulatory framework you are going to have to be more aggressive about those who say they are forensic scientists but who are not. It is no good just saying, "We have accredited these people and we are going to be dumb about those people over there." Those people over there are the people who, according to yourselves and the evidence you have given us, threaten your standards and, indeed, threaten the livelihood of real forensic scientists.
Professor Fraser: Absolutely. Answering part of your question, the test is against the agreed standards, so whoever comes along from private practice has to meet those agreed standards, and I accept there is a possibility that if they get such a critical mass they could begin to influence them, but we still have this issue where the final arbiter will be the courts. So we cannot confirm—

Q217 Mr McWalter: We all know there is a little bit of a loophole in here as well because sometimes agreed standards are really difficult. Whether it is cot death or brittle bone diseases, there are issues here about actually what the experts think at all.
Professor Fraser: Yes.

Q218 Mr McWalter: And you can rubbish the expert just as quickly as the person who knows nothing at all about bones and that also is a toe-hold for a company that is trying to say, "We are going into this market and we are much cheaper than those people over there who are the old school.
Professor Ebsworth: One of the things you have to recognise, and I am sure you do, is that being a highly competent scientist does not mean you will agree with another highly competent scientist. There has to be room for difference of view, even between properly accredited experts. I hope the courts will see that someone who is on our register has been through a test of competence which will stand up and which is against objective standards. Someone

who has not will have to prove themselves and have to prove themselves by showing that they can meet the same standards. There is no room in the court for cut-price evidence. I am sure no court would stand for that if the evidence itself was therefore undervalued and under-valid. It may be possible to produce services more cheaply, but, in the end, if they do not stand up under proper examination to the standards of quality determined by the needs of justice, I do not think they will be a threat.

Q219 Mr McWalter: But you yourselves have said that sometimes people can sound very plausible and actually not have the scientific knowledge to back that up.
Professor Ebsworth: Yes.

Q220 Mr McWalter: And judges and other people do not know enough science to be able to distinguish that someone is in fact not competent. There are these dangers here which come directly from privatising the service, because we know how privatisation can drive down standards because people will provide a cheaper product than is available in the sort of gold standard system that you are advocating.
Professor Ebsworth: That is certainly true, but not all failings of this kind come from private organisations. There is no defence fundamentally against failings in evidence. All I can say to that is that the system already has a lot of quality private companies, private organisations working in it; there are some that are perhaps less good. I believe that the process of registration is already making a difference there in sustaining the good and discouraging the less good. I hope it will continue to do so.

Q221 Dr Iddon: The General Medical Council often discipline doctors and even strike them off their registers. Could I ask both of your organisations how often this happens in your case.
Professor Ebsworth: It is a bit early to ask us because we the register has only been open for four years. But we have how many disciplinary cases running at the moment?
Mr Kershaw: We have two running at the moment. Those are our first two and we are finding our way and learning as we go. It is a matter of people's consciousness of the ability to complain. But there is a major drive this year to make the register better known within the courts and elsewhere to people who Commission services, so we would expect more. I can say that the practitioners concerned are putting up a pretty robust defence and it shows the value they place on being registered.
Professor Ebsworth: But it has always been an essential component of our system from the beginning that someone who breaks the rules in a serious way should be removed from the register.

Q222 Dr Iddon: Does the Forensic Science Society have disciplinary procedures?
Professor Fraser: We can claim to be even younger in some respects that CRFP. Only in November last year did the Forensic Science Society change from being a learned society to a professional body. Up until then pretty much anyone who was interested in forensic science could join it, whereas now there would be hurdles to get across. But we will have a strong discipline code and we will effectively kick in at those who fail to meet the standard determined.
Chairman: Thank you very much indeed. We will be watching this arena in the press and talking to comrades in the Home Office, ministers and others, about what is happening in this arena because it is a very topical issue and it concerns many MPs as it obviously does you too. Thank you very much for taking part.

Witnesses: **Dr Angela Gallop**, Chief Executive, and **Mr Tom Palmer**, Managing Director, Forensic Alliance, **Dr Nigel Law**, Director of Group Operations, and **Mr Richard Treble**, Forensic Quality Manager, LGC, examined.

Q223 Chairman: You have been sitting in on the session before, so you know about our inquiry, what we are interested in and why we are doing it. We are proceeding with the questions to begin with of the privatisation and how it might affect your business, for example, if it happened. Who knows. However you want to answer this—perhaps all of you could dig in at the beginning and get into the mood.
Dr Law: I do not mind referring to LGC's position on this. We think, with the market as it is, with an 85% market share player, the important thing is how the market is regulated such that there is a level playing field for all concerned. Whether the body is within the public sector or the private sector I think is less important than just the way that body is allowed to compete in the market place, because anyone with that level of market share has opportunities to distort the market to the disadvantage of the customers. One of the

objectives, as I understand it, of the PPP is to try to attract further investment money into forensic science and that of course can be within the context of the Forensic Science Service itself but it can also be within the context of the private sector companies that are participating in this market. In order to have the confidence to invest significant amounts of money, two things have to be clear. The first is that the market will become available (that is, that the work that is currently with the Forensic Science Service in the main will be tendered) and the second is that that tendering process will itself be fair. Providing those things happen, then I think the development of the market to the advantage of the police forces will continue.

Q224 Chairman: Do you do things that they do not do or do they do things you do not do?

Dr Law: We have research and development projects that are unique to LGC for sure, but many of the services that we provide day in and day out will be similar services to those provided by the other players in the market.

Q225 Chairman: How many companies are we talking about here in the private sector?
Dr Law: I would say there are three principal players: the Forensic Science Service, the Forensic Alliance and ourselves, although there are other participants in the market also.

Q226 Chairman: Do you compete? Of course you do.
Dr Law: Absolutely. We are rivals.

Q227 Chairman: How do you compete with each other? Fairly nicely or what? How does it work?
Dr Law: Actively, I think is the right word. I think the playing field, if I may describe it as such, has developed such that three key elements determine where the work goes. One is whether or not good value is being provided. One is the speed with which the results are returned to the customer. The other is the overall level of service that encompasses the forensic offering. I think the way that the market unfolds, whether the Forensic Science Service is public or private, each of the players I think will get as much of the market as they deserve ultimately in their ability to do well in each of those areas.

Q228 Chairman: Do you think they should be privatised?
Dr Law: I think there are benefits in privatising it because the regulation of such a market becomes that much simpler and clearer when you have private organisations competing for the work.

Q229 Chairman: Are they successful in delivering the service that hitherto has been delivered or would it be an improvement?
Dr Law: I think it would be an improvement because, as I say, if there is an objective to attract investment money into the market, confidence on the part of all the players there that the market is being controlled in a fair way is easier to achieve when the parties are in the private sector. It is less important than effective regulation of the market; it is just that regulation of that market can be more straightforward when the participants are private sector players.

Q230 Chairman: Let's see if we can bring someone else in.
Dr Gallop: For Forensic Alliance, I would like to underscore the principle that the playing field should be level because it has been quite difficult entering into this market. Forensic Alliance was established in 1997 and it was really established for professional and not commercial reasons. I think, had we taken a commercial view, we never, ever would have done it. It was to provide a more responsive service and more to provide a supportive and science-focused environment for scientists. They were really the drivers behind Forensic Alliance. It is absolutely

right that if the playing field was more level it would be more attractive commercially, and then the market would open up more effectively than it has to date.
Mr Palmer: The market has become rather more sophisticated, certainly in the last two years. The customers are getting more intelligent; the use of tendering has made quite a difference to the market place. I think the Forensic Science Service, along with us, have had to be more commercial and our promises to the police through a tender process have encouraged competition. That is going to carry on whatever the nature of the Forensic Science Service. I think the key thing is that we will need to maintain the quality of the science; we will not be able to go down the "pile 'em high, sell 'em cheap" route. We must keep that policy up; if not, the criminal justice system will suffer. The Forensic Science Service, along with us, will need to keep the standards of the science high so that we can provide a service that the police and the courts deserve. But I do not think really in the end it matters too much what the animal looks like, as long as it behaves properly.
Mr Treble: The only point I would add to that is that the police, as customers, are becoming more aware of their role as a customer, and they can be more challenging in the requirements they place upon their suppliers by having a number of suppliers in the field. In addition to expanding the capacity that is available for their use, it means that they can take advantage of some of the benefits that have already been alluded to in terms of the overall service provision, particularly in terms of timeliness and the way the service is provided, with the standards of quality taken as a given, that have to be there before anybody can be a credible supplier in this market.
Chairman: Thank you all very much indeed for that.

Q231 Dr Turner: You are obviously in agreement that there needs to be a regulator. Could I ask you your feelings on (a) whether you think it is important for the regulator to be independent and (b) what powers they should have.
Dr Law: There are two elements to a regulator's role. I think you need two sets of regulation. The first one would refer to standards within the sector to ensure that these need to be maintained at the highest possible level. I do not think any of the participants currently involved in the market would say anything other than that. The role of the regulator in that sense could be strengthened further. The way that needs to happen is further independence. It just does not work having the regulation of those aspects of forensic science within the hands of one of the providers—ie, the major provider, the Forensic Science Service. That aspect of regulation has to be seen to be organisationally, geographically and emotionally independent if it is to be effective. The second area of regulation is the bit that was alluded to in the opening remarks which is to do with the level playing field and commercial aspects of how the market runs. This is more difficult because I do not think the size of the market warrants a sledge hammer to crack a nut. I would not advocate a very expensive body being set up to oversee, monitor and

regulate the market. It is possible to contemplate something perhaps within the Home Office or something within the DTI where they are charged with overseeing what is going on in this market place to ensure that its future development is properly encouraged.

Q232 Dr Turner: Dr Law, you have argued that large contracts should be split between suppliers which would be a nice, cosy arrangement if you manage to get them.
Dr Law: Yes, or rather no.[1]

Q233 Dr Turner: What criteria would you advocate for making these decisions? Why do you suggest it is better than a private company taking the line one would expect, which is to let market forces do it?
Dr Law: Market forces do it. The experience we have is that the competition is most intense when you are looking over your shoulder at your competitor on the same account. It has big advantages for the constabularies as well because, first of all, with that proximity in terms of service provision, everyone's standards are elevated. Turn round times would be shorter with that level of competition, day in, day out. Also, if there are any difficulties in the service provision of one of the providers, it is more straightforward for the constabulary to ensure that the delivery of forensic services is not compromised because providing a sophisticated contract is set up it is possible to switch the work from one supplier to another if one, for whatever reason, is under-performing. Far from being a cosy arrangement, we find that the constabularies who operate this—the Metropolitan Police would be the most obvious example—make the competition even more intense.

Q234 Dr Turner: As separate, private companies operating in the sector, what constraints do you find on information sharing between different forensic science providers? Are you able to share data with other providers where necessary without any hindrance?
Dr Law: There are areas where data is shared on an open basis but others where it is not. We find our ability to participate in certain aspects of forensic science is compromised where particular pieces of intellectual property, where something is developed in one area and is not available broadly, are an issue. The way that the market develops to make such things available on a broader scale is quite an important matter. There are precedents for this. There are ways of doing it. For instance, licensing of intellectual property rights would be a typical way that industries find of disseminating to the public's benefit advances made in a particular organisation.
Dr Gallop: Forensic Alliance is slightly different from the LGC because it is very broadly focused. It covers the whole gamut of forensic science expertise. We find ourselves fairly frequently working with

Forensic Science Service scientists, particularly on individual cases where there is a very free and easy exchange of information and data because, after all, we are all interested in the same outcome: that the case is solved one way or another. We do not have those difficulties at that sort of level.

Q235 Dr Turner: The principal objection is where intellectual property rights become involved. Can you think of examples where it has impeded the progress of investigation of cases?
Dr Law: There are examples of this. One would be to do with familial searches of the National DNA Database where the intellectual property resides with the Forensic Science Service and for others to participate in that is really very difficult.

Q236 Chairman: Can you say something about regulation?
Mr Palmer: In terms of the regulation, first of all, you can regulate by trying to get CRFPs for scientists. Probably as important is being able to control and monitor laboratories. It is not just the scientists; you can do accreditation of laboratories and that is another key way to prevent cowboys coming into the market and to make sure that there is a regular check on the quality of science that is provided. Going back to the sharing of information, we have had problems with the Forensic Science Service being the custodian of databases and we are very strongly in favour of that being moved to a separate controlling body, preferably kept in the public sector. For example, in firearms, we have been restricted from using the firearms database in terms of entering data onto the database and getting data back from it. There has been a problem in terms of data being shared.

Q237 Dr Turner: That clearly is not a desirable situation so, provided a mechanism for paying a licence fee or whatever to get around any IPR considerations is put in place, is there any further reason to suspect that there may be difficulties in information sharing?
Mr Treble: The example that has been developed with the National DNA Database where there is one central database and a number of suppliers—certainly there are three major suppliers—feeding information into that for the benefit of the police forces has worked exceedingly well and forms a model for what could be used in other areas where we all accept that intelligence is an increasingly important part of the work of forensic scientists in working with the investigation phase of the police's work as well as taking the cases through the court. If we have common standards for intelligence so the information is being supplied by a number of suppliers and the information resulting from that is fed on to the police forces, it can only be for the benefit of the justice system.

Q238 Dr Harris: Which of your two companies is the "UK's leading private sector supplier of forensic services"?

---

[1] *Note by the witness*: The response "yes" referred to our argument that large contracts should be split. The response "no" indicated strong disagreement that this would be a "cosy arrangement".

Dr Law: I think we would both say yes but you are alluding to the submission I made. I can tell you the basis on which it was made. We were looking at the last published accounts and the various forensic activities that we were involved in. Of course we provide forensic services to the police forces but we also provide them to Her Majesty's Customs and Excise. In our capacity as the Government Chemist, which is a statutory role, we also find ourselves represented in court in a referee function. It was a comparison of our relative size at the point at which published accounts data was available.

Q239 Dr Harris: Does the other expert witness agree with that?

Mr Palmer: No. The range of services that we provide is certainly wider and I would suggest that the volume of work that we do is greater as well.

Q240 Dr Harris: You say that you are one of only two providers of full forensic services in England and Wales, the other one being the Forensic Science Service. I do not want this to be seen at this point as pejorative but you do cherry pick because there are some things that you do not do, are there not?

Dr Gallop: Right from the very start, the one thing we decided we would not do is cherry pick. Although it was extremely complicated, very difficult and extraordinarily expensive, when we set up the Forensic Alliance we had the five main aspects of service provision that we need: forensic biology, chemistry, drugs, toxicology and DNA. We are the only company that has ever done that. We went right across the board, right from the very start. To that we have added more specialist areas like, for example, firearms. We have introduced a whole new discipline into forensic science. There is the discipline of forensic ecology which includes areas such as pedology, which is soil, entomology, which is insects, palynology, which is pollen grain and diatoms. We have introduced that as a new area so I think we can hardly be said to be cherry picking. The other thing we did was to say to the forces, "Give us whatever kind of work you like. You can either give us certain specific sorts of cases or you can give us geographic areas" so confident were we that we would be able to cope with anything that they cared to throw at us. That was right from the start.

Q241 Dr Harris: What do you say to an independent body like the Royal Society of Chemistry who do not have an axe to grind, who say, "Currently the FSS is obliged to accept all incoming case work while other (private sector) providers can and do 'cherry pick'. By comparison this leaves the FSS vulnerable to criticism for taking longer or costing more for the more difficult work while being denied the commercial advantage of the high throughput routine work."

Dr Gallop: I suppose that is correct. Private companies could come and cherry pick but we certainly never have.

Dr Law: LGC does not provide the full range of services. The last thing we would wish that to be described as is cherry picking. If you take the report from the National Audit Office on the performance of the Forensic Science Service, it was highly critical of the turn round times to return work to the police forces.

Q242 Chairman: If it became private with more private companies, they are bound to cherry pick, are they not?

Dr Law: No. I disagree. In terms of our participation in the market therefore, we have gone to areas where there have been problems and made quite a dramatic improvement in such areas. In terms of the rate at which we unfold our portfolio of services and add to that, that is done in consultation with the constabularies in terms of meeting whatever needs they have. As time has gone on, additional services have been provided so that we now do not have the full spectrum of services but we have a very broad spectrum of services.

Q243 Dr Harris: Angela, I do not why you are so defensive about this because if I am your shareholder I would say, "Cherry pick. Specialise. Do what you are good at. Corner the market. Give us a return on our investment. That is why you are in the private sector. Behave like a private sector organisation."

Dr Gallop: Our shareholders have been extremely happy with our performance. We have done extremely well and I am glad to say it has never, ever been an issue.

Q244 Chairman: Do you trust your shareholders? Many chief executives do not now.

Dr Gallop: We are quite content with ours.

Q245 Dr Harris: On the issue of education and training, you have criticised the quality of forensic science degrees. What action have you taken? I understand there are degrees in forensic science and music at the South Bank University. There is another one at Anglia Polytechnic University, which is different from Cambridge. There is one on media studies and another one on theology. What have you done to complain about this because this is ridiculous, is it not?

Dr Gallop: Absolutely. I preceded Jim as president of the Forensic Science Society and I worked very hard in setting up this university accreditation scheme. I personally have talked to employers' groups and university lecturers' groups about this very fact. There seems to be a difficulty here because the government on the one hand is exhorting the universities to fill seats, to get more and more people through their doors, and the only way they can do that is by putting on courses that are attractive to them. Forensic science at the moment is a very attractive option because of all the television programmes you were alluding to earlier. That is why universities are sticking the words "forensic science" onto almost anything and that is proving to be an excellent way of doing it.

Q246 Mr McWalter: The attraction is it is a nice title but all the hard bits are removed. Would that be fair?

Dr Gallop: Yes. The huge danger is that so much time is spent on teaching pseudo forensic science that all the basic, pure science that you need to operate as a really good forensic scientist is missing.
Mr Palmer: The most effective way we have found to protest is not to recruit people from pseudo forensic science courses.
Dr Law: You have picked some graphic examples there. I do not think we should rubbish all these courses. There are some very good people that come forward from some of them. We are concerned at the reduction in pure chemists and other scientific disciplines that are available. The model that we tend to prefer is the one that Dr Turner was alluding to earlier, where it is very good if someone has the basic analytical and scientific discipline on a pure course that is then enhanced with perhaps an MSc to learn forensic practice above and beyond that. We also have perhaps a greater need than most organisations for the pure sciences because we are broad based in the scientific services that we provide. On the one hand, we do forensic science but with, in addition to our roles as National Measurement Institute for chemical and biochemical analysis we do a lot of work in food safety, BSE testing, sheep scrapie genotyping as well, and a lot of work for pharmaceutical companies. All those disciplines tend to benefit from someone with a higher level of pure scientific skills.

Q247 Dr Harris: The worrying thing is that the APU announced last November that it would cease to offer its chemistry provision except perhaps to support its forensic science degrees. We are very concerned about the loss of chemistry departments. What would you be saying on behalf of UK industry if you had the Higher Education Minister or the Education Secretary for ten minutes in a corner?
Dr Law: Something has to be done to prevent the continuing flow in this way. If that requires support for the traditional skills in one form or another, I would recommend that that be put in place. I know that individual universities have their budgets to meet and that is one of the reasons why they are making these decisions, but I think there is a risk that they are short term decisions. In the longer run when there are too many forensic scientists who find themselves perhaps unable to find suitable employment because of over-supply, maybe even those courses will start to come under pressure. I think a longer term view needs to be taken from the various academic institutes and government to ensure that the traditional disciplines are not lost.

Q248 Dr Harris: What training do you offer the police and other key players in the criminal justice system in the use and interpretation of forensic evidence? Do you see this as a way of getting a profit as well as providing an important service, or do you see it as a drain and something you have to do?
Dr Law: The way that we try to ensure that our prospects in the sector are served to best advantage is to provide our police customers with what they need. I know it is a well worn term but the partnership approach is the one that we think works

best. We find some constabularies would very much benefit from us providing training services, and we do, and others where they do not see that need. It is to do with having an effective dialogue with each of your customers to ensure you are providing what they require.

Q249 Mr McWalter: You will have heard from my line of questioning to the last panel that I am very interested in the use of market forces in this sector but not necessarily whether it is private or not because we just heard about how universities will down trade standards repeatedly to get paying customers in, to get their bottom line right. They are in the public sector but they are in a market. It started off as a very regulated market and slowly those regulations all were pulled away. The concerns that we have are about privatisation and how those markets evolve because at the moment it seems to me you are saying you are almost indistinguishable from the FSS in the sense of your aspirations, your commitments to quality and your happiness at strong regulation; but a private market will allow sharp forensics. They will end up being able to cherry pick if you do not. They will end up, for instance, doing things like recruitment from overseas of cheaper people. FAL do that, do they not?
Dr Gallop: Yes.

Q250 Mr McWalter: Far from worrying about the resources here, you are perfectly happy to do that. Is that because they are higher quality or is there a shortage of UK scientists or is it cheaper than training them yourself?
Dr Gallop: It is for a number of reasons really. It is partly because there is a shortage of UK scientists but it is also very much to enrich the scientific culture in this country because scientists coming from overseas bring with them a slightly different mix of skills and experience. This is absolutely brilliant. We have introduced some new techniques and reintroduced old techniques, interestingly, with a rather more modern cast to them that have been tremendously effective in solving some of our recent cases. It is a really good thing to do, not always comfortable in a laboratory because every scientist thinks they do things best so there are some very heated discussions about things but, at the end of the day, I think we end up with a very good model for developing best practice.

Q251 Mr McWalter: We have heard there are hundreds of applicants for each place. Then you give it to somebody from overseas. That does a fat lot of good for consolidating the expertise we have in this country.
Dr Gallop: It is a mix. We recruit an enormous number of graduates and put them through basic training courses, training them from scratch, but at the same time—

Q252 Mr McWalter: 25%?
Dr Gallop: Yes. Probably slightly more than that now. You have to keep a balance between experienced forensic scientists and new recruits. Otherwise you have too much youth and inexperience.

Q253 Mr McWalter: We have heard how important it is to have overseas people. Why do you not have them?
Dr Law: We do. I would echo Angela's words.

Q254 Mr McWalter: A much smaller proportion?
Dr Law: I do not know.[2]

Q255 Mr McWalter: 25% plus?
Dr Law: Maybe it is a little less than that but certainly we have an active recruitment programme for overseas candidates. You made a point regarding a sort of cheap and cheerful potential in this market place but there are two major things that will mitigate against that. The first is that any organisation's reputation is the most priceless thing they have. If that in some way becomes sullied and tarnished by having a down beat, down grade service, where the quality is in some way compromised, that would not stand them in good stead for the medium to long term. Laboratories have to be accredited to meet certain standards. If one were to drive down those standards in an attempt to foolhardily reduce costs, you would lose your accreditation and you would not be able to participate.

Q256 Mr McWalter: Is there anything special about the forensic science market which is different from, say, the broadcasting market where you start up with all sorts of guarantees about quality and end up with *Big Brother*?
Dr Law: Providing there are these effective controls, appropriate opportunities to reduce costs will be sought. That will be to the benefit of the police customers because it will mean that the same or a better service is being delivered at lower prices.

Q257 Mr McWalter: In broadcasting, we had and still have a big public sector, quality driven organisation which sets a tone for that market which, as I have indicated, is now being attenuated. That is what has happened at the moment in forensic science. We are worried that the erosion of the FSS could have the effect of pushing the market down in that way and you would be faced with new challenges which compromise on quality would be a solution to.
Dr Law: Maybe there are a couple of other things that will mitigate against that fear. The constabularies are now becoming increasingly sophisticated in the way that they tender their work and the scrutiny of organisations coming

forward to respond to that tender is now pretty intense. As part of that process, the quality of the service will be a principal part.

Q258 Mr McWalter: Chief constables are now experts in chemistry, are they?
Dr Law: I do not think chief constables need to be experts in chemistry. Our experience is that the forces have some fairly sophisticated people in charge of these areas.

Q259 Dr Iddon: How much does each of your organisations invest in R&D based on turnover?
Mr Palmer: Three per cent for us.
Dr Law: If you take LGC as a whole, I mentioned earlier there is a broad spectrum of analytical services. It would be about 12%. Some of that is contracted; some is not totally funded. If we take the forensic area, it includes both capital and operational expense and this year that would be running at about 15%.
Mr Palmer: Could I add a small warning? I know the FSS were saying they invested 12% in R&D. If you look at their accounts, they invested about £2.6 million last year and that is 1.8% of their total revenue so I am not quite sure where their 12% came from. Our 3% compares with their 1.8%.

Q260 Dr Iddon: If the FSS became a PPP, do you see that figure changing? Yes or no?
Dr Law: There is advantage to be had in a market that can benefit from rapidly moving technologies, for organisations to develop technologies that will be to the benefit of the police forces and the public. Since those opportunities are prevalent and commonplace, I would not anticipate a reduction in R&D, but you may even argue there could be an increase.
Mr Palmer: I am not too sure because the FSS have certainly benefited from public funds to help their R&D. Most of ours is privately sourced. We have to find it ourselves so I think there would be a reduction if the FSS became a PPP.

Q261 Dr Iddon: Does any of your R&D percentage go externally—for example, to universities?
Mr Palmer: Yes, it certainly does.

Q262 Dr Iddon: Do you invest any money in blue sky research, which is long term rather than short term?
Mr Palmer: Yes.

Q263 Dr Iddon: Finally, how many scientific papers do you publish or have you published?
Dr Gallop: I would have to give you a written answer on that, but certainly several.
Dr Law: Several.[3]

Q264 Dr Iddon: Is it a policy of your organisations to allow your scientists to publish?

[2] *Note by the witness*: Non-UK citizens form 5–10% of LGC's Forensic division, and approximately 20–25% of LGC's total operations.

[3] *Note by the witness*: LGC currently published an average of 30 papers per year.

Dr Law: Absolutely.
Dr Gallop: Absolutely.

Q265 Chairman: You do not have an assessment of them in terms of their work and the number of papers they publish?
Dr Law: We do not have that as such but to make sure that they are not inhibited by getting on with the next piece of work we find space in their budgets in order for the individuals to publish.
Dr Gallop: We insist that all the work they do is written up. Otherwise, it is a waste of time and money.
Chairman: Thank you very much for that information which was novel and new to us and very helpful in our inquiry. Thank you for coming and taking time to give us your professionalism.

Witnesses: **Mr Mike Sparham**, Negotiations Officer, and **Ms Helen Kenny**, Prospect FSS Branch Secretary, Prospect; **Mr Jeremy Gautrey**, Negotiations Officer, and **Mr Alan Organ**, PCS FSS Branch Secretary, PCS, examined.

Chairman: You are very welcome. Thank you very much for coming. You heard some of the questioning and the areas that we are interested in and your views are very important.

Q266 Mr Key: Could I start by asking if you all accept that there is a need for the Forensic Science Service to increase its commercial awareness and customer focus?
Mr Gautrey: We all accept that any organisation needs to improve standards. We believe the Forensic Science Service is the market world leader in the provision of forensic science service. The FSS as an organisation does not cherry pick. It provides a full range of forensic science services and does not turn any work away. The private sector organisations in the forensic market can turn that work away and have turned work away where they do not have the capacity. The FSS as a public sector organisation takes on all work and provides the customer with a full range of forensic services all the time.

Q267 Mr Key: Does Prospect share that view?
Mr Sparham: Yes.

Q268 Mr Key: Do you have any other comment that you would like to add?
Mr Sparham: We do see this argument about a market being developed as somewhat unreal. There is very limited demand for forensic science work, mostly from police forces, Customs and Excise and law enforcement agencies. The potential for growing the market therefore is very limited.

Q269 Mr Key: Do you think that the FSS is constrained by its trading fund and really should have more access to external finance?
Mr Sparham: We think it is constrained by general government constraints regarding the public sector borrowing requirement. That would apply whether it was a trading fund or just an ordinary government department. There are somewhat bizarre rules in the Treasury regarding what counts against the public sector borrowing requirement and what does not. There is no doubt that is a constraint. When the decision was announced to privatise the Forensic Science Service one of the man reasons given at the time was the need to raise £30 million of investment.

Q270 Chairman: Do you believe that figure or was it drawn out of a hat?
Ms Kenny: I do not think Prospect would deny that there is a need for investment in the Forensic Science Service but we do not know where they got the figure from.

Q271 Mr Key: How do you think that would change once you become a government company and would it change again if you then become a full PPP?
Mr Organ: I would argue that even if the Forensic Science Service became a private company, because it would still be primarily a public service provider, it would still be governed by much the same rules, particularly procurement rules, the same as it is now.

Q272 Mr Key: Do you think that in principle increased competition between providers of forensic services could benefit the criminal justice system?
Mr Sparham: No. It could well be detrimental because a lot of the work that is currently done in the Forensic Science Service relies on cooperation and team work. This was very much announced in the M25 Silver Acres case last year when the Forensic Science Service said that a lot of the work done on that relies on the different laboratories cooperating together and drawing the links that existed, that showed that apparently different cases were done by the same person. The more you get competition, you are less likely to get cooperation and sharing of information between different providers.
Mr Gautrey: If the FSS was put into the private sector, there would be an organisation to make a profit and it would be very reluctant to share information with its competitors and would probably take an aggressive stance to get rid of any competitors in the market.

Q273 Dr Iddon: Can you tell us why FSS staff mind whether their employer is a trading company or a PPP, because both would operate in a businesslike way and the jobs they would be doing would be essentially the same.

Ms Kenny: The objection that most staff have—I use the word "objection" rather than "concern"—that has been communicated to the trade unions is the objection to carrying out this work for profit. At the moment, we carry it out as a public service. We do not carry it out to make money for shareholders. The staff have a lot of concerns around that, on how the work would change, whether they would be required to use more lucrative techniques to maximise the profit, but their objective is around the profit motive.
Mr Gautrey: People working in the Forensic Science Service have chosen to work with the Forensic Science Service. They have an alternative. They can go and work for a private sector but they have chosen to work for the public sector which delivers FSS on a not for profit basis. The majority of our members object to the FSS being privatised because they believe they do their work as public servants and they want to continue as public servants.

Q274 Mr McWalter: Is it not reasonable for chief constables quite often to place these contracts with the private sector because they seem to get faster turn around times, for instance, so maybe your desire to work in the public sector is partly because it is a cosy existence in which no one hassles you too much; whereas in the private sector if you do not get the job done quickly they will sling you out and get someone else.
Ms Kenny: Forensic scientists working at the bench in the Forensic Science Service would dispute that they do not get hassle from their customers. The difficulty is that we are under resourced. We cannot turn work away. We take everything and it leads to backlogs.

Q275 Mr McWalter: Would a recommendation that you would want this Committee to make be that the staffing levels in the FSS are looked at with a view to being significantly increased, if proper turn around times are to be achieved?
Ms Kenny: I am not sure that simply recruiting staff is the answer, partly because it is all about demand. You cannot predict demand levels. Some things take longer as well and just throwing people at it is probably not going to help.
Mr Gautrey: Part of the reason why sometimes there are delays is because the FSS cannot cherry pick. It has to undertake the full range of duties. It does not turn work away. The private sector competitors can do that. They can control their turn around times to a certain extent, whereas the FSS cannot.

Q276 Mr McWalter: It has been said that if the FSS became a PPP that would damage public confidence in forensic science services. What evidence have you for that?
Mr Sparham: If we can go back a stage, it starts from the assumption that as a PPP it would be private sector classified and dominant in the market. In that way, we would argue that it would therefore act in the same way as any private sector monopoly company would act. It would want to maximise its returns for shareholders and look at ways of doing that. One of the ways it would do that would be to

increase the level of charges to a level that the market would bear and the police force would be willing to pay. That, we believe, would lead to a reduction in the number of referrals.

Q277 Mr McWalter: The main force of your service is to provide evidence for the courts and justice is the ultimate outcome. What you have just said is not associated with that side of the business, is it?
Mr Sparham: Yes. If the police forces decide that the charges have become too high—they already do to some extent decide what evidence to submit and what not to submit—it would not be long until a vital piece of evidence was not submitted for analysis which should have been. I do not know how you can ever prove that but we believe it is a risk.

Q278 Mr McWalter: That is a better answer.
Mr Organ: What we have here is an artificially produced market place that essentially profits from crime. That is what the FSS staff mostly have against this. They look at providing a service rather than making a profit.

Q279 Mr McWalter: Can you tell us what your alternative model for developing the FSS as an independent, publicly owned corporation would be instead of a PPP?
Mr Sparham: We believe an independent, publicly owned corporation which would still be in the public sector but would be released from the public sector borrowing requirement rules would be a much better model. It would be able to operate on a not for profit basis. It would have stakeholders who would be on a body of governance which could include staff representatives. We believe it would meet the government's requirements but without introducing the profit motive into forensic science.
Mr Gautrey: A key point would be that the government would set a charter about the standards that the FSS would be working towards and the board would be responsible for delivering that charter. The government would receive reports on the progress of that throughout its term.
Dr Turner: You must take some degree of satisfaction from the Home Office's statement yesterday that the immediate future of the FSS is as a GovCo.
Chairman: Do you believe that?

Q280 Dr Turner: That of course does not preclude at some point in the future its transmogrification into a PPP. Either way, do you think that either as a GovCo or as a PPP there will be any question of forensic material being restricted for the purposes of criminal investigation? What crucial differences do you see between the two states and how do you think that, whichever state you are faced with in the long term, you can maintain public confidence that there will be no barriers to forensic investigation to bring criminals to book?
Mr Sparham: We do welcome the government's statement of yesterday. A GovCo is not that far removed from the IPOC model that we were suggesting. It does not have the same governance

issues but it is a wholly owned government company and it remains in the public sector. Our concern about the statement yesterday is that it was said that this was a transitional measure and that further consideration would be given to changes in the future, although not for at least two years. We are not sure that the PPP has disappeared entirely. We believe it has not but certainly it is a better option than what we would be faced with. The difference between a GovCo and a PPP is simply in the question of ownership. A GovCo is wholly owned by government. In a PPP, the majority of shareholders are in the private sector and it is the ownership that we believe would mean a difference in the way in which the organisation behaves.

Q281 Dr Harris: I read what the Home Office said. Do you think there is any real change here in respect of what the government statement was yesterday and what they have always said, which was that they would go to a GovCo, assess that and then go to a PPP? Are they just trying to keep you happy until May?
Mr Sparham: I am not sure that keeping us happy is the primary aim.
Mr Gautrey: There is a change. It is not an absolutely massive change because they did originally say they would go to a GovCo before a PPP. The emphasis is that it will be given an opportunity to work as a GovCo before moving to a PPP and that is quite different from what they originally said. It is going to be like a stepping stone. You could put different slants on it. It is probably not as far as we would like them to go.

Q282 Dr Harris: This will be a transitional structure. I do not think personally that you could be clearer than that. I do not know what the difference is between a transitional structure and a stepping stone. I am suggesting you are looking for something here that is not here and you may even have been—I will not say "deceived"—but perhaps spun.
Mr Sparham: There is always spin in these things. The letter we received from the Minister which is the same effectively as what was in the Minister's statement does not refer to a PPP, so we do see a difference in emphasis. She does say that access to private sector capital and partnership is likely to be critical for longer term needs but the final decision to move forward will be determined in the light of the FSS performance as a GovCo. There is therefore no final decision yet. She tells us that there is no irrevocable decision to be taken for at least two years and the future form and direction will depend on agreement of key stakeholders. There is a pulling back from the very broad announcement that the previous Home Secretary made that we are going to PPP. This letter does not say we are. It clearly does not say we are not either but it is a change in emphasis.
Ms Kenny: Members are slightly reassured by the stepping back that we have seen but they do hold exactly the same concerns that you do, that this is simply an attempt to quieten our protests against privatisation and not a real, genuine turn round.

Q283 Dr Harris: Do you think you are a key stakeholder, referred to here, with a lock or are you a stakeholder where the government is encouraged if the unions are against it because it shows they can get the centre ground?
Mr Sparham: We do not know. We have replied to the Minister and asked precisely that question. We have had meetings with the Minister.
Dr Harris: Feel free to share the reply with us.

Q284 Dr Turner: I am inclined to think that memories of the air traffic control saga may also have been a factor in this. Whichever structure you are going to end up with, there is clearly a need for regulation of the forensic science market because it is still going to be a forensic science market whatever the structure of the Forensic Science Service is. What are your views on the nature of the regulators and their powers?
Mr Sparham: One of the things we have been very critical of is the lack in the government's previous proposals of any effective regulation. We believe there is a need for a regulator in two areas. If it was to become a PPP, we believe there would be a need for some form of economic regulation because it would be such a huge player in the market that the case for an economic regulator to oversee prices or profit or those kinds of things would be required. The other issue is standards.
Ms Kenny: All our members feel very strongly about standards. We heard from the CRFP earlier. They are not going to regulate the providers. They are simply going to regulate the individuals. It is a minimum standard of competence. I have concerns. Every time we have raised this, the Home Office have referred to the CRFP as a possible regulator. Unless their role changes significantly, I do not think they would be the best people to do that and they do not think they are.
Mr Gautrey: The FSS deals with highly sensitive investigations: crime, terrorism and internal police investigations. FSS staff are all security cleared. The prospect of a wholly privatised forensic market would potentially mean that there would be no checks in terms of who is undertaking some of these highly sensitive investigations. Currently, you could argue that there are people working in the private sector or forensic market that are not security cleared. The reality is that a lot of people who work in the private sector companies have already been security cleared because they worked for the Forensic Science Service previously, apart from that small, overseas contingent that you referred to, which would be a concern in some of the highly sensitive investigations that are undertaken by the FSS.
Dr Iddon: When the previous witnesses were in front of us, they challenged your figure of 12% investment in R&D based on turnover.

Q285 Chairman: Is it your figure?
Mr Sparham: I think it was in the FSS evidence.

Q286 Dr Iddon: The figure of 1.8% was mentioned. Are you able to challenge that?

Mr Sparham: I do not think we gave a figure.

Ms Kenny: There is a target to invest 11% of turnover set by the Home Office.

Q287 Dr Iddon: The figure of 1.8% was mentioned this morning, based upon FSS turnover and accounts. I wonder if you could look at that figure which the previous witnesses gave us and agree or disagree with it?

Mr Organ: Obviously that is a question for the FSS itself to answer. A substantial amount of the FSS's profit or return every year goes back to the Treasury and goes back into the system; whereas if we become a company I guess that would go to our shareholders.

Q288 Chairman: Helen, you work in the service at grass roots level. What is it like in there? Do people turn over quickly? Are they demoralised? Everybody is always demoralised but would you like your son or daughter to go into the service? Does it feel as if it has a future? I know you are doing a worthwhile job and you all believe that but what do you feel about the future? Are people wary about it?

Ms Kenny: There is a lot of uncertainty and a lot of staff thinking, "If I am going to have to work in the private sector I might as well join one of the competitors." Competitors are recruiting quite aggressively at times. As staff members, everybody is firmly committed to the criminal justice system. The difficulties that we are experiencing are around the uncertainty and the amount of work. It never seems to change. We feel like we have been operating in an uncertain environment since the McFarland Review was announced.

Q289 Dr Iddon: You told us in your memorandum that the government would bail the FSS out if the PPP failed financially. Does that not mean there is a guaranteed future for the FSS in any case?

Ms Kenny: Our belief is that the government could not allow the FSS to fail but it is not a stated fact. I believe there will always be work for forensic scientists but whether that work will be within the public sector or the private sector, within the FSS or one of the competitors or even somebody who has not entered the market yet is impossible to say.

Mr Organ: I represent the non-scientific staff. We have already been through, about a year ago, a restructuring process to gear up for this. We suffered from some redundancies so that has undermined staff and they are very worried about their jobs and the future.

Chairman: Obviously that has been a very important contribution because you are the people who do the essential work. I guess everybody in the country thanks you for the work that you do. We want to make sure the service continues, whatever the arguments might be over the economics and politics and so on. Thank you very much for taking the time to come and give your views to us, face to face.

Wednesday 26 January 2005

Members present:

Dr Ian Gibson, in the Chair

Dr Evan Harris   Mr Robert Key
Dr Brian Iddon   Dr Desmond Turner

Witnesses: **Mr David Coleman**, Chief Constable, Derbyshire Constabulary, **Mr Clive Wolfendale**, Deputy Chief Constable, North Wales Police, **Mr Barry Taylor**, Deputy Chief Constable, Dyfed Powys Police and **Mr Gary Pugh**, Directorate of Forensic Services, Metropolitan Police Service, examined.

Q290 Chairman: Can I thank you very much indeed for coming to help us with forensic science. I promise not to mention binge drinking or 24 hour boozing, but you are very welcome to help us in this inquiry we are doing into forensic science which is becoming very interesting. The new Home Office minister has already said that he is not going to privatise it in the near future, so who knows? We are on the edge of trying to get some help and support, and some of the issues we are raising do seem to be an open door anyway. Thank you for bringing your expertise and professionalism to it. I do not know how you want to answer us; one spokesperson would great but certainly I want everybody to indicate if they would like to add something or amplify or whatever. Let me start off by asking you what you think are the best qualifications or educational background for scene of crime officers and other police forensic staff. Do you need a double first from Cambridge or Oxford, or is that too highly qualified? Or do you need no education at all? Where do we pitch it at? What do you think is best for the kind of person you are looking for?

Mr Coleman: Perhaps I will just give a few brief remarks there and then I will ask Clive Wolfendale who specialises in training to say more. Our discussions have been around the breadth of roles and the difference between a need to have very academic, intelligent kind of qualifications and the ability to show practical competence in dealing with what are some very basic processes at the basic front end of forensic science in terms of scene searching and recovery of evidence. They are indeed extremely basic processes which a normally competent individual with a moderate level of education and attainment can actually be quite successful in. However, we then move right across the spectrum to the interpretational arena where particular scientific processes have to be undertaken. Of course, the further one moves across the spectrum the better qualifications one requires.

Q291 Chairman: If you are looking for somebody tomorrow—obviously it could be a man or a woman of any ethnic background and so on, there are no issues like that that we are going to raise with you because I assume that you handle that—what would you look for? What would they have in their education and qualifications that would make you throw the paper in the bin?

Mr Wolfendale: Perhaps we can just put some context around this. Early in my career I had the experience of directly managing about 100 scene examiners in the Greater Manchester Force and my observations are these. Most of the nuts and bolts forensic work—scene recovery work—currently undertaken in England and Wales is performed by volume crime scene examiners. Their job training consists of a three week course currently undertaken at our training centre in Durham, after which most of those individuals are perfectly competent to deliver a satisfactory service. Most of our results in volume crime and detecting vehicle crime come from those individuals. That is the sum total of their job bespoke training. The people that we find who are best equipped to take advantage of that training and deliver a good service are simply individuals who can read, who can count, who have good interpersonal skills—because they are dealing day in day out with members of the public in distressing circumstances—and who have an inquiring mind.

Q292 Chairman: What about the basic science that they know, for example?

Mr Wolfendale: Science qualifications for those individuals are not, in my view, necessary in any way.

Q293 Chairman: So somebody could come from a literature degree, for example.

Mr Wolfendale: Yes, and many do. Many take a career switch perhaps at the age of 30 from a completely unrelated discipline and work very successfully in the field. The ability to write a good report, to be able to deal with some of the numerical challenges associated with the job but also to communicate with the complainant is a fundamental requirement of the discipline. A little while ago in my own force—which is now in north Wales—we had a selection process. There were about 50 applicants for some volume crime scene examiner jobs. About half the individuals coming forward had BSc forensic science and for the three posts on offer we did not take any of them. Our own internal selection processes weeded them out. We found they were simply not measuring up to the skills we were looking for.

Q294 Chairman: Coming to you having done a forensic science course, would you be suspicious of that, given what you have said about how you can take a native born person, as it were, and turn them into a good practitioner.
Mr Wolfendale: That is a view shared by both the Police Service and the forensic science providers who are, of course, looking for people with a definite scientific bent and some knowledge. As far as we are concerned we cannot tar everybody with the same brush and we take each person on their merits. However, the point is this, we find the courses that are on offer—and I speak here from the police perspective and from the SEMTA prospective where I chair the forensic science group—are largely neither vocationally relevant nor academically rigourous.

Q295 Chairman: So you are laughing at them, are you?
Mr Wolfendale: Occasionally, yes.

Q296 Chairman: It is a university wheeze to get more students in because of television programmes, do you think?
Mr Wolfendale: That is unquestionably the case. There are now probably over 300 combination BSc forensic science courses and combinations available in about 50 institutions. Many of those have been established unashamedly to attract numbers of students to university.

Q297 Chairman: If you had a child who wanted to be a forensic scientist what would you advise them to do, if they wanted to go to university?
Mr Wolfendale: I would get them to the best university possible to study chemistry.

Q298 Chairman: If you could find a department where there is chemistry any more. That is a very interesting point you make.
Mr Pugh: My background is as a forensic scientist and I think there is a spectrum of ability required both within forensic science laboratories and within the Police Service. For me I think the issue in terms of how we look at potential applicants, we are looking for people who have very practical skills. We do not need boffins certainly within the Police Service, if I can use that expression. We are looking for people who have an inquiring mind and who also have a basic academic ability; we do not necessarily look for a degree but nowadays most of our applicants come with a degree. Within the Met the important thing for us is really about competence and we need people who can work at a crime scene on their own, can deal with victims of crime but also can have the technical ability to recover evidence. I think there is an increasing demand in terms of technical knowledge. Going on from that, I would add to Clive's point as well, certainly moving from the volume crime and certainly in London with the volume of serious crime, we need staff with interpretive skills. They need to be able to understand what has happened at the crime scene. They need to be able to interpret events effectively.

Q299 Chairman: The same people who do it?
Mr Pugh: Yes.

Q300 Chairman: You look to them to interpret the evidence and give you a "could be this, could be that" sort of thing.
Mr Pugh: I think we are looking for them to interpret the events at the crime scene to gain an understanding of how the crime was committed, to inform the decision making within the inquiry.

Q301 Chairman: Is it successful?
Mr Pugh: Yes.

Q302 Chairman: It really works well?
Mr Pugh: Yes.

Q303 Chairman: It is a new lively enterprise you think.
Mr Pugh: I do not think it is new; I think it is an innate skill that has always been there. What we have tried to do is encourage that interpretive contribution, particularly within homicide, supported by forensic scientists and other specialists where required.

Q304 Dr Turner: At the same time as university chemistry departments are closing students who might have gone there in the past are being seduced into glamorous looking forensic science courses—maybe they think they are going to play the Amanda Burton role or something—but these courses are in fact of little value in any practical terms. You are not the only witnesses we have had suggesting that. Do you feel this is a matter of great concern because it is in fact undermining your own potential recruiting process and that of the real Forensic Science Service? If you agree with that proposition, are you doing anything to feed back to the universities that they are offering a very poor false product?
Mr Wolfendale: We are definitely doing just that on behalf of the Police Service and on behalf of SEMTA (the sector skills council with responsibility for this area). You may be familiar with this document which is the *Implications for Higher Education* which was published about three months ago now and which explores just that topic. Following on that I have personally taken interviews to major newspapers and our director has spoken to Radio Four about this very problem. Can I make a point so far as the Police Service is concerned on this? As well as a waste in young people's time and a waste of parents' money, as well as the degradation of science within higher education, there has been a tendency in the last ten years for some of these institutions to begin to suborn police forces in their locality and our training establishment to trying to get their hooks into us as some sort of testimony or accreditation of their competence and relevance. This, in itself, has been injurious because it has meant an overhead on forces in terms of the training that they have begun to undertake without full knowledge of the consequences. Again it has led to training which is irrelevant and not fit for purpose. There is an additional danger there but it is one which we are

now alive to and most forces are beginning to resist. My final point on this is, as a matter of interest, of the over 300 courses now available two-thirds require no A'level science qualification at all to get on them. I think that tells its own story.

Q305 Chairman: So you are really sceptical; you think it is just way to get students into the university.
Mr Wolfendale: I think it is a savage waste of young people's time and parent's money.
Dr Turner: And tax payer's money.

Q306 Dr Iddon: As a former academic teaching chemistry and one who has planted quite a number of my former students into the Forensic Science Service I am very pleased to hear what you said about chemistry. Can you tell the Committee, for the benefit of other members who may not know, what is special about chemistry graduates in the Forensic Science Service?
Mr Pugh: I am a chemist myself and I think chemistry—certainly from my experience going into the Forensic Science Service—gives me a base of knowledge around the main processes and techniques that forensic science uses. Nowadays perhaps there is more bias towards bio-chemistry with DNA profiling, but I think the analytical sciences—which is my particular specialism—are under-utilised and I think that having a good sound chemistry base allows you to understand the analytical techniques that are used to compare fibres, glass, paint and so on.
Chairman: I think I have got the message on that one, thank you very much.

Q307 Dr Turner: There is, of course, an enormous range of scientific forensic techniques available now to police officers. Are you satisfied with the level of awareness of non-scientific staff and investigating officers in the police? Are you happy that the police themselves are in a position to make the best use of the forensic support?
Mr Coleman: I think in broad terms the answer to that would have to be "no". I think we can never really have the level of awareness that we would ideally like—which is near a 100% awareness in every one of our operational staff—for a number of reasons, not least of which is because we have people with such a broad range of experience out on the front line from the first day probationary constable to the hard-bitten 30 year officer who has been there, seen it and done it. It is a constant process really of trying to ensure not only that that basic long-term awareness is there, but when new techniques arise, new abilities to seek evidence in different ways, that we are able to disseminate that evidence properly to staff. Working as we do in an organisation which is multi-site 24/7 it is very, very difficult to get large groups of people together to give them the information and also to take them from day to day duties for any sort of training. It is a battle to raise that awareness. There is so much other information that police officers need to receive in addition to

forensic awareness that there is a tendency for information overload and therefore perhaps some of the key messages do not get through.

Q308 Dr Turner: Obviously you cannot expect every plod to be completely aware of all that is going on in forensic science, but equally any investigative team must have access—one would think—to somebody with that knowledge, not necessarily to know how to do it, but to know what is there and how to use it. What steps do police forces take and does ACPO make any recommendations to provide this sort of forensic liaison so that any investigating officer knows who to ask in his force at a moment's notice if there is anything that can help him?
Mr Coleman: I think that would be a feature of every force, that every force would have its scientific support department or whatever that particular force might call the department. Within that department would be a range of people with particular types of expertise from scene managers to fingerprint experts to people with expertise in DNA. I would be very surprised if any force did not have the facility for officers attending a crime scene to get first-hand advice from somebody of that nature.

Q309 Dr Turner: There is still obviously a need for, say, a detective sergeant to know that he needs to ask these questions so there is a minimum level of awareness which is obviously needed at middle to senior police ranks.
Mr Wolfendale: That is the key.

Q310 Dr Turner: What steps do you take to ensure that that training is given?
Mr Wolfendale: Once again I start by suggesting to you something which I always preface any conversation of this kind. About 30% of primary volume crime detections in my own force arise from forensic science of one type or another: DNA, fingerprints, footwear principally. I suspect that is the same in most forces. That is how important it is in terms of the overall crime fighting effort. The steps we have taken are broadly speaking these. About ten years ago the Police Service, together with the Forensic Science Service, developed a package called *Think Forensic* which was a series of fact sheets and a video which gave every officer a basic understanding of techniques in dealing with volume crime. That was updated about two years ago principally by the Hampshire police and it is undertaking a full revision and bringing it up-to-date with new techniques and that will be produced in April 2005 (in about three months' time). In the last two years we have also revised the probationary training arrangements in terms of the information given to officers in their basic training so that they have an understanding of the basics before they undertake patrols and start investigating crime. On top of that, in terms of the access to advice which you were specifically alluding to, that advice can be gained through any internal force scientific department. There are broadly speaking four layers of expertise within most departments starting at the bottom with the volume scene examiner doing

essentially vehicle crime; then a fully-fledged scene examiner doing a broad range of violence, burglary, robbery; then there would be a scene manager who would take responsibility for managing a team perhaps at the scene of a very serious assault or a murder; on top of that there is a scientific support co-ordinator who is a very skilled and experienced individual who will be able to manage multiple scenes and bring various disciplines together and co-ordinate the entire scientific input. Those ranges of advice and expertise are available now in just about every force. This model has been developed under the auspices of the National Training Centre for Scientific Support which is at Durham and is broadly established and accepted force-wide. On top of that the Forensic Science Service, through the DNA expansion funding, has offered additional training throughout the country. Unfortunately I agree with David Coleman that the take-up for that was disappointing from my point of view but, as an enthusiast, you would not expect me to say anything else. That is an indication, I think, that the spread of expertise and interest is not as wide as we would want it to be.

Q311 Dr Turner: Is there a cost consideration in forces taking up training provision from the FSS? Do you think this could be adversely affected by commercialisation of the FSS either to its projected form of the GovCo or even it were finally privatised?
Mr Coleman: The current round of training that is being offered by the FSS has been funded through the DNA Expansion Programme so there is no cost to forces. However, one can imagine in a future situation when the FSS status changes that they will certainly not be wanting to carry out those sorts of activities for free. Unless that funding continues from a government source—which the FSS will presumably then have to be contracted to deliver—we look to move into a situation where I think forces will be paying for trainers. There are a number of forces who have their own forensic trainers, including my own until recently when the individual left. We found that to be extremely effective.
Mr Pugh: The challenge in London in trying to reach 35,000 officers formal training is not really effective and we have to make more use of our own intranet and other means of doing that. We are trying to do that in London to try to raise basic levels of awareness. I think the key issues are around scene preservation and management and the need to make sure that officers do not compromise what comes later and all the good work that goes on. Also, in key groups of staff, particularly senior investigating officers in homicide and serious crime, we need to target groups to make sure they have the level of forensic awareness to make use of the tools.

Q312 Mr Key: Are the numbers of scientific support staff rising or falling across the country?
Mr Coleman: I would think they are probably stable at the moment. They have risen significantly in light of the funding that has been available from the DNA Expansion Programme and that is where we have managed to recruit increased numbers of forensic

vehicle examiners, for example, who are the people who receive rather less training. They have been extremely effective, but with the budgetary settlement this year it would be my guess that there would be very few forces that will actually increase their scientific support staff and it may be that some of them are under great pressure to reduce staff.

Q313 Mr Key: Are you saying they would have liked to have but they cannot afford to have because of the settlement?
Mr Coleman: Most forces I think would, given the opportunity, take on extra scene examiners. I think there is a problem with that in that you have to look at the process holistically and if you are more successful in recovering evidence from scenes then, as a consequence, you will need more fingerprint examiners, you will need to spend more money on DNA analysis, for example, and if you have a chemical lab as well it may put pressure on that. In work we have been doing with the Police Standards Unit we have argued very strongly to look at the whole system holistically.
Mr Wolfendale: I think the most authoritative study which is relevant to your question was undertaken about 18 months ago, the Occupational Mapping Study, by an independent consultant revealing that there are about 5,000 people currently employed in police scientific support units—much the largest overall employer—and probably about 4,500 people employed in the Forensic Science Service and other forensic science suppliers. That number I think marked the end of a huge expansion during the 1990s when departments upgraded with the advent of DNA and opportunities that afforded. As Mr Coleman said, the numbers have now broadly speaking stabilised. However, there are other disciplines here that begin to creep in and I refer particularly to digital technologies and computer examination which is becoming a huge requirement on forces in terms of investigating internet crime, e-crime and the rest of it. Those figures are still not particularly well understood but certainly every force to my knowledge is expanding its operation in that field.

Q314 Mr Key: Is it possible to identify any forces across the UK where they are short of scientific staff?
Mr Coleman: I am certainly not aware of any from the soundings I take.

Q315 Mr Key: What impact would privatisation of FSS have on the numbers we have been talking about? Would you anticipate that it would be harder to retain as well as recruit or would it just not make any difference?
Mr Coleman: I think that rather depends on how the salaries move. It is entirely possible that if competition arose between providers competition would also then arise for staff. It may well have the impact of pushing salary levels up which may well attract some of the staff currently employed by the Police Service to go and work for the forensic providers. But it is highly speculative at this stage I think.

Q316 Mr Key: Are you saying that you would anticipate that if the private sector pays higher salaries then the Police Service will have to pay higher salaries so there would be fewer people in the Service?

Mr Coleman: It is possible but we already have difficulties in some areas for instance fingerprint examiners where there is quite a bit of competition for fingerprint examiners when forces seek to recruit them. Many forces find themselves paying market supplements in order to retain their existing staff.

Q317 Mr Key: Mr Pugh, I believe the Met has a problem with retention. Is that the case?

Mr Pugh: Yes, in several ways. We are overwhelmed with applicants for many of the reasons we touched on earlier. It is really about retaining staff and offering them– not least because of the particular issues around working in London—a career development opportunity within the Met Police which we are seeking to do. Our staff—certainly our scene examiners in London—work on a 24/7 shift system and that has demands on them and they look for other careers. Interestingly they also move in to become police officers so even though there is a benefit to the Metropolitan Police I find there is a steady drift of staff who come into the Police Service as a scene examiner but they then see and understand the packages that are available for police officers and move in that direction.

Dr Turner: My own police force is the Sussex Police so they border onto the Metropolitan area. They suffer a very severe retention problem because the Met keeps coming and poaching their officers because the Met can offer them more money and free travel. Does this sort of thing happen with forensic workers as well?

Chairman: Are you asking them to stop it?

Q318 Dr Turner: They have been asked to stop it.

Mr Pugh: I do not think I could comment on the police officer issue. With regard to the forensic staff, we do not offer any particular packages. There is clearly a market for forensic staff and particularly experienced staff, whether it be fingerprint experts or scene examiners or crime scene managers. I think there is a movement between forces certainly in the south-east but there is not at the moment, if you like, a bidding war going on between them.

Q319 Dr Turner: You do not actually go poaching?

Mr Pugh: No.

Q320 Dr Turner: Why is CRFP registration not compulsory?

Mr Coleman: The ACPO position on CRFP registration is that we support it and we are very keen to ensure that people are independently accredited as being of the expertise they claim but the only way of making it compulsory for staff who are already in employment is to get them to agree to change their contract and that presents some significant difficulties. There are a number of forces now that are taking on new staff on the basis of a

contract that includes a requirement to be CRFP registered and the signs are that it will not be too long before all police scientific staff are registered.

Q321 Chairman: We have been told by several sources that there are great variations in gathering and using forensic data between different police forces. I guess that is probably true.

Mr Coleman: Yes, it is.

Q322 Chairman: Why is that? Is it because the Met is poaching all the best people?

Mr Coleman: I would certainly not subscribe to that view. There are many reasons why that should be and that is something around the way the Police Service is structured into the 43 forces which have different financial backgrounds, they are at different stages of development, they have different kinds of leadership and leaders who have different interests and emphasis.

Q323 Chairman: That is a bit worrying. That would mean that somebody has a greater chance of getting off in Kings Lynn, for example, than in Ipswich.

Mr Coleman: It is possible but in a service that is delivering across the country with as many people as we have, it is inevitable that some people will be more skilled than others I guess at the bottom line.

Q324 Chairman: That is not good enough, is it?

Mr Coleman: No, it is not.

Q325 Chairman: What are you doing to sort it out?

Mr Coleman: One of the things we have been working very hard on in the Forensic Portfolio is to try to ensure that forces are all driving up standards. We have done a lot of work with the Police Standards Unit on process mapping. We have a simulation model now that actually simulates the whole of the forensic processes which can be taken to any force and it can be laid against their performance. That will enable them to diagnose where their performance needs to improve and what particular aspects of the process they need to sharpen up on or put more resources on and so on and so forth.

Q326 Chairman: You said "we"; is there a person or two people whose job it is to drive it together and make sure there is unanimity across the country? Or do you just talk about it when you have a joint meeting?

Mr Coleman: It is not either of those. Across the Forensic Portfolio—which includes the witnesses today and a number of other senior officers—there is a general drive to improve standards and raise the profile of forensic science and increase investment in forensic science.

Q327 Chairman: Who is the best? If there were a league table who would be the best?

Mr Coleman: I am sure you would not expect me to answer that, Chairman, and I am not going to.

Q328 Chairman: Give me a clue. Is there a best and a worst?

Mr Coleman: I would not care to say who is the best and who is the worst. There are some people who are good at some things and some people who are good at others and a few who are good at everything and I would certainly not choose to pick out colleagues.

Q329 Chairman: Would you say that DNA analysis is better done in one place than another?

Mr Coleman: I think there are some people who manage the process better than others. If you look at the DNA process for example there are a number of opportunities sometimes missed to collect DNA.

Q330 Chairman: If you could tell me who was the worst, could I send my DNA to them? If I was picked up say at Riverside in Norwich on a Friday night with 25,000 others and they insisted on taking DNA, have I the right to choose who that DNA gets sent to?

Mr Coleman: No.

Q331 Chairman: Does it have to be done locally?

Mr Coleman: The DNA will be taken by the force which arrests you and the analysis will be done by the provider that that force normally uses.

Q332 Chairman: That takes me to my next question. The provider might be different in different areas as well and there must be good providers and bad providers. How does a force make the decision?

Mr Coleman: In terms of DNA then the custodian of the database sets the standards by which the DNA analysis has to be conducted and has a regime of quality control which ensures that all the providers analyse DNA to the same standard and the same quality.

Q333 Chairman: Do you keep it in the family? Are you a family unit, as it were, in the police? Do you say that a certain provider is better than another?

Mr Coleman: There are a variety of views on that. Forces who use a particular provider through choice would say that they feel that that provider is the best provider for them. That does not necessarily mean that the other providers are bad, but that force feels that that provider gives a better service.

Q334 Chairman: If I was making that decision for a force, what criteria would I use to decide who was the best for my force?

Mr Coleman: I think we are firmly in an era of best value now.

Q335 Chairman: In money? Would it be the cheapest?

Mr Coleman: No, best value is not about money it is about the relationship between turn-round times, quality of service and cost and I think that the cheapest is not necessarily the best.

Mr Taylor: Picking up on that forces are driving up performance themselves through regimes such as using the Police Standards Unit who are monitoring force performance, HMIC recommendations in reports such as *Under the Microscope Refocused* and so on. Coming back to the forensic providers, in some of the work I am doing at the moment in relation to procurement issues we need to articulate clearly the standards we expect forensic providers to perform to. That work is being undertaken at the moment. Standards are important in all of this but in terms of the evaluation of contracts, the evaluation is an important feature in relation to standards, timeliness and other services that providers can and will offer to forces. Forces will articulate to forensic providers what their evaluation criteria will be as it suits them because there is no one size fits all, depending on locality, geography and the nature of the crime or incidents that occur in that particular area. There may be different criteria that forces would want to assess.

Q336 Chairman: Can you give me an example?

Mr Taylor: My force is Dyfed Powys and is a huge geographic area. We are a very low crime area too. Geography is a difficulty for us and in terms of timeliness for collection of forensic exhibits that may be more of an issue for us than a more compact force where transportation is easier. Thankfully we do not have a gun crime problem in Dyfed Powys but other forces do have a substantial gun crime problem. Our evaluation criteria of particular types of services or products would take that into account. The evaluation criteria would very much be tailored to suit a locality and the policing need of that locality.

Q337 Chairman: Do you have to bid for money depending on those decisions. You might want more money, for example. We are battered by the police as you well know in terms of budgets and so on, but I have never heard them ask for extra money for this kind of service.

Mr Taylor: I think by and large money is nearly always made available for forensic budgets with police services. I am not sure that forces have fully understood the nature of their forensic spend at the moment. Some forces slightly under-spend their budget but most tend to over-spend and so perhaps the budget has not been set appropriately in the first instance. There is increasing reliance upon forensic evidence and there is a realisation across the board— and certainly at chief officer level—that we clearly need to take the best possible advantage of forensic science and when we re-assess our budgets throughout the year we would make that provision available to us and if necessary make further bids to the police authority to increase the budget for that particular service.

Q338 Dr Iddon: There has been quite a lot of criticism in recent years of the Forensic Science Service itself. What difference do you think conversion of that service from its present operation to a GovCo would actually make? Will it be sufficient to ensure that the FSS is competitive in what is now after all a forensic science market?

Mr Coleman: Firstly I think that some of that criticism has been unjustified over the years because if we examine what the FSS has achieved over the last five or six years for example in terms of automation and mass-production of DNA analysis then they have moved into a world leading position very rapidly as a result of pressure from the Police Service on turn-round times and costs. Amongst the problems there is a success story in some of the major areas of business they achieve. However, turn-round times have been a particular issue and from my perspective as the Forensic Portfolio Holder I have not had anything like the amount of complaints around turn-round times in the last two years that I had earlier in my tenure so it is my belief that that has been improved. To the question specifically, the difficulty that the FSS is under at the moment is that it works on very much the basis that it has always worked with the Police Service. It is on a very much non-contractual gentleman's agreement type of approach and it has therefore never felt the need to sharpen up its act commercially. It is restricted by rules on where it can obtain capital from for reinvestment and therefore it is operating in some facilities which, although I would not necessarily say they are anti-diluvian, they are fairly ancient and certainly need to be addressed. My feeling in moving it to GovCo and potentially later to the public/private partnership firstly it will get its commercial act together and it will become much sharper in its negotiations with forces in competition with other providers because if it does not it will very quickly start to lose business and we have already seen examples of where that will happen. Once it becomes more commercially aware and more competitive it will secure business and it will then be able to re-capitalise and invest in some more modern equipment and buildings and so on. I think that the benefits will be seen within three or four years.

Mr Pugh: Just adding to David's point, clearly the focus is on the privatisation of the FSS or the move of the FSS in terms of its commercial development but in my experience certainly from working in the Met for the last four years the issue is about the commercial development of forensic science and within that the privatisation of the FSS. We have a market place and I think that certainly from where I sit we need to manage that and manage the risks that there will be continuity of provision and that standards will be maintained. I think importantly—certainly in my role—the forensic science community have to deliver services that the police need to tackle crime. In my view you have to start from that end.

Mr Wolfendale: The point I would like to make is that since agencyisation I think the Forensic Science Service has been living in a twilight world for 10 years and in that position I think it has done extremely well in the face of having to try to find its way commercially but also being constrained by still being part of the Home Office. For me the big downside in that period for it and other suppliers has been that because investment has been limited R&D has been stifled and whilst we can point to DNA as being a huge success—and so it is—in other areas such as digital technologies and biometrics there have not been the developments which I think there might have been and which would now be benefiting

crime investigation throughout Britain. Personally I look forward to some aspects of the new world where this might be freed up and we might see some very quick developments. What I see then is a rich opportunity for an expanding business both in this country and abroad.

Q339 Chairman: How do you see the state of bio-metrics research at the minute with the ID cards and all this business? Where do you think it is at? Are we half way there to getting it accurate or what?
Mr Wolfendale: I think about half way is where I would put it and there are some centres of excellence around the country where there is some first class work being done, but it is not being translated into a commercial product at the moment.

Q340 Chairman: So you do not use it.
Mr Wolfendale: No, we do not use it.

Q341 Dr Iddon: You have argued for a regulator. Could you expand on that a little and tell the Committee who that might be and what powers they should have?
Mr Coleman: At the moment we are in the process of negotiating the separation of the National DNA Database from the Forensic Science Service so that the NDNAD remains public ownership with direct access to the Police Service. With that will go what is known as the custodian who is the arbiter of the rules and regulations and standards surrounding the database. What we are arguing is that that role ought to be expanded firstly to become custodian of other forensic databases and we are thinking of issues such as the National Fingerprints Database and others that will come along. Then that role could actually be broader in terms of standard setting for new players entering the forensic market and one of the benefits of commercialisation of the market is that one would expect new providers to come in with new technology, new ideas and so on. They need to be accredited and we need to be reassured before we start trading with those people that the way they conduct their business is proper.

Q342 Dr Iddon: Who would do the accreditations?
Mr Coleman: That is the debate that is going on at the moment. In terms of DNA what we are looking at is the custodian becoming part of the Home Office which is directly linked to government as it should be in terms of provenance in the public sector. The custodian will operate probably by some form of contracting out an outfit that actually accredits and ensures quality standards in DNA providers. We see that as being a principle that could be expanded to cover people entering the forensic market and also periodical re-accreditation of players who are already in. We need to bear in mind, of course, that many of the providers—in fact all of the providers—have independent assessments through UKAS and so on so we know that the players in the market at the moment are well accredited and are capable of delivering a product that has integrity. What we

need to do is have something in place that ensures that new people coming in are able to satisfy us the same.

Mr Pugh: I would add that quality and public confidence in forensic science and the databases are paramount. I think we have to start from there and therefore the regulatory function—or whatever the function is described as—is an issue around the forensic databases. However, we do have a situation where the market—as Clive mentioned—has been around for around 10 years. We have a near monopoly provider and we have two other providers who really have their roots in the public sector so it is not as if a major multi-national has come into this particular market. In my view—and I think we have seen this—there are some risks around how the commercialisation of forensic science develops and therefore perhaps a broader role being on the custodian in terms of dealing with those kinds of issues I think would be beneficial. I would return finally to the point as well about looking at this in a strategic way in terms of what technology and science does the Police Service need in order to improve its performance. That strategy could address that issue as well.

Q343 Dr Iddon: Do any of you have any experience either directly or knowledge of police forces who use different suppliers of forensic data? If you have, can you tell us what problems those police forces might experience in getting the results on time and the application of those results? Are there any problems with multiple supply?

Mr Coleman: There are a number of forces that use different suppliers to the FSS and there are a number of forces that use a mix of suppliers.

Q344 Dr Iddon: It is the ones who use a mix that I am particularly interested in.

Mr Coleman: There are some that have done it on a geographical basis. Thames Valley, for instance, used to put half of their work to FSS and half of it to Forensic Alliance on a geographical basis within the force. Some forces have put a particular kind of work to a different supplier, for example all their drugs work to one supplier and many of their other pieces of work to other suppliers. I think the experience by and large is that if forces have experienced problems with a supplier on a particular sector of work they have tended to move that work to another supplier at an appropriate time. The feed back I get from forces about different suppliers is that most forces are happy with their particular supplier at the time. I think the Met is probably distinctly different in that it has a particular strategy and Gary might want to enlarge on that.

Mr Pugh: We use all three providers and we have approached this from the perspective of how do we get the best service to support tackling crime in London with a heavy emphasis on improving timeliness. The procurement exercise and the contracts we put in place focus on securing improved timeliness from the forensic science providers. We use all three providers in order to do that, to deal with the volumes of material particularly DNA in London. I have to say that using all three providers—including the FSS in a particular area of routine analysis—has delivered benefits to us. By putting it within that framework it also brings a discipline to both sides in terms of us having to manage demand into the providers and they have to deliver to the contracts and service agreements that we have set up.

Q345 Dr Turner: Expert witnesses have to perform in courts. Sometimes things go wrong. The most blatant example I can think of is the most notorious murder in recent years in the Brighton area when the prosecution expert witness was being savaged by a sharp barrister who pointed out that the sample bag he was holding up and discussing was actually empty; the sample had gone missing. That is a fairly grotesque miscarriage of practice but nonetheless clearly expert witnesses have to be able to handle themselves in front of some very sharp legal sharks. How significant is the number of cases that are affected because the expert witness is not able to get the forensic evidence across to the court sufficiently well?

Mr Coleman: I think what that particular example demonstrates is the need for some sort of checks and balances to be in place to satisfy the court that when somebody appears as an expert he or she is actually an expert. The problems that sometimes arise in that regard are that experts in particular fields are so few that it is actually very difficult to find somebody who is in a position to challenge an expert on an equal footing. I can think of people in soil analysis and issues like that where in some fields there are only two or three experts in the world on a particular topic so it does become extremely difficult. I think it does demonstrate again the value of independent accreditation by such bodies as the CRFP and bodies of that ilk. What we have found in our membership of the CRFP Board of Governors is that there are rival organisations that seek to claim themselves as organisations which can accredit expert witnesses and in a sense there is competition between two or three bodies that is not actually helpful. What we have tried to do is to encourage the CRFP to work with the other bodies to make sure that they understand what each other's boundaries and responsibilities are.

Q346 Dr Turner: Gary, you would perhaps like to comment because the Met have submitted written evidence on this very point. Can you comment on how much impact the use of the CRFP register has had in getting consistency of performance in expert witnesses and is there any need to establish clear practices for the courts in dealing with expert witness evidence?

Mr Pugh: I will defer to Clive who sits on the Council, but in terms of our particular experience I think there is an emerging issue in terms of registration and how we deal with individuals who are called into question. I have unfortunately one or two examples in London where expert evidence has been called into question. We have then carried out very extensive reviews of the work carried out by the individuals in terms of the contribution it makes. This takes us into a discussion with the Crown Prosecution Service around disclosure and whether or not there are previous cases that the defence need to have disclosure of. It links also into issues around where perhaps the individual may have been employed by the police service as a finger print expert and how that interacts with the discipline process. I think there are a number of inter-connecting processes here that we perhaps need more clarity on. What I think we also need is an early warning system or a mechanism to alert us to where an expert is called into question so that we can take action to mitigate any effects of that on current cases. The CRFP, which I fully support, is still perhaps in its infancy in terms of its ability to manage the professional standards.

Mr Wolfendale: I endorse everything Gary has said, particularly that the register is still very young. I now believe that the right organisations are involved in CRFP and are fully involved in its implementation. The pilot study which was undertaken in the north-west region proved successful and free of any controversy which I think is a good sign. Given that, I do think now that we have reached the point where the register should be seen as the principal and prime guarantor of quality to the criminal justice system. As Gary has said, there are other organisations that would seek to query and muddy that ground and so that will have to happen within the next two years in my view. Finally, expert witnesses do fail sometimes and are not satisfactory but overall a lot of evidence telling is that cases that go to court with forensic evidence attached are more secure and they are more likely to succeed. We must never forget that.

Q347 Dr Turner: Finally whilst we are on expert witnesses, what do you think could be done about making sure that the courts and juries have a sufficient knowledge base to be able to interpret the forensic evidence that is placed before them, and what do you think you can do to stop distortion arising from the adversarial nature of the judicial process?

Mr Coleman: I am tempted to say change the adversarial nature of the process because the very essence of adversarial processes is to discredit the other guy's evidence. Unfortunately I think that creates doubt and uncertainty in the minds of the jury when often there is no need to do that. We have an independently accredited expert who is using techniques that have been well proven over many years and if the defence brings an expert who seeks to challenge that and put a different interpretation on it then there is not much that can be done about that in an adversarial system. It is a question of who presents the most powerful picture to the jury and who convinces the jury. Regrettably that is the nature of the system.

Q348 Dr Turner: To be fair you are arguing from a prosecution perspective. Do you think the defence gets a fair crack in terms of handling forensic evidence?

Mr Coleman: They have full disclosure of the forensic evidence; they have the opportunity to have the original material independently examined by their own expert and they have the facility to get experts in almost every case I would guess of equal standing to the person who is giving evidence for the prosecution. I think on the whole the defence does have a fair crack.

Q349 Mr Key: How aware are people at all levels in the Police Service of the potential of forensic intelligence as opposed to traditional forensic evidence gathering?

Mr Coleman: Not as aware as one would like them to be. I know that is not a particularly slick answer but forensic intelligence as a concept is relatively new. We have traditionally used forensic material in evidential mode, ie to support a particular prosecution case. What we are now moving into—particularly with the aid of digital databases—is the ability to spot patterns and connections between different crimes and different individuals. It is very important that we actually increase awareness particularly at front line level where officers miss opportunities sometimes to seize forensic material or to take DNA samples from individuals because they do not realise the value of actually doing that. There is a gap and we need to improve awareness.

Mr Taylor: I think the National Intelligence Model is beginning to help here and it links back to an earlier question you raised about awareness. General awareness is important; we do not need to have experts in every field but general awareness about how to secure and preserve evidence and to secure scenes in order to call in people with relevant experience to forensically recover evidence or raw material that may be advantageous. The National Intelligence Model permeates the whole of the police organisation but at different levels. Officers are governed or conduct their daily business in accordance with the National Intelligence Model making the best of the information they have available to them but certainly making links between crime scenes, individuals, trends and commodities sometimes. That is helping focus attention to this particular area now quite well.

Q350 Mr Key: Is evidence on these databases available to different suppliers of forensic services? What happens, for example, if a privatised sector has staff who are not security cleared? Do you check that?

Mr Coleman: Speaking in terms of the National DNA Database and the National Fingerprint Database that is not accessible directly to suppliers; it is operated within a secure environment.

Q351 Mr Key: Would it be available to a privatised forensic service?

Mr Coleman: No, it would not. Not directly, no.

Q352 Mr Key: I see. That is rather important, is it not?

Mr Pugh: Yes. I think with regard to security clearance that may be one of the by-products of putting in place more formal contractual relationships with providers, that it is a requirement that their staff are security cleared and, for example, are CRFP registered so it provides a vehicle for doing that.

Q353 Mr Key: How much research and development is going on into forensic intelligence at the moment?
Mr Coleman: There is a significant amount of work going on in terms of developing the ability to miniaturise the DNA process for example which will increase the through-put of DNA profiles into the DNA database. There is work going on to implement a new National Fingerprint Database which is going to take place next year. We also have some work going on in relation to footwear and the potential to create a new footwear database; there is a new National Firearms Forensic Intelligence Database. So there are an increasing number of databases that are actually being put into place.
Mr Wolfendale: As far as intelligence is concerned, could I just urge a note of caution here? There are a lot of agencies and a lot of suppliers who look to thrust the notion of forensic intelligence upon the Police Service. Part of the reason for that is because it is a good earner. I would like to remind us that in itself intelligence has no value; it only translates into value when it is transformed into evidence in terms of investigation or preventing a crime. Individuals and companies who promote the notion of forensic intelligence for its own worth ought to be treated with some degree of caution.

Q354 Mr Key: Thank you for that. What input does the Police Service have into the Engineering of Physical Science Research Council's *Think Crime* grant programme?
Mr Coleman: ACPO sits on the body that considers the bids and awards the grants and puts the Police Service view.[1]

Q355 Mr Key: Finally, are there any problems with allowing the presentation of novel forensic techniques in court?
Mr Coleman: In terms of technology available there often are problems. Many of the courts are not equipped to deliver the latest means, DVDs and so forth. Many courts are not equipped to deliver evidence through those means. I think we will see an increasing move in the service towards trying to produce evidence using those media for ease of reference.

Q356 Mr Key: Is that because of a shortage of resources for the court service or is it because of resistance from the judiciary or, indeed, from the Home Office?
Mr Coleman: I do not think it is resistance; I think it is probably shortage of resources. Technology moves so rapidly that public investment just has not caught up with it.
Chairman: Thank you very much for being good expert witnesses. Can I just say that it has been very helpful from your point of view because we hope we will be able to influence some of the policies in this area that you slightly touched on at the end. I think we got the messages about education in this field and the resources and support and we will do our bit in our report. Thank you very much for coming along today.

Witnesses: **Professor Sir Alec Jeffreys**, Department of Genetics, University of Leicester, **Professor Stephen Haswell**, Analytical Science Group, University of Hull, **Professor Tony Sammes**, Centre for Forensic Computing, The Royal Military College of Science, Cranfield University and **Professor Sue Black**, Department of Anatomy and Forensic Anthropology, University of Dundee, examined.

Q357 Chairman: Can I welcome you to the Committee. I understand you are not all experts in every area so you can answer in any way you like. I hear, Professor Sue Black, that you have been involved in the Tsunami episode.
Professor Black: I have, yes. I came back from Thailand last Thursday.

Q358 Chairman: We are quite interested in that, what the problems have been in terms of how government, for example, and the departments within government have been interacting together on it. Have you seen any results of deliberations that you have that that could be effective? In other words, do we need to do anything at our level to make it better?
Professor Black: I think that is now in hand, I am delighted to say. When forensic practitioners watch the news they watch it slightly differently from other people; we look at it as we are packing our suitcases expecting to be deployed. As an organisation who receive funding by the Foreign Office we began on

26 December to assist the UK. We had a considerable number of contacts with the Government which resulted in an absolutely deafening silence. In fact my deployment, as I went out to Thailand, was not on behalf of the UK Government but on behalf of a commercial company. It gave me an opportunity to assess things on the ground and having come back now I have a meeting this afternoon with the Foreign Office and a local authority later one this afternoon with the Metropolitan Police to take this matter forward, so it is in progress. Yes, we could have moved quicker; yes, we could have done things differently, but hindsight is a wonderful thing that must of us just do not have the grace to hold.

Q359 Chairman: Thank you for that. We welcome also the man who is responsible for DNA and you will be gratified I am sure to hear that DNA is being

---

[1] Mr Coleman subsequently submitted a written reconsideration of this answer. See Appendix ??.

used all over the place now in helping forensic teams. Let me start off by asking you what input any of you have into the forensic science degree courses. I am not going to repeat what was said in the last session but calling them useless was pretty close to what a lot of people thought. What are your views about this up-swell of courses going on to increase student numbers?

Professor Jeffreys: I have no direct involvement but I have a real concern that there is an explosion of courses. I had a quick look at UCAS yesterday and I found 422 single and combined degree courses are now on offer in the UK involving some aspect of forensic science. The courses are offered by 58 universities, most of them new universities. I have no idea what the quality of those courses is like. I think the Forensic Science Society which is the professional body has a major job on its hands in terms of accrediting some of these courses and these courses seem to really contradict the recommendations specifically from the Forensic Science Service and the Forensic Science Society that people entering into forensic science should have a basic degree—for example in chemistry, biology, physics or whatever—and then convert either through a masters mechanism or through in-job training. I have considerable concern about the value of these courses and about the fate of the people being recruited into them.

Q360 Chairman: Chemistry was pinpointed by the previous witnesses and you will know I am sure that chemistry departments are struggling because of the RAE and other factors as well. Do you have a very strong view on that?

Professor Jeffreys: Yes, I have an extremely strong view and it is not just for forensic science. A lot of forensic science is chemistry and you need chemists coming in there, not people trained on exceedingly broad forensic courses that attempt to cover the whole science and the technology which in my view is basically impossible. However, it is not just for forensic science. The pharmaceutical industry for example absolutely depends on a very vigorous chemical base. Given the expansion within forensic science and within pharmaceuticals, to start closing university chemistry departments just does not make sense.

Q361 Chairman: Can I ask the others if you have alternative views or other views about this whole situation which we have been examining?

Professor Haswell: I support and echo the views as a chemist and as someone involved in teaching forensic applications of chemistry. It is fair to say though that the forensic science courses are tracking students into science at some level that perhaps would not have been there at all. I have a good example. We have a young man who is now finishing his PhD who originally went out and was working in the commercial world but went on to do forensic science, understood his limitations and came and did more chemistry, built it up and has now finished

something which is very worthwhile. It is a gateway in for people. I think it is a question of how universities look after that.

Q362 Chairman: What would you do if you were vice-chancellor at Exeter University and you were closing a chemistry department and developing forensic science departments? How would you attract them into the basic sciences when you have these competing forces of money considerations and so on?

Professor Haswell: Students applying for the forensic science courses are twice that for chemistry and chemistry with other subjects so there is a need and a demand from the consumer. I think it is a question of how you deal with the expectation of that customer, how honest you are with them and how you deliver and prepare those courses.

Q363 Chairman: Is there anything we can do to merge them together other than just insisting that they must do it?

Professor Jeffreys: There are a number of chemistry departments that do offer combined degrees in chemistry and forensic science. These are fairly recent developments and it is clearly a mechanism for attracting people in. You are absolutely right; kids are very excited about forensic science now for whatever reason and if we can use that to bring them into the basic sciences I think that is extremely valuable.

Professor Sammes: I go along entirely with my colleagues on this. I am not absolutely convinced though that a first degree is appropriate for forensic activity. I think a basic science or engineering degree is essential. The forensic activity is probably better coming at post-graduate level and that is precisely what we are doing. I run a MSc in forensic computing. I would state, however, that a chemistry or physics first degree is not necessary; in the area of forensic computing IT degrees are equally acceptable. I would stress that the scientific method is the vital issue that underlies all the forensic activity.

Q364 Chairman: When somebody sets up a forensic science course it is fairly obvious—it is hardly rocket science—that there must be basic chemistry or chromatography or whatever it is. Why does it not happen? That is what I do not understand.

Professor Black: I think you have to look at who is offering the course. For example, the sex appeal of forensic is not just a problem for chemistry and physics; it is a problem for biology as well. In my discipline our problem was that archaeology departments had seen a way of introducing forensic anthropology into archaeology. With the best will in the world the body that is brought out of a harbour has much more of a relationship to a patient in a hospital than it does an Anglo-Saxon warrior. We had people taking information that they felt was applicable but generally was not so it was being concentrated perhaps on areas that were least applicable. When we then took those students out of their courses and took them onto the front lines in Kosova, in Bosnia and in Iraq these students were woefully under-prepared for what was required from them as a discipline. What we then said was that if that is the case then we have a responsibility as a university and as a practitioner in that subject to take our own subject by the scruff of the neck and bring it into line. We have gone away from the one year master's conversion course and we provide a full eight year career progression pathway for people in our discipline. You come in at day one and we train you right the way through for eight years. At the end of the eight years you are ready to look at accreditations with somebody like CRFP. I think the practitioners in the disciplines have to take some responsibility for those people that they are training to come along behind them.

Q365 Chairman: How can they get that responsibility? How can they come to acknowledge this in themselves, given that universities have a certain amount of autonomy, for example?
Professor Black: They do but it takes a considerable amount of foresight in the university. When I went to my university with what I wanted to do, they said that the last thing they wanted was to have a cap placed on their head or a badge around their neck that says, "This is another one of those forensic courses". We do not want that. The credible universities are looking at, if we are dealing with this subject, what do we need to do to produce practitioners at the end of the day that meet the needs of the market where these people are going for further career involvement.
Professor Sammes: One way of doing this that we follow is to have an advisory panel which is advising the committee on the structure and the form of the course. That advisory panel is drawn from people who are practitioners in the field.

Q366 Chairman: Subjects in higher education blow hot and cold; they go up and they go down. Do you think forensic science will burn out?
Professor Black: Yes, I do. We have seen the first wave of forensics crashing and I think coming behind it is a wave that is much, much more aware that quality that is required. I think those universities who are now coming in on that second wave are in fact much more aware of the situation. They are the ones who are going to look to accreditation with professional bodies and when those courses become accredited those students who are aware will know where they have to go to look at this as a career progression. However, that does not stop the other universities who want to offer forensic investigation and music as a course to be able to do that; it is the students' right to choose it if they wish to go down that route. But if it is not accredited to somewhere that is going down a professional route then at least we would take away part of that problem.

Q367 Dr Turner: What do you feel are the most promising areas of research and development in forensic science at the moment? What new applications can you see in the next few years?
Professor Sammes: I think I can say that the digital area is taking off almost exponentially and is likely to continue to do so. Digital devices are becoming more and more common place in use and associated more and more frequently with crimes of one kind or another. I believe digital devices is one area where there is a considerable expansion needed.
Professor Haswell: In my particular area—I am involved with the EPSRC panels—it is in the areas of more reliable and rapid intelligent information on chemical and biological media and materials. One of the drivers in this is the ability to miniaturise a lot of the techniques we use, which allows us then to take them into the field to get much more rapid, real time information which aids in both eliminating and identifying potential perpetrators. I believe that that is a growing area and one this country is a leading player.

Q368 Dr Turner: I believe ACPO are members of that advisory panel. How useful is the input of the police perspective towards directing likely areas of research?
Professor Haswell: I think what you have to realise is that the academic community out there—which is a formidable resource in terms of the UK capability—are not guided well and they are not informed well of what the needs are. If you look at what has been funded through that EPSRC "Think Crime" programme I think out of the 29 projects that have been funded only four or five of them have been from biology or chemistry; most of them have come from digital processing data and manipulation. I think that is saying that that community of scientists are not seeing the pull towards forensic work. That is probably because it is not being explained to them in terms of what they can offer. I think we are not getting a lot of guidance—this is true in the course development and it is true in research—in what research needs are how they are perceived by the user and I think without that you are not going to draw on the vast resources there that could be used.

Q369 Dr Turner: Your comments lead directly to my next question which is what are our current strengths in forensic science research and practice and, given what you have just said, are you worried about us being able to maintain what is currently a world leading position in forensic science?
Professor Haswell: I am worried about us using it effectively. When I look around at what people do in their research profiles you can always see tremendous opportunities to develop forensic support and forensic technology. That is simply not being tapped into. I think it is a kind of management problem more than a science based problem. It is just not being managed properly and exploited properly.

Q370 Dr Turner: Another issue, given that forensic science is becoming marketised to a degree and may well be further marketised, can you comment on the funding base of research and development in forensic science because there is an obvious worry that with increasing commercialisation there will be less funding coming from the body that finally replaces the FSS for instance.

Professor Haswell: Absolutely, it is a great concern that you will lose that focus and drive that is fundamental. I heard the discussions earlier; it is key that you have people who understand the fundamental science, who understand measurement and can interpret and relate to that. If you do not do that, you will not be able to move the science forward; you will not be able to have a future in terms of the demands of forensic science. Unless EPSRC or who ever picks up that mantle and manages it appropriately with the right focus, it will be lost.

Q371 Mr Key: Who trains judges, lawyers and police in novel forensic intelligence technology? Does anybody train them?

Professor Sammes: I can answer that we train police in digital electronics and computers and so forth in the forensic techniques associated with those. That is the only part I can answer. We have trained in the last five or six years some 700 law enforcement students in that area.

Q372 Mr Key: So there is no knowledge of anyone training lawyers. Does that make any sort of sense? Surely if you are presenting detailed technological evidence in court and the lawyers and the judges do not know what you are talking about, it is not really a very good idea.

Professor Black: We have difficulty even in dealing with the repeated training of police officers because with the best will in the world they are here today and promoted to another force in six months' time and we have to start all over again. Certainly in some of the specialised areas in which we operate many police are unaware of what we are able and capable of doing. The knock-on effect of that is when you get involved in a major investigation there are often not aware of what the financial implication of that extended investigation is going to be from a scientific point of view. We have problems at the police level before even going beyond into the lawyers and the judges.

Q373 Mr Key: Are you confident that the Home Office understands this novel technology?

Professor Black: No.

Q374 Mr Key: No?

Professor Black: In many cases, no.

Q375 Mr Key: Therefore ministers do not either. That is clearly a "no" from all four of you. Well, we have a problem, Chairman, do we not? If the Home Office—the sponsoring department—does not understand what is going on in the forensic service, what on earth are they doing privatising it?

Professor Sammes: I did not respond to you directly but I am not sure that it is an entire "no" in the area of computer forensics. I think there is an understanding within the Home Office in that area and they certainly support what is now known as the Digital Evidence Group which is representatives of police forces, ACPO, Customs and Excise and is chaired by a Home Office gentleman. I do not think it is entirely true to say that the Home Office does not appreciate the computer forensics activities.

Professor Black: But there are black holes.

Professor Sammes: There are black holes, certainly.

Professor Jeffreys: It is certainly my experience in DNA that there are plenty of informal routes for education. When we first came up with the technology entirely voluntarily on a very active programme we had discussions with judges and lawyers and so on and I think that is something that continues. The information does get out.

Q376 Dr Turner: Your comments about the Home Office are somewhat worrying given that they are responsible for policy in this field. The comments that you have just made, Professor Black, about police officers moving around is equally true of civil servants. They are shuffled around as well. By nature they are generalists and not specialists so they will not start with a specialised background. Do we need some additional mechanism to ensure a consistency of expertise in the area of forensic science within the Home Office?

Professor Black: Certainly if you look at the overseas involvement where we are deployed quite often by the Foreign Office, we have to re-invent that same wheel at the Foreign Office every time we are deployed. We have new personnel to meet who do not understand perhaps what identification process is required, what depth of forensic investigation is required and what is possible within the country. We are constantly re-inventing every single time the UK is deployed abroad. To a lesser extent we are possibly doing that in many of the police forces.

Professor Haswell: The speed by which technology and the breadth by which science is developing is so fast that it is very difficult to capture the relevance of what is going on.

Q377 Chairman: Where does RAE fit in forensic science?

Professor Jeffreys: I know nothing about RAE ratings.

Q378 Chairman: Is there not a separate committee for forensic science?

Professor Jeffreys: No.

Q379 Chairman: So it falls away and does not get assessed research-wise.

Professor Black: Certainly within our university they are going through a process of wondering what on earth to do with me when it comes to the RAE.

Q380 Chairman: Who funds the research and development and do you feel that enough of it is going on? How is it done, for example?

Professor Jeffreys: Going back to the point about forensic science being an all-inclusive science that borrows technology wherever it can possibly get it, the critical thing is to ensure as strong as possible a line of communication from the forensic users—the Forensic Science Service or whatever—back to the academic community. I am not convinced that in Britain we really optimise that. Let me just give you one small example. The Forensic Science Service, if you go to their website or look at their annual report, it is great on the case work they are doing, they have a very active research programme there and it is almost completely invisible. As an outside academic I would like to open the window to see what is going on in there. Can we help them? Can they help us? Let us open up a far better line of dialogue. I do see this as a problem in the UK.

Professor Black: My recent letter to the Home Office asked that very question. I am not a chemist; I am not a physicist; I am a biologist, where do I go to seek funding for biological based forensic research? My response from the Home Office was that if I was in England and Wales then I could link into research at the Forensic Science Service or with an independent provider like Forensic Alliance, but the quote was, "We do not know what happens in Scotland". Of course in Scotland the forensic service situation is allied to each of the independent police forces so that as a tapping in of research potential for funding that is not an option.

Q381 Chairman: In England do these connections take place with the FSS and private providers of services?

Professor Black: I have no first-hand knowledge.

Professor Jeffreys: Certainly the private providers are really quite limited. I am not being rude about forensic scientists, but there is a culture of proud independence that you see right round the world in the forensic community. That sometimes stifles these interactions back into the academic community. Another example of that is: where are the Forensic Science Service headquarters sited? They are in Birmingham, really rather remote for many academic institutions. We are not optimising the interaction where we could take the incredibly vibrant and strong science base in the UK and have forensic science really capitalise on that in the best possible way.

Q382 Chairman: Like in your case with DNA—and many other people with new technologies I guess—it is funded by research councils.

Professor Jeffreys: My own research is funded by the Medical Research Council and it was made very clear to me that now that it had gone forensic it was a job for the Home Office and the MRC at that stage were no longer terribly interested in supporting it. Again I think that is a culture that is somewhat alarming, that forensic science belongs to the Home Office and medical science belongs to the MRC. That is a split which I do not think is helpful.

Q383 Dr Iddon: Professor Jeffreys, as the person who showed the potential for the use of DNA fingerprinting in forensic science do you feel personally that you have been fully involved in the development of the applications in forensic science down the years since the discovery?

Professor Jeffreys: Not at all, nor would I have wished to have been. The technology is way bigger than one person. I was privileged to have stumbled on this totally by accident 20 years ago. For me to claim ownership of the technology which has had such a remarkable impact would be wholly incorrect. I do keep a very careful watching brief on what technology is being developed and how it is being deployed, however. I am not washing my hands; I am just saying that it is way too big for me.

Q384 Dr Iddon: Have you been happy in the way it has been taken forward or have you been critical in some instances?

Professor Jeffreys: I have been critical in a few respects, particularly with some of the recent developments in the National DNA Database, for example.

Q385 Dr Iddon: You have been quoted in the media as having said that DNA fingerprinting is no longer foolproof. Is that a true statement or is there media exaggeration?

Professor Jeffreys: It is a true statement but I will get rid of the "no longer"; it never was foolproof. There is no such thing as a scientific technology that delivers foolproof answers. I think it is a trivial point, but it is an obvious one.

Q386 Dr Iddon: Do you think the custodians of the National DNA Database have taken that on board, that it is not foolproof and never has been?

Professor Jeffreys: Not to my full satisfaction. We know that that database will contain errors. There are no independent external audits of the nature of those errors or their frequency. The way the database is handled is primarily that the board of governors is essentially ACPO and FSS, I think with a member from the Human Genetics Commission as well. That does not seem to be quite as open and independent as I would have liked for a database of that size and that importance. I think there are issues about the quality of the database.

Q387 Dr Iddon: Those questions were obviously directed at Professor Jeffreys but I would like to bring everyone in now. Familial searching is enabling the identification of suspects on the basis of their relatives' DNA samples. DNA is starting to be used to identify the physical features—the hair, the eye colour, et cetera—of suspects. How does that potential balance with the civil liberty angle? GeneWatch, for example, has some extreme concerns about this extension of DNA usage.

Professor Jeffreys: I will happily comment on both. Familial searching I think is an interesting extension to the current use of the database. The database was established to retain profiles of convicted criminals so that if they re-offend they can be speedily apprehended. You are now using the database in addition for implicating relatives and I think that does raise some civil liberties issues. There is also one of practicality. Given the number of markers that are used in the current DNA database as soon as you start familial searching you lose a lot of the statistical discrimination, there are going to be an awful lot of people brought into the picture. That, I think, has potential adverse impacts on the way you use that information in a criminal investigation.

Q388 Dr Iddon: It is 10 markers now.
Professor Jeffreys: Yes, and I would argue that that is not enough.

Q389 Dr Iddon: You are arguing that it should be 15 or 16.
Professor Jeffreys: That is correct. If you look, for example, at the Tsunami disaster, the identification there is done on a 16 marker system and I would argue that the UK should be running at about that sort of number.

Q390 Dr Iddon: Do you have any idea of how much that would increase the cost of DNA fingerprinting?

Q391 Professor Jeffreys: In principle not dramatically. There are kits out there that will enable you to do a 16 marker test with no extra time or very little cost implication compared to the ten marker test at the moment. The major problem is what we are going to do with the two and a half million database entries that are primarily 10 marker. Do we go back and re-test everybody and get them up to 16 markers? That is the problem. As soon as you have opened very large databases it is extremely difficult to move into a new technological platform.

Q392 Chairman: What is your advice about that, go back and start over again?
Professor Jeffreys: In a perfect world yes, but again if you were to call me back 10 years from now there would probably be some other technological platform and there will be even cheaper, quicker and more effective methods.

Q393 Chairman: Somebody could stand up in court and say that then.
Professor Jeffreys: Yes. The science is never going to arrive at the ultimate solution. Somewhere down the line a line is going be drawn saying that this is as good as it is going to get and in the 20 years since forensic DNA started by definition we have not arrived at the right answer. I think the answers we have at the moment, the 10 marker system, is not quite enough for a host of reasons.

Q394 Dr Iddon: Do any of our other witnesses have anything to say on the line of questioning so far, particularly on familial searching?
Professor Black: No.

Q395 Dr Turner: Could you expand a little on reasons why uncertainties can arise in DNA evidence? Are you saying that it is normally presented in court in terms that there is a one in a million or whatever chance of this being somebody else other than the accused, does it affect these probabilities markedly? Are there technical reasons that completely pervert that evidence? Are we missing an opportunity with the database to use it also as a base not just for identifying people but as a pool of epidemiological research material?
Professor Jeffreys: Could I start with the second question first because the DNA information that goes into the National DNA Database carries no information other than identity and relationship and to a very small extent ethnic origin. If you were to somehow marry together forensic databases with medical databases, the sort of information that for example would come from Biobank (the proposal to survey 500,000 people), you would first of all have to use very different types of genetic markers and secondly that would raise major issues about the people who are entering into the criminal DNA database as to what right the police have of accessing genetic marker information that is important to them as an individual in terms of health risks. I would forever see forensic DNA databases and medical DNA databases being kept completely separate. I think it would be extremely difficult to see how one could sell to the public a forensic database which carries very sensitive medical information. How would you use it? How would the police look at a DNA profile?

Q396 Dr Turner: I am not suggesting the police should use it.
Professor Jeffreys: If they were to use it they would be faced with impossible decisions.

Q397 Dr Iddon: Let us look at the situation where the FSS may go through GovCo and eventually to PPP which appears to be the Home Office's planned route for the FSS. If we get a PPP out of the FSS and it goes almost completely out of the public service that alters the relationship with all the databases, not just the National DNA Database but the Firearms Database and all the other databases that are associated with the FSS at the moment. Do you have any views as to who should be the custodian of those databases should the FSS become a PPP?
Professor Jeffreys: As I understand it at the moment the owner of the database is ACPO and that I presume would not change. For a criminal DNA database I have no problems with that at all.
Professor Sammes: I would agree with that.

Q398 Dr Iddon: You have already commented on the access to the different databases; who should be the gatekeeper? Should it be ACPO for the access to the databases and set the standards and the rules of access to all these databases, not just the DNA database? It is not just the police who could have access to the databases; it is beyond the police, is it not?

Professor Jeffreys: If the databases are expanding to include people who are not criminal then simply allowing anybody in the police to access the database willy-nilly would be inappropriate so in terms of guardianship there would have to be some different mechanism, some separate agency.

Q399 Dr Harris: Professor Jeffreys, you just talked about the database being expanded beyond the criminals, but of course it already has expanded beyond the criminals. If you or I were arrested for protesting excessively by the standards of Mr Blunkett—which perhaps would not be very excessive at all—and that was a recordable offence, our DNA would be stored. Do you have concerns about the way that people never convicted or even charged with any offence appear to be on this database forever, uniquely, and that those people may cluster among certain groups in the population (ethnic minorities, social classes)?

Professor Jeffreys: I have repeatedly argued that I am totally opposed to the extension of the database. I regard it as highly discriminatory for exactly the reasons you say, that you will be sampling excessively within ethnic communities, for example. The whole thing seems to be predicated on the assumption that the suspect population are people who would be engaged in future criminal behaviour. I have never seen any statistical justification for that assertion; none at all. Yes, it is discriminatory. I believe there has been one case that has gone to appeal and lost in the UK and has gone to the European Court of Justice. It will be extremely interesting to see their ruling on this.

Q400 Dr Harris: Another issue that has been raised is the question of the fact that samples are retained indefinitely even when the data has been stored. Is it your view that there is a necessity to do that once the data—assuming it is protected and safe—does not have to be re-obtained? What are the benefits of retaining a sample and for example deciding whether to go to sixteen markers would you need the original sample again, versus the civil liberties issues of this indefinite retention?

Professor Jeffreys: You have just answered the question that you need to retain these samples to cover yourself for the eventuality of a change in the testing platform. If we go from 10 to 16 markers and you want to update a database, you are going to go back which means keeping all DNAs. The potential concern I have there is what would the police be allowed to do with such samples and not do with such samples. It comes back to the question for example, of medical information being pulled out by DNA. If you have a DNA profile it is just a bunch of numbers on the computer and it really does not matter, but if you have the original DNA sample then you have the potential to extract absolutely

every scrap of genetic information of that individual from that sample. I would be reassured if there was very strict legislation in place that would limit the police in what they could do with those samples that had been retained.

Q401 Dr Harris: We have also heard from GeneWatch which is not an organisation I usually agree with on these issues, but there is this question about research being done. There is no independent ethical oversight that you would expect and indeed require in respect of research ethics committees and so forth for samples outside the DNA Database and this research has been done for reasons of questionable purpose, for example the ethnicity profiling I guess of samples on the database. Do you have a view about the merits of that particular research project and can you comment on whether you feel there needs to be a greater provision for consent, ie some provision for consent in any research done?

Professor Jeffreys: Informed consent lies at the heart of using human material in research. How one would implement an informed consent protocol for sampling from convicted people I have no idea. There is a clash there.

Q402 Dr Harris: You could ask them.

Professor Jeffreys: You could ask them, yes, but I am not sure what answer you would get.

Q403 Dr Harris: Some will say yes and some will say no. What I am saying is that if you are interested you could ask them and as long as you asked enough people and you have a reasonable sample and it was not too biased by ID refusal rate—but that is always a problem with any such approach because some classes of people will not give consent to any research—then it is do-able.

Professor Jeffreys: We are going back to another question which I did not answer, which is the whole issue of extracting physical information on individuals from DNA. I think that is a real concern because once you start pulling up information—if it can be done genetically, and I have considerable doubt about this—for example on facial features or stature or whatever, if that could be done I am pretty confident you would now be accessing genetic information which would be important to an individual in terms of genetic defects, disease liability and the like. My recommendation and certainly my own personal bias is that the police should not be looking into such issues. That is an inappropriate area for genetic research for police.

Q404 Dr Harris: In almost every answer you have raised serious concerns about things that are currently happening or might happen. Do you think there is an argument for there to be, for example, a Human Genetics Commission to set up the public consultation and inquiry into this and recommend to government that things be tightened up? Or do you envisage an alternative way of improving what you have described as an unsatisfactory situation?

Professor Jeffreys: A Human Genetics Commission or some equivalent body would be exactly the mechanism that I would think would be able to identify the problems and make recommendations in terms of the proper way that the police use DNA information.

Q405 Dr Harris: I want to ask about the presentation of forensic evidence in court. I have a series of questions in this particular area which is highly topical. What do you think the weaknesses are of the current system? Such problems as there are, is that a problem of expert witnesses not understanding the legal process or not being able to communicate well enough to both judge and jury?

Professor Sammes: If I can speak personally for a moment, I have not found a problem in where I have requested to use technology, for example, to help put over a point. It has always been possible by talking to both counsel and to the clerk of the court and arranging with the judge to bring in equipment if necessary to do the presentation. It does seem to be that if you have a requirement to present in a particular way using modern technology you can arrange for it to happen. That has been my experience.

Professor Black: I have experienced no problems whatsoever in the presentation of evidence to courts.

Q406 Dr Harris: Some people feel that there has been a problem in the past and that is why arguably the CFRP was set up—Birmingham Six, et cetera—but perhaps the problem lies elsewhere and not in the issue of presentation.

Professor Black: I gave a half answer; the other half answer is that for many of the professionals who are considered to be expert witnesses in court they frequently receive no instruction on what is required of them. If you have been a lucky professional to have had no problems presenting your evidence in court, you are one of the few. Certainly a lot of my colleagues who are called into court have no experience and they find that very little is explained to them as to what is required of them and they find the experience to be wholly unpleasant and feel that they have not presented in the way in which they had anticipated they would.

Q407 Dr Harris: In terms of what is being done like the CRFP register, would you like to comment on whether that is having an impact here and, to be constructive, what should be done in respect of scrutiny, for example (someone watching what is going on and providing a report on performance in some way) or training for everyone who is going to enter a courtroom.

Professor Black: The trouble is that CRFP cannot answer all of the questions that I think you want to place before it. Where you have a small discipline like my own then we all know who is undertaking work and we are actually the ones who are the guardians of who becomes registered and who does

not any way. I have a problem with that but I do not see any other way around it when we have small areas of expertise.

Q408 Dr Harris: Is that because you have a vested interest in keeping the club small like private surgeons so there is not much competition.

Professor Black: I disagree with that. Quite the opposite, we have a vested interest in increasing the size of the number of individuals involved because only by doing that do you actually broaden the use of the discipline and bring more people into it. We do not have enough people trained in our discipline. We need to be able to get them the expertise to allow them to be mentored through CRFP. CRFP allow us to recognise that we are practitioners in the field who have reached a certain level of competence, but they do not in any way prepare us for the presentation in court.

Professor Sammes: There is courtroom training available and we do take advantage of that. There are commercial companies which will provide you with courtroom training, take you to a court and allow you to go through the whole process which will allow expert witnesses or developing expert witnesses to gain confidence and ability in carrying out this process.

Q409 Dr Harris: It is offered but not required.

Professor Sammes: It is not required by anybody but I would recommend anyone who is a professional in this area should be doing it.

Q410 Dr Harris: It is offered and recommended but it is not required. Do you think it should be required?

Professor Sammes: I think it should in due course. I, too, strongly support CRFP and believe that that is the kind of route and the kind of thing where there should be very strong guidance that this should be carried out.

Q411 Dr Harris: So it is strongly recommended, but not compulsory for people who are giving evidence about whether people are going to go to prison or not on a complex area to have training to be able to do that.

Professor Sammes: I believe that it is essential but I do not see quite at this stage how it can be mandated.

Q412 Dr Harris: Who should pay for it? The court system? The individuals themselves to get the work?

Professor Sammes: Partly the employer of the individual and partly the individual I would suggest.

Q413 Dr Harris: Can I ask Professor Jeffreys specifically and then expand it, using DNA fingerprinting as an example: what problems did you encounter when this was first used in court and how were they overcome? Then we can see whether there are any general issues about the new technologies and what sort of problems there are.

Professor Jeffreys: Obviously there were major problems with education in terms of getting lawyers and judges to get their heads round what this new technology was about. That was all done outside the courtroom. I have to say, I am personally a great fan of the American system of pre-trial Frye hearings (this was introduced after a debate about the polygraph tests back in the 1920s). It is pre-trial hearing to examine a new science to look for three basic criteria: the first is whether it is based on solid science; second, whether that science is generally accepted by the scientific community; and third whether technology delivers information which is robust and reliable. We are in exactly that position and we have to do that much more in the context of the open court where we are asking a jury to make decisions about issues which are essentially scientific and have nothing to do with the law. My view is that the jury is not only not qualified to do that but it is positively unfair to ask them to make those sorts of decisions. If you accept that the science is all right then you are in a position to put that scientific information from the tests into the context of a given case and ask the jury to decide; that is right and proper. However, the initial scientific deliberation belongs to science rather than law.

Q414 Dr Harris: Do you think psychological profiling which is very trendy at the moment would pass those three tests of scientific rigour?
Professor Jeffreys: My personal view is with a degree of difficulty.
Professor Black: I think that is true of many practitioners that deal not in the very basics of sciences—the chemistry, the biology, the physics—but are dealing with, for example, a professional opinion on how much force was required to cause an injury, how much somebody may have responded in a particular way to a circumstances, things that require the opinion of the expert. I think that becomes a very dangerous area in court.
Dr Harris: Do you think the judges are getting enough training? We heard in the previous session that it was questionable as to how enthusiastic judges were to go back to school in respect of anything, particularly anything not specifically legal.

Q415 Chairman: Are there challenges in court in the States, for example, between experts? They are always a bit ahead of us in that game.
Professor Jeffreys: The very first major challenge in the United States involved open court discussion between defence and prosecution experts. They were scientists and took an interesting decision to simply walk out of the court together and as scientists together to come up with a view as to whether the evidence was reliable. In that case they decided it was not, because it would not have passed some of the basic tests that scientists have applied to the rebuttal of evidence. I do not know whether we would even be allowed to do that in the UK without suffering from contempt of court. I think there is a fundamental gulf between the philosophy of science

and the philosophy of law and it does create a tension for scientists in an adversarial situation where everything is reduced to a blunt "yes" or "no" to try to convey a discipline which works on synthesis, on integration of evidence, on concensus and on probability as well.

Q416 Chairman: Is there a situation where one expert has more titles than the other one and therefore they are definitely believable, Sir Alec?
Professor Jeffreys: It depends on the chemistry between the witness and the jury. Totally. If you bore or if you confuse them they will switch off and they will ignore the evidence. It does not matter whether it is DNA or digital information or whatever, they will reject it. If you can somehow establish a rapport you can get away with saying anything and that worries me. I lost my faith in the adversarial legal system the first time I stood up in court because I simply did not realise that this was going on.
Professor Black: The other side of the adversarial system is that when the defence ask who is the prosecution witness on this then frequently there are a number of people who will back down and will not go up in court against them.

Q417 Dr Harris: Why?
Professor Black: Presumably because they believe that the person the prosecution has aimed for is going to have greater credibility, greater presence and greater ability in court. There is, in many ways, a great scrambling in a lot of police forces to make sure that they get the person they want in the prosecution.

Q418 Dr Harris: Do you think quite often the defence does not get a fair whack in terms of its own expert because the FSS has first pick, as it were?
Professor Black: I have first-hand experience of that, of being brought into a number of police forces to ensure that I was not brought in with the defence.

Q419 Chairman: What should happen? Should there be a ballot allowed? There is evidence to be presented here and you are telling us there is some bias in how it is received. How do you get round that? Have you thought about a way of doing it?
Professor Black: At least if we had registration of other professionals through the CRFP there are other options available, but there is unquestionably a league table among expert witnesses.

Q420 Dr Harris: I want to deal with the issue of risk and probability, and I want to come to a question that was not answered because the Chairman asked an even better question. In these high profile cases on Sudden Infant Death or infanticide one of the issues has been whether the issues of probability has been well communicated and well understood. It has been put that a witness would give their opinion and if that is misinterpreted or not sufficiently questioned by defence counsel in this case or a defence expert or the judge, then it is wrong to hound the witness as if they have been malicious in what they have done. I come back to the question, how do we deal with getting across this issue of probability and is there more training that judges should have in order to make sure they understand the basics of this so that they can step in?

Q421 Professor Jeffreys: In a perfect world you get rid of probability and statistics. Coming back to DNA, if you have a sixteen marker system you can basically say, "That DNA came from that person. Full stop. There's no-one else on the face of the planet unless that person has an identical twin." That is a facile solution to the problem but if you are left in a world where you are having to describe probabilities, then there are two issues here. The first is the description of accurately derived probabilities and that is the job of the expert. If you come to the cases of Sudden Infant Death and the probabilities that have been cited in cases there, they were completely incorrect; I think any statistician would have picked that up. Secondly, if the probabilities are correct—in other words the expert has done his job properly—it comes down to how those probabilities are appropriately explained in court without unduly unbiasing the jury one way or another. That is a tricky one which still has not been adequately solved; it is a very difficult area. Unless you want me to go on for the next hour on a diatribe on statistics, I will stop now.

Professor Haswell: A comment I have is that you can shorten the odds if you increase the quality and robustness of the data that you are using. I believe that rolls you back to the research front of this, which is to develop that capability.

Q422 Dr Harris: Mistakes will always be made not necessarily with malice and I was wondering what safeguards there are. If, in the example you give, a statistic in this SID case was clearly wrong, I do not understand why the defence witness did not point it out and the judge could not have understood. If we are thinking about the same thing, it is not a difficult concept to anyone who has a basic knowledge of statistics. I am concerned about miscarriage of justice and wondering what extra safeguards could there be around judges being there and defence witnesses being competent and not intimidated. How can we deal with this problem because it is a current problem?

Professor Jeffreys: In the case of Sudden Infant Death that was a failure not only of the experts but also the courts and how one rectifies that I have no idea. I was amazed that that was not tracked right at the beginning. It was obviously statistically flawed. To make a statement that DNA matches and that

the profile is present in one person in a hundred million or whatever is not a useful way of stating the strength of DNA evidence unless you know how that DNA match was found in the first place. Was just one person tested? Was the entire database looked at, in which case you are going to get extremely rare matches given the size of that database? The statistics have to be put very accurately into the context of how that information is developed in the first place.

Q423 Chairman: Lab-on-a-chip technology would really help the police so that they could do the tests. How is that developing?
Professor Haswell: It is painfully slow. We have taken quite an early lead in this I believe in this country and it has all slowed down, part of that is due to the very slow through-put through the research councils. It can take two years from an idea to funding, by the time you have gone through an outline and a full proposal. Fast-tracking has to be looked into; we need better focus; management has to be looked into.

Q424 Chairman: That is so you can do the tests at the scene of the crime.
Professor Haswell: Technology is capable of doing that now. The capability is there, what it requires is a concerted focus to develop that and to deliver it to the people who want to use it. That is obviously going to require funding. That funding is more or less there if used wisely, if you do not spread it so thinly that you cannot achieve anything.

Q425 Chairman: If you were Charles Clarke for a day what would you say?
Professor Haswell: I would asses what it is going to take and the timescale you can do it over and focus and manage that piece of research pulling the expertise, the research basis that you have already funded (they are in the universities) and make it happen. That is what is happening in Korea; that is what is happening in Japan.

Q426 Chairman: We are ending on a unanimous note here because I see the previous witnesses absolutely in agreement with you on this. I think that is a pretty solid recommendations.
Professor Haswell: It comes down to management, it needs getting hold of and dealing with.
Chairman: Thank you. I wanted to finish on that kind of note and I think we have done it. Thank you very, very much for your expertise and raising some of the problems that you meet first hand, and giving us your advice and professionalism to help us move it forward.

Monday 31 January 2005

Members present:

Dr Ian Gibson, in the Chair

Dr Evan Harris	Mr Robert Key
Dr Brian Iddon	Dr Desmond Turner

Witnesses: **Ms Karen Squibb-Williams**, Lawyer and Policy Adviser, Crown Prosecution Service, **Mr Nimesh Jani**, Lawyer and Policy Adviser, Crown Prosecution Service, **Mr Graham Cooke**, Barrister, Bar Council, and **Judge Anthony Thorpe**, Resident Judge, Chichester Crown Court, examined.

Q427 Chairman: I am tempted to say the court is now open but this is not a court. As you know, this is a parliamentary scrutiny committee whose job it is to look at forensic science, how it is practised in this country, the possibilities of PPPs and so on, and I think you are probably aware from the minutes that we have had some briefing on it. The questions today are going to be all for you in terms of your professional knowledge and what experience you have in this very interesting field. The first question is about your training in terms of understanding and interpreting forensic science. I will ask each of you in turn to be as brief as you can please. Is it too much, too little, or just about right? How good are you at forensic science, I guess I am asking.
Judge Thorpe: There are two difficulties for a judge in forensic science. One is, is somebody an expert and, if he is an expert, how well he can put the evidence before a jury in a fair way? I am afraid that for most of the judges, apart from the lecturers which you get at the seminars run by the Judicial Studies Board, it is probably on-the-job training. You will appreciate, Chairman, that we go back every year for one day of training and every three years for three or four days and in the next six weeks every single judge in the country is going back for three days dealing with criminal justice reform. It is in the context of those lectures that the Judicial Studies Board are the people who run the training for judges in this country.

Q428 Chairman: So you understand what DNA gel looks like, do you?
Judge Thorpe: The answer is yes. DNA is obviously very important, but the point I would make is that unfortunately sometimes in the way scientists put it they use big numbers and big numbers really affect juries, so a judge has to try and put it in context for a jury, saying, "This actually means he is one of 20 people who matches the crime stain". That is all it means and then you have to go further, but the minute you start talking about one in a million— police officers have tended in the past and do occasionally now say, "Oh, that means it is a million in one chance against it being anybody other than you".

Q429 Chairman: Karen, what is your view on it all? What do you know about forensic science?
Ms Squibb-Williams: I think there is a distinction, whether we are talking about my understanding of the scientific side of forensic material or my understanding of how it is presented in court, how it fits with training provided to lawyers presenting it in court. Is your question directed at my training?

Q430 Chairman: Yes; how do you feel about it? Do you just sit back and dream of DNA gel and believe everything you are told? How acquainted are you with the kind of evidence you are given? Do you feel confident with it?
Ms Squibb-Williams: I feel a level of confidence. The broader answer is that there is some good information out there to give you a basic understanding of the meaning of DNA and some of the forensic science issues. I personally have not been on the receiving end of detailed scientific training but I have a grasp, a basic broad level, of the issues involved, whether it is the technical issues or the delivery for lawyers prosecuting in court.

Q431 Chairman: Okay. Nimesh?
Mr Jani: On a personal level I think I have a fairly good grasp of DNA issues but that is because I studied A-level in biology and then moved over to the law. In terms of the scientific background of lawyers on DNA, etc, I did have some knowledge of it before I moved into the law. I share Karen's views in terms of saying that my experience of DNA and its use in courts has been the main basis upon which I have developed my knowledge of DNA and forensic science within the law but it is wider than just DNA. I tend to have experience of dealing with fingerprints and also of experts in other fields such as pathology. On a broad level I would say I have a fair bit of knowledge of how it is used in legal terms.

Q432 Chairman: Graham?
Mr Cooke: I am troubled by the approach the Bar takes at large. We are supposed to be capable, whatever our seniority, of picking up whatever special scientific issue appears in a case, very often DNA but nowadays many other things as well, of being able to mug up on it, perhaps overnight because it was not our case and we are going to do the trial the next day, with little or no access to a relevant expert to find out what the true issues are. When it comes to DNA I am afraid, although personally I was originally a mathematician and an actuary so that part of it I obviously have training in and an aptitude for, that the Bar in general is innumerate, senior judges are innumerate—

Q433 Chairman: We will excuse Judge Thorpe then?

Judge Thorpe: No; I would agree.

Mr Cooke: Although it can come out in the literature elsewhere, there is a case called *Pringle* in the Privy Council and the five Law Lords came out with an astonishing proposition which everybody would agree would be wrong in arithmetic terms, on DNA. I have pressed in the past the Director of Public Prosecutions to think of having a special group of barristers or prosecuting solicitors (it does not matter which) to prosecute who have to pass some minimum qualification of understanding of the hearing.

Q434 Chairman: Why do you think that is important?

Mr Cooke: Because cases are lost in my view by the prosecution which should not be lost because the prosecuting barrister is insufficiently aware of the issues and the right way to present them.

Q435 Chairman: Put it round the other way: does a bit of scientific wizardry win cases?

Mr Cooke: It depends on the defence. If the defence do the job properly it should not. There is a real overall worry, and I suspect my colleagues will share this with me, in that once the jury has seen an expert, particularly when it is to do with DNA, without more, the evidence tends to be very persuasive.

Q436 Dr Harris: Can I just clarify what you were saying there because you argued that people should have to pass a test of competence in order to prosecute in this area. Could the same ever apply to the defence and on that basis are you arguing that people have got off on the basis of inadequate prosecution? Could not the same be said about the failure of either the defence to point out an arithmetical nonsense in the prosecution case, or indeed one of your innumerate judges to point out that something has been said that cannot really be sustained?

Mr Cooke: Your logic is impeccable but the mechanics are different because defending is down to individual high street solicitors who can go into a police station and pick up a client and, "Oh, there is a scientific issue", and it goes off to the favourite chambers and it is allocated within chambers on a very broad basis. It is not allocated, as far as I can tell, that it goes to a specialist.

Q437 Dr Harris: So the defence is particularly reliant on a judge being able to step in and point out where the prosecution is going further than can be justified or indeed is plain wrong on the arithmetic or the logic?

Mr Cooke: Yes and no. Yes, they are dependent upon an informed judge doing the right thing, but there is a duty on defence lawyers to read up the relevant case law and principles. One of the things that I have handed in to your committee today is a DVD of me talking for 20 minutes to some 200 barristers telling them off in terms of the way they do

not prepare cases and cases are a disgrace when they go into court. That is my experience and out of that come convictions that should not have occurred.

Q438 Chairman: Is there research on this level of ignorance in the professions?

Mr Cooke: Not that I am aware of.

Q439 Chairman: So you are really citing anecdotal experiences from your own experience or you have talked to many others about it?

Mr Cooke: Yes, certainly my own experience and reading the other cases that go up to appeal. Also, because I have written a lot about DNA in particular and there is a tradition in the Bar of sharing knowledge and helping, people ring me up and ask me for help, so I become aware of their level of ignorance on the issue.

Judge Thorpe: The key test I think is the judge grasping the case at the pleas and directions stage right back before a trial. He should not allow the scientist's evidence to go forward saying, "This is strong support that it was the defendant who left the crime scene". The Court of Appeal said in a case called *Hinman v Evans* that the scientist should never express an opinion. It is not his business.

Q440 Chairman: We will certainly come back to the case. I want to know how much you know before we start that.

Judge Thorpe: What I am saying is that if you grip it one stage back before we reach the Graham problem, you will do a lot better.

Mr Cooke: I suspect I have not answered your question. Can I do it briefly? I have historical forensic experience. I have worked with DNA. I go to the laboratory and I talk to scientists and I go and look at the papers myself. Out of that has come a layman's understanding of the various issues sufficient to cross-examine their expert.

Q441 Chairman: But that is because you are a serious professional. You do not have to do that.

Mr Cooke: That is true, and one does not get paid for doing it either.

Q442 Dr Iddon: The adversarial system that is practised in this country in criminal justice can be quite intimidating for expert witnesses, I understand, who go to court and have not got much experience of court and may be in an unusual area, not as common as DNA. Have you any views on that?

Judge Thorpe: You have to test the evidence; there is no better way. I personally, as a judge, and I know Graham is about to disagree with me, will say that the experts should get together without the benefit of lawyers and see if they can produce a joint statement on what they agree or disagree on. You very often find that what they disagree on is a very small part. In some cases you do not even call the expert because what they disagree on is a matter for a jury. I would like to give you a practical example: a death by dangerous driving case. A pedestrian is knocked down crossing the road. The car, from striations on the road, the scientist says was doing 45 miles an hour when the brakes locked up. The throw of the body shows it was doing 38 miles an hour when the car hit the body. This is a 30-mile-an-hour limit. The first part is totally agreed. Was that dangerous driving? It is not a matter for the expert; it is a matter for the jury. Once you get down to that point, they are all agreed on the first bit, you do not need the expert at all.

Q443 Dr Iddon: Assuming the expert is required to appear in court. Do you find in practising in court, either as a judge or prosecutor or defence lawyer or barrister, that the expert witness can frame his evidence to support the case, whether it be the prosecution case or the defence case? Are they influenced by the party they represent?

Mr Jani: Can I start on this one, on behalf of the prosecution as it were, and then the judge and the defence can have their say on it? I find that the question is perhaps wrong in terms of what is the intention of having an expert witness in court. The purpose for which I would call an expert witness, and what I would expect from them in court, does not require them, hopefully, to feel under any pressure, nor should they feel obliged to do anything more than tell their view independently, objectively and clearly of their own expertise and their view (if they are entitled to provide a view) of the conclusions they find from it. Within the adversarial system it is clear that there is going to be an opportunity for the defence to cross-examine, or for the prosecution to cross-examine if it is a defence witness, and some, depending upon their ability to cope with cross-examination, may find that that is a serious pressure. However, if it is clear from the outset within all the parties concerned, the judiciary, both defence and prosecution, that the aim is to get merely a clear view of that expert's opinion (if he is providing it) and to try and clarify the specific issue on which that opinion is required, I do not believe it is necessary for that level of pressure to be so significant that the expert witness would feel obliged to say one thing or other just because it is something that is being put to him, either by the prosecution or the defence.

Q444 Dr Iddon: So the expert's duty is to the court and that is the way they mainly play it?

Mr Jani: That is certainly the way I would have it if I were prosecuting a case. I would not have it any other way.

Mr Cooke: I will give you a couple of quick examples which are right at the limit. One was a DNA scientist who worked for the FSS (who contract themselves out to prosecution and defence). In cross-examination I said to him, "You rejected a particular finding, did you not?" "Yes". "If you had been working for the defence you would have reported that, would you not?" "Yes". "Why did you not report it when you were working for the prosecution?", to which there was no answer.

Q445 Chairman: Did he look embarrassed at all?

Mr Cooke: He knew it was coming and did his best not to look embarrassed.

Q446 Chairman: Is that frequent?

Mr Cooke: This is one of the difficulties, and that was a case where I had found that particular thing by going to the laboratory and looking at it. That was the only way we found it. The other one was a case of sexual abuse where a defendant was charged with buggery of an eight-year old boy and rape of his four-year old sister. Both children were examined by a doctor, a specialist in this work and working almost wholly for the police. She sat in court where, under cross-examination, the boy said, "Everything I said to the police was lies". The Crown did not stop the case but carried on and called this doctor who then upped her evidence from saying, "My findings were consistent with buggery and rape" to saying, "They were diagnostic of buggery and rape", which is the technical term for meaning that they themselves prove it. She was in difficulty because she made a witness statement at this level and now she was up here. I asked her why she had done that and she said, "I believe the boy". She had sat in court hearing the boy saying, "It is all lies".

Q447 Chairman: How much do these experts get paid, for example, for this game?

Mr Cooke: I do not know, I suppose is the strict answer, but the worry I have in that second case is that for professional reasons, which it would not be fair to her to go into, and I realise that this is a public but protected setting, she was as far as I knew completely dependent upon police work to earn her living and there is a zeal sometimes, whether it is conscious or subconscious, which can appear in a witness, particularly in the child protection area.

Q448 Dr Harris: Is there not something similar in the defence, because the defence can shop around for witnesses until they find one who backs up their view rather than the other? They do not have to disclose at the moment, as I understand it, the expert views they have got which do not support their case, as I understand from the case of Damilola Taylor, but is there not a vested interest under "no win, no fee", for example, that they are not going to get any money? I do not know if that applies to the defence. Is there a financial incentive around winning now as well as around reputational issues?

Judge Thorpe: Not in crime. In criminal cases they get paid for the work they do. It is more sinister than that. It is the Crown expert who has done the examination. It is the Crown expert who has measured the marks on the road or looked at the child. The defence expert by and large is looking at work the Crown expert has done. He was not there, he did not see the child, he did not see the road himself. He is at one remove.

Q449 Chairman: He is challenging the original expert?

Judge Thorpe: Absolutely, but he is basically looking and saying, "There is the data. I would have come to a different view". He is not in a position to say, "Actually, it was not there in the first place". That is the worry one has, I think, because he is at one remove. He is checking the Crown expert's data.

Q450 Chairman: Karen, what are they getting paid? Do you know?

Ms Squibb-Williams: I was cannot answer on that, Dr Gibson. I want to take up a slightly different angle if I may. All of this needs to be seen in the context of the criminal justice reforms that are going on because in many cases many of these points have already been taken and have already been built into the reforms as they are going through. They are starting to play out except that we do not yet have the evidence and to a great extent the anecdotal information is only just filtering through. I think it is very important, particularly on the question about adversarial proceedings and the effect of that, combined with Judge Thorpe's response, that if the case is dealt with much earlier on, combined with how the new criminal procedure rules will swing into effect, the criminal case management framework, that that removes an awful lot of the courtroom adversarial pressure come the day. It also saves the public purse an awful lot of money and you do not have to consider so highly the costs involved: who is going to win, who is going to lose.

Q451 Chairman: Who decides on the fees for these experts? Who would know?

Mr Cooke: May I help? May I come back to the issues you raised, Dr Harris. We are talking about £600–£700 to £1,000 per day for an average expert. We have a problem in many fields with defending because whereas the prosecution system—and I am not saying it has a limitless budget; that is not what I mean—allows for the expert to be seen by the barrister if it is necessary beforehand, for the expert to be at court at relevant times during the evidence, whereas the defence will not be able to shop around because they will not get the money. Of course, if it is privately paid it is different. When you have only got one shot at it—and now with the new legislation a failed expert, if you follow this Bill, is disclosable to the prosecution who could go and get it if necessary and use it—it is a lot of money and the defence are on the back foot, and particularly, bearing in mind that many cases that turn on scientific evidence, the suspect is arrested and interviewed but is not charged immediately. He has the benefit of a free legal aid lawyer at the police station, but thereafter until he is brought back on police bail to be charged he has no lawyer working for him.

Q452 Chairman: Has it always been like this, this system?

Mr Cooke: No.

Q453 Dr Iddon: That leads me into my next question. The committee is seeing evidence that the defence does not get the same forensic experts or quality of experts as the prosecution gets. Obviously, the prosecution has access to all government agencies, including the FSS, and because the quality of the lawyer on the defence side may not be high enough, they may not have enough knowledge of forensic evidence, we feel that perhaps the defence is let down in this sense.

Judge Thorpe: I think that is unfair because the Legal Service Commission approve payment for a defence expert and certainly in the cases I have been doing, the rapes and so on, the experts are very good. My problem is that they come into the case late. It is not that they are not good and the person does not know what he is doing. That is not really the problem. It would be unfair to say that the defence always gets a second-rate barrister or a second-rate expert. That is not true.

Ms Squibb-Williams: I also think there is a dimension to add that the prosecution do not get an unlimited choice of which experts they can use and an unlimited budget, having come relatively recently from the coal face, as it were, and sat there with my files in front of me wondering how we are going to find an expert and being limited to a very narrow budget. It may well be different at the higher end of cases but at the volume end of cases where ideally you would want an expert, at least to address the issues, budget constraints are every bit as much of a problem there. I agree with Judge Thorpe's point about timing in that the defence are on the back foot in that respect but not as much as I think the picture is painted on the volume end in terms of budgets.

Q454 Chairman: Are experts growing in numbers now in court cases in your personal experience? Is there one per case almost now?

Mr Cooke: It is a growth industry but it is still not that often.

Mr Jani: I think it might perhaps be growing in terms of the obvious problems we have had in relation to pathology.

Q455 Chairman: Which pathology?

Mr Jani: Home Office pathology, trying to find pathologists who can provide evidence for the prosecution. In terms of the experts available to the prosecution, in the whole country we have probably about 35–40 people we can approach to provide this evidence. Therefore, in terms of the specific question you asked about whether it is easy to find, the answer is no, it is not any easier for the prosecution to find experts.

Q456 Chairman: If they are getting £2,000 a day or whatever it is not a bad number, is it?

Mr Jani: I cannot answer that, obviously. Certainly I would be happy with that sort of money.

Judge Thorpe: At the pleas and directions hearing if the judge is alert he will say, "Yes, the defence needs an expert. This is a proper charge to the Legal Service Commission", so you can shorten the process quite dramatically if they go and get approval for the money. Then you have got to find the expert even before you can pay him.

Mr Cooke: There is a different aspect to all this which can bring an unfairness on a defendant. The statutory basis of credit for guilty pleas means that the clock starts running from the moment he is in the police station. If he waits to see if the Crown can properly prove their case, which of course is still the system, then by waiting he can lose a substantial amount of credit.

Mr Jani: That is right and proper in my opinion because at the end of the day if the defence are putting the prosecution to the cost of going through and proving the whole case, even on paper, they should lose some of their credit.

Judge Thorpe: It is not just some. Graham was right. If you plead on the day, the Sentencing Advisory Panel, which we know have taken account of that on behalf of the Criminal Justice Act 2003, says 10% is the best reduction you can give on a sentence. That is one third right at the outset, so it goes down quite dramatically.

Q457 Chairman: Who sorts out all these high finances?

Mr Cooke: It is in the hands of the legal aid people, as I still call them. Sadly, the rates at which they will pay are far less than many of the experts want. Many of the experts themselves are working in the National Health Service or wherever. They are working somewhere as paid professionals. I have not the remotest idea how they account for what I call these private fees, and I do not mean that unkindly. I raise the point. I certainly do not have the answer to it.

Q458 Dr Iddon: If the defence consult more than one expert witness is the forensic evidence trail always made available in its completeness to the prosecution?

Mr Cooke: To the prosecution or by the prosecution?

Q459 Dr Iddon: To the prosecution.

Mr Cooke: If you are going to use an expert for the defence you must give notice of his report, so you must give that to the prosecution as soon as he has made the report. If he himself has come up with some new tests, new results, then he is as much duty bound to disclose to the other side the underlying work and papers and principles he has worked on as are the prosecution to the defence.

Q460 Dr Iddon: And that would be the case if two expert witnesses were consulted by the defence on the same issue? Both reports would have to be made available to the prosecution?

Mr Jani: No. Under the current rules the only obligation on the defence to disclose an expert witness is where they use his evidence. Where they have not used that evidence there is no obligation to disclose any of it.

Judge Thorpe: That is going to change, is it not?
Mr Jani: That is going to change.

Q461 Dr Iddon: I am glad you said that.
Judge Thorpe: It is in the Act and that is going to change.

Q462 Dr Iddon: When is that going to change?
Ms Squibb-Williams: I believe it is scheduled to be some time in 2006. It is a rolling introduction and that part is next year.
Judge Thorpe: This is all under the Home Office. They will implement the Criminal Justice Act 2003 in stages, as you will appreciate.

Q463 Dr Iddon: I have one final question and that concerns the complexity of some forensic evidence. We have already referred to DNA. That could be complex for lawyers and the jury and the judge, of course. Do you think that the technical aspects of evidence are always put across in court or are there some difficulties with that, and in cases where there are difficulties how does the court proceed?
Judge Thorpe: There have been difficulties, as I identified right from the outset. For instance, if he matches the crime stain and you look at the probability that someone unrelated to the defendant having the same profile as the crime sample is one in a million, for example, it is probably best expressed by saying, "there are 20 million people on the database and he is one of 20". If you say to the expert, "put it to the jury like that", then it becomes comprehensible. Then you find he was in Adelaide at the time, or actually he is the victim's mother's boyfriend—you can see the difference at once. In my view, you want to get away from talking about one in a million, one in a billion; it is big numbers which cause real problems with juries because you can see the shutters come down, because the police will say to the defendant, "it is a million-to-one chance against it being anybody other than you, Chummy; now admit it."

Q464 Dr Turner: Mr Cooke, you have told us that lawyers, more often than not, have very limited understanding of forensic science. What about the reverse situation: how do you feel about the ability of expert witnesses to operate the legal system successfully, in terms of getting their evidence across in court and not getting lost in procedure?
Mr Cooke: It is very difficult. Courtrooms bring their own pressures. We have very complicated rules, perhaps like some other places have complicated rules, and procedures. I have seen witnesses get quite flummoxed just by being there, so it is not easy to know what you can do about it. There is a duty on us, whether prosecuting or defending, to get the evidence out clearly. It is never ever a duty on me, when I am defending, to confuse the witness. If the witness's evidence at the end of cross-examination is confusing, there it is. I am afraid I have to say that some scientists do not know the right way to give evidence, particularly on DNA. They say things off the cuff that they should not say, as so many appeals have demonstrated. What I

recommend, and have done for many years now, is that every judge in a DNA case, or its equivalent if it is some other scientific discipline involved, should thrash out with both sides, before the case starts exactly how it is going to proceed. That is not to pre-judge what the evidence is going to be, but it sets limits and in particular avoids statements by experts to a jury that are fundamentally wrong. That could apply to both sides. History has shown—and forgive me for going to the Professor Meadow problem—that there was a similar error—I say, and many others do—in his logic and numeracy—basically logic in the way that you should attack, and lawyers should be logical, but once you get figures it seems to drive logic out of the window.

Judge Thorpe: Since the judge in a sense speaks last, when both counsel have finished if you have a feeling that the witness's evidence is confusing, you do have a duty to say, "is what you are saying to the jury this, put in simple terms?" and try and get it put in those simple terms. I think that the judge has an overriding duty at the end to say, "I am confused, which means the jury are probably confused; is this what you mean?"

Mr Jani: You have touched upon one of the core issues in relation to expert witnesses in my opinion that needs to be approached and resolved fairly quickly with the expert and criminal law field. The issue is, first, whether the experts understand what the lawyers are saying. Second, do the experts understand what is their role when they provide evidence within the court process, and where their level of expertise should remain? I particularly touch on Professor Meadow when I say this because the issue was not so much whether Professor Meadow in Sally Clarke was qualified to give the evidence he gave—clearly he was qualified to give that—but the only issue is whether he went beyond his expertise when he went into the realm of statistics? It is the duty of the prosecutor, the defence and the judge to ensure that any expert when they give their evidence, give the evidence because it is probative, relevant, and within the field within which they are qualified to give that expert evidence. The failings that have recently been highlighted show those failings, ie, the expert did not know his role; the judge, the prosecutor, nor the defence spotted it, and therefore it has got to that stage. It is encumbent upon all parties therefore in the criminal justice agencies to make sure that they are from the very outset—and I share Judge Thorpe's views about giving directions properly—to get a plea and directions hearing and make sure experts from both prosecution and defence outline the issues that they have and make those very clear. At the end of the day, the whole point of the criminal system is not about experts talking to each other or lawyers talking to each other, it is about making sure juries or lay people can understand and make a factual judgment. It is about nothing else. If anything, DNA is an example where it is easy, because it is normally just a statistic; but if you go into the realms of pathology and other areas, normally you will be in a position where a number of experts are giving evidence in a number of specific

issues, which has to be combined for a factual judgment to be made by the jury. That is why I say it is such a key issue.

Q465 Mr Key: Chairman, forgive me, but I really must get this straight! Professor Meadow was not qualified to give statistical expertise.
Mr Jani: That is right.

Q466 Mr Key: You said he was.
Mr Jani: No.

Q467 Mr Key: Then I misheard you.
Judge Thorpe: Can I give you a practical example—one against myself? Some years ago I conducted a trial of a rape case. The defendant produced an expert who was a 68-year old retired professor of gynaecology, with qualifications out of the door. At the last moment, I said to him, "when did you last see a rape victim?" He said, "ah, when I was senior house officer at St Thomas's." I said: "Is that over 40 years ago?" "Yes." He was not an expert and should not have been allowed to give evidence as an expert in rape cases.

Q468 Chairman: Who hired him?
Judge Thorpe: The point is, it was my fault, as judge. I should have said right at the outset, because you appreciate that since 1894 the courts have said it is for the judge to decide (a) whether you need expert evidence, and (b) if the man you have got is in fact an expert.

Q469 Chairman: This is the question. Just because his qualifications were out of the door he must be believed. Is that your point?
Judge Thorpe: Hitherto, I suspect that had been part of the approach. I am not beating the drums for the CRFP except to this extent, that I am terribly grateful for the Government support for CRFP and the way in which Jack Straw, when he was Home Secretary, set it up. Judges can now say, "Are you registered?" That means that you have been through an assessment process by your peers, and you are in date, because you have to re-qualify every four years. I suspect that he would not have been registered, because his peers would have looked at him and said "no".

Q470 Chairman: A lot of people might have been convicted under unregistered people, inside or outside or whatever.
Ms Squibb Williams: Chairman, I was going to add a caveat in my mind that registration cannot be a panacea for exercising a judge's discretion, which I am sure nobody is saying, but in support of the principles of registration, in my view there should be absolute independence and integrity in the auditing of that registration and validation of the accreditation that goes with it. Providing one can be confident that there is independent auditing of the standards and the application of professional codes, and accreditation of continuing training and so

forth, then registration would have some merit. Registration on its own would not be sufficient to allay the sort of concerns we have had.

Q471 Dr Turner: What provisions are made at the moment for training expert witnesses in how to conduct themselves in courts? Do you think this should be mandatory? Do you think it should be a requirement before they should have a sufficient level of expertise in witness presentation before they could be registered, and do you think the CRFP is making any significant difference yet?

Ms Squibb Williams: I do not know what provision of training is out there. I am not convinced that you actually need training. My concern is that with the criminal justice reforms as they are, you are not going to need the same kind of witness box skills as you might have needed in the past, because many of the issues should have been ventilated, and either agreed or admissions made, before getting to court. If the expert is doing their job, serving their primary duty to the court, then it is not a matter of knowing how to do it as best you can, or being trained at being a witness; it is about knowing your subject well and many of the contentious issues being pared down, just to the very essence of them, if that part has to go to court.

Mr Jani: In relation to training, it is very difficult to generalise because experts come from all fields and they are part of an institution such as a police force area, the FSS or Forensic Alliance or one of the other forensic science providers. I am fairly certain that there is a basic level of training given to them about court processes and procedures and how to process these things. That is not necessarily to say that everyone will go through that sort of process. I agree with you to the level of saying it is important that any expert who gives evidence in a criminal court should know what is expected of them and should be ready and aware of how to approach questioning and the answers.

Judge Thorpe: In addition to the point you made about CRFP, as a judge I can tell you that it does make a difference because you have now got a tool. I accept at once that you do not preclude somebody because they are just not registered, but you do know that if he is registered he has been the assessment process. You will have seen the letter that I received from the Prime Minister, putting his support behind it. I really do feel that the CRFP is a way ahead to help judges decide whether he is an in-date expert—and I stress "in-date".

Q472 Dr Harris: You have just argued that you should not have someone as an expert witness just because they are not on the CRFP but I have heard it suggested that in Legal Services Commission-funded cases one should only go to expert witnesses who are CRFP approved; and indeed you describe that in the letter that you copied to us of 12 November to the Lord Chancellor. You said: "This is an attractive proposition from the CRFP and I hope you will give it your support."

Judge Thorpe: I think that is the way the Legal Services Commission are looking at it. They decide who they are going to pay for, and they are probably saying, "if he is registered, we need not worry about going any further into detail." From the judge's point of view he is registered, and that is over one hurdle; we know he is in date and we know he has been currently assessed. If he is not registered, one starts to ask a lot more questions—"convince me that you are an expert".

Q473 Dr Harris: Do you think there should be a requirement in Commission-funded cases at least, of CRFP registration, when it has got over the backlog?

Judge Thorpe: That is a matter for the Legal Services Commission. I meant to say that that is the route they seem to be going down, but only they can decide that.

Ms Squibb Williams: Can I make two points on that? CRFP does not cover all the specialist areas, and whether or not the Commission is going down that route, is there absolute certainty of who is assessing the assessors? How independent is the quality control?

Q474 Dr Turner: Some expert witnesses are going to make a better impression on juries than others. Juries naturally are human and are going to be affected by the apparent professionalism of an expert witness. What do you think can be done to prevent the style or appearance of the expert witness unduly influencing the jury's perception of the value of his evidence?

Mr Jani: That is not necessarily unique to expert evidence in any event. That may be true of any evidence that juries will hear, and it is probably true whether it be the defence lawyer or the prosecution lawyer, if they have the charisma to entertain the juries properly. In terms of what can be done to ensure that the jury performs its task properly, I believe it is necessary for them to have as sanitised as possible a version of the crucial issues. I do not think you will ever get to a position, certainly within the adversarial system, where you will be able to remove totally personalities, nor would it be appropriate, in my view. At the end of the day, juries are there to judge the facts, and that includes how people come across—inappropriately of course not, but appropriately yes.

Q475 Chairman: Experts are tutored on how to behave and so on, like people who come in front of us get coached as well! Do experts get coached in the same way by lawyers?

Mr Jani: There is certainly no coaching.

Q476 Dr Turner: Is there not a temptation for people such as yourselves who are employing expert witnesses to choose the witnesses that present well as far as a jury is concerned, rather than on the basis of the quality of their science and the validity of their evidence?

Mr Jani: I can only go back to what I said at the outset. If I am doing my job properly, which is to prosecute, as an officer of the court, my role is merely to present the evidence and to ensure that the best evidence of the prosecution is available for the jury to decide. I am not there to try and get a conviction, or to get an expert who I think will get that conviction. I am there, performing the task of making sure the expert can provide his opinion. As long as he does his role properly, that is all that should be there. It would be wrong of me if the line that you take is the line I follow in prosecuting a case; then I would be unprofessional in what I do.

Q477 Dr Turner: There must be a temptation. As we heard from one previous witness who is an expert witness, it is not uncommon for the prosecution to go and grab a convincing expert witness in order to prevent the defence from being able to use them. That temptation is clearly out there, is it not?

Mr Jani: I cannot speak for the whole of the criminal justice system of course. All I can say is that if there is a position where—and this has been defined as "hawks and doves"—certain experts appear to opine towards the prosecution, whereas certain experts appear to be more towards the defence, that is clearly not in the interests of the criminal justice system as a whole and it should be prevented.

Judge Thorpe: It is one of the advantages of getting experts together before trial. I know the Bar do not always agree with judges about this, but it happens commonly I know, and I regularly direct that they are to get together and decide on what they are agree on and disagree on. You would be amazed how little disagreement there probably is at the end of it.

Ms Squibb Williams: I fully support that.

Q478 Dr Iddon: Why can the court not call an expert witness rather than the defence or the prosecution, because the expert would be neutral and produce the scientific evidence straight to the court and not act for either party?

Mr Jani: This has been considered by the Auld Review. It depends on what exactly you mean by "why can't the court provide the expert opinion?" Within the adversarial system, if you are going to suggest that the only expert available is one that the court appoints for a specific issue, and the defence and prosecution are going to be bound by it, my understanding of it would be that if the defence did not agree with it, they may then decide to get another expert in any event; and if we tried to stop that, there would be ECHR implications which would impact on that. The reverse argument of that would be that the prosecution would similarly be inclined to getting their own experts if there are issues arising out of that expert evidence that the court had appointed which required further clarification.

Q479 Dr Turner: It would be like asking the court to act as an examining magistrate, as they have in France.

Judge Thorpe: I am bound to say to you that you will have been told that in France they call one expert—not true. They start down that route, and they finish up just as Nimesh said.

Mr Cooke: An important postscript to all expert statements, prosecuting and defending, is, "I have made this report in an open-minded way and I am not partial". That is paraphrased, but that is the gist of it. That is why it was so disappointing for me when I had the FSS scientist who did not disclose something when he was prosecuting scientist that he would have disclosed . . .

Q480 Chairman: It sounds to me like Alex Jefferies, who would be everybody's choice and he could not fail—

Mr Cooke: I will not be drawn! Can I just give one dreadful illustration of how bad an expert you can end up with? It was a carbon monoxide poisoning case and a gas-fitter who did not do whatever he should have done, and somebody sadly died. My expert, who I had only met on the day of the trial, because he was too expensive to see beforehand, wrote every question down before he answered it. It was the most unnerving experience, and it was almost funny. The cross-examination was: "How many cases of this type have you done before today?" He wrote it down; he thought for a long time; and then he said, "about two". The prosecutor then said: "Is this case one of them?" He wrote that down and then said, "Yes". You did not hear any more about that because the defendant was acquitted, but I did apply to the judge to have a brand new expert in the middle of the trial.

Q481 Mr Key: In roughly what proportion of cases do you say there are major disagreements between expert witnesses?

Mr Jani: I do not think I can answer that question, because in terms of the volume of work we deal with—the CPS prosecutes 1.2 million cases—I would say the majority are cases where there are not experts involved, certainly to the level of having huge fights on that specific issue alone. In terms of numbers there is no way I can answer that question.

Ms Squibb-Williams: We do not have any figures on that question. What always seems to happen of course is that the very serious cases float to the surface, and tend to set the tone, which is quite different from the volume of cases that go on underneath. The vast majority do not involve experts—the large middle tranche that do. Very often, there can be agreement sought, and it is only those where there is an issue and then a further issue on top that would float to the top, which distort the picture.

Q482 Mr Key: How are jurors meant to decide whose evidence is more credible? Does the judge intervene to guide the jury?

Judge Thorpe: In the DNA cases and rape cases, you have probably got one on each side, and road traffic you have one on each side. The real problem is the baby-shaking cases, when you have three or four on each side. All you can do, with the best will in the world, is summarise to the jury what each side said; and I think they are in a very difficult position, I honestly do.

Mr Cooke: Judges are enjoined not to try and guide witnesses on one side or the other, and they get criticised in the Court of Appeal. It is a very real problem in court where you see an imbalance, particularly where you have a persuasive prosecution—and I speak because I obviously defend, but a prosecution expert can be very persuasive, and that, after all, is what the jury hear first.

Q483 Mr Key: Judge, could I probe what you said about pre-trial meetings. This is really important. How would it work in practice? I could see that it could be very important to set up an early-warning system to identify somebody who perhaps might be giving dubious evidence, but how would it work in practice?

Judge Thorpe: What happens now is that serious cases come to court for a pleas and directions hearing in advance, by which time the Crown should have served primary disclosure including all the experts, obviously. You ought really to have had a defence case statement to see what the defence is; so then the prosecution can say, "now we have got this we can go away and look at it again". That is the moment I think a judge can say, "right, now we get experts together. We know what the Crown say, and the defence have got all that; we know what the defence say and the Crown have got that; now let them get together." That is the point you do it, before you ever get to trial. Then you bring it back a few weeks later and say, "where are we now?"

Mr Jani: I agree with Judge Thorpe, but in terms of practice one plea and directions will never be enough. What is really needed is the initial plea and directions hearing to get the lawyers to bang their heads together to try and get to the issues, and following that certain directions perhaps by the judge to highlight what needs to be done by both parties in terms of the expert evidence, hopefully with a view to having a further plea and directions hearing where both parties have complied, and got to a position where you have narrowed down the expert issues to such an extent that it is clear or not whether to call the expert witnesses. The problems I have with the approach currently is that the timetable is such that the pleas and directions hearings are not happening or are not as effective as they should be to ensure that the issues are narrowed down quickly. I do not think, with due respect, that judges have the teeth they need.

Judge Thorpe: One of the difficulties is that I rarely do a serious case like a rape without three pleas and directions hearings, but I am being criticised by people saying "that is taking up court time; why do they not do what they are told the first time round?" The plain fact is that they do not.

Q484 Chairman: Who said that?

Judge Thorpe: I will not tell you who is criticising. So you bring it back, and I have no qualms, if this is a 10-year old girl who says she is raped by her uncle;

this is really important; he is facing a sentence probably in double figures and there are a lot of issues, about saying: "I will see this three times before trial to make sure we get it right." Nimesh is right; some judges do not because perhaps they are under more pressure.

Ms Squibb-Williams: At the risk of sounding a little bit like a stuck record, it is important to note that the changes that are coming through as a result of the criminal case management framework—the introduction of the Criminal Procedure Rules due in April of this year, and the impact of statutory charging, which is slowly rolling out to CPS areas, is attending to exactly the problem that Judge Thorpe is referring to. It is really important to understand that all of these processes are being put into place throughout huge agencies across the country, and it will take a little bit more time to see the results. I do not think we need to assume that none of this has been attended to. Very careful attention is being paid to doing just that; making pleas and directions hearings—or they will be from April pleas and case management hearings—effective by proper use of what would be case progression officers. They are already there—it is just a slight change of name. The impact of statutory charging is an important factor because the CPS will be deciding on the charges much earlier on in the case and considering the expert issues far sooner. We should be seeing the improvements that the Judge is talking about.

Judge Thorpe: We hope so. Currently, I am an overpaid case progression officer, and I have no qualms about saying that that is exactly what I do, because that means that when it gets to trial, you stand a better chance of having the issues clearly understood and put before a jury.

Q485 Mr Key: Judge, I know you are here in your own right today, but can I ask you about the Council for the Registration of Forensic Practitioners. In your letter to the Lord Chancellor of 12 November 2004 you said at paragraph 21, on the subject of digital evidence: "Shortly we will be holding a round-table discussion and we will be able to define and promote an agreed standard of safe, competent practice." Did "shortly" mean six months? How far have you got?

Judge Thorpe: I am not sure I can answer that entirely, and I will give you a written answer if necessary—last Friday is the answer.

Q486 Mr Key: This is clearly very important because in the long list of practitioners who have applied and achieved registration, the largest category was scene examiners, followed by laboratory scientists, fingerprint examiners; and then there was a huge drop until you get to fingerprint development specialists, road transport investigators and so on, and even an archaeologist, but none were registered in computing.

Judge Thorpe: I have updated those figures and supplied the Committee with them beforehand, and no doubt it has been circulated.

Q487 Mr Key: Are you now building a register of experts in computing?

Judge Thorpe: We are certainly looking to do just that. One of the things we are doing in the CRFP is under pressure—and I put it mildly from the court—as they identify areas we need to look at, then we are looking to see if we can find assessors and open the register and so on. This is an ongoing process, which will continue. Computing is very important, particularly of course with all the pornographic image cases that have been flooding through the doors.

Q488 Dr Harris: Going back to the issue of disclosure, Mr Cooke, in the example you gave of finding out the evidence that had been gathered by the prosecution that was never put—that is just an issue of disclosure. Should judges not be coming down hard on the prosecution where they do not, in an obvious case like that—you felt it was obvious and did not have to interpret it—should judges not becoming down hard on failure to disclose things that could make a significant difference? That is a failure of the system, as well as your heroics!

Mr Cooke: Yes, it is a worry, but what are the judge's powers and what can he do? First of all, the non-disclosure has to be found, otherwise you run the whole trial without it. During the trial the judge will stand back from criticising the scientist because it is for the jury to make what they will of the scientist's evidence. It was to some extent perhaps a cheap jibe by me about that point, but the bit that he did not disclose was so much in issue and very important—although it was not definitive of the case—that I had—

Q489 Dr Harris: It was not him that did not disclose it; it was the prosecution.

Mr Cooke: No, no, the prosecution do not go and look through a scientist's files. They do not get the scientist's files.

Q490 Dr Harris: They should send everything.

Mr Jani: In relation to that, from the prosecution point of view there has to be a clear distinction drawn between that which we know about and which we do not disclose and that which we do not know anything about because the expert did not tell us, and which we cannot disclose because we do not know about it. Whilst I accept readily that if we know about it and we know it undermines the prosecution case or assists the defence case we should disclose it, it would be wrong to criticise the CPS or any other prosecutor for failing to disclose something of which they had no knowledge whatsoever because the expert failed to disclose it in the first place.

Q491 Dr Harris: Are experts being told by prosecutors that they are not to do that?

Mr Jani: Certainly there is a disclosure project. That is one of the areas that will be looked into to make sure that we are aware of their obligations on disclosure.

Q492 Dr Harris: Perhaps you can send us information on that.

Judge Thorpe: If there was a serious non-disclosure to a trial, which a judge felt affected the—I would have not the slightest qualm in discharging the jury and saying, "go away and we will start again".

Q493 Dr Harris: The CPS tell me they are under pressure; they are not allowed just to dump, in spite of what I have just said, huge amounts of stuff on the defence. They now have performance targets to sort through all this stuff and at least file it and present it in a reasonable way to the defence. They do not like having to do that because it takes a huge amount of prosecutor time, so they are not meeting their own performance targets or their real performance targets on efficiency. Is there a problem with performance targets on prosecutors that prevent adequate disclosure to the defence in respect of expert witnesses among other things?

Mr Jani: The first thing I would challenge is your reference to performance targets. I do not get paid for the number of people I put away, and there are no performance targets for me to that level.

Q494 Dr Harris: The performance targets that I am aware of are around speed and staying within budget and that sort of thing.

Mr Jani: On the ground, as a prosecutor we do not take those issues into account. Certainly, I am happy for you to talk to any prosecutor you wish to, but they would not be talking about performance targets to that extent. What they talk about is if there is enough evidence, and is there a public interest in prosecuting it. The issue in terms of experts and how we approach those cases is not unique; it would be the same for cases where there are no experts. We have a function to provide and it is not guided by performance targets in the way you have raised.

Q495 Dr Harris: I was rather depressed to hear you say that you, as an idealist perhaps, expected juries to reach their judgment on the basis of fact, including how people come across. I happen to think that those two are different concepts. I hope that this Committee listens to the evidence and not how well people come across, although I suspect that has to be determined! Can you clarify what you meant by that, because I thought I heard two different things from you then.

Mr Jani: What I said—and perhaps it is the way I phrased it which has been misunderstood—is that it is unavoidable when you are talking about people giving evidence that their personalities will come across with that evidence. Just as this body cannot avoid having our personalities coming across when we give our evidence, so the jury will, as part of the evidence they hear, see the personality. I do not think you can have a position where you have a sanitised—apart from having a robot perhaps giving evidence—version of the evidence where there is no personality involved—

Q496 Dr Harris: It would be best if they stuck to the facts. It would be good case management for a judge to step in if there is over-performance perhaps, and seek to—

Mr Jani: If you have someone who is interested in amateur dramatics, of course you are right; but in terms of expert evidence, they are clearly not just giving evidence of fact, but they are giving evidence of opinion as well as fact, based on objective criteria in whatever expertise that they have.

Q497 Dr Harris: I just wanted to pin down the position of CRFP and its role. On the assumption that the CRFP has had the register open for a long time in the area, and there is no backlog, does anyone disagree that it would be a reasonable proposition to insist as a matter of policy, whether that is the LSC doing it or Parliament deciding, that Commission-funded experts should be registered with the CRFP? Does anyone disagree with that?

Mr Cooke: Only with a slight caveat as the thing rolls forward, which is simply that if you have an expert for one reason or another who has not joined or been accepted—it is probable he has been refused—then at least he or she should be able to make out, despite not being on the register at this stage, that they are suitable. There is an important timescale on this; you have got to find experts who are available for trial dates and so on. There are practical problems with that, but in principle I wholly support it; it is a major step forward and a major resource for everyone.

Ms Squibb-Williams: The principle of the Council is a good one. I would still want to preserve judicial discretion, however and wherever that is to be applied, and would not want to see someone excluded simply because they were not on the register. I do not agree with automatic registration, mostly or until such time as we are sure of the auditing process upon the assessors. There is no evidence that I have seen as yet that the auditing of the assessors is independent and that it has clearly set-out criteria, and where the power to sanction any breach of the code has come from.

Q498 Dr Harris: Where that was the case, would you be happy, because we do not allow people to unleash themselves on people's bodies or teeth without registration.

Ms Squibb-Williams: Precisely.

Mr Jani: Times have moved on in relation to where we get our experts from. I pointed out earlier that there are certain areas where the expertise is such that there are very few people who can provide that evidence. In fact, the prosecution and defence have to go to experts overseas. The overseas experts will not be registered with the CRFP for obvious reasons, but to prevent them giving that evidence just because they are not registered with the CRFP would be detrimental to the criminal just system as a whole because it would be preventing world-renowned experts who can assist with the case giving their evidence, simply because of this requirement to register.

Judge Thorpe: I hope in time that they will become a minority, and I agree with you to that extent.

Q499 Dr Harris: You agree with me?

Judge Thorpe: Sorry, I do agree the point you are making. I am hoping in time the situation that Nimesh is talking about will go down; in other words we will have a pool like that. However, there is a sanction. If experts breach the code and do not come up to the right standard, the CRFP has the power to strike them off the register. There are currently two cases being considered, so it is really significant. I would really like to place on record, Mr Chairman, that I think the Government's approach to this was extremely far-sighted in 1999, and they are still funding it to a considerable extent, which is a tremendous step forward.

Mr Cooke: Feedback of scientists or experts is I think non-existent. Whether I am prosecuting or defending, I am not asked to report back on a good expert or what-have-you. In fact I do because I think it is part of my job, but I suspect many other people do not. It would be helpful to have scientists' feedback on the lawyers and judges. It would be quite interesting; but none of this is ever done, as far as I can tell. I know some judges who simply should not be let loose on certain technical cases because they are just not up to it, but what am I to do with that? As for barristers, you have already heard what I said. If any of you listened to the 21 minutes of me banging on about the way that the Bar and judges behave in DNA cases, I used words like "appalling".

Q500 Dr Turner: I was going to mention DNA yet again, since I want to look at the adoption of the novel techniques and establishing their validity in court proceedings. DNA is a good example; it is still fairly new. When it first came in, the public at least certainly thought it was a magic bullet that was absolutely infallible. Now we have become a bit critical, and now we are careful to mention it in terms of probabilities. Those probabilities are determined by the fact that standard procedure uses a 10-point identification. Dr Jeffries suggested that 16 points would be more appropriate. Do you have any mechanism for reviewing the validity of techniques? Would you, for instance, want the use of DNA evidence to be updated so that the analyses were presented in terms of 16 points, which would narrow the probabilities of it being a different person?

Judge Thorpe: One of the problems with the committee that I chair and which Graham and Nimesh are on is that we are rather concerned, as things improve, when we go back and look at old cases that people were convicted when DNA was under a different mechanism. Frankly, people on the FSS say, "perhaps we ought to go and look at it but nobody has asked me and nobody is paying". It is a matter of considerable concern to Graham and I whether you have cases in the system of people that perhaps should not be—I would not put it as high as that, but which should be re-examined with new hits on the database.

Mr Cooke: Can I answer first as a statistician. The 10-point improved system uses of the order of one in a billion. The reason why it is put in those vague terms is because there has not, and probably cannot be, a large enough study to make sure that each of the ten positions is independent of the other nine. To use a completely different example, if you work with statistics on Scandinavians with blond hair and blue eyes, you would see immediately that those two things are not independent. We know that from observation; but in other areas you have to do a statistical study. It is just not feasible, at the level of ten points, to conduct a study that would demonstrate that these things are independent. There is no biological evidence, as I understand it, that demonstrates that that position of DNA will be independent, and therefore going to 16 points, however attractive it may seem to Dr Jones, is not going to help in court.

Q501 Dr Turner: That is interesting.
Mr Jani: Speaking very much as a prosecutor on this, I am trying to make sure that DNA evidence when I present it gives a fair assessment of what that DNA will prove, i.e., "the probability of somebody having that match is this". Ideally, I would like what the lay understanding of genetics used to be, that is that the genetic fingerprint is unique. It would solve all the problems we have been talking about in terms of these probabilities. Once you get to the point where the science is capable of giving a DNA match that is unique, then clearly I would be in a position to openly say what would currently be a prosecutor's fallacy, ie, "the crime scene matches your DNA; you are the one who did it". Ultimately that is the position which, as a prosecutor, I would like to be in. We are not there yet, and until we get there, in terms of the database I agree with Judge Thorpe and Graham Cooke that it is important that we try and monitor for miscarriages which may occur because we are only matching a certain number of DNA strands, and therefore there may be a possibility that there is more than one person who has that match.

Q502 Dr Turner: You are clearly saying that you would be unwilling to press convictions on DNA evidence alone.
Mr Cooke: You should not.

Q503 Dr Turner: And it needs other evidence to place it in the context.
Judge Thorpe: All it should say is one of a pool of people. It is not the way that in the past, and probably today, the police approach it. They will say, "it is a hit; it has to be you".

Q504 Dr Turner: Let us say that the other evidence relied on fairly novel techniques as well. How would you wish to see those novel techniques validated for court purposes? Would you want to see a system such as the Fry test, as used in the US courts?
Mr Cooke: I have taken the view, as DNA has used further technology—we think DNA has been around for 15 years in court work—it is different steps, and as new technology has come along I have

taken the view of asking in appropriate cases to have chapter and verse from the FSS as to what their error ratios have been and things like that. The Fry test, as it is called—and a similar test is used in England and Wales, which is broadly the same—has it been peer-reviewed; has it been accepted? There has to be a first time for everything, but I have challenged it and had a judge rule that it is accepted; it has moved along. Forgive me, but Nimesh said something which I fundamentally disagree with, which is the way it is presented at the moment as the right one. Ian Evett, who is one of the most respected statisticians and scientist in the whole area of this and also fingerprints, has said in public that when it is presented in the FSS way, which is still being done today, that all journalists get it wrong. I was speaking at the same meeting after him and I spoke of that and said, "for journalists, read jurors". I have here an example, which I am happy to leave with you, of a newspaper report that said: "Semen found on the body had only one in a billion chance of being from someone other than the man accused of strangling her." That is the prosecutor's fallacy. All journalists, in my experience, get it wrong. I rang this chap up and he said: "Oh, dear, have I got it wrong again?"
Mr Jani: Can I just say that, clearly, I am not responsible for the members of the press or the journalist there. In terms of the approach the CPS takes and the wording we use in our statements, it is not something that is done off the cuff; and clearly we want to make sure that any evidence we present is in accordance with *Doheney v Adams*. Graham is right that we have had a fair exchange of words, and I am sure they will continue, in relation to what is or what is not falling foul of prosecutor's fallacy. However, it is a question of wording, not a question of whether the CPS is saying "we do not believe that *Doheney v. Adams* is right. We do believe it is right, and we want to be sure that the wording we use complies with it. As far as I am concerned the wording we use does comply with it. I am happy to have that validated by a court judgment if necessary.

Q505 Mr Key: You said something, Mr Cooke, that is very important: you said "for journalists read jurors". Could you not say, "for journalists read jurors and policemen"?
Mr Cooke: Yes.

Q506 Mr Key: And does it matter? In my experience, during the Sally Clarke case, a family that lived in my constituency—we all knew her as a little girl and went to school with my children and so on—during the course of that trial Angela Cannings, also a constituent—well known as a Tesco's check-out girl—I was talking to a senior policeman who said: "Well, Angela Cannings has got to be the same as Sally Clarke." I said: "Why?" "Well, one baby, possibly two—come on, three—it stands to reason." This was a senior police officer.
Mr Cooke: Seniority either in the ranks of lawyers or police officers does not absolve people from—

Judge Thorpe: I will give you a practical example, if I may, just to reinforce exactly what you said, Mr Key, of a recent rape case, with a stain and so on—one in a million chance. The policeman said to the defendant in interview: "There you are, million to one chance against it being anybody other than you. Now, what have you got to say?" That was from a policeman in interview. Not having got as far as Nimesh and the CPS, this was right at the outset.

Q507 Mr Key: Does that make any difference then, in the end?
Judge Thorpe: Yes.

Q508 Mr Key: How does it make a difference?
Mr Cooke: Because the solicitor will say to the man, "come on, now, you are bang to rights; it is DNA; you are guilty, and if you plead guilty now we will get a bit knocked off, or we will probably get the offence brought down a bit"—because plea-bargaining goes on at police stations as well as elsewhere—
Ms Squibb-Williams: If it was not his DNA he is not going to plead no matter what his solicitor says.
Mr Cooke: I am not so sure. I suspect, Karen, if you—I have spent time with more defendants than you have, and I do not mean that unkindly—

Q509 Chairman: There is no hierarchy here among witnesses, please.
Mr Cooke: I have a fear about that, and that is where some of the miscarriages might emerge eventually, if we are able to go back.

Q510 Dr Turner: Judge, I have a fair idea of what you might say from your earlier remarks, but when you are hearing a case how will you decide whether to admit evidence from a new and emerging field of forensic technology? You yourself clearly, because of your involvement in CRFP, have some level of expertise probably over and above that of most judges. Do you think that judges are really competent to establish the credentials and competency of expert witnesses?
Judge Thorpe: It is a very difficult area. As I said, this test was laid down in 1894, and they mere said that judges will decide someone is an expert. Fine, but then you are going to have to go into the details, as best you can, of what is involved and so on, and come to a value judgment. With emerging techniques you are quite right; it may be very difficult, and it may actually be an area where you do not need an expert at all, or are not clear, and then, if you do need an expert, have you got one? I would not minimise it. I know that the Judicial Studies Board is responsible for all aspects of training, and they have for instance had some lectures from people in the FSS, some judges—I do not know about DNA, but it leads on to it. I would not pretend it is easy, and I would not pretend to get it right all the time—I would not, really.
Mr Cooke: The defence do not often take the lead.
Mr Jani: It is probably an obvious point, Dr Turner, to you as a scientist, but science moves on and what is happening in certain areas is that we have what we could possibly call an organised field of science and

expertise. However, something comes along which may change that. That state of knowledge will have to be reassessed. There will be nothing that lawyers and judges can do until the point comes where that level of science has moved on to the question of what is something that is currently considered organised and well created to be a level of expertise.
Judge Thorpe: Can I put one caveat on what Karen said, that he would not plead guilty if it was not his DNA. How many years ago do we know about false confessions? People do, I am afraid, put their hands up to things they have not done.

Q511 Dr Turner: I am sure there are those who would suggest that in highly complex cases, where the scientific evidence is highly complex, you cannot expect an ordinary juror to understand it. There have been suggestions for instance that complex fraud cases are better heard by a specially qualified judge rather than by a jury. What do you think of the proposition that in cases involving highly complex scientific evidence they should be heard by a suitably qualified judge, assuming one exists, rather than by a jury?
Judge Thorpe: I am going again, I am afraid, to say that that is a matter for government policy, not for me as a judge.
Mr Jani: I am going to go a little further than that and say that it sounds great, if you think about it in those terms, but if you think a little further about just how wide a field of expertise you are talking about, it will not be so easy to create a jury that is suitable that is suitable for the position. Currently, we are having problems finding enough experts, forget about a group of people who will understand those experts, which is what you are suggesting. By example, I give the computer experts. Just because you are a qualified medical practitioner does not mean you will know about computers and IT crime. That is the issue you will face with that sort of situation when you are trying to get a specialist jury.
Ms Squibb-Williams: Perhaps also there is a view that by maintaining juries and not going down the specialist judge road such as in a complex fraud case, it is a good discipline to impose on the advocates because the public has a right to understand what goes on in court and what the results are, so that when they hear the case reported it still has to make sense. Having to present what is a complex case to a jury in a way that they understand it assists with that public confidence in working towards keeping it as simple and straightforward as possible. There is a risk, if you have specialist judges that advocates will put in more and more complex arguments and thus make it harder for the public to understand.

Q512 Dr Turner: Are you satisfied that the facility for presenting digital evidence to courts is adequate? Does digital evidence get presented properly in court? Do judges understand it, and advocates?
Mr Cooke: I had the distinction of working with the new equipment at one of the Crown courts in south London, which was the worst hotchpotch I have ever seen. It was extraordinarily badly introduced, and the poor jury sitting in the front row were stuck

with lights shining down on their screens and that sort of thing—in that sense, if you are talking about introducing exhibits and working with them in that way. Other than that, I have stayed deliberately away from fraud in my career. I have done one and I never want to do another one. Its only merit was that it was extremely well paid! I am all for, in that field, having a judge who knows what he is doing. It is much more difficult to find a suitable judge, I think, in the various disciplines that will crop up and have cropped up. I do not think there is at the Bar enough people, at trial stage, or at the judicial stage, who can fit the bill.

Q513 Dr Turner: Judge, do you get much digital crime in Chichester?
Judge Thorpe: No. They just tend to hit people over the head with iron bars! Can I go back to the point you were making. The plain fact is that none of us knows why a jury comes to the decision it does, whether it is complexity or not. We just do not know. We know the Lord Chancellor is talking about jury investigation. Maybe we should wait and see if he stets those studies in train.
Mr Cooke: I am wholly in favour of that, wholly favour.
Judge Thorpe: Me too.
Mr Cooke: We can only but learn from that process.
Judge Thorpe: You might then find whether the expert who came across well actually carried the day—the question you were asking earlier on.

Q514 Dr Harris: I trained in medical epidemiology, and there is a well-known joke about the epidemiologist who is up in court for a serious offence. "How do you plead, guilty or not guilty?" He said: "I don't know; I haven't heard the evidence yet." That illustrates perhaps the gulf between some branches of science and law—which is a binary decision—guilty or not guilty. Do forums exist between judges and scientists to discuss, with the idea of building up training courses, how that gulf can be bridged? Do you know of any work going on?
Judge Thorpe: Funnily enough, one of the things we are doing –I am chairing a working party of judges, lawyers and scientists, and we met last week. We set it up in the margins of the CRP just to address this issue because we had suddenly woken up to the fact that there is a gap. We are trying to come up with a sensible recommendation that I can put to the Lord Chief Justice and senior presiding judge, where we go from here. You are absolutely right, Dr Harris, that it is a problem that we are starting slowly, and rather late in the day, to address.
Ms Squibb-Williams: There is work that is going on which joins up exactly those groups of people you referred to. In the work I have been doing, I have found particular support from the judiciary in trying to get whatever material is available from the Forensic Science Service or other providers, out to the judiciary to understand better for example what the prosecution are doing. In addition to that, I have seen a lot of enthusiasm from, for example, the College of Law, which has already put together a video package and a learning module for students,

teaching them the new DNA prosecution process. There is work afoot, and the more groups get together to design a larger and broader system of training, the better.
Judge Thorpe: There is one problem, if I could just flag it up. I am off this week for three days with another hundred judges doing the training, and we are all being trained, which means there are a hundred courts not sitting for three days trying serious cases. All this training is not without serious cost, and I do not mean in money but in cases just not coming on.

Q515 Dr Harris: We started this session with this question—and I am not sure we got a specific answer, on the issue say of prosecutor's fallacy—of what training lawyers, both prosecution and defence, and judges get. Is it covered? Can we expect, as parliamentarians, that every single judge has had training in this question—any judge that is liable to hear a case like this—and similarly Crown prosecutors; or is it work in progress?
Judge Thorpe: The Court of Appeal laid down the standard directions as clear as day in 1997 in *Doheney v Adams*, and all judges should be aware of that. I certainly address it in lectures, and Dr Pope from the FSS does as well, so the answer is that there are some, but basically the law is actually clear.
Mr Cooke: But not being applied. There is a real problem with DNA evidence. First of all, judges are taught in their occasional sessions—and I am not a judge and I do not know how often it is—but perhaps once a year or two, but every judge sitting will have gone through a session on DNA evidence, taught, I am afraid to say, by two FSS statisticians. They will be taught the FSS line, which I wholly disagree with. I say it is disloyal to the Court of Appeal decision in *Doheney v Adams*. The CPS knows my views, and I have persuaded—rather he has been persuaded, that is Dr Evett and Dr Bramley, who was at the time the Deputy Director of the FSS that the move ought to be made away from the way that the FSS expressed it in court. That is a very important issue indeed. We have yet to carry, those of us in favour of that change, the CPS. That is ongoing, and it remains to be seen whether we carry the CPS or not. Returning to the Bar, the Bar is taught nothing. It relies upon its general principle of doing the right thing, which is that in any area of law you should check your case and look up the authorities. I have said publicly, and I say it now, that the Bar is a disgrace in this; it will go and prosecute in a DNA case without knowing that there is a guideline case of the Court of Appeal which dates back to 1996. It is a disgrace.

Q516 Dr Harris: Maybe the CPS can respond.
Mr Jani: I certainly hope so! I am not going to rehearse the issues in relation to whether we are going to comply with *Doheney v Adams*; the short answer is that we are, although there may be some dispute between myself and Graham as to how we will do this. On the issue of whether there is training for prosecutors, there is training. Guidance was sent out following the decision in *Doheney v Adams* to all

the 42 areas that the CPS prosecutes in. In addition, I hope it is clear that we are not just talking about DNA here; apart even from the issue of DNA we are talking about *Doheney v Adams* when you are talking about issues of continuity and use of assistance in situations where you have DNA evidence, and guidance as regards all three aspects has been sent out, which respects the decision of *Doheney v Adams* and complies with it. In terms of whether the CPS will comply, the answer in short is that we do have training, and guidance is sent out to all the areas. The intention would be that everyone complies with it.

Q517 Dr Harris: Maybe we can reach a conclusion on that if we have more information. I would be interested to see what the dispute is, because I have not seen any documentation around this last issue, and we do not have time to explore it further here. What has happened since? What effect has Meadow had? All this training that people get, and judges ought to know; yet it appears that the judge in that case did not step in and say "it is obvious that that is a fallacy"—in fact more than one fallacy as I understand it—and the there is a bunch of judges in the Court of Appeal first time round who said it is not an issue. What is going on there? We know that the public flaying of Meadow, even before he has had his hearing and been able to defend himself, is having a very damaging effect on the willingness of experts to come forward in child protection, to the detriment of every other case, and justice in these cases. What is happening to the judges in those cases, which I have implied really ought to have a responsibility to step in?

Mr Cooke: Any judge that has been the subject of an appeal as a result of a trial or a ruling, gets the result from the Court of Appeal upheld in the first place or not upheld in the second place. I speak largely from ignorance here, but there must be a hierarchy of judges that basically descend on that chap who got it wrong, somehow to make sure that it will not happen again. Will the same happen to barristers? Who knows! We are all independent practitioners, whether prosecutors or defenders. We will get work from somewhere. People generally do not examine that. Who knows who was the prosecuting silk in the *Silverman* case? I do not. They all got it dreadfully wrong.

Judge Thorpe: I can say this much about judges; Graham is right, you get the thing back from the Court of Appeal, and if it is a really bad case your presiding judge will certainly talk to you. In an ultimate case, you will probably appreciate that before you try rape cases or murder, you have to have a ticket effectively from the Lord Chief Justice.

Q518 Dr Harris: An ultimate case?
Judge Thorpe: Really serious cases. He says: "Right, you are now clear to try cases of attempted murder and rape." But if I made a complete hash of one, the remedy is that he would say, "right, you do not try any more rape cases". One or two people have been stopped from trying very serious cases, but that is the

ultimate sanction. The cases you quote, I do not know—you would have to talk to the Lord Chief Justice.
Mr Cooke: One of the forensic scientists in the *Doheney v Adams* case got it so wrong, it is inconceivable how wrong he got it. He was not alone. He held his view right through the appeal, and even wrote to me—I was defending—insisting that he was still right. Later, when I had the opportunity I asked Dr Evett: "How on earth did that man make that mistake and go to court as an FSS scientist?" His answer was to me: "I told him he was wrong but he wouldn't have it." That man had kept going to court as an FSS expert—analogous to your question about judges and barristers.

Q519 Chairman: What use are experts, then, in court cases?
Mr Cooke: Enormous use most of the time. Every now and again it is the opposite.

Q520 Chairman: Judge Thorpe, what do you think?
Judge Thorpe: I do. I gave you the case of death by dangerous driving. It is very difficult because without the expert we would not have known how fast the car was going or how fast he had hit the pedestrian. That is all the expert told us. They could then say: "Right, has he fallen substantially below the standard of the careful driver?" They would not have known he was doing 45 in a 30-mile limit when he hit the pedestrian without the expert.
Mr Jani: The whole point of the experts being there is because they know something they can provide an opinion on something which the jury cannot make their own minds up on, on the basis of the facts. If they could, quite rightly the expert should not be allowed there and should not be there at all. The only point for which they are called is because of either their professional training or experience or whatever—they have an opinion which the jury cannot form of their own experiences—and they are needed to provide that opinion objectively.

Q521 Dr Turner: It is still critical that judges and advocates have sufficient knowledge themselves to be properly critical of what an expert witness says, which I am sure—
Ms Squibb-Williams: Again, with the increased emphasis on robust case management everybody's knowledge should improve as they go through canvassing the issues at an earlier and earlier stage in the process.

Q522 Dr Harris: If there is an ultimate case where an expert gets it wrong—and I am not going to personalise the case—and the judge gets it wrong obviously by not spotting the gross error that is allowed to go unchallenged by well-paid lawyers as well—then should there be an equality of opprobrium placed on both the expert, assuming the expert was not being malevolent and made an honest mistake, in so far as a mistake can be honest, and do you think that is what occurs? I have never heard of a judge being publicly attacked—maybe it is just not our style—for gross errors or attitudes—in the way that some expert witnesses are attacked?

Mr Jani: Can I approach it on this basis? You have given a hypothetical situation, and in a situation like what you really need to examine is, if you are looking at fault, if an expert goes beyond his own expertise then clearly he is not an expert and cannot do so, and somebody should prevent him from doing so.

Q523 Dr Harris: Particularly if he is doing so in good faith.

Mr Jani: There is also the other situation, which I do not think we have touched on but which is equally possible, of an expert who within his own field gets it wrong in terms of the knowledge within his own expertise. Both those issues need to be addressed by all criminal justice agencies. It is not just an expert that gets it wrong, and if that situation gets to the point of a miscarriage, clearly there are a number of people who have failed to spot it. That is why it has got to that stage. However, you must look at that in context, in terms of the seriousness and complexity of these cases. Hindsight is a wonderful thing, when you are looking at these things in the cold light of day, without the full picture of how many months and days the persons are involved and their volume of work when this case is being heard. All agencies have responsibility to try and spot where an expert goes beyond their expertise, and to spot where an expert perhaps has failed to give the appropriate evidence in relation to his expertise.

Q524 Chairman: How many appeals are there against experts' evidence? Who appeals?

Mr Jani: I cannot say I know of precise figures, but the recent ones are those you have already heard about—Cannings, Clarke, and another recent one in Brooks as well, which may not be quite—

Q525 Chairman: Do you think they are rarities?

Mr Jani: Whether it is a rarity or not, it is something we should try and avoid.

Q526 Dr Harris: We know that some lawyers say, "I will not take that case because that judge is on it". Maybe that does not happen, but we have heard cases of people saying, "Who is the expert on the other side? I am not going to go against him/her." Do you think there should be ways of ensuring that that sort of reputational prejudice is sought out and dealt with?

Mr Cooke: Can I try and cope with this in terms of DNA and, for example, the FSS. I will not use an FSS expert when I am defending because I believe—whether I am right or not is not the point—there is a corporate spirit that will mean an expert from the FSS will not go against the party line. That is my belief, rightly or wrongly, but I will do for my client what I think is right.

Q527 Chairman: You would not agree, would you?

Mr Jani: I would certainly hope that there is no such leaning because it is going into that situation where you are talking about hawks and doves, ie, you have experts who are not doing their role to the court and independently giving evidence but are siding with one side or another to ensure they have a pay-packet, in essence; and that is not the right way of approaching it at all.

Judge Thorpe: That may not be right. I say as a judge that I very rarely see an expert for the defence who is an FSS man. It may be that they all share Graham's view, and find independent experts from somewhere else.

Mr Cooke: From what I know of the Professor Meadow case—and one must be very careful, working on chat in the newspapers—to my mind it is not Professor Meadow's fault. So far as I can tell he gave that evidence honestly and thought he was right. One of the problems we have with experts and other witnesses is that witnesses who think they are right are very convincing because they are convinced that they are right. It is the lawyers' job, and particularly I would single out the defence lawyer—what on earth he thought he was doing letting that go unchallenged. I assume it was unchallenged. If he challenged it and the judge ruled, then it is not his fault, but as far as I know it was unchallenged. That is basic defence work, in my opinion.

Q528 Chairman: Maybe there are people in the world you just do not challenge.

Mr Cooke: Well, the bigger they are the—

Judge Thorpe: It is very difficult as a judge if nobody challenges the evidence and both sides agree they are happy with the evidence. It is quite tricky to step in and say, "this is absolutely statistical rubbish" if it is.

Mr Jani: I do not agree with that line, I have to say.

Q529 Chairman: Perhaps you could get together afterwards and fight it out.

Ms Squibb-Williams: Mr Chairman, can I submit some of the training materials that have been produced for the prosecution team?

Mr Cooke: I have brought a book—

Q530 Chairman: Bedtime reading!

Mr Cooke: Yes!

Chairman: This has been quite interesting.

Mr Key: It has indeed.

Chairman: It is a new world for us but it involves science, technology, and things that we are scrutinising, and the applied use of them. The questions they raise are indeed very interesting. I do not know that this has ever been done before but it will certainly raise questions and perhaps suggestions of new ways of doing things. Thank you very much for your time.

Judge Thorpe: If you were pressing that there should be more training for judges and so on, your recommendation should really be directed towards Lord Justice Keene, Chairman of the Judicial Studies Board.

Wednesday 9 February 2005

Members present:

Dr Ian Gibson, in the Chair

Dr Evan Harris
Dr Brian Iddon
Mr Robert Key

Mr Tony McWalter
Dr Desmond Turner

Witnesses: **Caroline Flint**, a Member of the House, Parliamentary Under-Secretary of State for Reducing Organised and International Crime, Police Science and Technology, Anti-Drugs Co-Ordination and International and European Issues, **Dr Lyn Fereday**, DNA Expansion Programme Manager, and **Mr Tim Wilson**, Head, Science Policy Unit, the Home Office, examined.

Q531 Chairman: Welcome, Minister. Nice to see you again, Tim, and welcome, Lyn, to the Committee this morning. I think you know we have been looking into forensic science and it has been quite absorbing and interesting. I am finding out about things I never knew went on in courts, so I must go some time and see how it is used, the evidence. There is some confusion, Minister, about the statement that has been made on 11 January of this year about the future of the Service. Is it a change of policy, for example, or is it just a statement of previous policy? What is the situation, please? Is PPP still an option?
Caroline Flint: PPP is still an option, but what we said in the statement, and I took over this portfolio around June of last year, is that it was the intention originally, as you are probably aware, that going to a government-owned company was part of the transition stage towards a PPP and that was always open and transparent. What we have said, and this was in discussion with the previous Home Secretary and endorsed by this Home Secretary, is that we are making that move, but what we have said is that if the FSS can compete, given what we know from McFarland and what I have actually seen in the last six months of the problems facing FSS, then if it did succeed, it would not necessarily need to move to a PPP. At the moment we do think that even though a government-owned company does give some benefits, certainly in terms of FSS and its contractual arrangements with its customers, we are still worried about the problems about getting investment and equity to develop the Service, so we have been clear about that. Having said that, I think in the statement that was issued just before Christmas we were prepared to see if the GovCo could make a go of it and we have given a sort of two-year cycle for that to happen, so we are not going necessarily to move straightaway. We would have to be convinced that it could not succeed in order to move, but we still think that has to be an option at the end of the day.

Q532 Chairman: It still feels like it has been a change in policy. Is that because there is a new Home Secretary, the charming chap that we all know?
Caroline Flint: It is not a change in policy because actually the statement was agreed with the previous Home Secretary before Christmas, so it is part of the discussions about this areaome Ho Ho and we have met with MPs and others to hear their concerns. At the end of the day, when I took over in June, I said

to people, "What's going on here? Why are we doing this? Why is this happening?", and I have seen the evidence you have already received and read other people's testimonies and it seems clear that the world is changing around FSS and, therefore, I have always been clear that actually the status quo was not an option. If the GovCo can deliver, then that is fine, but I still have doubts about that—particularly the injection of sufficient funding for it to develop and for it to innovate in the future. I have to say, I think there are two sites I have not been to so far and, for example, the accommodation that people are working in is an issue, I think, for the future and there will be significant capital investment for that.

Q533 Chairman: So if I said to you that really it was a stay of execution, do you think I would be over-egging it a bit?
Caroline Flint: I think what we are saying really is that we are willing to see if the GovCo can work, but it has to prove it can work and it can deliver. What we have said also is that if we did think we should move to a PPP, we would be absolutely clear about the reasons for that and what the benefits would be in terms of FSS, but would not be delivered by a GovCo. I think really the GovCo does give an opportunity for both the management, the staff and, for that matter, the unions to see if that can work. It will provide some benefits that we cannot currently provide under the trading status, particularly in terms of its contractual relationship with its customers, but it still has limitations in terms of, for example, the threshold that is placed on it in terms of the contracts it can carry out independently.

Q534 Chairman: But you will understand the nervousness of people who work within it given that there is a general election, who knows, perhaps new ministers and a change of direction again, so can you allay any fears that might appertain to those events?
Caroline Flint: I cannot foresee the outcome of a general election, but I have to say I think there has been both before I took over this role, but also since, considerable discussion about the problems facing FSS. Now, I do believe that whoever has this responsibility after the general election, when they see the information, they will realise that actually the status quo is not an option and, therefore, we have to make some changes, and I think that is in the best interests of FSS, but also in terms of our criminal

justice system as well. I think for someone to have to change the pattern of direction, they would have to have access to something I have not had access to in order to suggest that things should stay as they are at the moment, which I do not think is practical and I actually do not think that even serves staff in terms of their future service and stability either.

Q535 Chairman: Has the Chief Scientific Adviser to the Home Office been involved in these decisions and been consulted?

Mr Wilson: Yes, Paul Wiles, as Chief Scientific Adviser[1], is clearly aware of the way in which corporate policy is being developed and will have been copied into quite a lot of material. The overall direction is reflected in the Police Scientific and Technology Strategy which Paul was very much involved in, and we have a strategic group that pulls together the Home Office's own scientific and IT experts with some outside participants, the police and a wide range of stakeholders, including the Police Federation and the Chief Superintendents Association, so this is all taking place reasonably openly within the broader corporate Home Office.

Q536 Chairman: Are negotiations taking place with the trade unions, for example?

Mr Wilson: He has not been involved in negotiations taking place with the trade unions.

Q537 Chairman: Is that planned?

Mr Wilson: That is primarily a matter for the Chief Executive of the Forensic Science Service because he is responsible for those people. I have had a limited involvement with the trade union side in discussing the outline business case and trying to explain that without breaching commercial confidentiality and also listening to their own alternative proposals where we established some common ground, recognising that there has to be some way of bringing development capital into the FSS. There are issues about its vulnerability in that because it is at the moment without a broader revenue base, it is highly dependent on expenditure by the police and a quite narrow range of criminal justice participants.

Q538 Dr Harris: You just said I think, Minister, that the statement of 11 January was not a change of policy, as I think was the implication, that the new Home Secretary changed the policy, but I got the impression from reading the newspapers that it was a change in policy and indeed some people have interpreted it as such. Can you just clarify exactly what the difference is between the plan post-11 January and before?

Caroline Flint: The McFarland Report, as you will be aware, when it looked at FSS, did think that the end result should be a PPP, but it did say within that

that the organisation would have to go to a government-owned company as part of that step-by-step process, so that was always, always there.

Q539 Dr Harris: Government policy is not the McFarland Report.

Caroline Flint: No, but we accepted the recommendation of McFarland on this issue. Obviously there have been a number of discussions about how we would go forward on that. In terms of what we have said in relation to declaring that we are going to move now to a government-owned company, what we have said is that the only difference is that if a government-owned company can provide the sort of stability and the opportunity for FSS to compete in this changing market, then, all things being equal, we do not necessarily move to a PPP, but what I have said is I do think still, and we have been open enough about this and how the media interpret it is entirely up to them, what people say and voices off, but we have said and I think it is clear in the written statement, which I do have here before me, that, "The timing of the next stage will depend on reaching agreement with key stakeholders that conditions are favourable and the move would be advantageous to the business". What it also, I think, says is that if the government-owned company can succeed and succeed in terms of the problems we have identified, then we would not necessarily move, but, as I said to the Chairman before, I think one of the problems that I see and understand in terms of a government-owned company is that there is still this problem about injecting sufficient capital and private investment for the organisation.

Dr Harris: There may be other questions on that. I am sure we are going to explore the GovCo issue. That is interesting because my next question is: who decides? Your answer, and I would like to quote you, Minister, your answer suggested that it would "depend upon reaching agreement", this is what the statement said, "with the key stakeholders that conditions are favourable [for the development of a PPP] and the move would be advantageous to the business", so that seems to suggest there is going to be agreement with the key stakeholders that the GovCo does not deliver everything that you need it to deliver. Then in answer to a further question we put to you in a written sense, this is question 10 of our further questions, we raised that quote and you say that, "The views of stakeholders will be taken into account", that is, FSS, ACPO, APA and TUs representing the FSS staff, "when determining the next steps, but the main focus will be on the interests of business, the cost—

Chairman: Can you make a question out of this, please?

Q540 Dr Harris: The question is that that looks as if it does not depend on key stakeholder agreement because you say that the main focus will be on blah, blah, blah.

Caroline Flint: The problem is that I did not want to read out the whole of the written ministerial statement, but perhaps I can refer to another

---

[1] *Note by the witness*: In addition, one of the Chief Scientific Advisors was a member of the Project Management Group responsible for overseeing the transformation of the FSS until November 2004. He remains on the copy list for all the Committee's papers.

paragraph in the written statement. It says: "This will be a transitional structure. In the light of FSS performance as a GovCo the Government will consider what next steps are necessary to facilitate the growth of the business, ensure the future of the FSS, maintain its position at the forefront of forensic science, and maximise its contribution to reducing crime and the fear of crime". That has to underpin everything that we do, but of course, as Tim just said before about our engagement with stakeholders on a number of issues, procurement issues, the development, innovation and science, of course we connect with stakeholders, but underpinning all of that has to be about how the Service will deliver primarily in helping to reduce crime and obviously detect crime and get people in court and prosecute them.

Mr Wilson: Can I come back on the previous question just to clarify that. There is no change of policy, but there is a distinctive change of pace. Normally when the Government cedes the majority control of an entity, the government-owned company corporatised stage takes place a minute before midnight and a minute after midnight, it sells 51% or so of its stake. What we are trying to do is expand that window of opportunity to work with the FSS to see how it can transform itself, running under a corporate structure, not an accounting officer's structure, with people with the right kind of commercial discipline and experience in order to see what can be achieved from the revenue that the organisation itself can earn as it develops to face a competitive market. We think the time is propitious for that because ACPO and the APA, as the main funders of services purchased from the FSS, are working very hard to adopt a strategic approach to procurement which is not about getting people to rush to procurement willy-nilly, but it is about trying to have a controlled approach to tenders coming onto the market. That provides a window of opportunity for the FSS to adjust to changes that are being driven by value for money, in its broadest sense, including changes in the criminal justice system that require a staged approach, as the CPS were explaining last week, which would put great demand on all forensic providers to actually begin to report in on a whole case basis in a much more structured and timely manner than we are seeing on the whole now. Therefore, we have two important windows of opportunity and we are seeking to maximise the benefits that can be obtained for the FSS and forensic science in general by managing it in this period.

Q541 Dr Turner: Minister, you have set a target date for transforming the FSS to a GovCo of 1 July of this year. Is this a realistic target date? What else do you have to do to get it there? Why has it taken so long to set this date when you said two years ago that you were moving to change the status of the FSS?

Caroline Flint: Well, perhaps Tim can talk about before I took on this role in June 2003, but I think you are right. I think it is an ambitious target in terms of reaching that by 1 July of this year, but, having said that, obviously there has been considerable discussion going on for the last couple of years. One of the things I felt that I had to address, as the Minister, was to make some progress because I think the longer we just left it and did not make a decision about the move to a GovCo, the more uncertainty I felt there was for the FSS at the end of the day. I really felt that both from obviously official submissions I get, but also when I went out to some of the service providers themselves and having meetings with staff and talking to staff as well, so I thought that was important. I think also, linked to what Tim has just said, is that parallel to this is the work that is going on with ACPO and the APA in relation to procurement because one of the things that really struck me in taking over this role was the very sort of *laissez-faire* attitude from sometimes the customer towards the Forensic Science Service and the ability of the Forensic Science Service to have far tighter procurement and contracting arrangements that did not put them in, I think, a weak position and a bad place. I really felt that that was something that they were suffering from in the position they were in in terms of a trading fund status. As I said, having come into this in June, most of my discussions over the last six months have been about trying to establish for myself what the problems are and trying to make progress on discussions which have already happened, on work that had already been done on the outline business case in July of last year when the workshop was had with the trade unions on the outline business case, and I think some of those activities have just fallen into place in the last six months which I think allowed us to make this decision. I felt really there was not a lot more that needed to be said in making that decision. I think making the decision itself is helpful because I think it galvanises people to get on with it and helps the FSS and, I think, the Home Office, the police and others to work towards what I hope will be some successful benefits of the GovCo.

Mr Wilson: It is an ambitious target and not everything within the process is under the control of the FSS or the Home Office. There will be contracts to be reassigned, licences and property rights to be adjusted, so there are issues that we cannot control, but unlike many such commercial processes between government and the private sector, we have not got to bear in mind that people bidding, as it were, to deliver something need the certainty of the programme because they are committing resources in the same way, and most of this is controllable in terms of Home Office, and the implications will affect Home Office and FSS business performance, but not external third parties. I think it is important, given the window of opportunity is very narrow, to move to a restructured FSS as quickly as possible and for that reason we are being quite ambitious in setting our target.

Q542 Dr Turner: Can I just explore the commercial prospects of GovCo in the market. You are sending it out there with a remit to compete, but are you going to expect it to continue to offer the full and complete range of forensic services or will it be able to choose what it offers because some of its competitors today obviously have the ability to cherry-pick the most profitable bits if they choose to?

Caroline Flint: I think the short answer is yes, the full range, but I think what is important here is that the GovCo gives an opportunity for the FSS to have far clearer and tighter contractual arrangements with their customers and I think that also puts a duty actually and a responsibility on the customers to recognise that FSS has to operate in an environment where it is competing and, in the same way as they have contractual relationships with other providers, they should provide the same sort of, if you like, tightness and professionalism to the way they deal with the FSS. As I say, in the past, I think some of that has not been as tight as it should have been. However, I think there have been improvements though I do think sometimes that the FSS has been taken for granted in the way it has been used but the FSS needs to look clearly at what services it is offering and make sure it can identify the best way in which it can provide that service and the price for that service. Also, there have been discussions about looking at contracts where, for example, a police force gives, if you like, a sole contract to FSS and what they would provide for having that advantage. Then I think there are other issues around, if something breaks down in a police force with another provider, if they then come to the FSS as, if you like, a last resort because the capacity was not there, then I think it is quite fair for the FSS to say in that situation that they should look at a realistic price for providing that back-up service if there was no original contract with them. It seems to me—and Tim can probably elaborate on this further—that that has been missing to a great extent from the engagement between the FSS with its main customer, the police and the police forces. Hopefully GovCo can give that a greater professionalism in the way they carry out their contracts on both parts, both the customer and also the provider as well.

Mr Wilson: What we are working with in terms of developing the market requirement with the police and the CPS is an offence-based approach to services being sold, so that, quite properly, the forensic provider is concentrating on the offence in question, the offender in question and the judicial timescale and has to offer the full range of forensic services that may be required in that particular case. So, they are competing to provide a service based on meeting all requirements for the case rather than being able to cherry pick in terms of disciplines although clearly, in a highly complex case, any provider, even the FSS, may need to bring in specialists such as, for example, forensic anthropologists and you would normally look to people like Professor Black for that kind of assistance. In terms of provider of last resort, there is a very strong perception that the FSS is having to carry that burden. Any such burden has a cost. It is quite right, if the FSS has to carry that burden, that the FSS receives fair remuneration for the cost rather than distorting prices that it has to charge to its customers who decide to put all their demand with the FSS in order that the FSS can

provide them with an efficient service. So, we are trying in effect to reduce cross-subsidisation and for individual forces or groups of forces to recognise the consequences of their procurement decisions.

Q543 Dr Turner: Obviously charging mechanisms are quite a crucial issue but who is going to actually determine these charging mechanisms? Will GovCo be free, as would a normal business, to set its own price structures?

Caroline Flint: Yes.

Q544 Dr Turner: And likewise the implications for pay and conditions of the staff. At the moment, I take it that they are getting Civil Service pay scales and obviously a company would not necessarily do that. What would happen to these issues?

Caroline Flint: It would be the FSS that could determine its own prices and they would have to look at that in terms of obviously what the competition is out there but also the quality of what they are providing as well because I think that is an issue here and the quality is also linked to the people at the end of the day. These are issues that to a certain extent the FSS has had to deal with in the last few years, that is not something new, and the problems about having the flexibility to respond to some of these areas does raise some challenging questions but it is also about their ability to be flexible to provide the sort of services at the right price and at the same time having the qualified people to do that sort of work. It is interesting that, when I have visited some of the different establishments, the range of different skills is quite enormous and I am not a forensic scientist and I am not claiming to be by any stretch of the imagination. If I look at, for example, a presentation I had up in the North West—I think it might have been the Chorley establishment—on the sort of service the Forensic Science Service was offering to deal with, for example, sexual crimes, rapes, a holistic service to police forces and all that that involved in terms of analysis and in terms of the evidence collection and everything else, that sort of service, a sort of bespoke service, that they could provide compared to the work that at one time was incredibly labour intensive but is changing in terms of sampling, that is the range of different services that is on offer in FSS and some of them elsewhere that do require a much more defined pricing and what came across to me was that sometimes what was happening was that you could have a rather lower price than I would expect for a bespoke service and a rather higher price than I would expect compared to some of the other providers for some of the testing of samples and it is not for me, it is for the FSS to, if you like, grapple with those issues and find a better way in which they can get a good return for what I think are highly skilled and qualified services as well as recognising that, in some of the other services, the competition is out there and maybe their prices have to reflect the marketplace better and then decide how it will provide those different services in the round as a corporate body.

Mr Wilson: On the second point of your question, we are seeking to maintain maximum flexibility for how the FSS manage their business including the pay and conditions for their staff. These issues have yet to be discussed with the trade union side, so I do not think it would be proper to go into any detail, but it is important given that the key assets of the organisation are the staff themselves in terms of the quality they provide and their ability to adapt to new working practices in the more demanding world and the skills that they have acquired over time. That is a very important investment which the organisation has made. It is central to the future prosperity of the business. However, they will need to adapt to change and demands in the business as time limits begin to change as far as their customers are concerned. So, there is a lot of work for FSS management to do there with their staff.

Caroline Flint: May I just add a note to that because I think running alongside that, as well as the work we are doing with the police in the APA on procurement issues, the other area of discussion is about issues around quality assurance as well and I think that is an important part of this too which should apply to whether it is the FSS or any other provider out there, but where do we go in terms of a regulator, if that is the right term, and you might have some questions on that later.

Chairman: We will come back to that.

Q545 Dr Turner: If a GovCo is judged to be successful, you are saying that it would be able to continue its future life as a GovCo, but of course that depends very much, does it not, on your criteria for success and it is also not irrelevant that the Government are the sole shareholder, so the Government have considerable influence over the direction of the company in any event. So, it is actually a controlling factor in its success or otherwise, is it not? How has this worked out with other GovCos? How many other GovCos do we have left?

Mr Wilson: It has been a declining number in recent years and I think the approach to GovCos has changed in recent years; it used to be very much one minute to midnight, and seen very much as a second-best solution. We have been working very hard with the Treasury and the Shareholder Executive and continue to work in terms of what this generation of GovCos will achieve. As you are probably aware, it is a vehicle that the Treasury has selected for the modernisation of the Royal Mint and the Shareholder Executive, with whom we work very closely, and has been created to seek to ensure that there is a common approach across Government to maximise value and I think that there the interests of the organisation, its employees and Government come together because we wish to see a strong organisation that increases in value under Government ownership and that value will be generated by its ability to convince its customers that it is the supplier of their choice.

Q546 Dr Turner: The big point that has always been advanced about PPP was the access to capital. It was that which was a supposedly great advantage. It has

not always been a great success. I do remember Air Traffic Control—I have that t-shirt as well. Why is it that this difference has to persist? Is there any reason why GovCo should not be able to borrow, prudentially of course, to invest as needed? After all, just as Air Traffic Control did, it has a sufficient revenue to deal with borrowings and I am sure that GovCo FSS will likewise have a sufficient revenue stream to be able to handle capital borrowings where necessary. Is the Treasury putting barriers to this?

Mr Wilson: As a Government-owned company, any borrowings are classified to the public sector and therefore access to capital for future development will be determined by fiscal policy rather than necessarily the needs of the business. The Minister has been extremely frank about that in saying that we are determined to seek to make a success of GovCo, but ultimately it may not be achievable. It may not be achievable because of quite proper fiscal stability that the Government are determined to achieve which may not create the opportunities for the level of investment that the FSS may require.

Q547 Dr Turner: I appreciate that argument but it always seemed to be a slightly false one and I would like your view because it is public money anyway, it is public money that is paying for the service, so whether capital is being borrowed by a now privatised company or by a GovCo, it is still being serviced by public money.

Mr Wilson: It is the value that we extract from that investment that is key to the issue and I think that many of the reports by the NAO have indicated, in PFI delivery of projects on time without cost overrun in a way that is extracting better money in many cases from that capital investment than Government itself has tended to achieve for its direct capital investment. I think that the Air Traffic Control situation was a highly geared undertaking that faced circumstances[2] that perhaps understandably people had not put into the model when they were looking at the sensitivities of the deal and I think they were stuck with an arrangement where they could only adjust the income from the people funding the service once a year. So, I think Air Traffic Control had particular circumstances applied to their project.

Q548 Dr Turner: Would it be fair to say that, at the end of it, it comes down very simply to Treasury rules?

Mr Wilson: I think the rules are there as an important framework for fiscal stability. This Government are in a very strong position compared with many of our fellow EU States but, within the fiscal stability rules, I think it actually comes down to making the right decisions by identifying potential risks and taking early realistic steps to think through the financial consequences of those and how you best manage and mitigate and how you best structure the financial arrangement in a bespoke manner for the risks that the task you are seeking to

---

[2] *Note by the witness*: The disruption of trans-Atlantic air-travel following 9/11.

achieve through capital investment is best managed because ultimately the risks will drive up the cost of capital and the value of the returns extracted.

Q549 Mr McWalter: Where is the definitive argument for the extraordinary claims you have just made about PFI to be found? What evidence do you have that those advantages will be secured long term? What evidence do you have that the extraordinarily low rate of investment in private companies in Britain compared, say, to private companies in Japan and America will not continue to vitiate any investment gains that you think you might make in the immediate to longer term?
Caroline Flint: In terms of a move to PPP and private investment, one of the issues will be, is there the sort of private investment interest out there? What sort of private investment interest are we talking about? We are not looking for people who come in, sort of venture capitalists, and take what they can and move out. We will be setting conditions about any move to PPP that would involve that sort of private investment in the service.

Q550 Mr McWalter: It was explicitly a claim made about the advantages of PFI made by Mr Wilson that I would like him to answer.
Mr Wilson: I was referring to a report that I read I think about 18 months ago or it may have been longer.

Q551 Mr McWalter: Could it be read into the record, please?
Mr Wilson: I will provide a reference published by the NAO and no doubt examined by the PAC and I will seek to provide a reference.[3] It is something that I read without studying it.

Q552 Chairman: We will need a lot of convincing, I think.
Mr Wilson: In terms of investment in areas like forensic science, one witness at a previous hearing indicated that his company on average was investing about 12% of their turnover in R&D but felt that within the forensic science area it was near to about 15% but, in terms of coming to general levels of investment in areas such as R&D within the economy, I think there are much broader issues than the Home Office can claim to be responsible for.

---

[3] *Note by the witness:* A key conclusion reported by the Select Committee on Public Accounts in its Thirty-Fifth Report during the session 2003–04 was that "PFI is delivering greater certainty on timing and on the cost to departments of their construction projects". It made it clear that while this was an important benefit, the use of the PFI approach needs to be assessed in each case alongside all other benefits, costs and risks of PFI to determine overall value for money. The Committee's report followed the publication of C&AG's Report, "PFI; Constriction Performance" (HC 371, session 2002–03). This indicated—after interviewing a number if contractors, construction industry bodies and academics— that the PFI approach was leading to improvements in built assets "this through the better integration of design, construction and maintenance, leading to the better management of construction cost risks".

Q553 Mr McWalter: I think it is interesting that the actual source of those claims is in fact obscure and indeed they are highly contested by, for instance, people like Alison Pollock in her recent book called *NHS plc* who tears those arguments to pieces. I do just want to indicate that if that rather folk wisdom lies behind this decision and if in fact in unmasking that folk wisdom you arrive at a very different view about the benefits of moving to privatised or semi-privatised companies, would that, as a result, make the Government think again about the arrangements they were making to potentially dismember our excellent Forensic Science Service?
Caroline Flint: We are not trying to dismember the Forensic Science Service, we are trying to make sure that we put it in the best place it can be to deal with what are the constraints. I suppose, in discussing this issue, one of the areas is actually whether you do believe that there are problems in the way the Forensic Science Service is currently operating. You might have a different view to that. You may think it is all right out there.

Q554 Mr McWalter: It needs investment.
Caroline Flint: When I look at the issue that, for example, it depends on six police forces, albeit they are big ones like the Metropolitan Police Service and some others, for the bulk of its revenue, when I know that people like the MPS and Thames Valley have altered their contractual arrangements with the FSS and when we know that there are people out there who can provide and are already providing in terms of evidence in court the product of their businesses towards forensic science and the evidence that is used in court, that is already happening out there, and we know, for example, that of the police spend, over 50% of it on forensic science is in force, then you have to address those issues. One of the questions is about the way in which the FSS runs itself, its relationship with its client and what-have-you but also at the end of the day there are issues about just what level of investment is needed, not just for the next two years but for the next 20 years. I do not think that is something that is an easy question to answer because technology is rapidly changing out there, innovation is happening all the time, the needs of the service are changing as well, the way they want the service provided is changing too and competition is in-growing. I think I am right in saying—and Tim can correct me on this—that in the last two to three years that FSS has lost 10% of its market share to other providers. That might seem relatively small but I think that is potentially a growing area. What we do know though on the positive side is that some of the ways in which the FSS has been addressing how it runs its business and, where it has lost some services in certain areas, it has won it back in other areas, I think Avon and Somerset Police Force areas is one of those examples. So, it is trying to change. The problem is, just how much can the Government at the end of the day, given all that, just have, if you like, a blank cheque for whatever might be needed? That is not to say that we do not feel that the FSS is important, there is a public service ethos that is important and also a Government commitment to

be engaged with the FSS in the future and that is why we are not privatising it but we are looking for a model that will allow that sort of engagement and access to the private funds whilst making sure, not just in the FSS but also in all the other providers, how we can improve the quality assurance across both the private and public sectors in this field.

Q555 Mr McWalter: I would like to place on the record that the 12% figure which was mentioned by Mr Wilson is itself under intensive scrutiny by this Committee and some have suggested that it is not 12% but 1.8, so we are going to get ourselves into the analysis of exactly how you arrive at a figure of private investment.
Mr Wilson: The 12% was the FSS figure. The comparable figure for the FSS with the figures provided by the other suppliers I understand was 1.8%. I think it is 3% for Forensic Alliance and, if my memory serves me right but it is in the record, I think it is 13/14% for LGC but this goes up to 15% for their forensic science areas.

Q556 Dr Iddon: Minister, it seems to me that the success of any business, whether it is a GovCo or a PPP, will be determined by the potential for expansion of the market. How do you square that with an increasing use by all the police forces of miniaturised and handheld devices? In other words, there seems to be a tension between developing the FSS in any form or shape and the police acquiring on-the-spot instruments and chemical techniques which means they can do the job themselves without going to the Forensic Science Service.
Caroline Flint: That is part of the nub of the situation we face ourselves. As I said before, I think it is 52% of police spend on forensic science is done in-house and, as the Minister also responsible for PITO and looking at issues around the use of technology for policing, as you say, the handheld equipment but also if you look at things like Livescan and other equipment that is helping the police to do their job, the reality is that that is the direction in which the police are going. I think that one of the issues there has been—and I know that the FSS is addressing this—is how best the FSS could help provide services more locally to the police and also back-up support for the range of equipment that the police might use at the end of the day because I think again there is an important issue here around how the police make sure it also has quality standards in terms of, if it is going to do work in house, which is fair enough, what are the quality standards for the people carrying out those jobs where forensic science is involved and may therefore be used in court at the end of the day and that again is something we are trying to work on. You are right that one of the issues around DNA is the use of miniaturised units—and Dr Lyn Fereday is here and she can talk more about this as she is an expert in this area—which is another example of where people could do sampling much closer to where the police are rather than sending work away and to take these

samples at, if you like, the source rather than sending them away. So, yes, I think that illustrates part of the issue we are dealing with here.
Mr Wilson: I think that is a very good example of why the FSS needs to be able to operate differently. It needs to anticipate the very big changes that will come from miniaturising in a way that a Government accounting officer organised trading funds are not. As miniaturisation DNA begins to become robust and acceptable, perhaps some of its service will change from providing commodity laboratory testing to the provision, maintenance and calibration of instruments in police stations or, as they are developing already, mobile resources for crime scenes. There are new areas. The Tsunami has drawn to our attention the growing importance of being able to identify dead bodies in mass disasters. A number of UK forensic people are involved in that. We are very much in a position where the UK lead in forensics across the board is recognised internationally. I was in The Hague before Christmas at a conference and they talked about "a NAFIS"—they have created a common noun out of the name we use in the UK for our national fingerprint database. This, I think, is an indication of the regard with which British forensic science is held as a practical service supporting the police. It is very difficult to compete with the US in terms of high levels of investment for pioneering R&D but I think we have been very good as exploiting R&D developed in the States and the DNA techniques that they use in the States.
Chairman: It would be nice to hear the dulcet tones of the Minister somewhat more, if you feel you can help!

Q557 Dr Iddon: You have half-answered my next question which is, do you see a growth of British companies, including the FSS as a business, in the international market? Have you measured that at all? It sounds as if you have.
Caroline Flint: I would hope we could see that sort of innovation, yes. The Government are very committed overall—true, the Committee has looked at this as well—in terms of science and technology and how we can stimulate the interest in this area and ensure that companies in the UK are at the forefront. We think actually there could be some real opportunities for the FSS—and Tim might want to add to this—in the future to do partnerships more with industry and others and look at how it can develop new techniques and new innovations in the same way as on DNA. Clearly, we are a world leader in that area and we continue to be and one would hope in the future that will be continuing.

Q558 Dr Iddon: What are the barriers to growth on the international market, Minister? Do you see any?
Caroline Flint: In terms of the FSS?

Q559 Dr Iddon: In terms of any of our British companies because they will be in competition, obviously.

Caroline Flint: In terms of barriers to growth, I am not completely sure about the answer but what I would say is that it is in terms of, is there the connection between those providers like FSS and others to engage with companies and engage with academia to come up with the ideas that are going to take us forward in this area? I know that, in terms of looking at what the service wants, I think that is really important. Sometimes, in terms of law enforcement, one of the issues has been, and continues to be sometimes, that what we do not look at is, what is it that the customer wants? What is it that the police want to be able to do? Therefore, they define what outputs they want at the end of the day and then go to those people who can provide the solutions and answers. I think that is the sort of engagement that is really important in this area rather than people just working away and developing something they think the client might want at the end of the day. I think it is really important that there is that engagement because I think that would (a) save a great deal of time and (b) certainly would provide outcomes, if you like, of product that the police would ultimately use at the end of the day and I think sometimes in the past a great deal of work has been done and then the police have not said what they want and the police have not used it.

Q560 Dr Iddon: It sounds as if we are going for an international market and, if we are, we cannot prevent international companies, US companies for example, penetrating our market more and, if that is beginning to happen and we have a full international market here, have you considered the security risks involved in that?

Caroline Flint: Tim might want to add to that but I would just say that there is already international collaboration in terms of forensic science in the UK particularly from America and I accept your point, security issues are important and that is something we are going to have to work through, but I think it is important that the risk assessment takes place in terms of what security is appropriate and that is something we are discussing at the moment obviously with the move to the GovCo as well.

Mr Wilson: The Government are signatories to the Government Purchasing Agreement which, under the World Trade Organisation's rules, means that we cannot close up our gates to forensic science providers from any countries including the United States. As far as going abroad is concerned, in addition to the points made by the Minister, I think you need to get the right local partners because you cannot succeed in foreign markets unless you have very sound partners indeed. A number of UK private firms have run into trouble precisely because of that problem. It also requires capital. As far as the Home Office is concerned, while we wish to encourage that, we also need to consider the risks involved and we need to ensure that that is done through ring-fenced arrangements in order that any problems—people are never 100% successful in developing new business ahead—do not affect the core business within the United Kingdom.

Q561 Dr Iddon: Let me turn now to a key question and that is the question of a regulator which came up earlier. Many witnesses have told us that the need for a regulator is getting quite urgent now and indeed the Royal Commission on Criminal Justice recommended establishing a Forensic Science Advisory Council both to provide independent impartial advice and fulfil the function of a regulator. Why has that recommendation not been implemented, Minister?

Caroline Flint: We are working through at the moment. First of all, we agree that there is a need for a regulator, some regulation, which is different to the Council for the Registration of Forensic Practitioners in that it will be looking at the sort of quality assurance of services rather than just registering individuals, things like lab accreditation and what-have-you. We do think, as I said earlier, that, in order to, within a competitive marketplace, at least have some sort of level playing field, both in terms of what the customer is providing but what the country and the public can have confidence in, we need to address this in both the public and the private sectors in terms of providers. We are working through that issue at the moment in discussion with ACPO and the APA but also as part of our forensic integration strategy as well about how we can come up with the best model. So, we have not reached that point yet of finally deciding; we have not ruled out different options but we do agree in principle that that is absolutely right. I think again, in terms of the changes that we propose to FSS, quite rightly, the public and Members of Parliament have raised the issue about confidence and I think this particular part of our discussions is absolutely important to that. Can I just mention one thing in relation to what you said before about international companies coming in. Also, we would see the FSS have an opportunity to also be involved in what it can do abroad and Dr Fereday just mentioned to me that the FSS at the moment are involved with the Dutch on DNA and that is where they are obviously getting work going outwards rather than just receiving it internally and domestically.

Q562 Dr Iddon: I want to bring Dr Fereday in on this question. ACPO have told us that the withdrawal of Home Office funding from the DNA expansion programme would have a catastrophic effect. We are looking at a sum of about £30 million. Do you agree with that statement of ACPO and can you give us any guarantee that that will not happen, namely the withdrawal of £30 million worth of Home Office funding to the DNA expansion programme?

Dr Fereday: Certainly the withdrawal of that funding would have a distinct effect. The funding to date has been exemplary in the way in which DNA samples have been analysed and the money has been used to analyse samples from individuals and from crime scenes to ensure that the database works effectively. It is also used to support the police forces in the provision of forensic support for DNA and crime scene examinations.

Q563 Dr Iddon: We have the catastrophic effect agreed, so you are in agreement with that, but, Minister, is there any threat to that £30 million or not?

Caroline Flint: There are pressures on police budgets as has probably been said to you by ACPO. What we are doing is ensuring that there is what we think is focused funding and adequate funding for DNA. I think that there are some issues here again about the extent of the use of DNA and the impact on the price as well and one of the things that we have been looking at is what is changing in terms of the pricing costs for the work involved in DNA. To be honest, some of the prices have gone down because the fact is that it has become I would not necessarily say commonplace but it has actually become a much more used tool. The costs in terms of staffing and everything have changed and the technology is changing. So, what we are trying to look at is, what is a real appropriate cost for the work in this area and reflect that, but we obviously are committed as a Government and as a Department to making sure that we remain a world leader in DNA, hence our work with the Dutch and hence that, during our UK presidency, that is one of the issues that we are going to promote through seminars and other work with our European partners. I do think again some of this discussion comes back to some of the earlier points about how, in some of the areas, technology has changed and, as a result, the use of something which has become more commonplace affects the cost and the costs today are not the same as they were a few years ago as some of those prices have come down.

Q564 Dr Harris: Before we continue on DNA databases, I will take the Chairman's advice and ask you this succinctly and it could be a "yes" or "no" answer. In *The Guardian* on 12 January in response to the headline "Science Sell-Off Drop", it is stated, "The Home Office has backed down over plans to create the world's first privatised Forensic Science Service." Is that accurate or would you like to take the opportunity to put the record straight?

Caroline Flint: First of all, I would dispute the words "privatised Forensic Science Service". It was never our intention and is not our intention that the Forensic Science Service would be a totally privatised company, it will be a public/private partnership, so I think that is wrong. What we I hope clearly said this afternoon is that the transition into a PPP was always going to include a GovCo. What we have said—and the Home Secretary said at the time—is that we are going to give an opportunity to GovCo to see what it can prove in terms of the benefits. In that sense, if it were able to deal with all the problems that we have identified and I think are commonly accepted, then, if the GovCo worked, so be it. However, as I have said, we have also been very clear about the limitations of a GovCo and those are limitations that are placed on us by Government but also there are issues there in terms of competition as well and in terms of fair trading and what-have-you and we have to be mindful of that too.

Q565 Dr Harris: I think that is helpful. So, when it says, "Whitehall Trade Unions welcome the decision to drop the scheme", you can disabuse them of that, can you? You have not dropped the scheme.

Caroline Flint: We have not dropped—and that is clear within the statement—that a PPP might still be necessary at the end of the day, but what we have said—and the Home Secretary said at the time—is that we want to make a successful GovCo. In fact, GovCo has to be a success if we were to keep PPP anyway but, if GovCo can exist and can deal with the things that we think are real problems facing the staff working at the FSS at the moment, then so be it. We are not tied to a dogmatic view but we cannot escape what some of the problems are and GovCo gives us opportunities but they are limited. I think we have said a two-year period from this December to get into a GovCo and 12 months to two years to see if that will work.

Q566 Dr Harris: Finally, will the move from GovCo to PPP depend on reaching agreement with key stakeholders including the trade unions? Yes or no?

Caroline Flint: Not on its own.

Q567 Dr Harris: On DNA, do you have any qualms about the civil liberties issues around the way the database works, both who accesses it, what it is used for and the fact that people who have never even been charged let alone convicted have their details on that forever more?

Caroline Flint: No.

Q568 Dr Harris: Professor Sir Alec Jeffreys argued in his evidence that the extension of the database to people who are not convicted or even charged he regards "as highly discriminatory" because "you will be sampling excessively within ethnic communities, for example. The whole thing seems to be predicated on the assumption that the suspect population are people who would be engaged in future criminal behaviour. I have never seen any statistical justification for that assertion; none at all. Yes, it is discriminatory." You do not have any qualms?

Caroline Flint: I disagree with what he is saying. What we are trying to do is tackle offending behaviour and it has been useful to have those DNA samples because they do sometimes have an effect in a criminal case. We have had discussions in this House on the use of DNA and we feel that what we are doing is right and important in the same way as we do on taking fingerprints in other areas as well. So, I disagree with what he is saying. At the end of the day, DNA is used for criminal proceedings to see if people have been involved in a crime and I think it is important that we have that database of information in the same way as in other areas we take fingerprints and we do drug tests.

Mr Wilson: This issue has been specifically tested before the House of Lords, who are not shy at expressing a view about the preservation of civil liberties, and they fully agreed with the arrangements that we have in place and I understand from the work that we have done in the past that— and I do not have the figures exactly in my head—

something like 600 fairly serious crimes have been solved because we have retained DNA from people who are not proceeded with including a number of murders and serious sexual offences and we will gladly provide those statistics as we did to the House of Lords.

Chairman: Yes, please.

Q569 Dr Harris: I do not think anyone argues that there is not a good crime-solving reason to do that or do anything on the basis of that but there is the balance. There is the further issue about familial searching which might involve taking DNA from multiple relatives of the person on the database. There is the Human Rights concern that that sort of testing can raise issues of paternity and establish non-paternity with your kids and their relatives as well as disclosing the fact, which might be considered damaging, that a relative has a criminal record. So, do you accept that there are concerns to be engaged at least, even if they do not override your policy?

Caroline Flint: The way in which DNA is used is very controlled. It is about the prosecution and detection of crime. Therefore, I cannot see how the examples you have given of establishing paternity could link in with the detection of a crime. It is estimated that from the roughly 175,500 DNA profiles on the database which would have previously fallen to be removed, 7,005 profiles of individuals have been linked with crime scene stains involving 8,498 offences and these involved 68 murders, 38 attempted murders, 116 rapes, 52 sexual offences, 78 aggravated burglaries and 80 for supply of controlled drugs. So, as Tim has said, this issue has been tested in terms of the House of Lords opinion and it is felt that on the balance of what is reasonable against obviously individual human rights and this particular issue in relation to detection and prosecution of criminal offences that the safeguards that exist, the restricted way in which the DNA can be used has given confidence to the House of Lords, who as Tim says do not always agree with us on these issues, that is proportionate and reasonable in these very tightly controlled circumstances—

Q570 Dr Harris: I just want to pursue this, if I may, and feel free to add in. If we can be persuaded that just as many detections or indeed more can be achieved by putting everyone on this database, would you have any qualms at putting everyone on the database? Why stop at people who are never charged but who have been picked up and questioned? Why not just stick us all on?

Caroline Flint: Because I think it is about being proportionate and what you make the case for at the end of the day and what we have made the case for is that people who have been picked up by the police and come in contact with the police, that is an issue, in a way, that does not apply to just saying that every single other member of the public should have their DNA sample ... Personally, I would not mind. In fact, I had my DNA taken whilst I was down at one

of the forensic science labs, but what I personally would not mind is not necessarily appropriate as a policy for the whole of the public.

Q571 Dr Harris: You talk about controlled access for the purpose of crime detection but what about research? There is no formal ethical overview for the use of this DNA database for research purposes. I am happy for anyone to answer that.

Mr Wilson: The Human Genetics Commission are represented on the National DNA Board; they ensure that nothing is done as far as the database and the retained samples are concerned that would compromise ethical standards in research; they are our conscience, as it were.

Q572 Dr Harris: On that basis, why do we bother with Research Ethics Committees? Why do we not just have everybody's DNA research project passed by one member of the Human Genetics Commission if that is the way of ensuring that a conscience is there and it is all sorted out?

Mr Wilson: I think this is in the area where we need to make sure that we have the arrangements in place that are appropriate and it is not necessarily the case that the current DNA Board arrangements are fixed forever.[4] If I might just make two points. Familial searches are extremely controlled; they are not used without the agreement of the Chairman of the DNA Board itself; they are not something available to policemen in any case.[5] Techniques similar to familial searches were very important for reversing a miscarriage of justice in South Wales which Dr Fereday may be able to say something about.

Dr Fereday: I would just like to reassure you that the way in which the database is accessed is extremely well controlled. The oversight of the database is managed through a board which is chaired by an ACPO lead in forensic science. The custodian of the database is a member of that board as is, as Mr Wilson said, a member of the Human Genetics Commission. Research cannot just be undertaken. Requests are made and routinely turned down for research projects.

Q573 Chairman: Roughly what percentage?

Dr Fereday: I think very few; I could not give you a percentage but it is a very, very small number potentially going forward. That board is very controlled in the way that the database is used.

Q574 Dr Harris: What you are saying is that there are plenty of applications which are dodgy.

Dr Fereday: There are not that many applications. The situation is that the database is used for intelligence purposes for the investigation and prosecution of crimes. Hence the access is controlled and the use of the data is controlled in a most ethical

---

[4] *Note by the witness*: For example, discussions have been initiated with the Central Office for Research Ethics Committees (COREC) about their ability to support the ethical oversight of research proposals.

[5] *Note by the witness*: Correction: The protocol controlling the use of familial searches confines this to serious crimes, but authorisation is within each force—by an officer of ACPO rank—not the NDNAD Chairman.

manner. I feel very concerned about public perception of how this data is held and how the samples are retained and I think this gives public confidence that that data is managed carefully.

Q575 Dr Harris: Has an independent group been asked to judge whether there is adequate ethical oversight? Has the Human Genetics Commission been asked by the Government, "Is this the appropriate way forward?" or is it just that you say it is ethical and therefore it is ethical?
Caroline Flint: They might not sit on the Board.
Dr Fereday: The Human Genetics Commission visited the database and were satisfied with the procedures. In addition, a member of the Commission routinely attends and is able to comment and so far there have been no negative comments.

Q576 Mr Key: I have been trying to remember, Minister, whether, under the Identity Cards Bill, there are any circumstances in the categories covered under which a person's DNA will be recorded on their ID card. If you cannot remember, will you let us know?
Caroline Flint: I will let you know.

Q577 Dr Harris: What are the arrangements going to be of the custodianship of the national DNA database because this was supposed to be finalised in summer 2004 and yet there seems to have been a delay?
Caroline Flint: The arrangements are that it will be obviously separated out because we are going to make sure that does remain within the Government's ambit and arrangements are being sorted out as to where that will be located and how it will exist and how it will function separate from FSS.
Mr Wilson: And we are negotiating currently with the Association of Police Authorities[6] tripartite governance to ensure that, if anything, the database is managed in a more transparent and accountable way.
Caroline Flint: Which might bring some pleasure to you!

Q578 Dr Harris: My final point is this question of the number of marker issues. We heard evidence from Professor Sir Alec Jeffreys with whom I know you do not agree with on civil liberties—
Caroline Flint: No, on that one statement.

Q579 Dr Harris: And there is some issue here about whether ten is the right number. He argues that particularly if you are doing relative searches and issues around physical characteristics, it simply is not enough to provide the accuracy that our system requires. Is there any cognisance of this being taken in respect of going to a 16 marker, say?
Dr Fereday: At present, the 10 marker system has been researched and the chance of getting an advantageous match is low, hence the 10 markers will continue. With the specific examples of cases of

parentage or the sorts of cases that you have mentioned, there are other systems available that can be used in those circumstances. What you have to remember is that the database is used as an intelligence tool and those 10 markers are adequate at present.
Caroline Flint: It is important to remember that DNA is not just a tool that we can use in terms of finding someone guilty, it is also about establishing someone's innocence as well. Clearly, DNA has been quite crucial in terms of what can be miscarriages of justice. I think that is important. The other issue as well is cold cases where DNA can play a role in a way that obviously was not available at the time when those cases were first investigated.

Q580 Dr Harris: When Professor Sir Alec Jeffreys says, "I would argue that that is not enough" when Dr Iddon said to him that it was ten markers now, do you think that he was wrong and that you have good evidence to suggest that he and people who agree with him are wrong in that statement and that you are right?
Dr Fereday: Statisticians have researched the database and the position is that the ten markers are adequate.

Q581 Chairman: What do the Americans use?
Dr Fereday: The Americans use 13 markers using two different systems, so they do analyses to provide those 13 markers, but they also say that it is an identification which is something we do not do.

Q582 Dr Harris: In terms of physical characteristics, do you understand the point that, when you move to try and get physical characteristics from the database, there is an argument that you need more markers in order to get the same statistical powers? Have I misunderstood that?
Dr Fereday: That work is not possible at the moment; the database is not used for physical characteristics.

Q583 Dr Harris: But, if it were—
Dr Fereday: No, it is not. It is not for debate.

Q584 Dr Harris: So, it is never going to be used?
Dr Fereday: At the moment, that is not the use of the database.

Q585 Dr Harris: If it became a suggested use—and people have suggested it because we have had evidence to that effect—would there be an issue around whether ten markers is sufficient?
Dr Fereday: Then it would be appropriate to go through an ethical committee to work out exactly what procedures should be laid down and the standards to be adhered to in order to make sure there is the exact control that you need to give public confidence and to make sure that everything you do is accurate.

Q586 Chairman: What about other national databases that do not have the personal samples, the firearms and so on? Is there any change there or any

---

[6] *Note by the witness*: omitted "and ACPO".

consideration or any discussion about changing them or the protection of them? Is anything happening in that arena?

Mr Wilson: This is something we are discussing with ACPO in the context of the forensic integration strategy. What we are seeking to achieve with that is getting the same kind of enhancement and detections from the use of forensic science more effectively as we have achieved with DNA. In the case of burglaries where no DNA is recovered, we are looking at a clear-up rate of about 15%. Detections rise to about 48%, if my memory is correct, when DNA is found. Over the next 18 months through the forensic integration strategy, we will be working with ACPO to see whether there are any steps that the Government can take to support the police and police authorities in actually getting better value out of the various sources of forensic information, firearms, footprints[7] and fingerprints themselves to improve performance of what are seeing now.

Q587 Chairman: You can understand why we are asking questions in that people are a little worried about the protection of the data and so on. What is your general feeling, Minister? Is it that it will stay as it is?

Caroline Flint: As Tim says, we are working through some of these issues about those other forms of data as well, the access to them and how they are controlled and that is something we are working through. Obviously DNA is the most personal thing somebody can have at the end of the day and, for the reasons that Evan has outlined today, there are concerns. My worry is that he is actually putting out there concerns that are not actually happening in relation to the way in which the whole process is managed. All I can say at this stage is that we are looking at other issues such as fingerprints, we are looking at firearms and we are looking at footprints and trying to work through how best that can be managed and how that data can be stored with changes to FSS in the future.

Q588 Chairman: Do you consider financial matters at the same time as you consider these questions or are they divorced?

Caroline Flint: I think that we do have to consider financial matters at the same time. For example, on the issue of the footprints, there is a system at the moment whereby there is always a manual way, just as it used to be with fingerprints, that you can look at the footprints to establish if that is connected to an individual and I have to say that it has been quite fascinating to see how you connect a shoe to someone but we are looking to that on a computerised system, so we do have to be thinking at least one step ahead all the time but, if we do want to have a computerised system where you can just literally scan through and see what it picks up, there are costs to that. Again, in terms of the other work we are doing with the police forces around the use of new technology—I think some of these issues do

dovetail into each other—we have to look at what it is we want this for, how is it going to be used and what are the added benefits and therefore, at the end of the day, then negotiate what is a fair price for the police forces to pay for this because it should actually speed up detection in other areas and be an added value for money as well as what we might need to look at as Government in stimulating the growth of these technologies in certain areas. In the same way as if you look at something like Airwave, clearly the Government underwrote the cost for that, but again that was also done on the basis of looking at what the product was, how it would be used, whether it would change working practices and whether it would improve efficiency and value for money. That was a long answer but the short answer is that cost always has to be alongside these discussions.

Q589 Chairman: Yes, but you understand that that nub of our inquiry is to see if you are reacting quickly enough to the new technologies and sciences that come along and what drives that. Is it getting better information, better prosecutions or releases or whatever, or does that come second best to the financial considerations in a police force which considers itself starved of money?

Caroline Flint: I would not say that police forces can say they are starved of money.

Q590 Chairman: You must have been lobbied by your Chief Constable and others.

Caroline Flint: People will always lobby. It does not matter how much money you are going to give them, they will lobby forever. David Coleman has given evidence to your Committee and I visited David in Derbyshire and I have been really interested, for example, in the work that he has done with his in-house forensic science services and how they actually have come up with a model which has cut down on wasted time and used their staff better. I am sure he can provide you with information on that. We know that value for money is not necessarily about being on the cheap, it is actually about, are we using the equipment properly, which is really important, and therefore are the staff able, if it is in-house in the police force, to use the equipment, but also what are the end products at the end of the day? Does it speed up detection? Does it deal with problems quicker? Does sampling, instead of sending it away for so many days or weeks, come back quicker and therefore they are able to use that information in real time rather than unnecessary waiting times? At the end of the day, it is about looking about the practices in which the science is used and applied and what the outcomes are. Yes, at the end of the day, there is a price with that but I think the price always has to be measured against the value and ultimately, at the end of the day, the public are going to say in terms of prosecutions and convictions, "Are we getting value for money from the amount we put in to the number of actual arrests that become charged but then actually go to court and, where forensic science fits into that, is it delivering?"

---

[7] *Note by the witness:* "Shoemarks" is the term used by forensic scientists.

Dr Turner: Minister, I assume you are aware that there are 401 degrees out there available at 57 different universities which have the word "forensic" in their title, most of which we are told by forensic scientists who have been witnesses are simply Mickey Mouse degrees as far as forensic science training is concerned.

Chairman: Not a word we use a lot on this Committee!

Q591 Dr Turner: Does this worry you? Have you discussed any steps to deal with this issue with colleagues in the DfES?

Caroline Flint: What worries me—and obviously we are not the lead department in this area—is if young people apply for courses and, at the end of the day, those courses do not equip them in what they expect to be their future career. I think that goes for anything that universities are providing at the end of the day, whether it is forensic science, media studies or any other course that is currently out there. I think that is important. The other issue is about recognising. I do not claim to be an expert in this area but, from my limited involvement in terms of meeting different people over the last six months, there is a range of different skills that are required for different sorts of engagement in forensic science or forensic intelligence. I read through some of the transcripts of your sessions. I cannot remember which witness it was, though it was a police officer, who did talk about the fact that they were interviewing for a particular job in terms of crime scene investigations and three people with forensic science degrees did not get the job because actually the sort of skills they were looking for in terms of application, analysis, practical hands-on involvement was what they were looking for and clearly other people with other qualifications could provide that, as far as they were concerned, on the day better than those with forensic science degrees. I think these are issues again whereby our work with ACPO and CPS and others, who at the end of the day want to purchase the product, should have an influence in the same way as any other employer in any other sector should seek to influence our academic institutions as to what they want at the end of the day and I think that engagement is as appropriate to this area as it is to other areas of how higher education institutions develop the courses that they provide. They should have an engagement with the people at the end of the day who will be recruiting for particular jobs and make sure that the people they provide can do that. Again, I would say that I do not think there is a one-size-fits-all for people who work in this field and I think that again is something that needs to be looked at. There clearly is, for some people, a grounding and background in hard science is absolutely key and chief to their central role but there are other issues as well and other skills that that person may need to have that they may not clearly get from a pure science degree and I think again this is about engagement, about what the jobs are out there and how our academic institutions can understand that and equip people so they are not let down by thinking that they can go

along and get a job and it is going to be enough because they have a forensic science degree. I think that, in terms of our role, obviously through the work we are doing in terms of tackling the procurement issue and tackling what is necessary and what is needed in terms of the criminal justice system, hopefully through the DfES, we can have some influence in that debate even though it is not primarily an issue for us.

Mr Wilson: We also maintain links with the Forensic Science Society and I think it is very important in terms of degrees with forensic science in the title to recognise that they are not all the same and that there are some degrees that have accreditation or are seeking accreditation with, for example, the Royal Society of Chemistry to indicate that there is a solid hard-science component in that degree and that perhaps it is more in a forensic context and then one can look at the people who are teaching, whether they have forensic experience having worked in one of the providers or having worked for the police and Professor Fraser, the Chairman, is a good example of that because I believe that is the approach that his department at Strathclyde are seeking to adopt for their first degrees and they are also offering higher degrees that will convert non-forensic science degrees into a more forensic focus.

Q592 Dr Turner: Is the Home Office supporting the FSS in their efforts to produce an accreditation scheme for undergraduate and postgraduate degrees?

Mr Wilson: We are supporting it but not financially.

Q593 Dr Turner: I was not imputing that either way. What is the Home Office doing or has done in trying to ensure that the best practice in the use of forensic science is spread amongst police forces? Are you satisfied with the quality of training that the police forces have and their competence in the use of forensic evidence?

Caroline Flint: We are working closely with them. We have a forensic integration strategy where that is looking at a whole number of issues which includes best practice as well and David Coleman, as the ACPO lead, has been a very important influence. I think I am right in saying that there was a conference in October of last year which David pulled together which was actually looking at some of these issues you have raised about the quality assurance and the training at force levels of those in-house services. I do think it is very important and, as I say, we are trying to work with ACPO and the others to make sure that we can spread that good practice and raise the standards in those areas.

Mr Wilson: It is also work that is being pursued through the Police Standards Unit and the Inspectorate. Very valuable work was undertaken by the Inspectorate looking at the whole approach with police forces to forensic science in two reports that were published a couple of years ago which actually provide very important templates and which we actually picked up again to remind police forces about in the conference. The Police Standards

Unit is working on specific issues where perhaps the performance has been sluggish in some respects by forces.

Q594 Dr Turner: Can I ask you about the training that the FSS currently delivers to police forces in the use of forensic science. As a GovCo, I assume that you would still expect them to carry out this function. Do you think there is a risk, having introduced the profit element to it, that it may become too expensive for police forces to use as much as they should?
Caroline Flint: I think it is important that—and again this comes back to some of the issues about procurement issues as well and having a realistic discussion but which is also based on quality as well—when you are wanting to provide an in-house service, then actually the training to do that is absolutely important and key and, at the end of the day, it is going to be about whether police forces are able to meet that underlying issue of solving crime. What we do not want—and the police are also mindful of this—is that, if their staff are not properly trained, then that could create all sorts of problems further down the line in terms of an offence coming to court and I think that is absolutely important. I do not think that in itself the issue of looking at value for money should actually say that we would not want a quality product for what is your money at the end of the day and I think that is absolutely key. I think that issues around best practice and the discussions we are having about a procurement model for the police forces is certainly something that should be addressed as part of that raising of quality of standards.

Q595 Dr Turner: In a market with a range of different suppliers, quality of standards is quite important. Will you want to make the Council's registration mandatory for forensic practitioners?
Caroline Flint: No, we have not felt that was the appropriate way forward. We opted for a voluntary situation partly because I think there are some difficulties in terms of the range of people who might be necessary to give evidence in court could be people, for example, who work in industry who have a particular knowledge in metals or what-have-you and therefore it would not be appropriate for them to necessarily be registered by the Council for Forensic Practitioners. That being said, we are encouraging and supporting more people to be registered who, if you like, I think fit the bill so to speak and I think one of the issues in relation to what you said before about standards at force level is again the registration of those people at force level who fit the bill registering with the Council too.

Q596 Mr McWalter: Just to follow on from Des's question, this whole business seems to me just illustrative nonsense of the current way of doing things because you have a purchaser/provider split. Police forces are increasingly seen as purchasers and then these other people, companies, FSS, whoever and all the people who can train are providers. Then you say, hang on a minute, that is no good because,

if the police only become purchasers, they end up losing the expertise to even be very good purchasers but in addition we want them to be implicated in provision in all sorts of ways. Would it not be best to just drop the whole nonsense of having purchaser and provider splits and actually understand that police forces need a huge amount of knowledge and involvement in the provision of the service and equally that forensic scientists need an awful lot of involvement in policing functions?
Caroline Flint: Of course, one cannot exist without the other, I suppose, at the end of the day, but—

Q597 Mr McWalter: They have been split by Thatcherite politics which you have then incorporated and are carrying on implementing.
Caroline Flint: I would dispute that. The relationship has always been that the service is there and the police avail themselves of that service. The question is, is the service that the FSS is able to provide today the same as it was 20 years ago? No, it is not. Is it going to be the same in 20 years' time? No, it is not because basically the science technology is changing, the idea at the end of the day that some services could be provided in a force area in a custody suite in terms of fingerprinting or what-have-you, we are moving in terms of issues in the future of face recognition and some of these issues face the service with questions they have to answer and one of the questions they have to answer is, how best can we solve crime? How best can we deal with certain functions ourselves? What are those other functions that we need to have provided by other agencies? That is nothing to do with Thatcherite economics, that is about the pace of change in the technology and the science and the better way in which actually the police have, to be fair, invested in their own forces in people who are qualified to be there at the right place at the right time on the ground when a crime is committed to get people out there. If you are burgled or if something terrible happens to you or your family is a victim of crime, you may be extremely upset and distressed if you felt that the police force was not able to respond quickly to, for example, scene of crime investigations, to be able to take some sampling at that crime scene.

Q598 Mr McWalter: This is going well beyond my question.
Caroline Flint: This is the issue about what people want and therefore how we can best deliver that in the public interest at the end of the day.

Q599 Mr McWalter: I put it to you that the purchaser/provider split is not the way but equally the American Service has changed out of all recognition but they keep a huge amount of this activity in the public sector, well away from the WTO rules that Mr Wilson talked about earlier, because the Americans emphasise the security that my colleague Brian Iddon has pictured and, as a result, it is the America defence system that provides a huge amount and the American security system that keeps the research, the university work and the forensic services all with a very, very strong public sector investment and I think that maybe that might be a much better model than the crazy model that has produced effectively a half-privatisation of a service that ought to be in the public sector.

Caroline Flint: I say three things on that. First of all, there is a mixed economy in the American system.

Q600 Mr McWalter: Not of this service.

Caroline Flint: They do provide other providers. If I can elaborate my point. One of the issues is that their turnaround times are in many cases deplorable and one of the issues is where there is not the capacity in the public sector provision, they then have to go to private providers to deal with those samples because actually their police forces say, "It is not acceptable for us to wait weeks and weeks on end while we are trying to pursue a criminal investigation to get some results back." So, three reasons. They do have a mixed economy; they do involve the private sector. Secondly, their turnaround times in some cases take months and months and months in terms of sampling and therefore they have had to engage the private sector. Thirdly, if you ask them, "Is there enough money?" they say, "No, there is not enough money."

Q601 Mr McWalter: If you ask them if it is better, the answer is "yes".

Caroline Flint: I would dispute that.

Q602 Dr Iddon: Can I bring you back to the world of academe. It is difficult to get research funding from the research councils for forensic-related research. Does the Home Office have perhaps sufficient knowledge within it to be able to commission and encourage research in universities and, if so, does it fund any?

Mr Wilson: We are very much involved with the Engineering and Physical Science Research Council in a programme where we were able to make an input into the first round of discussions, but we are not involved in the second round that takes into account the academic quality of the research being proposed, so we have tried to work with the Council[8] to get some focus research but inevitably there is the risk that it is not seen as sufficiently advanced or blue sky to qualify for that kind of work. We have very modest amounts of investment going into forensic sciences but we do invest directly and about £500,000 a year has regularly gone to the FSS to support their R&D work and they have been able to supplement that from other sources. I believe that they usually get £1 million from other sources in addition to their own revenues. The Home Office more widely is engaged in a very broad range of scientific technological research but clearly that is very much prioritised. Priorities at the moment include devices for obtaining information through intercepts of various sorts, protection of police, so it is a very big agenda.

Caroline Flint: Perhaps if you want some more detail, we can write.

Q603 Dr Iddon: My understanding is that it is very difficult to get funding for forensic science research in universities, that is what the witnesses have been telling us. I just wonder, following on from Dr Turner's question, whether you hold quite regular discussions with the OST and the research council.

Mr Wilson: I think these are all the things we should be doing. We have quite regular liaison with the research council through the programme I have mentioned and we are also beginning in my unit to have more direct engagement with universities. I went to Sheffield before Christmas to see the range of work that they are engaged in and Sheffield, for example, are engaged directly in some fingerprint transmission research with Lincolnshire Police under an ACPO aegis, so it is also ACPO who are involved in this area and part of the integration strategy is to seek to get databases better integrated. We are also establishing a database to try and make sure we know where the research activity is going on which we do not at the moment.

Caroline Flint: It is a work in progress.

Q604 Dr Iddon: Quite recently, we had Professor Steve Haswell in front of us who is a Professor of Analytical Chemistry at my old university, the Department of Chemistry University at Hull. He gave us the impression that there was a lot of useful work out there which the Forensic Science Services could pull in but there is a lack of communication between the researchers and the people who could use the research, particularly in the world of biology and chemistry, and I hope that, Minister, you would take that criticism of Steve Haswell on board and perhaps do something about it.

Caroline Flint: I will take that away.

Q605 Dr Iddon: In the present climate, the police do their own in-house work and the FSS complement that obviously. There is a limited amount of money for the police forces, so it is difficult for them to do their own R&D in house, so who should do the R&D? Should it be the Home Office?

Caroline Flint: I think this goes back to the point Tim was making. Part of our forensic integrated strategy is that we are talking with the police and others about how certain forensic science services are provided but also looking at this issue around research as well and, as Tim has just said, we could do more in this area. One of the issues is what is currently happening out there and how we engage with universities as to some better understanding about what the police might want and therefore the research that might be helpful to that and therefore being clear about what the priorities are in terms of taking any steps forward and working together better in a more integrated way rather than necessarily the police going off down one stream and us going off on another and so on and so on. I think that is something we are working on and hopefully there will be improvements in the future and, as I

---

[8] *Note by the witness*: Should have said "police focused research but inevitably there is the risk that it is not seen as sufficiently advanced or blue sky to qualify for research council funding."

say, I think some of those discussions we have set up for these sorts of discussions on a tripartite basis are going to help.

Q606 Dr Iddon: The research and development investment even in the private sector is not brilliant compared with some other industry or sectors. Are the Government doing anything to stimulate private sector R&D? You have the tax credit system admittedly.
Caroline Flint: I would have to come back to you on that. I know that the Treasury has, over the last few years, tried to stimulate R&D in science, but I will come back to you on the details of that.

Q607 Chairman: If you do not talk much to the DTI, you will not know about small businesses, the problems and all the rest of it. That is a huge enterprise for this Government and you have not really phased in with them at all.
Caroline Flint: In terms of where we are, obviously we have discussions with some of the service providers into it in terms of providing forensic science services but I suppose as an issue of itself, that is not something we have hugely been involved in. Maybe it is something that we should be.

Q608 Dr Iddon: What Britain has been very poor at in the past though it is getting better now is transferring research and development from the laboratory into practical usage. Again, Professor Steve Haswell, when we had him in front of us as a witness, referred to "lab-on-a-chip" technologies of all kinds. Britain has certainly had the lead in that area but Professor Haswell flagged up the warning signals that the research in that area is painfully slow at the moment, partly as a result of the lack of investment in R&D in forensic science. I do not know whether you were aware of that, Minister, but do you have any comment to make on that?
Caroline Flint: I am not aware of that particular criticism. I will have to go away and look at what the Professor said. Again, I think one of these issues here is about having that better joined-up thinking about what the developments are and how they can be used and therefore collectively how some of the organisations that sometimes operate apart from each other can invest in some of those areas or direct research in a certain way that they are prepared to pay for it at the end of the day. I think that is important. If you do not have that basis of engagement, then it is very difficult, I think, to be proactive in some of these areas. Further to the point raised before, I understand that the DTI do have a place on our Science and Technology Strategy Group, so there is some input from there. I am sorry that I did not mention that earlier.

Q609 Chairman: Do they turn up though? That is the question.
Mr Wilson: Yes, they do and make valuable contributions.

Q610 Chairman: Lyn, you might have something to say. You were against 16 markers and you were quite vehement about that. What do you think about this chip technology?
Dr Fereday: I think that with all these new methodologies and research techniques, it takes time to roll out and implement.

Q611 Chairman: But you have nothing against it in theory?
Dr Fereday: I think nothing against it. I think what we have to look at is that technology is changing and we need to move on and take advantage of the opportunity that the new technology brings.

Q612 Chairman: Are we in danger of falling behind in your estimate?
Dr Fereday: I do not think so.
Mr Wilson: There is a broader economic issue to do with the size of our economy. Compared with the US where most of this is taking place, perhaps affected also by the way in which the taxation laws are changing in the States which encourage people to invest there because of transfer taxation laws rather than in the UK and we can see the Chinese, which at the moment have a smaller economy than our own, doing phenomenal work in areas such as e-forensics. That has probably something to do with the amount of private consumption that has been taken out of their GDP growth. I suspect that it is much less than in this country. What we are trying to do is talk much more to our European colleagues and our G8 colleagues about these issues to ensure a more pooled approach.

Q613 Mr Key: Minister, do you think that solicitors, barristers and judges are adequately trained in forensic science?
Caroline Flint: I understand that there has been some work done in this area to build the awareness and training but I think it is an area that could grow. I think that is where we are. I understand that there have been specific courses that have been run for those working in these areas and again I think that, as in other areas, it is an area that we need to develop.

Q614 Mr Key: We have had evidence that the English adversarial court system really does not make best use of the forensic science, it is just not like that, and maybe the use of specialist judges would be better. Would you agree with that?
Caroline Flint: I would have to think about that. I would have to look at that and think about this area. We have the system that we have and how it works. I know that there are some issues here that concern people about one expert being set up against another and how that influences a jury and I understand people's concerns about that. Again, the issue of the registration of forensic practitioners may be helpful in that regard, so that at least a jury would know who is registered and who is not registered. That will not deal with all the range of different experts that might be brought to a court, but obviously it is an issue in our system that someone will give their

evidence for the prosecution and of course the defence can have their own expert and the jury are left wondering what to do in that situation. As I say, registration may help and the jury being aware of that registration may help but also, at the end of the day, you have to give someone the defence and there are different expert views and, as we know in terms of cases, there are different expert views.

Q615 Mr Key: We have had evidence from forensic scientists and of course nobody knows why juries reach a particular verdict and it is unlikely that a jury will understand complex forensic science, particularly perhaps digital forensic evidence and so on, but are you bothered that the outcome of a trial may depend on the prosecution and the defence finding the most attractive and articulate expert witness rather than examining the facts of the case because we have had specific evidence on that?
Caroline Flint: That is interesting if that is the evidence that you have received. At the end of the day, given the complexities of what you say about juries understanding the forensic evidence before them, there are issues for the judges also to play a role in giving some directions to the jury in terms of the evidence that is presented before them at the end of the day. Tim might want to say a little more about some new CPS rules in relation to this area.
Mr Wilson: I think that will help curb some of the extravagancies of the adversarial system in the sense that the new rules that the CPS and courts are working on mean that the issues are flagged up earlier in advance which creates the opportunity for prosecution and defence to identify what is being contested and what is not. I think that is a much more rational way of trying to approach this and actually using the expert evidence in an informed way that perhaps takes it out of courtroom rhetoric to what is agreed between the two sides, what is disagreed and how you focus on those specific technical issues and how you try and ensure that they are presented in the least rhetorical manner.

Q616 Mr Key: So, we are talking here about pre-trial agreement in front of the judge between the prosecution and the defence.
Mr Wilson: Yes.

Q617 Mr Key: And the admissibility of the forensic evidence.
Mr Wilson: Yes.

Q618 Chairman: Do you think that works well, Minister?
Caroline Flint: It is coming in, I understand, but I think as a basis for trying to deal with some of the issues raised, that seems to me to be a pretty good idea to have those sort of arrangements and I think if it can, as I say, get to the facts of the situation and provide that in a way that is not just rhetoric—

Q619 Chairman: How do you equalise experts when you have somebody with a knighthood against somebody who is just a lowly teacher in an academic university or something because that was an issue?

Caroline Flint: Again, I think it is about competence and that is where I think the registration comes in but also I think in terms of these CPS rules to come into force, we are going to have to see how that will help that situation. It may be something that has to be come back to in the future.

Q620 Mr Key: Who should be responsible for training forensic scientists on how to present evidence in court? Again, we have heard evidence there that very distinguished forensic scientists can be completely thrown off course by a skilful barrister.
Mr Wilson: I think we can all be thrown off course by a skilful barrister, whatever our background. The providers take that very seriously indeed. CPRF take it into account in the accreditation of individuals. We are thinking about this in terms of what we are requiring as we begin to improve the arrangements for the registration of forensic pathologists because, on the whole, the strongest part of accreditation of individuals is the technical part, whether it is medical or scientific, there are well-established paths there. The tricky thing is actually getting right people's ability to operate sensibly and constructively within the interests of justice within the criminal justice system and I think that we all need to do more work there.

Q621 Mr Key: Does the Home Office have any plans to establish some form of scrutiny on the presentation and use of forensic evidence in courts?
Caroline Flint: Not as far as I am aware, no.

Q622 Mr Key: Do you not think it would be a good idea in view of the discussion we have been having?
Caroline Flint: I will certainly go away and think about that issue.
Mr Key: I am very grateful!

Q623 Chairman: Will you talk to other departments about all these kinds of issues as well?
Caroline Flint: Yes. It is not just obviously the Home Office—

Q624 Mr Key: Indeed not!
Caroline Flint: There are issues in terms of DCA and of course the Attorney General's Department.

Q625 Mr Key: Of course that is right. Minister, who do you think should be responsible for the quality control of the Council for the Registration of Forensic Practitioners because this is absolutely crucial, is it not? They are busy attracting more and more registered practitioners and there is a huge new effort going into specialist digital analysis and so on. Who is doing to control the quality and the standards of the CRFP?
Caroline Flint: I think there are issues there about the regulator and I think there is an issue around the Standards Unit having an involvement in that as well in terms of how it would function and how it would operate. There will have to be a link between the regulator and the Council because there will be some issues there. For example, whilst the role of the

regulator—and we talked about this earlier—is more in terms of, if you like, the quality assurance of services and, for example, lab accreditation, there will be some issues about, for example, the provider if a provider is actually using qualified staff for their job. So, I think there is an issue there where the regulator could again have an influence on the quality assurance of those who are registered by the Council. Ultimately, at the end of the day, it is the people who underpin the quality of the service, so I think there will have to be cross-referencing there.

Mr Wilson: Can I briefly refer you to the membership of the Council that is responsible for the Council for the Registration of Forensic Practitioners. They are nominees of most of the scientific professional bodies in the area. So, to some extent it is self-regulating but it reflects very much the expertise that come from those bodies such as the Bar Council and the General Medical Council.

Q626 Mr Key: Can I just be quite clear as to whom you are referring as the regulator.

Caroline Flint: This is one of the issues we have been discussing earlier in terms of quality assurance. It is one of the areas we are working through at the moment about how we can come up with a structure and system in terms of public confidence to give reassurance about the quality of services whether it is in the public or the private sector. Therefore, that is a model we are trying to work through and what I was just saying is that the regulator's role will not be to register individuals, that is the role of the Council, but there will be a cross-reference because obviously those individuals ultimately underpin the quality of the services that the regulator will be looking at.

Q627 Dr Harris: I just want to come back to this issue of the Human Genetics Commission and the National DNA database, Dr Fereday. You said that they did not have any problems with the way things were being done at the moment. Does that mean they resile from their recommendation in their 2002 report that there should be an independent body with lay membership to oversee the database and a separate National Ethics Committee to review all research projects involving the use of DNA samplings?

Dr Fereday: I think that will stand as far as the Human Genetics Commission's recommendations are concerned. Those recommendations were made following a visit to the database and the custodian.

Q628 Chairman: Who got the recommendations? Was it the Home Office?

Dr Fereday: I think so.

Q629 Dr Harris: Are you planning to do both those things?

Dr Fereday: I think it will be taken forward in the separation of the custodian from the FSS.

Q630 Dr Harris: Is there a plan to have a national independent research ethics committee type process because it says in the annual report for 2003–04—

and I note, Tim, that you are on this board—that it will be exploring the setting up of a protocol with a central office for the Research Ethics Committee to obtain independent opinion for future research policy proposals to be presented to the board.

Mr Wilson: That is still being pursued. I cannot say from what I have received by way of reports that a great deal is happening very fast though but there is not a great deal of research by way of research proposals coming to the board and similarly the McFarland report was also in favour of some independent ethical advice.

Q631 Dr Harris: It is not a high priority.

Mr Wilson: It is more a question of trying to ensure that what you put in place actually reflects what the level of demand for R&D advice is and I think that, on the whole, the board's key intention is to make sure that the regular mainstream work of the board is operated in an ethical and transparent manner. So, we are more concerned with ensuring that, for example, the reference samples that are retained by the suppliers are properly secured and are only used for purposes permitted under the law. That sort of operation is a much higher priority in terms of the issues that are coming to the board.

Q632 Dr Harris: Do you think the prioritisation is right? Do you think that the reports and recommendations of the Lords Select Committee of 2001 and the Human Genetics Commission of 2002 about having independent ethical oversight for research should be given a higher priority to move on with this proposal?

Caroline Flint: I think, as Tim said, our priority at the moment is in terms of how we tackle the issues and the confines within tackling criminal prosecutions and the use of DNA. That is a priority about how that is used. I will have a look at that report and have to come back to you later on that. I cannot give you an opinion here and now without having a proper look at that report and what it is saying.

Mr Wilson: Could we also check how many research requests we have actually received. I think it is two or three.

Q633 Chairman: Give us some data. I think the line of questioning from this side has been that it is not just about getting numbers of prosecutions but they have to be fair and seen to be fair by the public and you have to have a system/regulator that makes sure that the process does deliver that.

Caroline Flint: Absolutely.

Chairman: We want no more Sir Roy Meadows either and these kind of issues. We are trying to ensure that there is a fair system out there related to other activities you are taking. Thank you very much indeed for helping deliver the Home Office position, Minister. Tim and Lyn, thank you very much as well. Our report will go out before the Election, I presume, and hopefully we will get a debate on it. Thank you very much and, if it helps, all well and good.

Written evidence

APPENDIX 1

Memorandum from the Home Office

SECTION 1: EXECUTIVE SUMMARY

1.1 Efficient, effective and innovative forensic science, delivered in a manner that ensures professional integrity and quality assurance, is critical for continued improvement in the extent to which offences are detected and offenders punished.

1.2 Over 50% of forensic science work (by value) is undertaken by police staff and the remainder by external providers, of which the Forensic Science Service (FSS), LGC Ltd and Forensic Alliance Ltd (FAL) are the leading entities (by market share).

1.3 The UK has been well served by its forensic scientists and police forensic staff. Their professional integrity, ability to work with police and other Criminal Justice System (CJS) colleagues, and innovative thinking have ensured the UK is a global leader in use of forensic science. As a result of targeted Home Office investment this country has set the benchmark for the exploitation of DNA.

1.4 There has been a market for forensic science since 1991. It is no longer an exclusively public sector provided service, but part of a mixed economy. Indeed, the new discipline as "e-forensics" has been developed predominantly through private sector technological and scientific capabilities. The pace of change is accelerating with the Police gearing up to strategically manage the supplier market in line with public sector procurement best practice and with strong competition among providers. This will be given additional impetus by imminent technological change as forensic services, particularly those assisting with identification become faster, more localised and automated, resulting in unit costs falling in real terms with the commoditisation of many analytical services.

1.5 Overall the FSS has made a success of its Trading Fund status. It is considered to be generally well regarded by stakeholders and has consistently met most of the operational and financial targets set by the Home Office. However there are a number of substantial risks to the status quo, not least of which is having to operate within the formal constraints of a Trading Fund, in the face of increasing competition from private sector providers and a fast developing innovative market.

1.6 There is a real risk that the disadvantage in which the FSS operates will result in sustained and accelerated loss of business. There are already indications that some forces are seeking alternative suppliers and it is conceivable that a cumulative loss of market share could result in managed decline. The situation is compounded by a number of important market trends impacting on forensic science delivery overall:

— rapid technological change, in particular miniaturisation of DNA related services;

— lower barriers to entry for commodity based forensic services such as DNA testing;

— increased pressure on Police and other customers to manage procurement against Best Value scrutiny, reinforced by the Gershon Review; and

— increased vulnerability of FSS in the face of selective competition and the difficulties it faces retaining key staff attracted by private sector inducements.

1.7 In taking the transition of the FSS forward, certain public policy objectives need to be protected, principally:

— ensuring reliable, high quality, responsive and good value for money forensic science support for the CJS;

— facilitating market reform, particularly in the light of specific targets for police forces set in the Gershon Review; and

— better integration of police intelligence handling in response to the Bichard Report.

1.8 The Government is currently considering in detail how the FSS can best make the crucial changes necessary to respond to customer demands and seize the opportunities presented by emerging technologies, in a way that is properly consistent with public policy objectives.

SECTION 2: BACKGROUND

Forensic science and the Criminal Justice System

2.1 Forensic science, particularly as an intelligent tool is transforming the work of the police and ability of the Criminal Justice System in England and Wales to bring offenders to justice.

2.2 Originally forensic science was focused on the application of science for the provision of objective and reliable evidence to the Courts. Today it may be the initial and only crime scene response by the Police to certain types of offence.

METROPOLITAN POLICE SOLE FORENSIC RESPONSE TO BURGLARIES

The ability to attend crime scenes at the earliest opportunity maximises forensic retrievals, reduces evidence loss and contamination risk. In 2003 the Metropolitan Police conducted a successful pilot study in two boroughs in which civilian crime scene examiners provided the sole response to burglary.

— Crime scene examiners were tasked by a Telephone Investigation Bureau and targeted to attend the scene within four hours from receiving the call in order to minimise delays to victims and ensure the forensic potential of the scene was preserved.

— Initial results from the pilot included:

  — 80% of burglaries attended by crime scene examiners.

  — 79% of which were examined within four hours.

  — 40% increase in forensic evidence or intelligence recovered.

  — The number of forensic detections for burglary in the two pilot Boroughs averaged 38 per 1,000 crimes compared to an average of 26 per 1,000 crimes across the other 30 Metropolitan Police Boroughs in the same period and 28 per 1,000 crimes nationally.

— More generally it demonstrates how a more victim focused approach utilising modern communications enables people to get on with their lives more quickly, coupled with the reassurance that every effort is being made to catch the perpetrators.

2.3 Forensic science has always encompassed many scientific disciplines and their use in the analysis, interpretation and comparison of a wide range of evidential materials. It has traditionally been applied to the identification and examination of evidence such as body fluids, fingerprints, illicit drugs, fibres, glass and documents. This (the basis on which the term "forensic science" is used within this document) is predominantly rooted in biological, chemical and physical sciences but there is an increasingly important interface with ITC and e-forensics. The scope of the latter includes video enhancement and the interrogation of both mobile phones and computers, and is based on computer and electronic sciences.

2.4 Most forensic science work is either undertaken by police forces using their own in-house resources or by purchase from external providers.

Figure 1—Market segmentation among the three types of providers of forensic science in England and Wales (2004 estimates)

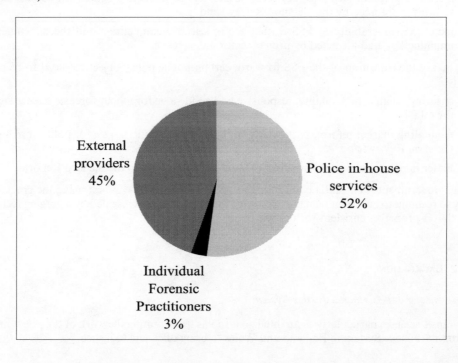

2.5 Overall expenditure on forensic science is estimated to be in the order of £400 million pa. This amounts to a 0.04% of police expenditure (central and local) in England and Wales. Within police forces expenditure on forensic science is estimated to account for some 20% of their scientific and technological spend. The major external providers are the Government owned FSS, Forensic Alliance Ltd and LGC Ltd; some other commercial entities are engaged in analytical and testing work, especially drug testing and analysis.

2.6 There has been a steady increase in the contribution that forensic science makes to the delivery of justice, as both the demand for independently verifiable evidence (through statements and as witness) has increased, whilst the use of traditional investigative methods by the Police has become more difficult due to increasing reluctance within the CJS to rely on some forms of evidence without forensic corroboration. Although the use of forensic science by the prosecution is more widely recognised, the Defence can equally apply its provision of impartial analysis and interpretation. Moreover, with the proper preservation of evidence, "cold case reviews" are resulting in justice for the victims of serious crimes committed years ago.

> The "cold case review" programme, led by the Home Office Police Standards Unit in collaboration with the Home Office Science Policy Unit (SPU) managed DNA Expansion Programme and the Forensic Science Service has identified two hundred and fifteen cases that had early DNA crime stains and were mainly undetected serious sexual offences (92%). To date, with samples taken from individuals 25% of these cases have matched on the National DNA Database® (NDNAD) and produced thirty-four named suspects. One in four cases worked on so far have resulted in either a match to a suspect or another crime scene. The oldest offence having occurred in 1989. Some police forces are now undertaking similar initiatives, including a £2 million (2004–05 budget) cold case review of 740 unsolved cases in West Yorkshire.

Government investment in forensic science: the record

2.7 Cold case reviews are one example of where this country leads the World in the exploitation of DNA as a powerful new forensic tool. This reflects targeted funding (£182 million between April 2000 and March 2004 via the DNA Expansion Programme) to support enhanced sampling and improved integration of forensic work with other aspects of intelligence led policing; funding work on process improvement; and the introduction of new legislation.

Table 1

PROPORTION OF THE POPULATION ON CRIMINAL INTELLIGENCE DATABASE

UK	EU pre May 2004	EU May 2004 onwards	USA
3.7	0.68	0.57	0.48

2.8 The Government is working with fellow EU member states, the European Commission, Europol, Eurojust and Interpol to assess via a pilot project and technical studies how added value from the increased coverage of national databases can be obtained through improved international co-operation. Initially the focus will be on unsolved sexual offences.

2.9 While there is important added value to be gained from better international co-operation, the main benefits are domestic. The increased use of DNA technology coupled with the improved handling of forensic intelligence within forces has delivered significant improvements in England and Wales in volume crime detections.

Table 2

DNA DETECTION RATES FOR 2003–04

Crime Category	National (crimes recorded/detected)	DNA rate ("detections" when DNA recovered)
All Recorded crime	23%	43%
Domestic burglary	15%	45%
Burglary (non-domestic)	10%	53%
Theft of vehicle/TWOC	14%	26%
Theft from vehicle	6%	61%
Criminal damage	13%	54%

2.10 The UK is also among the World leaders in the use of fingerprints. This has been largely the work of police crime scene examiners and fingerprint bureaux working to scientific standards and other guidance issued by the Home Office's Police Scientific and Development Branch (PSDB). The Government has funded, via the tripartite managed Police Information & Technology Organisation (PITO), the National Automated Fingerprint Identification System (NAFIS). This contains 5.7 million sets of individuals' fingerprints and approximately 930,000 crime scene marks. Working with private sector suppliers, PITO will provide through the next generation of technology (IDENT1) an ability to automatically match palm prints with palm marks left at crime scenes.

2.11 Livescan—also developed by PITO in partnership with commercial specialists—is a system used in custody suites that enables fingerprints to be taken and submitted electronically from suspects on arrest and searched against the NAFIS database in a matter of minutes. This enables searches to be made against marks from crime scenes as well as verifying the identity of individuals. Mobile technology is already being trialled that will enable the electronic transfer of fingerprints from crime scenes to NAFIS, speeding the identification of suspects soon after committing offences.

2.12 Information Technology (IT) can ensure that the police have easier access to the information they require and reduce bureaucracy. The Government will continue to invest in key national IT systems like the Police National Computer. It is equally important to ensure that local systems are linked and not developed in silos. The introduction of the first National Police Intelligence Computer system—entitled "IMPACT"—will ensure that all forces use the same system to manage and share intelligence information

2.13 Forensic pathology is an important discipline provided mainly by individual practitioners. The Home Office is working in partnership with: the Association of Chief Police Officers (ACPO), the Association of Police Authorities (APA), the Coroners' Society, the Royal College of Pathologists and Home Office registered forensic pathologists to deliver better quality services to the coroninal and criminal justice system.

2.14 The Home Office has also funded the recruitment and training of specialist registrars seeking to become Home Office registered forensic pathologists. In addition, it is providing £10 million for the three years to 2006 to finance:

— improvements to mortuaries for the conduct of forensic autopsies; and

— an IT system to provide management information relating to suspicious deaths.

The IT system will also facilitate the management of forensic pathologists' workloads and act as a mechanism so that evidence presented to the criminal justice system can be subjected to critical findings review.

2.15 More generally the Government has supported the independent accreditation of professional and technical standards by supporting the work of the Council for the Registration of Forensic Practitioners (CRFP) (£1.2 million since April 2001 to date).

Government investment and policy for forensic science: future plans

2.16 Forensic science, together with its effective use and management by the Police, will have a significant impact on the Government's ability to achieve two SR2004 PSA targets:

— PSA target 1: Reduce crime and the fear of crime; improve performance overall, including by reducing the gap between the highest Crime and Disorder Partnerships (CDRP) areas and the best comparable areas.

— PSA target 2: Improve the performance of all police forces, and significantly reduce the performance gap between the best and worst performing forces; and significantly increase the proportion of time spent on frontline duties.

2.17 More specifically, the Government's Strategic Plan for Criminal Justice 2004–08 includes a shared vision for criminal justice reform. Underpinning this overarching vision are key commitments, two of which, namely:

— To have reduced crime by 15% and further in high crime areas; and

— To improve the delivery of justice by increasing the number of crimes for which an offender is brought to justice to 1.25 million by 2007–08.

The delivery of such results will be dependent to a significant extent on impartial and effective forensic intelligence and forensic science.

2.18 In order to support the delivery of these targets the Government is committed to build on the achievements of the DNA Expansion Programme in order to improve all types of forensic science. A conference held jointly by the Home Office SPU and ACPO in May 2004 helped to identify how this might be done. At this conference views were sought form 180 participants—police officers, forensic scientists and police specialist staff from the UK and abroad to draw on their direct experience in order to shape a successful policy. (A record of the proceedings of this conference will be available shortly from the Home Office.)

2.19 Following this conference, the Government announced in the Home Office Strategic Plan for 2004–08 its intention through the Forensic Integration Strategy (FIS) to ensure the police optimise their use of forensic science, extending the UK global lead in the use of DNA to all forms of forensic intelligence. The strategy will bring about changes in the operational management and workforce practice as well as exploiting IT and scientific developments, in order to raise the level of detections.

2.20 FIS will be developed under the aegis of the Police Science & Technology Strategy, which the Government launched in 2003 to ensure the police service is equipped to exploit the opportunities in science and technology to deliver effective policing as part of a modern and respected CJS. (Copies of the Strategy are available from the Home Office.) The principle focus of FIS will be the police use of the available and emerging forensic techniques within the context of police reform and the integration of forensic intelligence systems in response to the Bichard Report recommendations.

2.21 As indicated above the foundations for the success of this initiative are in place both within police forces and the forensic science community, but there is still substantial scope for improvement in three main respects, namely to:

— Deliver more, faster, and better support and intelligence contributing to increased detections, whilst achieving substantial (real) savings in unit costs;

— Standardise and optimise the techniques and processes in a manner that results in benefits realised within the entire CJS; and

— Support and learn from international colleagues to ensure that domestic investments in forensic capacity and capability gain added value from effective international co-operation, and represent or reflect global good practice.

2.22 Such an approach based on strategic leadership by ACPO and backed by highly focused investment by Government will ensure that the relatively small expenditure on forensic science will continue to yield disproportionate benefits in terms of detections and judicial disposals.

SECTION 3: THE FORENSIC SCIENCE MARKET

3.1 The total forensic science spend by police forces and other parts of the CJS in England and Wales in 2003–04 was estimated to be in the region of £400 million. Some £210 million (or 52%) of this is in respect of services provided in-house by police forces in particular fingerprinting and scene of crime officers. The balance of £190 million (or 48%) is provided by third parties. The balance is provided by third parties, chiefly the FSS, FAL and LGC Ltd, but also individual forensic practitioners.

3.2 The main services provided by third party organisations are forensic testing and more bespoke, labour intensive casework. Both services have expanded on the back of the enhanced use of DNA testing. The value of work placed with third parties was estimated at some £170 million in 2003–04. The key players are FSS, which has some 85% of this market with the two other principal providers being LGC Ltd and FAL.

3.3 The current structure of the market reflects the way in which it has been shaped by historical circumstances, not any intrinsic division between internal or external providers, or the public and private sectors. Virtually all forensic work was originally undertaken within police forces and the greater part continues to be provided on this basis today, with the rest via a mixed economy. Increased specialisation resulted in the emergence of the FSS as a major public sector external provider.

3.4 As new requirements have been identified, particularly, with the need to ensure ITC integration and the emergence of new disciplines such as e-forensics, the private sector has generally been better placed to innovate, undertake research and development, and rollout the delivery of new services. It has worked in partnership with police forces, central bodies such as PITO or a combination of both, where appropriate to scientific standards and quality assurance standards set within the public sector by PSDB and the NDNAD Custodian.

3.5 Within the European Union, the closest parallel to the mixed economy of the UK forensic market appears to be found in Germany. Here arrangements will vary between länder, for example, Baden–Wüttemburg invite tenders for all reference samples that need to be analysed for the DNA database. Some other länder only resort to external laboratories if their own facilities are short of capacity. The United States also follows a mixed economy approach, and is a powerhouse for R&D in both traditional forensic science and new fields relying on ITC and electronic sciences.

A rapidly evolving market

3.6 The market for forensic science has grown rapidly in recent years due mainly to the increased use of DNA. The rate of market growth slowed significantly in 2003 and 2004, however, as the process of populating the NDNAD has been achieved in line with the Government's target of completing this by April 2003. Thereafter, some DNA work will decline as individual sampling is confined mainly to those beginning a criminal career in this country or to reflect more extensive sampling permitted under the Criminal Justice Act 2003.

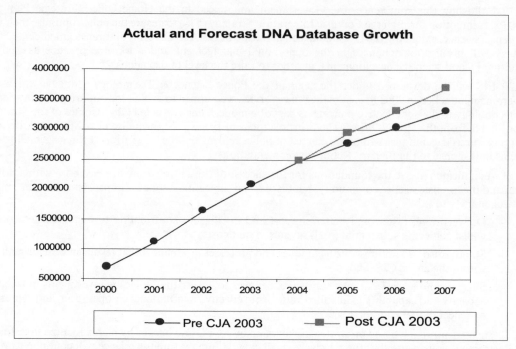

3.7 The market will continue to evolve rapidly because of technological change and in response to the intention of police authorities and police forces to achieve more strategic market management in line with public procurement best practice.

3.8 The delivery of forensic science and technology is likely to continue to change over the next few years. In particular, there is significant potential to move to "real time" support of the criminal justice system at the crime scene or in the custody suite. Much of underlying science needed is already available from areas outside the forensic science sector. A key issue for police forces will be to identify future priority requirements and how these might be met by several suppliers competing to meet output specifications.

Strategic management of the market

3.9 As expenditure on forensic science has grown, so has the pressure from police authorities and within police forces to manage both the procurement of external services in line with best procurement practice and the management of internal forensic resources against Best Value scrutiny. The most significant initial development was a review undertaken for the Metropolitan Police Authority (MPA), The Mayor of London and the Metropolitan Police by external consultants in January 2003. This resulted in the Metropolitan Police ceasing to purchase all its external forensic science from the FSS. Instead it has multi-sourced those services from three providers, namely the FSS, LGC Ltd and FAL. Other forces have put out other such work to tender, most recently, Thames Valley Police, which having previously obtained services from both the FSS and FAL, now works exclusively with FAL. While the brunt of these changes has been borne by the FSS, it has responded to a more competitive market, winning back some DNA work in Avon and Somerset from its major competitor LGC Ltd. There are other examples where work has been retained following a competitive process, eg Derbyshire, and Devon and Cornwall Constabularies.

3.10 The Government is contributing to the drive for better value by its general expenditure policy and support for market reform by ACPO and APA. The Gershon Review set specific targets for police forces to achieve 3% (1.5% cashable) annual efficiency savings over the next three years.

3.11 Recently, 18 months work by ACPO culminated in a conference held on 7 October 2004. It was agreed that key customer requirements are for increasing the timeliness of supply, greater consistency of service delivery within an intelligence-led approach and enhanced innovation in particular ensuring the effective application of technological advances.

3.12 Work is now underway by ACPO, supported by the APA and the Home Office, to take forward the process of restructuring the forensic services market in line with the following strategy:

— Clear articulation by police forces of their strategy towards the forensic science service market and likely volumes/nature of support from suppliers;

— A co-ordinated and structured approach to tendering to facilitate greater competition including encouraging the entry of new suppliers to the market;

— The greatest use of standardisation possible covering standard industry classification of services and contractual terms and conditions;

— Recognition of the need for individual forces to maintain some flexibility as to the precise nature of services they require and the formation of local, regional and possibly national consortia for different types of services reflecting the experience of the new arrangements;

— Prices to be determined through competition and with those forces willing to provide a more attractive basis (eg in terms of volume commitments) for suppliers being expected to benefit; and

— Facilitation of a national approach to areas of common interest across forces (eg security of supply issues).

It is anticipated that these significant reforms will be introduced across England and Wales during 2005–06.

Section 4: The Forensic Science Service

4.1 Forensic science emerged as a separate discipline in the 1930s. By the early 1980s there were six regional laboratories that, together with the Metropolitan Police Forensic Science Laboratory (MPFSL) in London, serviced the whole of England and Wales. A central research laboratory was established in 1967. These laboratories were run by the Home Office, except the MPFSL, which was part of the Metropolitan Police.

4.2 The FSS became an Executive Agency of the Home Office in 1991 when charging was introduced for the purpose of creating a "purchaser and provider" discipline. In 1996 the FSS was merged with the MPFSL. The FSS was granted Trading Fund status in 1999.

Performance to date

4.3 FSS has experienced strong revenue growth, principally on the back of the DNA Expansion Programme. It has invested in an automated testing capability for DNA and has put in place significant additional processing capacity. In respect of casework the FSS national coverage and the long and close relationships between its forensic scientists and individual police forces make it a valued supplier and give it a strong market presence.

4.4 Whilst FSS does not have the benefit of guaranteed income streams, its trading performance benefits from its former status as the "preferred partner" to the Police. Its relationships with Police customers tend to reflect a producer led arrangement, both in respect of pricing and the standards to which work is carried out.

4.5 In the last two years, the FSS has experienced slower growth as a result of increasing competitive pressure and slower market growth as a consequence of having reached the peak volumes for populating the NDNAD and a reduction in turnaround times. The later mainly being achieved with significant gains in the DNA automation and better management of discretionary costs.

4.6 Overall the FSS has made a success of its Trading Fund status. It is considered to be generally well regarded by stakeholders and has consistently met most of the operational and financial targets set by the Home Office. FSS can take particular credit for:

(i) Its response to the significant increase in demand for forensic services over the last decade;

(ii) The development of the forensic application of DNA, and the setting up and managing, with ACPO of the NDNAD; and

(iii) Pioneering new ways of working with, and in support of, the Police.

4.7 There is a strong consensus within Home Office and FSS however that Trading Fund imposes constraints that materially impair the ability of the FSS to match the approach to winning and delivering work of its competitors. For example:

(i) It is unable to contract directly with the Home Office and other Central Government customers; more generally, trading arrangements with police customers are not on a secure legal basis.

(ii) Public sector procurement obligations that apply to the FSS as a "contracting authority" and detailed Home Office procurement rules have to be followed within delegated financial authority limits.

(iii) Pay and conditions are subject to formal Treasury controls and policies that are applied to all departments and agencies.

(iv) It is unable to access funding for its business plan on a secure, certain and timely basis.

(v) There are limitations on the scope for new business opportunities or to development joint venture arrangements.

As a result of this the Government commissioned the McFarland Review and subsequently an Outline Business case for a new organisational structure.

The McFarland Review

4.8 The McFarland Review of the FSS reported to the Home Secretary in July 2003. The main thrust of the Review focused on the emergence of a more competitive market for forensic science services driven mainly by police authorities seeking better value and the ability of FSS, as a Trading Fund, to compete effectively in the face of increasing pressures from competitors and the dynamics of the market. The Review was also supportive of measures to increase competition, which it was felt would, over time, bring benefits to the CJS.

4.9 McFarland concluded that the main risk from the continuance of FSS as a Trading Fund was a sustained and accelerating loss of market share should it not prove possible to provide the right kind of management, the appropriate governance framework, the necessary freedoms to compete effectively and access to capital investment sufficient to remain at the leading edge of rapidly advancing science and technology.

4.10 Given that FSS generally delivers scientific support services, which can and already are being delivered by competing private sector organisations, McFarland concluded there was no reason in principle why such services could not be delivered by a private sector classified organisation. More specifically the Review recommended that:

(i)   That the FSS should be formed into a Government-owned company (GovCo) as a precursor to development into a private sector classified Public Private Partnership (PPP); and

(ii) Consistent with the reform of the forensic science market, the arrangements for the operation of the NDNAD should be restructured with regulatory and accreditation functions being separated from the day to day operation of the NDNAD and left under public control.

4.11 The key recommendation that the FSS should be developed as a PPP was endorsed by the Home Secretary on 17 July 2003.

National DNA Database

4.12 Acceptance of the recommendation to separate the governance of the NDNAD from the FSS was announced to Parliament on 3 December 2003. In taking this forward there is also a need to ensure that plans for the future of the NDNAD dovetail with the Home Office's response to the Bichard Report in respect of police intelligence handling.

4.13 The key objective is to retain NDNAD exclusively under public sector control that will deliver the required services up to the necessary high standards, through new governance arrangements and a series of contracts that will ensure there is confidence among all suppliers that no single supplier can gain an unfair competitive advantage. The key drivers must be the continuity, quality assurance, forensic integrity, and the improvement of services to the CJS end users.

The Outline Business Case (OBC)

4.14 Since the Home Secretary's decision was announced the Government has been working with the FSS, ACPO and APA to identify how the necessary transformation can best be managed, taking into account the demands of the CJS, ongoing changes in the use of forensic science and the business needs of the FSS itself.

4.15 An Outline Business Case (OBC) prepared by PricewaterhouseCoopers LLP, the Department's commercial and financial advisers, has provided analysis of those needs and how they can be met in a manner consistent with the Home Office public policy objectives. Chief amongst these is the continued maintenance of FSS high standards of integrity and impartiality as well as a collaborative approach with CJS agencies.

4.16 The process involved consultation with the Home Office and ACPO as to their future requirements in respect of the forensic science market and with the FSS in respect of its financial standing and prospects. Other parties involved include other suppliers, FSS trade unions, management and staff, a number of potential investors and other public sector stakeholders.

4.17 While the conclusions of the OBC supported McFarland, they also highlighted a number of areas where further work was needed to ensure that the Home Office objectives for the future of forensic science services could be met. These included:

(i)   Further development and articulation by the Police strategy towards the use and procurement of forensic science;

(ii) The introduction of more commercial, contractually based trading arrangements between the Police and the FSS;

(iii) The design and introduction of arrangements to secure public policy objectives, including an appropriate governance structure for the FSS and changes to the NDNAD and other forensic databases; and

(iv) The corporate transformation of the FSS including further development of its business plan, commercial strategy and projections.

4.18 The OBC confirmed that the FSS is vulnerable to a loss of business for a number of factors:

(i) It has a highly concentrated customer group. This makes the FSS vulnerable to changes in the procurement practices of individual forces.

(ii) As a labour intensive business the FSS has high fixed costs. As was the case following the loss of work with the Metropolitan Police Service (MPS), further losses of individual contracts and tendering processes could be expected to lead to further reductions in headcount.

(iii) The FSS has no significant sales outside of its core CJS customers. This reflects the historical focus of the FSS in its desire to meet the needs of the CJS and a focus on its core business. However, it makes the business vulnerable to factors which influence CJS customers as a whole, for example changes in the level of funding.

(iv) The next technological change may well be miniaturised DNA analysis. Competitors could take a lead on the introduction of this new technology and its provision in custody suites and, in due course at the scene of the crime. This would have significant implications for forensic science providers, in particular the FSS given the size and nature of its laboratory facilities.

4.19 The OBC concluded that the Trading Fund model would not allow the FSS to deliver to its full potential. Restructuring the FSS will ensure that the organisation's potential to assist the police to exploit forensic science is maximised. A failure to achieve this objective and with sufficient speed, as changes in market conditions and technology accelerate, risk leaving the FSS with no future other than managed decline.

SECTION 5: CONCLUSION—THE NEED FOR THE FSS TO BE ABLE TO RESPOND TO CHANGING CJS CLIENT REQUIREMENT

5.1 The objective is for the FSS to remain at the leading edge of forensic science provision in the UK and internationally. This requires a more commercial, customer focused organisational structure. This is supported by a detailed analysis of the FSS business and its prospects, together with its strengths and weaknesses, confirming the conclusion of the independent review.

5.2 In particular, an analysis of the market has confirmed growing commercial pressures as the police have begun to spell out their requirements in terms of rapid accurate results, better more integrated intelligence and bespoke services tailored to meet local requirements. Their requirements for greater innovation and choice to achieve these objectives at reduced cost, reinforced by Gershon and Best Value requirements, is resulting in a greater sophistication by purchasers, including decisions by some forces to multi-source forensic services, and to possibly combine, or regionalise their procurement strategy. In these circumstances, the FSS' competitors, companies with similar reputations for scientific excellence and forensic integrity, and owned by financial investors with the resources and flexibility to respond quickly to evolving police requirements, present a considerable challenge to an organisation based on working practices developed in a provider dominated market, and dependent on investment capital from Government.

5.3 The organisational legacy and Trading Fund status leaves FSS more vulnerable than its competitors in the face of such pressures for a number of reasons. The size of its market share means that it is exposed to the emergence of stronger competition, particularly when almost half of its current revenue comes from only six police forces. High and inflexible fixed costs (staff and infrastructure) which may be difficult to manage down in the face of reduced revenues, together with significant surplus capacity in some areas and inbalance in its charging structures. Much of its accommodation is ageing, with the high maintenance costs and lack of flexibility impacting adversely on the business. More crucially, it risks being left behind in the introduction and deployment of new technology. In particular, and within a few years, miniaturised DNA techniques could revolutionise the location and speed of the work on which much of its revenue relies.

5.4 In short, the FSS cannot be as responsive to customer demands and to the opportunities presented by emerging technologies in a way that properly reflects its crucial role in the CJS. At the same time, the Government is aiming for continuity of service; enhanced delivery to CJS customers; a fully functioning competitive forensic science market; and a flexible, efficient, commercially astute FSS.

5.5 The Government acknowledges the scale of the challenge. The FSS needs to focus on meeting the demands posed by its core business in terms of enhanced service delivery and customer relations; keep pace with the proving and deployment of new scientific techniques; improve efficiency; re-balance charging structures and develop the commercial skills to fully utilise its key asset: a highly qualified workforce. Indeed, its present systemic weaknesses are such that it must begin making major improvements as soon as possible.

5.6 Such changes in the FSS will bring wider public benefits resulting from the reform and development of the forensic science market in England and Wales. These will include enhanced quality of service, innovation and value for money. Contractually based, formalised, trading arrangements between the FSS and the police in the form being developed by ACPO will serve to protect their interests and that of the Criminal Justice System in general, whilst a more competitive and efficient market continues to evolve.

October 2004

Annex I

EDUCATION, TRAINING AND SUPPLY OF SKILLED PERSONNEL IN THE FSS

The Home Office can only provide information on this issue in respect of the FSS. Other forensic providers are engaged in similar activities and may be submitting evidence direct to the Committee, as are SEMTA, the Sector Skills Council (SSC) for Science, Engineering and Skills, and the Council for the Registration of Forensic Practitioners (CRFP).

1 FSS training programmes are delivered in response to a whole range of developmental needs, but the main thrust of the training effort is focussed on scientific and technical areas in direct response to the needs of the Criminal Justice System. Consequently the training and development of scientists to deliver forensic support to investigations and provide expert testimony to the courts takes priority. The development of staff, known as Reporting Officers, and the training of those who show potential for the role carries a significant investment and attendant investment risk. There are about 625 of these staff leading the delivery of forensic casework (out of 2,070 frontline staff and a total workforce of 2,620).

2 Depending upon the type of evidence involved initial training can take between 12 and 18 months at a cost of £60–£100k per trainee. In the last three years (since October 2001) the FSS has selected and trained 280 new Reporting Officers over a range of 27 different evidence types at a total cost of approximately £22 million. Training programmes cover evidential searching, statistics and interpretation, case writing and courtroom and expert witness skills, as well as laboratory work, forensic methodology and scene of crime protocols.

3 Trainees are required to undergo competency assessment before deployment to casework and thereafter remain subject to appropriate supervision by experienced scientists until they are deemed capable of working unsupervised. Moreover the FSS requires that reporting staff are registered with The Council for the Registration of Forensic Practitioners (CRFP) which adopts and promulgates standards of professional competence agreed by the suppliers to the forensic science market. In addition the FSS operates a rigorous quality management system which is subject to scrutiny by the United Kingdom Accreditation Service (UKAS) which among other things assesses FSS processes for the training of scientists, accredits the organisation accordingly and reviews that accreditation on a regular basis.

4 To support the work of the reporting staff the FSS employs about 500 assistant forensic scientists whose main function is to recover evidence from material retrieved from scenes of crime, victims and suspects. Understandably their training needs are considerably less than those of reporting staff. Nonetheless in the financial year ending March 2004 some 4,000 training days were provided at a cost of nearly £0.5 million.

5 Training requirements in the FSS are dictated by forecast customer demand, succession planning, and the need to keep abreast of changing technologies, processes and good practice. There is therefore a constant need for significant investment in staff development. Much of the time the FSS needs to respond rapidly. It is difficult at this stage whether evolution of the forensic science market will affect the breadth of training. On the other hand, the freedom to operate more commercially would open the door to more varied services nationally and internationally together with improved reward and retention strategies unconstrained by Civil Service policies. Clearly as the market developed and employment opportunities increased staff retention would become a bigger issue. At present the FSS is not adequately equipped to tackle the drain on resources. It currently loses about 30 reporting staff each year (excluding early retirement and compulsory severance) representing a loss of £2.5 million in training investment and the same amount in lost income. By the same token greater commercial freedom and freedom from constraining procurement procedures in the Civil Service would put the FSS in a position to invest more innovatively in training opportunities with greater cost effectiveness and speed of response to customer needs.

Annex II

THE LEVEL OF INVESTMENT IN FORENSIC SCIENCE R&D

The Home Office can only provide information on this issue in respect of the FSS. Other forensic providers are engaged in similar activities and may be submitting evidence direct to the Committee.

1. Research and Development (R&D) in the FSS is driven by business needs derived from customer requirements and the need to apply new methods and technologies in support of those requirements. The culture of continuously improving service levels by delivering new and enhanced services that add value underscores all of the development objectives that the business strives to achieve. The FSS development plan is implemented through corporate change processes and programmes supported by a healthy and innovative research effort.

2. In the financial year ending March 2004 the FSS spent £18 million (source FSS) on development [12% of turnover] and business processes, representing in itself the achievement of an Agency target. Some 0.5 million of this was funded directly from the Home Office Police Science & Technology R&D Fund. Deliverables included remarkable advances in the automation of processes, new digital technology and the introduction of familial DNA profiling to identify suspects through links to people genetically related to someone whose DNA was found at the scene of a crime. It is difficult to separate entirely spending on research within the R&D budget, excluding funding for development work such as new ways of working,

partnership projects etc but it is estimated that of the £18 million spent last year the salaries of the 80 research staff and other costs accounted for about £5 million. In a developing market it is critical that R&D is delivered and not all suppliers can necessarily be relied upon to contribute to a co-ordinated R&D programme.

Annex III

USE OF NOVEL TECHNOLOGIES BY FSS AND CJS

The Home Office can only provide information on this issue in respect of the FSS. Other forensic providers are engaged in similar activities and may be submitting evidence direct to the Committee.

1. Since DNA science was first applied to forensic problems the FSS research programme has been dominated by the need to develop further this vital tool in the fight against crime. The FSS therefore continues to focus not only on research work on the science itself but more importantly on the use made of it to support the criminal justice system and add value to the services it provides to its customers.

2. Over the years the FSS has been responsible for the creation of many new technologies as well as the enhancement and development of existing ones. Perhaps the best known was the establishment of the world's first National DNA Database® in 1994 that revolutionised the war on crime. It has given rise to similar systems the world over but still remains the envy of the world because of leading edge improvements that are constantly being incorporated into it by the FSS. The database contains the DNA profiles of virtually every active criminal in the UK and everyday provides police with vital leads in investigations that previously would not have been possible. Over a year about 50,000 matches link suspects to crimes or crimes to one another where otherwise the links would not be made. Moreover the long established policy the FSS has of retaining evidential material from unsolved crimes, together with technological advances forged by the FSS, mean that old crimes can now be reinvestigated with startling success.

3. Automation techniques and the use of robotics to deliver DNA services more quickly and cost effectively have been at the forefront of FSS development work on DNA. When DNA analysis for forensic purposes first took place the process took 350 days to complete. Thanks largely to the FSS that process now takes a matter of hours. Shortly the FSS will complete the final phase in its automation project, delivering the world's first fully automated DNA service featuring the most advanced DNA laboratory the world has ever seen. As a result capacity will be more than adequate to meet demand and efficiency savings will begin to appear perhaps running into many millions over the next few years.

4. Similarly work carried out in the FSS on miniaturising DNA systems has meant that DNA recovered from the scene of a crime will soon be processed at the scene in a mobile laboratory and the results communicated to investigating officers there and then.

5. Although taking pride of place in the FSS research programme for many years, DNA science is however only part of the FSS success story. New technologies in digital research for example are being applied to computer crime, crime involving mobile phones and retail crime (eg chip and PIN), as well as digital techniques to establish similarity between facial images in the identification of suspects and culprits from CCTV and other monitoring devices. In other areas new technology developed or innovated by the FSS is being applied to fingerprint identification, drug profiling, analysing fibres and gun crime. In all of these fields the FSS makes use of the very latest technologies or creates better ones to ensure the best service is made available to the Criminal Justice System.

6. There have at times inevitably been frustrations both on the scientific front and in delays in acquiring technologies brought about by bureaucracy with which competitors both here and abroad do not find themselves burdened. This has resulted not only in adverse effects on the operational service the FSS provides but also on its cost base and its ability to keep one step ahead of the criminal. In addition the nature of the procurement procedures which the FSS is obliged to follow Government procurement procedures place it at a disadvantage. They not only cause delays in research projects but also expose in the process matters of a business confidential nature which the FSS would rather not disclose.

Annex IV

FORENSIC SCIENCE IN THE CJS

The Home Office can only provide information on this issue in respect of the FSS. Other forensic providers are engaged in similar activities and may be submitting evidence direct to the Committee.

1. The FSS supports police investigations by providing scientific services involving the recovery and analysis of evidential material and the interpretation of results. The findings then form the substance of statements prepared for use in Court supported as necessary by expert witness appearances. The FSS deals with every type of crime and offers services covering every type of offence from criminal damage to murder, sexual offences, and terrorism involving every evidence type from handwriting analysis to explosives and weapons examination.

2. For many years perhaps the major issue affecting police customers and others who serve the Criminal Justice System has been the extent to which the FSS has been able to respond quickly to customers' needs. While the FSS has accepted valid criticism of its performance on timeliness in the past, by and large it

experienced great difficulty improving because of problems with which it was beset associated with its rapid growth (sevenfold in 12 years) and its inability to match capacity with demand throughout that time. (There has been reference earlier to timescales for bringing on new talent.) The problems were highlighted by the National Audit Office (NAO) Report of 2003 and in the PAC report "*Improving service delivery: the Forensic Science Service*" published in January 2004. In its response the FSS was able to give assurances that measures were in place to improve timeliness in the light of a stabilising of demand and the introduction of automation in DNA processes. The target would be to achieve an almost 50% improvement and this did indeed happen by the end of the 2003–04 financial year. Further improvements are planned in the current year.

3. The FSS employs a robust quality management system. It involves scientists checking one another's critical findings, case audits, declared trials where cases are created in-house and put to scientists to process, and undeclared trials where cases are again created in-house but submitted by police as genuine cases in the usual way. The scientist's performance is assessed on completion of the forensic work and the production of a statement. Despite all of this there are occasions during the course of normal work either in the laboratory, at a scene, or in Court when a shortcoming might be revealed in a scientist's performance and appropriate action is taken. Happily such occurrences are rare.

APPENDIX 2

Memorandum from the University of Strathclyde

EXECUTIVE SUMMARY

The use of forensic science in England and Wales is relatively sophisticated compared to most other jurisdictions. Despite this, there remains considerable potential for it to contribute further to the criminal justice system. Optimum benefits are likely to accrue from a national approach that is integrated on the basis of aims that are agreed by the relevant stakeholders in the criminal justice system. Such an approach is predicated on the basis of clear user needs and service provision that meets required legal, scientific and ethical standards. To maintain such an approach requires the effective coordination of forensic science education, research and practice in addition to service provision. A Forensic Science Advisory Committee that represents the all stakeholders and co-ordinates activities is essential to achieving the maximum benefits from forensic science.

INTRODUCTION

1. The University of Strathclyde has been involved in forensic science education, research and practice for over 35 years. Currently it has two undergraduate forensic science qualifications in chemistry and biology in addition to an MSc in Forensic Science and an MSc in Forensic Informatics. Hundreds of graduates from the University of Strathclyde have become professional forensic scientists in laboratories around the world, a number of them in senior posts. The University of Strathclyde was a founder member of the European Network of Forensic Science Institutes (ENFSI) and also validates postgraduate diplomas in a number of forensic science disciplines for the Forensic Science Society.

2. The author of this report, Professor Jim Fraser, is Director of The Centre for Forensic Science and President of the Forensic Science Society. He has extensive experience as a forensic practitioner in forensic science laboratories and police forces in England and Scotland. He also has considerable experience in the development and application of policy and strategy in forensic science. Professor Fraser has carried out forensic and management consultancy for a large number of organisations in the UK, including police forces and the Home Office.

Provision of forensic science

3. The provision of forensic science at strategic level is generally a public service enterprise. Although there are a number of countries with elements of private forensic science provision, such as the USA, no other country is contemplating the complete privatisation of forensic science provision to its criminal justice system.

4. In Scotland, it is intended that forensic science will become part of common police services[1] and recent steps have been taken by the Scottish Executive to implement this.

---

[1] www.scottishpolicesupers.co.uk/ed12cps.htm

Forensic science provision in England and Wales

5. In England and Wales a private market already exists. There is at least one private strategic supplier and numerous niche suppliers of various sizes, that compete with the Forensic Science Service (FSS). Given that such a market already exists the potential PPP of the FSS should be seen in this context. The more fundamental question is: what infrastructure and safeguards are necessary to ensure effective provision of forensic science to the criminal justice system? Furthermore, given that this is a unique arrangement that raises issues of public confidence and trust, how are such perceptions to be dealt with?

The potential of forensic science

6. Part of the rationale for the development of the FSS as an agency was to break the traditional deadlock between the growing demands of the police service against the limited resources of the FSS. There is little doubt that agency status has radically altered the relationship between the police service and forensic science providers.

7. Breakthroughs in new technology, particularly DNA and the implementation of the National DNA Database (NDNADB), supported by government funding, have contributed to the substantial growth of the use of forensic science as an investigative resource and a contributor to criminal justice. In particular the NDNADB has facilitated an increase in the use of forensic science to identify previously unconsidered suspects rather than incriminate or eliminate those already identified by other means.

8. Forensic science has enormous potential to contribute further to the criminal justice process if used on a national scale, properly integrated with other forms of police investigatory practice and based on common policies and systems derived from evidenced good practice.

9. There is extensive published evidence that this is not the case at present.[2, 3, 4] These sources identify a lack of knowledge, poorly integrated systems, and cultural barriers that act as impediments to the large scale, effective use of forensic science. There is also unexplained variation in the uses made of forensic science by different police forces. Variation in usage of shoe marks is a good example of this.[5]

10. The issue of good practice merits particular mention. There are very few instances of practice being based on objective, published evaluations. Despite the availability of existing models,[6] there is a lack consistency in the approach to individual projects. There is no overall program focused on strategic aims that meet the needs of the criminal justice system. Furthermore lack of valid data[7] hampers the provision of information on which to base evaluations of tactical and strategic use of forensic science.

11. Future developments in the successful deployment of forensic science will rely on the integration and effective use of scientific information, the development of databases and good operational practice. However, given the above constraints, optimising the benefits of forensic science presents huge challenges. In this context it is essential that there is a focus on behavioural (as opposed to structural) change within organisations that play a significant part in the delivery of forensic science to the criminal justice system. Recent research[8] illustrates some of the complexities in understanding the behavioural aspects of forensic practice and the challenges that face this approach.

The Market

12. The forensic science market is relatively new and there are a limited number of published studies of its emerging structure.[9] However, there are significant benefits to be gained from a competitive market and competitive pressures on suppliers have resulted in increased choice, large reductions in turn-around times (DNA profiling in volume crime and drugs identification are good examples of such improvements). In these particular areas of volume crime, delivery times are so short that it is increasingly the case that delays in timeliness are attributable to delays in the receipt of items by a forensic laboratory rather than laboratory time itself. There has also been a significant reduction in the prices for DNA profiling.

13. However, this is a market that needs approaching with some sophistication. Although some individual products could be considered as commodities (eg DNA CJ samples and drugs identification), their delivery in a complex criminal justice context that means scientific standards, integrity and service

[2] Association of Chief Police Officers, *Using forensic science effectively,* 1996.

[3] Her Majesty's Inspector of Constabulary (2000), *Under the microscope: a thematic inspection of scientific and technical support.*

[4] Her Majesty's Inspector of Constabulary (2002), *Under the microscope refocused: a revisit to the investigative use of DNA and fingerprints,* London, Home Office.

[5] Rix, R (2004), *The contribution of shoe mark data to police intelligence, crime detection and prosecution.* Home Office report 236, London.

[6] Fraser, JG, *A framework for good practice* (2002), presented to the National Conference for Scientific Support.

[7] *Ibid* Under the microscope.

[8] Williams R, *The Management of crime scene examination in relation to burglary and vehicle crime,* Home Office Report 235, London, Home Office.

[9] Fraser, *Delivery and evaluation of forensic science,* Science and Justice, 2003.

profiles must always be taken into account when procuring products and evaluating benefits.[10] There is a danger that a consumerist approach, which may be appropriate for some forensic products, is applied to other more sophisticated forensic services, such as interpretation of blood patterns or investigation of fires.

14. It is also essential that aggressive competitive behaviour that could destabilise the market and consequently compromise continuity of provision or standards must be controlled in some way. Further risks include: the poaching of staff to the extent that they remove key skills from one or more competitors; attempted buy outs: and the use of patents or intellectual property rights that prevent wider benefits to the criminal justice system. Whilst all of these tactics are legitimate in wholly commercial enterprises, in this context it is essential that they are governed in the wider interests of justice, fairness to individual suppliers and maintenance of public confidence and trust.

Research and development

15. The primary sources of funding for scientific research are discipline based and consequently the research itself is invariably discipline based. This approach does not serve the multidisciplinary and practice based needs of forensic science well. Despite comments about support for practice based and multidisciplinary research[11] this trend seems set to continue. The exception to this is the relatively recent Engineering and Physical Sciences Research Council (EPSRC) "Think Crime" initiative. Other than this, there is no specific research council funding that is readily accessible to forensic science research.

16. Effective research in forensic science requires three elements:

— A framework for the implementation of new technology and methodologies that is agreed by laboratories and the various parties in the criminal justice system. This should take into account the potential risks and benefits of new technology and ensure that the process is managed effectively and in the interests of justice;

— A mechanism by which novel technologies of potential operational relevance are identified and evaluated;

— The identification of a set of problems whose resolution by research and development is likely to benefit the criminal justice process. The most likely source of such problems is the police service and other law enforcement agencies who are the main users of forensic science.

Education in forensic science

17. In the past five years there has been huge growth in the number of undergraduate and postgraduate courses with "forensic" in the title. This provision does not reflect the limited employment prospects in forensic science nor is it in response to employers in the sector. It is the view of the University of Strathclyde that the development of individuals who are to be effective forensic practitioners is secondary to a sound education in science. This is a view that is widely shared by forensic practitioners and employers. In educational terms this means a first degree in science ideally followed by a postgraduate degree in forensic science.

18. However, it is the case that the vast majority of the forensic courses in the UK are delivered by individuals and departments that have no direct experience of forensic science. The Forensic Science Society currently has an accreditation program open to universities that offer forensic courses that is in its early stages of implementation and which a number of universities have signed up to.

19. There is another important role that the higher education sector can play in relation to the development of forensic science. This relates to the ongoing education and competence of forensic practitioners. Sound education allied to training is required to ensure the highest standards in a dynamic and increasingly professionalised sector.

A proposed framework for forensic science in England and Wales

20. The Criminal Justice system requires forensic science provision that meets appropriate scientific, legal, ethical and service standards. It is possible to have a framework that meets the needs of the criminal justice system and users of forensic science that is applicable to public and private provision of forensic science.

21. Since the Royal Commission on Criminal Justice (RCCJ)[12] there have been many changes relevant to forensic practice. These include:

— The widespread implementation of formal quality management systems by forensic science suppliers;

— The creation of the Council for Registration for Forensic Practitioners;

---

[10] Fraser, *ibid.*

[11] Research Assessment Exercise, 2008.

[12] Royal Commission on Criminal Justice (1993) Report, Cm 2263. London: HMSO.

— The formation of a professional body for forensic science practitioners (The Forensic Science Society);

— The creation of the National Centre for Policing Excellence;

— Extensive changes to legislation, particularly the Criminal Procedure and Investigations Act (1996) and subsequent case law setting standards for disclosure of forensic evidence and materials.

22. All of these are factors that should support the integrity of forensic science in a private market (or otherwise) and help maintain public confidence in forensic science in the criminal justice system. Despite the developments described above, the recommendation of the RCCJ to create a Forensic Science Advisory Council (FSAC) is still relevant today.

23. A framework that incorporates the recommendations of the RCCJ and the recent developments relevant to forensic science could provide regulation and strategic governance of the market to ensure:

— Integrity and standards of supply and competence of practitioners;

— Continuity of supply in addition to healthy competition;

— Coherence of research and development based on a clear user need and technological opportunities;

— Planned introduction of new technologies based on an assessment of risks and benefits to the criminal justice system and evidence based evaluations of their effectiveness.

In order to be effective any FSAC would have to represent all of the relevant stakeholders in the criminal justice including academic institutions with a proven track record in forensic science, education and practice.

CONCLUSIONS

24. Given the growing private market in forensic science, irrespective of the future status of the FSS, it is essential that there is effective governance that ensures scientific standards, integrity, and continuity of provision of forensic science to the criminal justice system. The recommendation of the RCCJ for a Forensic Science Advisory Committee would be an effective mechanism by which to achieve these aims. Given the increasingly important role of forensic science such a body is essential to maintaining public confidence and trust.

October 2004

APPENDIX 3

Memorandum from the Council for the Registration of Forensic Practitioners (CRFP)

Ensuring high standards of professional competence of those experts called to give evidence is crucial to the credibility of the judicial system and the Register is a tool that can do much to underpin that credibility."

The Prime Minister, writing to CRFP Vice Chairman Judge Anthony Thorpe, October 2004

EXECUTIVE SUMMARY

1. CRFP operates a unique registration scheme, underlining the quality of UK forensic practice by defining and maintaining high standards of conduct and competence. Full details are on the website: www.crfp.org.uk.

2. The courts must be able to rely on the quality of professional evidence. Judges need an effective tool to help them decide who should give such evidence. No such tool existed before the CRFP Register, which offers a straightforward means of checking the current competence of individual practitioners.

3. A forensic scientist first has to be a scientist. Forensic practice demands a steady supply of graduates equipped with sound knowledge and skills in pure science or other disciplines.

4. In a diversifying forensic marketplace, published standards of competence and conduct are central to public confidence. The standards should apply to all practitioners providing forensic evidence—prosecution or defence, public or private sector.

5. This paper discusses measures to achieve these aims. It uses the term "forensic practice" to encompass not only traditional laboratory based science but all professional work done towards the preparation of evidence.

UK forensic practice: a quality product

6. UK forensic practice is respected throughout the world: our forensic scientists, anthropologists, police experts and others have a formidable reputation not only for technical excellence but for even-handedness and reliability.

7. The privileges accorded by that reputation bring a commensurate responsibility: to ensure that standards of professional conduct and competence are maintained throughout the forensic community. When things go wrong, the risks to the justice system, and to public confidence, are substantial and far-reaching. The financial cost of forensic mistakes can also be high.

8. A number of shortcomings in forensic practice have attracted public attention in recent years. CRFP is building a Register which will put a boundary around safe, competent practice in all the main forensic specialties.

Why CRFP?

9. Few events are as likely to erode confidence in the justice system as the discovery that a practitioner giving forensic evidence has fallen short of the standards the public has a right to expect. High profile miscarriages of justice which came to light in the early 1990s led to calls to set standards and police them effectively. The cases of the Birmingham Six, the Maguires and others still resonate in the public's mind.

10. Successive studies, and a strong initiative led by the Forensic Science Service (FSS), led to the proposal to establish CRFP. In 1998 Jack Straw MP, then Home Secretary, announced Government support to get the organisation off the ground. CRFP was established in August 1999.

11. A not-for-profit company limited by guarantee, CRFP is independent of the Government and of sectoral interests. The composition of CRFP's Governing Council is in Annex A. The Home Office have been providing deficit funding, currently some 60% of CRFP's needs. CRFP will ultimately achieve self-sufficiency through levying registration fees.

12. Most providers of forensic services have in place systems attesting to their organisational and procedural quality. These are not designed to test the competence and professional standards of individual practitioners. But it is individuals on whom the reputation of their organisations depends; and who answer for forensic work in court.

13. Systems of accreditation exist in other countries; but there is no model which matches the range, depth and rigour of the system CRFP has introduced. Charles Clarke MP, opening the Register in 2000, called CRFP "a unique concept and a real world leader".

14. Lord Justice Auld, in the Criminal Courts Review, recognised that membership organisations such as the Expert Witness Institute and the Academy of Experts are not equipped to fulfil the regulatory function that CRFP was set up to perform. He called on organisations involved with expert witnesses to collaborate with CRFP to give the courts a single point of reference on the competence of forensic practitioners.

15. These sentiments have recently been echoed by the Senior Presiding Judge and other judges exercised by the need to ensure quality in professional evidence. CRFP has secured the strong support of successive Lords Chief Justice, Masters of the Rolls, Directors of Public Prosecutions, ACPO, ACPOS, the Bar Council and Law Society, leading professional bodies and the main providers of forensic services.

The Register and how it works

16. CRFP has a single, overriding aim: to promote public confidence in forensic practice in the UK. It will achieve this in three main ways:

— publishing a register of currently competent forensic practitioners;

— ensuring, through periodic revalidation, that registered practitioners stay up to date and maintain competence; and

— dealing with practitioners who fall short of the standards expected.

17. The central function of a professional register is to define competent practice and put a boundary around it. Regulatory bodies receive most attention when a practitioner is struck off. But for the generality of each profession the purpose of the register is to underline and uphold good practice.

18. CRFP is building a single Register, emphasising the unity of the forensic process from the scene of an incident to the courtroom. The Register, which is open to all on CRFP's website (www.crfp.org.uk) makes it easy for anyone wishing to check a practitioner's credentials to see at a glance the forensic specialties in which they have demonstrated competence.

Getting on the Register

19. Applicants for registration have to provide details of their qualifications and experience, references from colleagues and users of their services, and declarations about their past and future conduct. They also provide a log of recent cases, from which an assessor from their own specialty chooses a sample for scrutiny against competence criteria. CRFP has developed these criteria in association with leading professional groups, who also nominate the assessors for training by CRFP.

20. The standard for registration is "safe, competent practice". Most achieve registration: generally, practitioners apply only when confident of success. Those about whom an assessor has doubts are entitled to a second opinion; but more usually they withdraw to address the issues identified, then reapply later.

21. While it is impossible to prove a negative, CRFP believe the scheme has been sufficiently rigorous to deter charlatans. Registration is voluntary; but once the register is used actively in connection with court proceedings it should become increasingly difficult to practise as a forensic practitioner without holding registration.

Staying on the Register

22. CRFP grants registration for four years at a time. Before that period ends, practitioners must demonstrate that they have stayed up to date and maintained their competence. There is another formal assessment of recent casework before a further period of registration is granted.

When things go wrong

23. No register can guarantee that registrants will never make a mistake. CRFP has disciplinary procedures designed to deal with information that calls a practitioner's fitness to practise into question.

24. The action taken will often be educational and remedial; but the ultimate sanction is removal of the practitioner's name from the Register. This would take place in public and be published immediately on the CRFP website.

25. CRFP will play a full part in the work commissioned by the Crown Prosecution Service to examine early warning systems to prevent possible miscarriages when concerns come to light about a practitioner's competence.

26. It is often said that lawyers and scientists do not understand each other, leading sometimes to less than satisfactory results. A regulatory body is by way of a bridge between professionals and the public. Although bridges tend to be trampled from both sides, CRFP offers a ready means to promote dialogue between scientists, lawyers and others.

27. During 2004 CRFP has brokered discussion between scientists, judges and lawyers about the presentation of DNA evidence, in which juries can readily be misled particularly by the way complex material is presented. The resulting guidance should improve understanding on all sides.

Why CRFP is different

28. There are various "registers" or lists of expert witnesses. These are held by membership organisations such as the Expert Witness Institute, or are commercial publications. Entry is via simple processes that may not include any appreciable assessment of forensic competence.

29. The very fact of a published list or directory suggests an authority that these lists cannot bear. The CRFP Register, by contrast, is based on a proper professional assessment, entries are regularly revalidated and the disciplinary procedures provide real teeth and a clear influence over standards.

The scope of the Register

30. Registration is for forensic scientists and others who use professional skills to provide reports and witness statements for court. The FSS have shown their commitment to the principle by making it a requirement that all their reporting officers are registered.

31. So far the Register, which presently contains 1,681 entries, is open to 18 specialties of forensic practice:

— Science (drugs; toxicology; firearms; human contact traces; particulates; questioned documents; marks; incident reconstruction)
— Scene examination (police scene of crime officers)
— Fingerprint examination
— Fingerprint development
— Collision investigation
— Vehicle examination

— Anthropology
— Archaeology
— Odontology
— Paediatrics
— Forensic medical examination (police surgeons).

32. CRFP is piloting schemes for extending registration to:
— Computing specialists
— Imaging specialists
— Veterinarians
— Fire examiners
— Geologists.

33. Discussions are under way towards the possible development of registration schemes for:
— Telecommunications specialists
— Psychiatrists
— Other medical specialists
— Rail accident investigators.

34. More specialties will follow. CRFP is involved in discussions brokered by the Civil Justice Council about the application of the Register to expert witnesses in the civil courts: this will necessarily take registration into new areas, including those professions and specialties where full time forensic work is rare.

The diversifying market

35. The group who undertook the review which led to the recommendation that the FSS be released from public sector constraints emphasised strongly the need for registration as a safeguard to underpin standards in a diversifying market.

36. This makes good sense. Over the past 10–20 years the market for science and other forensic services has already developed substantially beyond what was once a state-run service, closely associated with the police.

37. Like other professional regulatory bodies, CRFP is not concerned with the way forensic services are organised and delivered. CRFP's aim is to ensure that those who use forensic services and those who provide them make full use of the Register as an independent measure of the quality of individuals' professional performance.

38. Developing the FSS, from a single public sector provider into one or more companies less constrained by public sector rules, would not in itself have adverse implications for the standards of professional competence and conduct of its employees. But users rightly want a proper balance between the criteria of cost, quality and timeliness. It is essential that quality receives its full measure in this calculation.

39. The maintenance of the present FSS management policy, of insisting that all its scientists who report to court are registered with CRFP, would be a powerful answer to the suggestion that exposure to more overtly commercial pressures could lead to a fall in standards.

Education for forensic practice

40. There is at present no qualification which, of itself, equips an individual for forensic practice. Employers, and the sector skills councils which aim to provide a voice for them, express doubts about the value of some of the undergraduate courses offering degrees in forensic science, archaeology, anthropology and other disciplines.

41. Those doubts usually centre on the quantity of pure science a course contains; the depth in which individual subjects are studied; and the extent to which the university pays attention to the needs of employers.

42. To be a forensic scientist you first need to be a scientist—and a good one. Although CRFP has no direct responsibility for the education and training of forensic practitioners, the advent of a regulatory body to set and police standards has crystallised the arguments and been a catalyst for discussion.

43. The Forensic Science Society and the sector skills council SEMTA have both been looking closely at this issue. CRFP's concern is with the end product: whether a forensic practitioner is, in practice, able to do the things that should be expected of a person claiming competence in a forensic specialty.

44. The sequence of needs might be summarised as a series of successive responsibilities. It is the responsibility of:

— **CRFP** to register practitioners who demonstrate current competence in the essential elements of their specialty;

— **employers** to train their employees to a standard where CRFP can be confident about registering them;

— **universities** to provide graduates with the pure knowledge and skills essential for application to forensic practice; and

— **schools** to provide university entrants with the basic equipment necessary to cope with a rigorous course in an appropriate academic discipline.

Standards: the level playing field

45. Does the defence get as good a service as the prosecution? This question is central to the quality of justice. The diversification of the market for forensic science stands alongside the developing application of the human rights legislation, a growing combativeness on the part of legal defence teams, and a general climate of challenge to professional opinion.

46. Individuals coming into contact with the justice system have a right to competent professional support, whichever side they are on. CRFP has been concerned, since its inception, to develop registration schemes which ensure that all practitioners registered in a specialty have demonstrated competence to an equivalent standard—whether they work for the prosecution or defence, public or private sector, or are employed or self-employed.

47. CRFP has therefore been careful always to draw on the expertise of both the public and the private sectors in setting standards for registration and in selecting assessors for each specialty on the Register.

48. Whether any further distancing of the FSS from the public sector will increase the willingness of defence teams to seek professional advice from them—a service they already offer—remains to be seen.

The emergent specialties: What is an expert?

49. Courts call for expert evidence to fill gaps in their expertise. It is for the court to decide which experts to hear. But how, lacking expertise in a field, is the court to decide who is an expert? The CRFP Register provides a ready tool to help resolve this conundrum.

50. In the more established forensic specialties (laboratory science, fingerprints, scene examination), there has been little difficulty in defining standards of competence. A much more substantial task has been to define standards in emergent specialties where no agreed standard has been set down before.

51. Examples of this are the digital evidence specialties: computing, imaging and telecommunications. The part specialists in these fields play in court proceedings has increased enormously in recent years. The FSS has a growing capacity to undertake such work, as do the police forces with in-house teams; but demand significantly outstrips supply and law enforcement agencies are obliged to call on private firms to help manage the workload.

52. This is not a problem in principle. The difficulty lies in establishing the competence of individuals and firms to provide forensic evidence of adequate quality. The Director of Public Prosecutions has expressed particular concern about this area of work, and looks to CRFP to establish clear standards where none have existed before.

53. CRFP has no wish to sanctify areas of practice for which no scientific basis has yet been established. But in fields where a demonstrable standard can be defined the work is well advanced. CRFP hopes to be able to open the Register to forensic computing and imaging specialists in the first half of 2005; and to telecommunications specialists later that year. In such ways CRFP can contribute directly to the validation of emerging scientific and technical methods for the production of evidence.

54. The use of novel science in court should be approached with caution. If innovation is not to be stifled, a substantial investment in research is needed to establish the reliability of new methods, drawing on the expertise not only of the FSS but of other forensic providers and of academic institutions of sufficient standing.

Professional evidence in the civil courts

55. Justice is indivisible; and the standards to be expected of experts giving evidence in the civil courts should be identical to those of practitioners working in the criminal justice system. The professional institutions and leading practitioners helping CRFP with the registration scheme have universally expressed the view that the professional knowledge and skills exercised are exactly the same, whatever the nature of the court.

56. CRFP was founded in response to miscarriages of justice which occurred in the criminal courts. So the initial focus has been on registering practitioners who work chiefly in criminal or coroners' courts. But a growing number of registrants work also in the civil courts. This, together with concerns expressed by judges and others about the quality of expert evidence, is causing CRFP to look closely at extending registration to the wider expert witness community.

57. The Civil Justice Council is increasingly interested in the subject of expert evidence. CRFP will be playing a full part in their forthcoming seminars on this. Particular concerns surround the rapidly growing use of experts in the family courts, who need a straightforward means of examining the credentials and current competence of those who offer such evidence.

58. The Legal Services Commission spends some £135 million annually on expert witnesses and is anxious to find means of quality control. Its consultation paper due for issue in November 2004 proposes using the CRFP Register as an indicator, so that solicitors who use registered practitioners will have to provide less justification than those who do not.

59. CRFP strongly supports this proposal but recognises that it will need substantial extra resources if it is to move swiftly, working with the appropriate professional institutions, to extend registration to the range of specialties engaged in expert witness work.

60. None of this implies any shift in the view that registration should remain voluntary. In a free society no one should seek to constrain the courts as to the evidence they can hear; and there will always be situations where evidence is required from an expert in a very small specialty, or one whose expertise is needed in court too rarely to justify maintaining a registration scheme.

CONCLUSION

61. The issue of quality in forensic practice is too important to allow resource constraints, the difficulty of defining standards in the newer specialties, and cultural resistance to outside scrutiny to stand in the way of effective regulatory measures. CRFP has achieved a great deal, with very limited resources, in a short period. There is more to be done and further investment is required to enable the project to achieve its true potential.

27 October 2004

Annex A

The Composition of CRFP

Professor Evelyn Ebsworth, Chairman

Chemist: former Vice Chancellor of Durham University

Mr Peter Ablett

Head of Chief Executive's Office, Centrex: appointed to chair the Incident Investigation Sector Assessment Panel

Mrs Rosemary Barnes

Chief Executive, Cystic Fibrosis Trust and formerly MP for Greenwich 1987–92: coopted as a lay member

Professor Sir Colin Berry

Queen Mary Hospital, London: appointed in consultation with the General Medical Council

Mr Jeremy Carter-Manning QC

Barrister: appointed in consultation with the Bar Council

Professor David Croisdale-Appleby

Chairman, Buckinghamshire Hospitals NHS trust: coopted as a lay member

Mr Sean Doyle

Head of Forensic Chemistry and Research, DSTL Forensic Explosives Laboratory: appointed in consultation with the UK Forensic Science Liaison Group

Mr Roger Ede

Law Society Representation and Law Reform Directorate; Deputy District Judge (magistrates' courts): appointed in consultation with the Law Society

Dr Angela Gallop

Forensic Alliance: appointed in consultation with the Consultative Forum

Mr William Gilchrist

Deputy Crown Agent, Edinburgh: nominated by the Crown Agent

Mr Tom Harper

Scientific Support Manager, Essex Police: elected by fellow CRFP registered practitioners.

Professor Sir Peter Lachmann

Emeritus Professor of Immunology, Cambridge University: coopted in consultation with the Royal Society

Mr Tony Lake

Chief Constable, Lincolnshire Police: appointed in consultation with ACPO/ACPOS

Mr Mike Loveland

Chief Operating Officer, Forensic Science Service: appointed to chair the Science Sector Assessment Panel

Professor Alan Malcolm

Chief Executive, Institute of Biology: appointed in consultation with the learned societies with forensic practitioner members

Judge Anthony Thorpe, Vice Chairman

Resident Judge, Chichester Crown Court: nominated by the Lord Chancellor

Dr Robert Watt

Dr JH Burgoyne and Partners: transitional member

Dr Michael Wilks

Principal Forensic Medical Examiner: appointed to chair the Medicine & Healthcare Sector Assessment Panel

Mr Timothy Wilson

Head of Science Policy Unit, Home Office: nominated by the Minister of State at the Home Office

Mr Clive Wolfendale

Deputy Chief Constable, North Wales Police: appointed in conjunction with the relevant national training organisations

Dr Richard Worswick

Chief Executive, LGC Ltd: transitional member

Two further places are being kept available, to be filled by the chairmen of further assessment panels when we establish these.

Annex B

Good Practice for Forensic Practitioners

CRFP is the Council for the Registration of Forensic Practitioners.

CRFP is an independent regulatory body. Our objective is to promote public confidence in forensic practice in the UK.

We will achieve this by:

— publishing a register of competent forensic practitioners;

— ensuring through periodic revalidation that forensic practitioners keep up to date and maintain competence; and

— dealing with registered practitioners who fail to meet the necessary standards.

Registration with CRFP, which is voluntary, carries both privileges and responsibilities. The public will accept your registration as proof of your competence. Your responsibility is, in return, to maintain and develop your professional performance, adhering at all times to the standards in this code.

As a registered forensic practitioner you must:

1. Recognise that your overriding duty is to the court and to the administration of justice: it is your duty to present your findings and evidence, whether written or oral, in a fair and impartial manner.

2. Act with honesty, integrity, objectivity and impartiality.

3. Not discriminate on grounds of race, beliefs, gender, language, sexual orientation, social status, age, lifestyle or political persuasion.

4. Comply with the code of conduct of any professional body of which you are a member.

5. Provide advice and evidence only within the limits of your professional competence and only when fit to do so.

6. Inform a suitable person or authority, in confidence where appropriate, if you have good grounds for believing there is a situation which may result in a miscarriage of justice.

In all aspects of your work as a provider of expert advice and evidence you must:

6. Take all reasonable steps to maintain and develop your professional competence, taking account of material research and developments within the relevant field and practising techniques of quality assurance.

7. Declare to your client, patient, or employer if you have one, any prior involvement or personal interest which gives, or may give, rise to a conflict of interest, real or perceived; and act in such a case only with their explicit written consent.

8. Take all reasonable steps to ensure access to all available evidential materials which are relevant to the examinations requested; to establish, so far as reasonably practicable, whether any may have been compromised before coming into your possession; and to ensure their integrity and security are maintained whilst in your possession.

9. Accept responsibility for all work done under your supervision, direct or indirect.

10. Conduct all work in accordance with the established principles of your profession, using methods of proven validity and appropriate equipment and materials.

11. Make and retain full, contemporaneous, clear and accurate records of the examinations you conduct, your methods and your results, in sufficient detail for another forensic practitioner competent in the same area of work to review your work independently.

12. Report clearly, comprehensively and impartially, setting out or stating:

(a) your terms of reference and the source of your instructions;

(b) the material upon which you based your investigation and conclusions;

(c) summaries of your and your team's work, results and conclusions;

(d) any ways in which your investigations or conclusions were limited by external factors; especially if your access to relevant material was restricted; or if you believe unreasonable limitations on your time, or on the human, physical or financial resources available to you, have significantly compromised the quality of your work; and

(e) that you have carried out your work and prepared your report in accordance with this Code.

13. Reconsider and, if necessary, be prepared to change your conclusions, opinions or advice and to reinterpret your findings in the light of new information or new developments in the relevant field; and take the initiative in informing your client or employer promptly of any such change.

14. Preserve confidentiality unless:

(a) the client or patient explicitly authorises you to disclose something;

(b) a court or tribunal orders disclosure;

(c) the law obliges disclosure; or

(d) your overriding duty to the court and to the administration of justice demands disclosure.

15. Preserve legal professional privilege: only the client may waive this. It protects communications, oral and written, between professional legal advisers and their clients; and between those advisers and expert witnesses in connection with the giving of legal advice, or in connection with, or in contemplation of, legal proceedings and for the purposes of those proceedings.

When you register with CRFP, you accept these as the principles that must govern your professional practice. They are the standards against which CRFP would judge any information that called into question your fitness to stay on the register. You must therefore always be prepared to justify, in the light of this code, the actions and decisions you take in the course of your professional work.

In considering a complaint against a registered forensic practitioner, CRFP will be guided primarily by the provisions of the code. But they reserve the right to take action where a practitioner's fitness to practise is questioned for other reasons. This would include circumstances such as a criminal conviction or an allegation of behaviour which, while not specifically addressed in the code, might be regarded as bringing forensic practice into disrepute.

October 2004

APPENDIX 4

Memorandum from the Metropolitan Police Service

EXECUTIVE SUMMARY

The Metropolitan Police Service (MPS) has taken a strategic approach to securing the provision of forensic science services recognising its importance and the impact of rapidly identifying offenders. By adopting a business-like approach we have secured improved performance. Our experience highlights the need to manage the commercial development of forensic science at a strategic level through effective regulation and within this the privatisation of the FSS.

INTRODUCTION

1. The MPS welcomes the opportunity to provide a response to the issues raised by the Science and Technology Committee. We have been working closely with the Association of Chief Police Officers (ACPO) on the commercial development of forensic science and fully support the initiative taken by David Coleman, Chair of ACPO Forensic Science sub-Committee. Given the circumstances that prevail in the MPS with respect to the relationship with forensic science providers, we are providing an additional response to that from ACPO.

2. Forensic science is a vital and important tool in tackling crime and the administration of justice. In the MPS many thousands of perpetrators of crime are identified each year through the application of forensic science, equally important many individuals are eliminated from criminal investigations. This contribution combined with fingerprints and other forensic services contributes to tackling a wide range of criminality for vehicle theft through homicide and serious crime to terrorism.

3. To bring a focus to this contribution the MPS has developed, and is implementing, a forensic strategy that has the aim to maximise the forensic opportunities arising from priority crime, deliver improvements in performance to support crime reduction and add to an understanding of criminality in London. This will be achieved through innovation, continuous improvement, efficient use of resources and demonstrating Best Value. We seek to integrate forensic science within the investigative process and deliver outcomes and benefits that support the achievement of MPS strategic objectives.

4. Central to this strategy is the recognition that a strategic shift has taken place in the use of forensic science following the development of forensic intelligence databases that identify suspects rather than provide evidence for the courts. This has required a step reduction in the time taken for the completion of forensic examinations to minimise the risk of re-offending and support crime reduction. These databases can also provide an insight into particular areas of criminality where there is a high forensic intervention rate and information that can be used to link criminal commodities such as illegal drugs and firearms. Forensic intelligence contributes to the operation of the National Intelligence Model (NIM) through coordinating and tasking and the formulation of strategic assessments. In London we face the added challenge of tackling crime that has significant international and organised dimensions. The establishment or growth in criminal networks in the communities in London argues for more effective and rapid "point to point" exchange of forensic data at an international level to tackle organised crime and terrorism.

5. The MPS has developed an approach to securing the provision of forensic science that aims to meet these challenges with the emphasis on improved timeliness while maintaining effectiveness and securing value for money. Within this approach we recognise that the evolving market place for forensic science provision offers opportunities to improve performance. Our experience to date is that by adopting a more business-like approach we have delivered significant benefits and performance improvements that were unlikely to have been achieved by other means.

MPS response to issue raised by the Science and Technology Committee

6. The likely impact of the Government plan to develop the Forensic Science Service (FSS) as a public private partnership (PPP) on the competitiveness of the FSS and on the effective provision of forensic science services to the criminal justice system.

7. Following the introduction of direct charging for forensic science services and the establishment of the FSS as a Executive Agency in 1991 a market has developed in the provision of forensic science services. Over the last 13 years the FSS has moved to Trading Fund status and in 1999 the MPS agreed to the merger of its Forensic Science Laboratory with the FSS. The Metropolitan Police Forensic Science Laboratory was a significant intellectual asset to the MPS.

8. The MPS is the major customer, if not a stakeholder, of the FSS with over twenty thousands cases submitted for forensic examination each year and a spend of around £35 million per annum. We have come late to the commercialisation of forensic science and it is only in the last three years we have sought to secure improved service delivery and more effective use of forensic science through a more accountable business relationship. This was against the background of the spend on forensic science services increasing by 59% over four years.

9. The MPS was the subject of a critical review carried out on behalf of the Mayor, the Metropolitan Police Authority (MPA) and the Commissioner that highlighted the lack of a clear and accountable business relationship with the FSS. The MPS had introduced a submission policy prior to this review but the findings prompted the development and implementation of a wider commercial strategy. This involved assessing the current level of market development, establishing clear requirements and entering into a procurement process to secure provision of forensic science services to the MPS. A great deal learnt in this exercise about the operation of the market for forensic science provision, the strengths and weaknesses of the three main providers and the challenge of securing services that meet the needs of investigators and the criminal justice system.

10. The MPS has identified the strategic drivers for forensic science provision as:

— *Intervention*: there is potential to increase the volume of forensic interventions across all areas of crime and generate more useful outcomes for investigators and the criminal justice system.

— *Timeliness*: forensic science is about identifying suspects as well as providing evidence for the courts, this means results are required in hours and days not weeks and months.

— *Intelligence*: the potential for forensic databases to provide intelligence in digital/electronic format will enable a more effective contribution to intelligence led policing and an understanding of criminality.

— *Innovation:* scientific innovation will challenge current service delivery models allowing front line staff to provide more rapid and effective results at reduced cost.

11. Based on these, an approach that regards forensic science as an integral part of an overall process, the need to have strategic alignment with MPS objectives, the need for an accountable business relationship and with the overriding aim of improving performance the MPA commercial strategy for forensic science was established with three objectives:

— to put the relationship with the FSS on a more robust commercial basis by agreeing a contract with improved service levels, pricing and governance;

— to stimulate the market for forensic science by competitively tendering certain limited packages of work; and

— to continue to improve the internal management of the use of forensic services.

12. The procurement exercise that formed part of the implementation of the commercial strategy resulted in the award of forensic science work from the MPS to three providers with a limited reduction in work sent to the FSS. The implementation of the commercial strategy has enabled the MPS to embed an authorisation process that allows more informed use of forensic science, to improve timeliness and better understand the effectiveness of DNA (success rates). The MPS has also developed requirements for specific initiatives and focussed forensic science on operational requirements such as middle market drugs activity. The spend has been brought under control and working with forensic science providers and academic establishments the MPS has initiated development work to establish in-house testing of DNA and drugs.

13. The MPS has acknowledged that a market place for forensic science provision is a reality but it is not well developed nor managed at a strategic level. The main providers have their roots in the public sector and limited private sector investment has been made. The FSS is at present a monopoly provider that has massive leverage over the market in terms of defining services, controlling access to key data in the forensic process and managing its own professional standards. This was reflected in its approach to the MPS procurement exercise and a reluctance to participate and even challenge the process. What is clear from the MPS experience is that the current situation and position of the FSS is unsustainable if the commercial development of forensic science is to continue. The MPS fully supports the work of ACPO to bring a more strategic approach to the management of the commercial development of forensic science in England and Wales.

14. In recognition of the current market development and the FSS position a regulatory and strategic framework needs to be established to manage the risks that capacity will be limited, consistency in service delivery will be lost, standards will not be upheld and barriers to entry will be such that new investment will not be forthcoming. This will also manage the risk that the FSS is not competitive or undermined by the growth of current and new providers. The PPP of itself is not a threat to the competitiveness of the FSS this is more to do with quality of the forensic science services delivered by the FSS and its ability to operate in a commercial environment. The effective and continued provision of high quality forensic science services to the criminal justice system is also unlikely to be directly affected by the PPP providing the FSS is able to come to terms with the commercial reality and most importantly there is independent and effective oversight of quality and standards in forensic science. The MPS experience in the implementation of the MPA commercial strategy reinforces and supports the view that the commercial development of forensic science is at a critical point and strategic and direct management of this is required.

15. *The quality of forensic science education and training and the supply of skilled personnel in forensic science.*

16. The MPS has increased the numbers of forensic staff who undertake roles such as crime scene and fingerprint examination and we find the media profile of forensic services is such that there are always large numbers of applicants most with a good academic background to degree level. However, as with forensic science the full range of forensic roles require experience and a range of qualities in addition to academic ability. Changes in technology and the profile of forensic services will require a greater range of skills for forensic staff in the MPS. The knowledge levels and awareness of all police and criminal justice personnel as a major enabler to the effective use of forensic science should not be underestimated. Raising awareness and ensuring that forensic science is used effectively is a critical part of building capability in the MPS.

17. There are many academic organisations that offer forensic science at degree level but the emphasis on practical and applied knowledge for forensic staff is such that academic studies can only be regarded as a starting point for most careers as a forensic practitioner. Having said this, there is some illogicality in the need for a science degree to undertake for example footwear and ballistics examination which require pattern recognition skills more akin to that of the fingerprint expert. Vocational training provides the basics and the MPS Crime Academy which incorporates a Forensic Faculty is a centre of excellence in the provision of training to forensic staff and investigators. The MPS recognises that the emphasis of training forensic staff must be on the achievement of competence rather than attending formal training events, and underpinned by a professional development programme to encourage lifelong learning. It will be critical that the MPS forensic workforce is flexible and has a wide skill base as some of the barriers between tradition roles breakdown and technology enables front line staff to carry out work that would have been previously undertaken in a laboratory. The MPS is seeking to establish career development pathways for forensic staff supported by a competency framework approach and professional development that will meet future needs, motivate staff, provide flexibility and allow the most effective use of technology.

18. The issue with the supply forensic staff for the MPS is not recruitment but retention; particularly as the roles are heavily experienced based and interpretational skills are built up over many years. The MPS has lost staff to the FSS as it expanded its business into other areas of forensic services such as fingerprint examination. This was the loss of a significant investment to the MPS but we acknowledge that there will be movement between organisations and agencies as staff seek career development opportunities and higher rewards. The greater cause for concern is that the salaries for forensic staff both within forensic science organisations and police forces are driven up by commercial development. The effective regulation of forensic science where market forces come into play should provide some degree of control alongside a balance between internal and external provision driven by the need to improve performance of core police functions and Best Value.

19. *The levels of investment in forensic science R&D.*

20. Most if not all developments in forensic science have their origins in other areas of endeavour such as medicine or defence. The scale of forensic science is such that a large research base is not feasible. Recent Home Office funding initiatives are welcomed by the MPS and the science and technology strategy provides a strategic framework for research activity. However, with the pace of technology change and the opportunities for criminals presented by new technology we need to reach out to industry and academic establishments to devise new approaches and products that will speed up and increase the range of forensic technologies used to tackle crime.

21. The commercial development of forensic science should provide the impetus for investment in more efficient forensic science services. The MPS is encouraging the development of new technology to bring routine DNA and evidential drug testing into the police environment. This will have significant operational and other benefits but will have significant disbenefits to forensic science providers unless they can adapt and provide a range of enabling services to police forces.

22. *The use of novel forensic technologies by the FSS and the criminal justice system.*

23. We have already referred to our interest in new technology that could bring routine DNA and evidential drug testing into the police environment. This would speed up the processing of prisoners and in the case of DNA potentially provide the equivalent of "Livescan for DNA" where the DNA profile of a person in custody could be checked against the National DNA Database. With over two hundred thousand unmatched crime stains on the database this represents a significant opportunity to solve crime.

24. The main areas of science and technology that have novel applications in forensic services are the analytical sciences and digital technology. There is the potential to bring the laboratory to the crime scene or at least into the police environment and the use of computing technology and databases allows for forensic services to contribute to intelligence led policing and provide more effective evidence in court. The example given of DNA analysis in custody would have a significant effect on the current market for forensic science services and such a strategic shift will need to be managed if stability and the full benefits of science and technology are to be realised. On this note we would also wish to ensure that intellectual property currently owned by the Home Secretary is used to public good and not exploited in such a way that limits access by police forces or reinforces the monopoly position of a privatised FSS. The same would apply to the ownership, access and use of forensic data that forms the basis for forensic intelligence databases, it is critical to the future development of forensic science that this data is publicly held and securely available to all law enforcement agencies.

25. *The use of forensic science in criminal investigations and court proceedings and the extent to which shortcomings in forensic science have affected the administration of justice.*

26. Forensic services in general and forensic science in particular are major contributors to tackling crime. The standards to which forensic work is undertaken and the competence and integrity of the staff are vital to this contribution. It must also be recognised that much of forensic science is accepted and regarded as sound within the criminal justice process. A major error or loss of confidence would have significant implications not just for justice but the effective operation of the courts. If, for example, bulk analysis such as DNA profiling or alcohol analysis in Road Traffic Act cases were discredited then the cost of failure and disruption would run into millions of pounds.

27. The external accreditation of forensic science laboratories to ISO and UKAS standards and the increasing registration of forensic practitioners provide two key elements in assuring quality and competence. However, there is no strategic oversight or body that looks at quality and standards as a whole within what is the emerging forensic industry. The MPS commercial strategy and some recent experiences have highlighted this as a significant gap and the need for clarity in processes to deal with expert evidence that is called into question

CONCLUDING REMARKS

28. We have highlighted the important and critical contribution that forensic science makes to tackling crime in London through the identification of offenders, informing an understanding of criminality and providing evidence to the courts. The commercial development of forensic science offers many opportunities to improve the contribution of forensic science but comes with some significant risks. We believe that the strategic management of the commercial development of forensic science will deliver benefits, minimise risk to the MPS and support us make London a safer place.

October 2004

APPENDIX 5

Memorandum from Forensic Alliance Limited

EXECUTIVE SUMMARY

1. The FSS's move to agency status effectively initiated the market in forensic science.

2. This has already brought a raft of benefits to the criminal justice system including improvements in timeliness, reductions in cost, and increased innovation.

3. But to maximise available opportunities the playing field needs levelling. This could be assisted by developing the FSS as a PPP.

4. Becoming a PPP would require the FSS to relinquish:

— its custodianship of National forensic databases to an independent Custodian; and

— its role as sole Government advisor on forensic science. perhaps to a Forensic Science Advisory Panel including all (three) main forensic science providers.

5. The burgeoning number of university degree courses featuring forensic science does little to improve the supply of skilled forensic scientists. Training is still entirely dependent upon the main service providers.

6. Government should continue to invest heavily in forensic science R&D but funds should be centrally administered and coordinated—perhaps by the Forensic Science Advisory Panel.

7. The market will continue to drive the exploration of new technology. Its introduction into casework might be regulated at least in part through the new forensic databases Custodian.

8. Shortcomings in forensic science have centred on the presentation of unsafe evidence, and lack of timeliness in service delivery. The latter will be resolved by market forces. The former is best dealt with through second opinions commissioned by the defence, but this must be properly funded or risks of miscarriage will persist.

9. A system for accrediting laboratories to forensic standards should be considered—to augment scientist accreditation and as part of a proper regulatory framework for the sector.

10. An attempt has been made to lay to rest a number of popular myths about private forensic science.

INTRODUCTION

11. Forensic Alliance Limited (FAL) is a private Company and one of only two providers of full forensic science services in England and Wales—the other being the Forensic Science Service (FSS).

12. On the basis that, as Sir Winston Churchill put it "the farther backwards you can look, the farther forwards you are likely to see", this submission briefly rehearses the history of private provision of forensic science services. It goes on to comment on each of the topics that the Science and Technology Committee has identified. It then lays to rest some popular myths about private forensic science in general and FAL in particular before, finally, making some recommendations for the way forward.

HISTORY OF PRIVATE FORENSIC SCIENCE

13. Private forensic science services have been available for many years. In criminal cases they were historically focused mainly on the needs of defence teams because the large majority of the police/prosecution's requirements were met by the Forensic Science Service (FSS). Notionally the FSS was accessible by the defence too, but this was not a popular option since requests for work, and results emerging from it, were channelled through police.

14. Exceptionally, and reflecting its historic position in Government, the Laboratory of the Government Chemist (LGC) carried out mainly drugs and questioned documents work for HM Customs and Excise.

15. In 1991, the FSS became a government agency ending its prerogative as supplier of forensic services to police. The LGC exploited the new opportunities this presented and extended services to the police too. Albeit on a limited front, competition had arrived. The first tangible benefit to police was a sharp reduction in the price of drugs testing.

16. In 1995, the Government established the National DNA Database with the FSS as Custodian. The LGC moved into limited DNA testing for police, and introduced toxicological analyses too. A management buy-out supported by 3is and the Royal Society of Chemistry saw privatisation of the LGC and marked the start of real competition for the FSS from the private sector.

17. In 1997, and in response to pressure from police and scientists alike, FAL was established. It was then and is still the only full service alternative to the FSS (see Annex for details). The Company quickly established an enviable reputation for innovative, high quality work and continues to make strong and steady growth. FAL and, in its restricted way, the LGC have captured approximately 15% of the forensic market. A few much smaller, niche providers have also emerged. Private sector forensic science is well established and thriving.

18. The emergence of competition has benefited the criminal justice system by:

— improving timeliness of forensic services and, connected with this;

— substantially expanding the national pool of forensic scientists;

— reducing the cost of some services;

— extending the breadth and depth of forensic science expertise;

— stimulating innovative approaches and methodologies;

— extending the range and scope of forensic research and development; and

— providing the police with choice of supplier.

The likely impact of the Government plan to develop the FSS as a PPP and on the effective provision of forensic science services to the criminal justice system

19. Turning the FSS into a government agency initiated competition in forensic science and produced the raft of benefits to the criminal justice system outlined above. To maximise these benefits there needs to be a levelling of the playing field between providers. Developing the FSS as a PPP would be a simple way to achieve this, by removing the substantial influence and commercial advantage that the FSS currently enjoys over other suppliers while providing it with the greater financial and commercial freedoms of the private sector.

20. As a PPP, the FSS would necessarily have to relinquish its roles as Custodian of National forensic databases, and sole advisor to Government on forensic science matters. The Custodian should be made transparently independent of all suppliers. The advisor role might best be transferred to a Forensic Science Advisory Panel—including all main forensic science providers, and which could serve a number of other functions too.

21. Importantly, such equality of terms might encourage investment in forensic science both by existing providers and new ones. This would invigorate the market and widen the range and choice of services available to the criminal justice system. It is perhaps no coincidence that FAL is the only new provider to enter the emergent forensic science market in the 13 years of its existence, and that it did so for mainly professional, not commercial reasons. Use of formal tenders has already given police forces the advantages of choice between suppliers and has reduced the commercial impact of the FSS becoming a PPP.

The quality of forensic science education and training and the supply of skilled personnel in forensic science

22. The media portray forensic science as an attractive topic, reflected in its popularity as a subject for study at university. Universities have been quick to exploit this, both to keep unfashionable but important subjects such as chemistry in their prospectuses and to help meet ambitious Government targets for university attendance. There are now several hundred courses across the Country featuring forensic science.

23. Very few of these courses make any significant contribution to the training that students require to practise. Indeed, there is increasing evidence that the teaching of pure science is compromised for pseudo forensic science. Recognising that they will have to provide virtually all the necessary training themselves, forensic science employers tend to prefer new recruits with pure science degrees over forensic ones. This runs counter to student expectations.

24. In addition to training, FAL has increased the national pool of skilled scientists by overseas recruitment.

The levels of investment in forensic science research and development

25. There are currently three main sources of funding for R&D in forensic science, namely:
   — direct grants from the Home Office for specific operational projects;
   — other grants from Government via, for example, the research councils; and
   — investment in R&D by supplier organisations themselves.

26. The FSS continues to be the traditional recipient of direct grants from the Home Office reflecting its historical position embedded in government. Although some of this money might technically now be available to other organisations, the FSS, as Government advisor, would automatically scrutinise bids. This generates concerns that ideas might be either hi-jacked by the FSS or, conceivably, dismissed if the FSS felt unable to support operational opportunities flowing from them.

27. Other grants from government come variously from the EPSRC ("Think Crime" initiative), NERC, DTI and from Europe. They involve collaborations with universities and/or other bodies and are all highly competitive. Again, the FSS can exert influence through their reviewing function.

28. Regarding supplier self-funded R&D, FAL currently invests 3% of revenue in a vigorous programme of internal projects and other, more ambitious ones in collaboration with a range of partners. Projects cover all aspects of forensic science from continuing method development for immediate improvements in service delivery, to medium to longer term initiatives involving both novel approaches, and the development of new instrumentation, software and consumables.

29. To make best use of funding—regardless of source, avoid unnecessary duplication of effort and ensure that resources are objectively targeted, there should be a centrally administered R&D programme—preferably through the auspices of the sort of Advisory Panel referred to earlier.

The use of novel forensic technologies by the FSS and criminal justice system

30. To be really effective as a relatively small specialism, forensic science has to rely to a large extent on advances in the wider scientific community. DNA profiling is an excellent example of an academic breakthrough which found widespread application in forensic science.

31. The FSS has made a significant contribution to the development of forensic techniques but it would be wrong to suppose that it had been behind all advances in UK forensic science or that it is necessarily the most likely source of future innovation.

32. For instance it was Cellmark—FAL's dedicated DNA profilers, who took the first forensic DNA case through the courts and who trained many FSS scientists in early DNA techniques. Similarly, it is Cellmark through FAL who is now pioneering the use in casework of the next generation of forensic DNA techniques—Single Nucleotide Polymorphisms (SNPs).

33. Like the LGC, Cellmark provides DNA analysis to markets other than forensic science and when synergies in operations and R&D can be usefully exploited in more than one direction.

34. The forensic science market is adding fresh impetus to the drive to invent and discover new technologies, but they must be fit for purpose. As the number of forensic science databases grows, so the Custodian role will expand, capturing and regulating an increasing number of technologies underpinning the data.

35. Importantly, not all advances stem directly from novel technology; while this is critically important, so too are imaginative new approaches using existing technology.

The use of forensic science in criminal investigations and court proceedings and the extent to which shortcomings in forensic science have affected the administration of justice

36. Forensic science provides the criminal justice system with an increasingly powerful tool for clarifying disputed matters, but shortcomings in it have occasionally adversely affected the administration of justice. These have been mainly associated with the presentation of what has later been discovered to be unsafe evidence, and late delivery of results which has effectively denied some courts scientific objectivity.

37. Competition in the market place should continue to reduce case turnround times so that timeliness should cease to be an issue, but it is important that there is a clear understanding of the interrelationship between timeliness, cost and quality so that service delivery requirements can be formulated on an informed basis.

38. Reliable laboratories have elaborate quality management systems which can be audited against National standards. These provide some safeguards but do not guarantee that evidence is automatically safe and sustainable. As new forensic science providers emerge, this is likely to become an increasingly important issue. The whole question of laboratory accreditation for criminal justice purposes should be properly tackled, perhaps through an extension of the database Custodian function, or the appointment of a Forensic Regulator or, conceivably, through The Council for the Registration of Forensic Practitioners (CRFP) which is already performing the vital analogous function of accrediting individual practitioners.

39. Currently the most likely reason for forensic science to prove unreliable is when findings are interpreted out of context, usually when the scientist offering expert opinion is not in full possession of all relevant facts. The position may become more complex if, as the forensic science market expands, scientific input is fragmented between suppliers.

40. The best safeguard against this—especially where forensic science evidence is likely to prove central to conviction, continues to be through second opinions commissioned by the defence. Historically, funding for such opinions has been poor and the work has been awarded on the basis of the lowest quote—a disastrous policy especially before CRFP accreditation has a chance to bite.

Exploding myths about private forensic science

41. Ever since FAL was established, a number of myths have been circulated about the Company in particular and private forensic science in general. It is high time these were formally laid to rest. They include:

42. *Myth*

FAL "cherry picks" its work, selecting only the most profitable lines and leaving the unprofitable ones for the FSS to pick up.

Reality

From inception, FAL has provided comprehensive services and police forces have been free to access these as they choose. Some prefer FAL to service geographical areas, taking everything that comes, while others choose to give the Company specific types of casework.

43. *Myth*

The FSS is the only training ground for forensic scientists and FAL simply recruits its scientists fully trained at the FSS expense.

Reality

Only 18 months after FAL became fully operational, it started to take raw recruits for training. It now has an advanced training facility running carefully structured courses covering all scientific aspects of forensic science, crime scene investigation and court work. It has trained 25% of its staff from scratch and augmented the training of many others.

44. *Myth*

The FSS is the only forensic science provider engaged in forensic R&D and any work transferred to other suppliers would endanger the research programme

Reality

FAL invests heavily in a vigorous and imaginative R&D programme which is enriched by similar efforts by its DNA profiling partner, Orchid Cellmark. This has already made a large impact on day-to-day operations and contributed to services not currently available from any other provider.

45. *Myth*

FAL recruits forensic scientists from overseas who are less competent than home grown ones.

Reality

Every country has a slightly different approach to providing forensic science services but increasing globalisation ensures that core competencies are roughly comparable. Moreover, overseas scientists bring other expertise and experience which enrich the scientific culture here and contribute to establishment of best practice.

46. *Myth*

FAL pays higher salaries as the only way to attract scientists from other organisations.

Reality

FAL is at a substantial disadvantage particularly compared to the FSS which currently has a very generous Civil Service based pension scheme. FAL merely aims to bring its total employment package as near to this as possible so staff are not unduly disadvantaged.

47. *Myth*

FAL's main driver is to make profits for its financial backers.

Reality

FAL's prices are similar to those charged by the FSS and LGC because it faces similar costs. Aside from gradually paying off the debt incurred in establishing the Company, FAL ploughs back all profits into its operations; it has not paid dividends to any shareholder. This is directly analogous to the FSS as a Trading Fund paying a dividend on public dividend capital.

RECOMMENDATIONS

48. The playing field in the emergent forensic science market place should be levelled, and developing the FSS as a PPP would seem to be a good way of achieving this.

49. Operational responsibility for all National forensic databases should be transferred to a Custodian transparently independent of any supplier of forensic science services.

50. To improve and maintain confidence in the safety and sustainability of forensic science evidence, laboratories and not just the scientists in them should be specifically accredited for the purpose. This requires a proper regulatory framework involving the forensic databases Custodian, the CRFP and, conceivably, a Forensic Science Regulator.

51. A Forensic Science Advisory Panel including but not limited to the main forensic providers, should replace the FSS as the source of forensic science advice to Government. The panel should also direct Government funding for R&D.

October 2004

Annex

Forensic Alliance Limited—Company profile

52. Forensic Alliance (FAL) was established in 1997 in response to pressure from police for more responsive forensic services, and from forensic scientists for a more supportive, science focused working environment. It achieved early successes with a number of difficult unresolved cases and this contributed to its now substantial and enviable reputation for solving the unsolvable.

53. FAL has 170 staff (plus 80 dedicated DNA profilers in its partner Company—Orchid Cellmark), and laboratories at Culham (Oxford) and Risley (Warrington). It is opening new laboratories in Tamworth, and an advanced firearms facility at Leeds with the Royal Armouries.

54. The Company provides an extended range of forensic services including all traditional ones and the wholly new discipline of forensic ecology, and it is moving towards integrated forensic science and forensic pathology through a powerful initiative with the largest group of UK forensic pathologists.

55. Forensic Alliance has served most police forces in England and Wales, currently providing routine services to fifteen of them on a geographical, or case-type-specific basis. For instance, it provides for all forensic science needs of the Thames Valley Police, the larger geographical part of Merseyside, and a third of homicides and half of crime scene DNA testing for the Metropolitan Police.

56. The Company is privately owned and backed financially by City bankers, Close Brothers and Lloyds TSB.

APPENDIX 6

Memorandum from Prospect and the Public and Commercial Services Union (PCS)

1. INTRODUCTION

1.1 Forensic Science is a highly specialised field and entry to the market for forensic services is difficult, requiring significant investment in laboratories and recruitment of specialist staff. For these reasons, the market is immature and likely to remain so with relatively few suppliers and relatively few customers. Its primary function is to operate as an arm of the Criminal Justice System to assist in ensuring that offenders are convicted and the innocent are exonerated. The Forensic Science Service (FSS) currently has about 90% of the forensic market outside of the work traditionally carried out by police staff. Its main competitors are Forensic Alliance, which arose from the closure of the FSS laboratory at Aldermaston and targets trained FSS staff for its recruitment, and LGC, which provides evidence examination limited to DNA, drugs and documents, and was itself previously part of the public sector. How this competitive market might develop is a matter for conjecture.

1.2 The FSS undertakes a wide range of work at crime scenes and at the laboratory, aiming to provide intelligence information and evidential material to the investigative team. The lists provided below are not exhaustive.

Scene work includes:

— the interpretation of murder/assault scenes including the assessment of the distribution and pattern of blood staining;

— the enhancement and retrieval of marks at serious crime scenes;

— the examination of suspicious fire scenes to determine the likely cause;

— the assessment of illicit drug production facilities.

Laboratory work includes:

— the comparison of marks left at scenes with questioned footwear, tools or, sometimes, a suspect's fingerprints;

— the examination of items for the presence of body fluids, the retrieval and analysis of any present and the comparison with samples from suspects or victims, including DNA testing;

— the recovery of particulate material, such as paint or glass, from suspects and their comparison with control samples from crime scenes;

— fibre transfer investigations;

— the analysis of drugs and comparison of packaged drugs with packaging materials and bulk drugs seizures;

— the analysis of body fluids and organs to determine the presence or absence of drugs or their metabolites;

— the examination and comparison of firearms and ammunition;

— the examination of documents and related work such as handwriting comparisons.

2. The Development of Competition

2.1 In our view, if competition develops in each of these fields it will do so at different rates. New entrants to the market may be attracted by straightforward work where there is potential for profit and fairly limited investment in equipment or staff training needs (eg DNA testing), but work which is interpretative, labour intensive or requires extensive training (eg work at crime scenes and the provision of expert testimony in Court) may not be so attractive to new entrants. In addition smaller suppliers may be less responsive to fluctuations in demand.

2.2 PPP will create a new private sector classified Company with a controlling 51%–75% of the shares owned by the private sector "partner". Assuming it is sold as a single entity, FSS plc will already have 90% of the forensic market in England and Wales. With full commercial freedom, it will be able to determine its pricing policy according to the competition and the need to make a return for its investors. It will also need opportunities for expansion if it is to attract investors. We believe the natural consequences of becoming a commercial body with a near-monopoly are as follows:

(1) Where there is effective competition (eg DNA or drugs testing) prices will be held down to a competitive level. Indeed, the Company may behave aggressively towards the competition in order to retain or increase its market share.

(2) On low profit items (eg firearms) where there is only limited competition, prices to the customer (primarily police forces) will go up considerably so the FSS fully meets its costs and can make a surplus. In order to keep down their own costs, police forces may have no option but to reduce the amount of evidence sent for analysis.

(3) Free advice given over the phone prior to the submission of evidence would have to be charged for.

(4) In order to be able to budget and control its costs, the FSS would have to be allowed to refuse work, as its competitors already do.

(5) External training given to customers, which currently is cost-neutral, would have a profit element introduced

2.3 Once the FSS has to satisfy its shareholders and investors, profit will inevitably become the driving force. At present, as a Trading Fund, increases in charges across the board are restricted by a Home Office target to 75% of the Average Earnings Index. We have seen no suggestion that any restrictions on pricing levels would be maintained if the FSS became Private Sector classified. It is fair to assume, therefore, that it would be free to charge whatever the market would bear.

2.4 Since the introduction of charging for forensic work police have had to balance their budgetary constraints against the potential for forensic tests to yield significant evidential/intelligence information. The ability of a near-monopoly supplier to set its own charges would inevitably lead to a shift in this balance, with a greater emphasis on budgetary concerns. The most likely consequence of this would be to limit the number of submissions to forensic suppliers, and, as a result, potentially vital evidential material might not be submitted. As it could take only one piece of evidence, not submitted for analysis, to make the difference to an offender remaining at large, or an innocent person being convicted, the potential consequences of this are only too obvious.

2.5 The degree to which this happens will depend to a certain extent upon the kind of investor attracted to become a "partner" in the FSS. The main interest so far has been from venture capitalists, who are more likely to be interested in a short-term gain on their investment than a long-term commitment to forensic science.

2.6 Longer-term considerations also are of concern. Competition developing at different rates in different fields means that a future Company may decide to sell one or more areas of its work, thereby splitting up the organisation and losing the valuable liaison that currently takes place within and between laboratories. Information is not likely to be shared between Companies, and the consequence would be a loss of communication and a reduction in shared intelligence. Such liaison is crucial, as was highlighted in the M25 serial rapist case, when more than 100 scientists and support staff from five of the FSS's laboratories were involved in carrying out work for six police forces.

2.7 This vital co-operation may also be put at risk where smaller companies enter the market place. Prospect and PCS feel that, in order to provide the best possible service to the Criminal Justice System, there should be a national policy with national standards providing a fully integrated service with full access to all databases, independent of the police.

3. Research and Development

3.1 Recent FSS research has been directly funded by the U.S. Department of Army Technical Support Working Group, the Science Policy Unit of the Home Office and indirectly through academic collaborations via the Engineering and Physical Science Research Council. Current Government status excludes the FSS from applying for some funding schemes but includes it within others (eg Public Sector Research Exploitation Fund). Whilst a change of status might open new opportunities for funding research it could also restrict access to current sources of funding.

3.2 When part of the MoD was privatised as QinetiQ, most of its Corporate Research was directed towards areas involving co-operation with Defence Departments in other countries. They cannot co-operate in the same way now with the USA but have to do so through another Government Agency. The FSS could encounter similar problems if it was no longer part of a Government body. In addition, the QinetiQ experience shows that DTI funding for their civil aerospace related research has reduced from 100% to zero. DTI can fund 50% of research at a private Company but only providing the Company can match the amount. QinetiQ have been unable to find a source of funding to match it and so have lost the DTI funding. The future arrangements for the funding of FSS research are unclear, but these rules would also apply to them as a private Company.

3.3 As the FSS is a Government Agency the Director is a member of the European Network of Forensic Science Institutes. This permits FSS scientists to sit on the Expert Working Group committees. The aims of the Expert Working Groups are "exchanging information and expertise, combining research activities, international access to data, promoting quality by proficiency testing and best practice manuals". Based on current ENFSI rules, there are no private organisations that are full members. Therefore, the FSS membership could be in question should it move into the private sector. Losing full membership would exclude scientists from sitting on these committees and would be detrimental to the scientific development of the FSS.

3.4 As a trading fund the FSS has targets set with respect to investment in research and development including a requirement to invest 11% of turnover in development and the generation of £1 million of external funding. As a private sector company the FSS will no longer need to comply with these targets.

4. THE USE OF NOVEL FORENSIC TECHNOLOGIES

4.1 The rapid growth in the forensic market since the mid 1990's has been largely the result of the development of DNA testing. The FSS has, and continues to, lead the world in forensic developments within this field, including the recent developments in the automation of the DNA process, increasing the sensitivity of DNA testing, and the examination and interpretation of DNA for indications of physical characteristics and ethnicity. The fact that this cutting edge research continues to be performed and integrated into the criminal justice system by the FSS, and not by its competitors, is evidence to refute the assertion made in the McFarland report (which initially recommended PPP) that the status of the FSS places it at a disadvantage to its competitors in researching new forensic techniques.

4.2 The FSS acknowledges that "the next DNA" needs to be found to enable it to remain at the forefront of research. The FSS is seriously investigating the possibilities of nanotechnology and a paper entitled Nanoforensics: a Vision of the Future will be presented to a forthcoming conference at the Royal Society.

4.3 FSS staff have been the inventors of several patents. Most recently a micro device that can recover and concentrate a sample from a surface, and also a novel use of pre-humidification to enhance the fingermarks visualised with latent print developer. The latter invention has added value to the service provided by the Specialist Location and Recovery unit, developing fingermarks that would previously not have been visualised at such an early stage in the forensic process.

4.4 Searches of the Internet journal database "the Web of Science" showed that in the years 2000–04 FSS staff have authored or been co-authors of 84 scientific papers. These papers have been cited a total of 300 times. One key paper, the validation of the DNA technique SGM + has been cited 36 times in four years. In the same time period Forensic Alliance have published only six scientific papers, only one of which has been cited and then only once.

5. TRAINING

5.1 A degree in Forensic Science or a related subject does not make a forensic scientist. Training of a new court-going officer in one discipline takes around 12 months. However, "on the job" development is then required, involving intensive support and mentoring from senior colleagues. It is impossible to put a timescale on this as it will depend on the person and the discipline(s) in which they are training.

5.2 The majority of active forensic scientists within England and Wales were trained at an FSS laboratory. At the end of September 2004 over 80% of scientists registered as Forensic Practitioners by the Council for the Registration of Forensic Practitioners were trained at an FSS laboratory. Of those scientists registered as Forensic Practitioners in human contact traces to provide expert testimony in biology/DNA evidence approximately 94% received their training at an FSS laboratory.

5.3 Additionally the FSS carries out a significant amount of training for police officers. In the financial year 2003–04 the FSS delivered over 450 courses to over 50 police forces/other bodies, training officers of all ranks.

6. Regulation

6.1 Currently the FSS security clears all staff to a minimum of Counter Terrorist Level as work is often highly sensitive including organised crime, terrorism and internal police investigations. As a private organisation there would not necessarily be the requirement to security clear all staff; in fact the McFarland report cited the delay in recruitment caused by security clearance as one of the "burdens" which would be removed from the FSS as a PPP. Therefore, as a result of the PPP, the UK could be faced with the prospect of having non-governmental and non-security cleared staff processing some of the most sensitive criminal and intelligence information in the UK.

6.2 Although the relatively recently established Council for the Registration of Forensic Practitioners should eliminate rogue forensic scientists, by setting minimum standards for individual registration, it is not a regulator. There is currently no regulation of the forensic marketplace in respect to training, or the use of new and novel scientific processes. The FSS as a Government Agency has effectively acted as a governmental regulator for forensic science by carrying out the training and internal accreditation of staff, holding down prices, and ensuring that new scientific techniques are rigorously tested. This lack of regulation in an entirely private sector part of the Criminal Justice System, with a monopoly supplier, would be untenable.

7. Conclusion

7.1 The creation of a PPP will not transfer risk to the private sector, because if the Company were to fail financially, the Government would be forced to step in for the benefit of the Criminal Justice System.

7.2 As a PPP, the Government would be a minority shareholder and will not have a controlling influence. Neither will other stakeholders have any say in how the Company is run, unless they themselves become shareholders. This we believe is a step too far for forensic science.

7.3 It could also impact on the provision of forensic services in Scotland and Northern Ireland. Although the current proposal affects only England and Wales, there will be nothing to prevent a private sector UK company competing for business in Scotland and Northern Ireland, and indeed they may well want to do so as a means of expanding the Company.

7.4 To meet the concerns we have over PPP, but also to try to meet the Government's objectives, Prospect and PCS have looked at alternative models and have proposed an Independent Publicly Owned Corporation (IPOC). Under this model, the Government would be the sole shareholder and all stakeholders would have an input to decisions on the long-term strategic direction of the FSS, and the setting of investment, efficiency, equity and performance targets.

7.5 Ministers have consistently praised the FSS. In 1999 Paul Boateng, then a Home Office minister, said: "We have a forensic service which we are proud of and it is widely regarded as a market leader in the way it meets ever demanding challenges. Its contribution is key to the delivery of justice through effective and efficient investigations." Former Northern Ireland Secretary, Mo Mowlam said: "The FSS is well known as a world leader in the forensic DNA field. I am grateful to their expertise."

7.6 Any structural changes must not put this at risk.

Executive Summary

(1) The Forensic Science Service currently has 90% of the forensic market and undertakes a wide range of work at crime scenes and at the laboratory. Competition in this market will develop at different rates in different fields, with new investors only being attracted by work where there is potential for profit and fairly limited investment and training needs.

(2) In a PPP, the controlling shareholder interest would be held by a private sector "partner". With full commercial freedom the new Company would be able to set charges for all its work, reflecting the level of competition, and building in a return for shareholders. A large increase in charges would strain the budgets of police forces so that potentially vital evidential material might not be submitted for analysis.

(3) Valuable liaison within and between laboratories would be lost if the Company were later to be sold on in its different parts.

(4) Future funding for research, and continued participation in European Expert Working Group committees, are matters which are unclear in a PPP structure.

(5) The rapid growth in the forensic market is largely due to DNA testing. The FSS leads the world in further developing the use of DNA. The FSS also acknowledges that "the next DNA" needs to be found, and is seriously investigating the possibilities of nanotechnology. The quality of FSS research is demonstrated by the publication of 84 scientific papers in four years, which have been cited 300 times.

(6) The majority of active forensic scientists in England and Wales were trained at an FSS laboratory. Initial training takes 12 months, but this is followed by a sustained period of intensive support and mentoring from colleagues. The FSS also trains police officers of all ranks.

(7) Currently the FSS effectively acts as a governmental regulator for forensic science by carrying out the training and internal accreditation of staff, holding down prices, and ensuring new scientific techniques are rigorously tested. The lack of any regulation over an entirely private sector market would be untenable.

(8) The Unions have put forward their own proposals for an Independent Publicly Owned Company, to meet our concerns about the impact of a PPP.

November 2004

APPENDIX 7

Memorandum from LGC

Following the Government's announcement of the decision to develop the Forensic Science Service (FSS) as a public-private partnership (PPP), the Select Committee has requested interested parties to comment on a number of key issues.

INTRODUCTION

1. As the UK's leading private sector supplier of forensic services, with a current turnover in the forensic business sector of approximately £12 million per annum, LGC has a major interest in the transition of the FSS into the private sector. We welcome the Government's overall decision, and the advantages that this should offer in the development of an open and competitive forensic market, but there are a number of aspects that we consider will need to be handled with care to sustain the (currently embryonic) development of a real forensic market. In particular, the FSS's current dominance of the forensic market (with a market share of 85% to 90%) means that opening of the market to other suppliers will need to be overseen by an independent body to ensure that the national interest is best served. In addition, the FSS's traditional position as both scientific advisors to their parent department, the Home Office, and custodian of national forensic intelligence resources, such as the National DNA Database, mean that careful separation of the commercial and strategic (national interest) functions of the FSS will be vital.

2. The market structure that has developed in England and Wales for forensic DNA service provision is an example to the rest of the world of what can be achieved. This now involves three major laboratories, competing with each other on service provision, all feeding results into a central database function. This competitive approach has delivered spectacular benefits to police forces, and the resulting expanded capacity, lower costs and faster turn rounds mean that England and Wales now lead the world in the application of forensic DNA testing. Meanwhile, rigorous application of national quality standards to all suppliers has safeguarded the integrity of the central database. We regard this "competition within standards" model as widely applicable within other forensic activities and key to the Government's requirement for maximising the benefits obtainable from the application of forensic techniques, within realistic budgetary constraints.

3. LGC wish to see the FSS established as a commercial supplier, in competition with other suppliers, within a market where national assets, such as intelligence databases, and the quality standards of the forensic "industry" are overseen by an independent custodian.

The five key issues on which the Select Committee has particularly invited comment are as follows:

Q.1 *The likely impact of the Government plan to develop the FSS as a PPP on the competitiveness of the FSS and on the effective provision of forensic science services to the CJS*

4. Market pressures have already obliged the FSS to become more competitive in order to survive in the new commercial environment and, in recent years, its service performance has improved significantly. There are additional freedoms to private sector organisations, particularly in aspects such as sources of investment, of which the FSS now wishes to take advantage.

5. There are, however, functions of the current FSS which clearly should not move into the private sector, as they involve issues such as standard setting and regulation of the forensic "industry". These functions must be operated independently and in the national interest.

6. The FSS is currently a near-monopoly supplier, with 85% to 90 % of the market. The ideal future structure is a flexible, responsive market with adequate capacity available to meet the expected continuing growth in demand for forensic services (independently estimated at around 8% per year). For other suppliers, and potential suppliers, to be encouraged to make the investments necessary to enter the market and to commit to the research and development necessary continually to improve service provision, they must be confident that the privatised FSS will be treated as one supplier among others.

7. When matters relating to forensic science arise, government bodies, such as the Home Office and the Crown Prosecution Service, routinely approach the FSS to negotiate, trial and agree new working systems on behalf of all forensic suppliers. Other suppliers are usually only informed when the new approach has been agreed. Once the FSS enters the commercial sector, we would wish to see a more open approach adopted. This should involve the independent authority ("forensic custodian") established to oversee the forensic industry, who could then instigate a wider consultative process.

8. The main customers for forensic services are the various police forces within England and Wales. As the forces are encouraged by ACPO's new forensic procurement initiative to move to competitive tendering on a national or regional basis, continuing with a "winner takes all" approach to awarding long-term multi-force contracts could rapidly destroy the market. A more viable approach would be to award such large contracts on a "split" basis, with, for example, a guaranteed 25% of a work type being awarded to each of two suppliers, and the remaining 50% then being switched between the two, based on their available capacity and demonstrated performance, including turn round times and service quality. This approach ensures that suppliers are encouraged to remain in the market and invest in service development, while encouraging both winning suppliers to continue to compete with each other to provide optimum services to try to increase their market shares.

9. The key to maintaining a healthy and expanding forensic market while the FSS changes status will be a strategy intended to develop a playing field which is demonstrably level. A national "forensic custodian" to oversee the market's operation and act as a central point for consultation, information and standard setting will be a vital component of this process. ACPO's developing initiative to support forensic tendering will need to ensure that a competitive market is preserved and encouraged.

Q.2 *The quality of forensic science education & training, and the supply of skilled personnel*

10. Forensic science is a system of working, rather than a separate scientific discipline. It involves using scientific techniques that can be demonstrated to be reliable and that are expected to be subject, and robust, to challenge. Additionally, forensic evidence has to be presented in a form which meets all legal requirements, including that for appropriate disclosure. Forensic scientists then have to be prepared and able to present their evidence in court, if required.

11. LGC's Forensic Division recruits scientists both externally and internally (that is, from other, non-forensic, areas of our business) and then trains them in forensic methodology, rather than routinely "poaching" trained forensic staff from other forensic laboratories. We are therefore expanding the overall resources available to service users. There is, however, some movement of staff, both into and out of LGC, as individuals move between suppliers to enhance their careers within forensic science. In addition, where new services are being established, it is usually necessary to recruit a few key individuals with the necessary skills to form the core of new businesses.

12. It has been LGC's experience that, for laboratories moving from the public to the private sector, there is also a requirement to employ individuals with commercial skills, such as marketing and sales, not least to ensure that services are truly focussed on customer needs, rather than available technologies.

13. The expansion of DNA service provision in recent years, mainly driven by the Government's DNA Expansion Plan, has resulted in a very rapid growth of the number of people employed in the forensic science laboratories. Many of these joined as new graduates, particularly from the biological sciences, and the effect is that the DNA laboratories, which now represent the majority of staff within the forensic service suppliers, are primarily staffed by younger people. Meanwhile, there are continuing moves to automate forensic processes, partly to reduce costs, but also to reduce analysis times. These influences are likely to result in limited career opportunities for this large intake of forensic scientists and a reducing requirement for future recruits.

14. However, the universities now offer several hundred different courses involving forensic science. These appear to be designed more to attract students by offering an attractive and interesting subject than to meet the needs of the laboratories. The number of students undertaking these courses vastly exceeds the future manpower needs of the forensic laboratories. Given the limited number of experienced forensic practitioners within the UK, we have concerns about the expertise of many of those who are teaching these courses and we regard only a few of the courses as being credible.

15. Most forensic training is via "apprenticeship" training within the forensic laboratories and experienced forensic practitioners are highly valued. The focus in universities should be on a more limited number of high quality courses.

Q.3 *The levels of investment in forensic science R&D*

16. The Home Office has traditionally regarded their main source of advice on forensic R&D priorities and requirements as the FSS and they have, not surprisingly, routed the majority of their funding for forensic development into the FSS. However, the Home Office's evolving policy, as set out in the Police Science and Technology Strategy, indicates that a broader consultation and range of research providers is

to be sought. At the same time, the police, through ACPO, have indicated their intention to become more "intelligent customers", setting the agenda on what their requirements are, rather than waiting for suppliers to offer them new products. We welcome these developments.

17. The establishment of the FSS as a commercial supplier—in a level playing field—offers an important opportunity to secure better value from forensic R&D investment, through drawing upon a wider range of advice to inform research policy, through more effective research stimulated by competition and through attracting additional private sector investment. The benefit of a competitive R&D market for Government is plain from the experience of DEFRA, FSA, DoH and DTI, all of whom consult widely to establish R&D priorities and commission work competitively. In each case, the stimulus of competition has re-energised the established suppliers and has broadened the technical contributions to national programmes. Government could also encourage private sector investment in forensic R&D by sharing the costs of near-market projects.

18. For suppliers, investment in research and development is fundamental to maintaining state-of-the-art forensic service provision and to winning work at both the national and international level. Private companies such as LGC have to fund their own research and development from their operating profits. LGC has a core commitment to remaining at the forefront of analytical science and, to this end, makes a substantial investment each year into new equipment and both in-house and externally placed R&D. In the last financial year, for example, LGC's total investment in research and development programmes was approximately £8 million, in both internally and externally funded programmes. A significant proportion of this investment has been made within our Forensic Division, including an on-going research programme into developing a system for portable, real-time, DNA processing, aimed at providing DNA evidence within twenty minutes. However, LGC operates in a variety of business sectors and has to decide between competing options for investment. The future market environment for forensic suppliers will therefore be significant in long-term investment planning for product and service development.

19. It is of course vital for any company contemplating investment that it has the confidence to do so through knowledge that it is competing on a "level playing field". Hence the importance of a regulatory body to oversee the forensic market, to ensure, for example, that competitor's accounts are not being selectively targeted by the use of discriminatory pricing or other inducements to customers. Such behaviour would be extremely anti-competitive and would stifle market development.

20. A privatised FSS is bound to seek commercial advantage from the expertise and techniques which they have built up while in the public sector. Although this will present problems to the other suppliers in the next few years, we hope that a more even-handed approach to funding by the Home Office and the influence of a regulating body for the forensic market will, over time, erode the competitive advantage inherent within the FSS's initial position and size as they join the private sector.

21. A competitive market for forensic research and development, pursuing objectives identified through wide consultation, will do much to encourage private sector investment in research and will secure better value for Government.

Q.4 *The use of novel forensic technologies by the FSS and the CJS*

22. The forensic suppliers each have their own programmes of in-house development and external "technology scanning" to identify new technologies, both to improve their existing operations and to develop new services. Subject to the need for extensive validation necessary to demonstrate that novel technologies are sufficiently robust for use within the justice system, there can be no doubt that innovation in forensic science will continue.

23. The new Home Office Science and Technology Strategy provides a mechanism for the wider community, including industry and academia, to draw attention to their products and research.

24. There is however a need to ensure that the introduction of new technologies and techniques does not destroy the market. If, for example, a single supplier either develops or purchases rights to a particular technique, service or database which then becomes essential to forensic service provision, and secures a monopoly in its use, it will effectively prevent police forces from using a supplier without access to that technique. A preferred approach would be for a licensing system to be put in place, so that developers of new techniques can be appropriately rewarded for their innovation, but all suppliers can, on payment of an appropriate licensing fee and demonstration of competence, use the technique.

25. Here again, we see a clear role for an independent custodian to oversee the operation of the forensic market.

Q.5 *The use of forensic science in criminal investigations and court proceedings and the extent to which shortcomings in forensic science have affected the administration of justice*

26. Despite the expansion seen in recent years, forensic science is still only used in a relative small proportion of investigations. ACPO is continuing its work to promote the value of more routine use of forensic science, partly in the expectation that competition between forensic service providers will continue to drive down unit prices. It is notable that, for example, as the unit cost of DNA work has decreased, while

the available capacity has increased and turn round times have improved, it has become possible to make use of DNA in volume crime investigation, rather than concentrating its use in serious crime. The Government's investment in expanding the National DNA Database® has resulted in a system, open to all accredited suppliers, where a DNA profile recovered from a stain from a crime scene now has an approximately 50% chance of producing an identification from the Database. The impact of this on volume crime detection and, therefore, subsequent crime reduction, is substantial. Similar investment in other integrated national systems, open to all suppliers who can demonstrate competence, should further enhance the contribution that forensic science can make to tackling crime.

27. One of the key drivers within the Criminal Justice System at present is the requirement to reduce the time taken to bring offenders to justice, both in the investigatory and the prosecuting stages. Forensic science providers are playing their part in this, both by speeding up their own processes and by integrating their operations into the police forces and the Crown Prosecution Service, primarily by the more effective use of IT. Further application of IT to improve the administration of justice will need to be effected in a way that ensures access to all suppliers.

28. The extremely successful system developed for operating the National DNA Database provides a blueprint for the development of further, nationally managed but multi-supplier, intelligence systems to improve the application of forensic science as an aid to criminal investigation.

29. National initiatives are also under way to develop an "electronic" Criminal Justice System, based on electronic transfer of data, including casefiles, to expedite the administration of justice. All forensic suppliers need to be able to participate, through common standards and an inclusive consultative system.

SUMMARY

30. LGC welcomes the decision to transfer the FSS into the private sector, but we urge care to ensure that doing so does not damage the developing market in forensic service provision, which is providing such marked benefits to the UK's Criminal Justice System. In particular, there is a range of activities, currently carried out by the FSS which, in the national interest, should not transfer to the private sector. An independent body to oversee the operation of the forensic market to ensure an even-handed approach to all suppliers is vital.

November 2004

APPENDIX 8

Memorandum from the Association of Chief Police Officers of England, Wales and Northern Ireland

INTRODUCTORY REMARKS AND SUMMARY

1. ACPO welcomes the opportunity to respond to the issues raised by the Science and Technology Committee. Forensic Science is an indispensable element of criminal investigations and as such, the future provision of forensic science and expertise is of fundamental importance to policing.

2. Current developments in technology and the development of the market place present huge opportunities to improve the contribution of forensic science to the detection of crime. Police requirements are changing. Independence of advice, the maintenance of standards, a sensible regulatory framework, and effective procurement processes are vital in order to ensure that maximum benefit is realised from the changes being made.

3. For the information of the Committee, ACPO's role is set out at Appendix A.

EVIDENCE

The likely impact of the Government plan to develop the Forensic Science Service as a public private partnership (PPP) on the competitiveness of the FSS and on the effective provision of forensic science services to the criminal justice system.

4. It is necessary to look back over the last two decades to trace the changing relationship between the FSS and the police service. Prior to the FSS becoming an executive agency in 1991, there was no charging mechanism for forensic services, no market for forensic science, and services were, effectively, free at the point of use. The creation of the FSS as an Executive Agency and subsequently as a Trading Fund introduced financial discipline into forensic science provision and procurement. Costs and value added by forensic support became clearer to police forces, where it had not been so previously. Timeliness targets arising from government policy objectives to speed up the administration of justice created a need to prioritise services and this led the FSS to charge premium prices for express services. Other providers began to see opportunities to enter the market, at first in specialist areas, but increasingly, offering a broader range

of services in direct competition to the FSS. Indeed, some emerging competition was from former FSS staff. However, ACPO's relationship with the FSS until about 2002 was so close that the FSS was considered "the preferred supplier".

5. Police service structures have led forces, historically, to act independently to procure forensic services, and despite competitors emerging, many forces have simply extended what was effectively a "gentleman's agreement" with the FSS to provide services, following the former ACPO policy line. In recent years "letters of understanding" have been signed between the FSS and many forces, as the FSS sought to bring a degree of certainty into its future business plans. Formal contractual arrangements have been a departure from the norm until recently.

6. It became increasingly clear that this position was untenable, given the responsibility of Police Authorities to obtain Best Value under the provisions of the Local Government Act 1999. Best Value requires that Authorities challenge, compare, compete, and consult when reviewing services, naturally leading to consideration of competing providers as an alternative to the FSS. In our view, therefore, there is a pressing need for a change in procurement practices, but with appropriate safeguards.

7. We estimate conservatively from a recent exercise that total forensic provision costs the police service in the region of £400 million annually, including staffing costs. Much of this expenditure is on in-house forensic provision such as crime scene examination, fingerprint services, photography, and simple laboratory processes. There is no current desire on our part to outsource these services. They are integral to our investigations, producing, for the most part, rapid turnaround times at reasonable cost. Any development in the immediate future is likely to involve improving efficiency by rationalisation of services between forces, rather than outsourcing, thus restricting potential market opportunities for commercial providers.

8. It is estimated that the external police forensic market is worth some £140 million. Of this, some £30 million per annum is funded by the Home Office DNA Expansion Programme, matched by a similar amount from forces spent on DNA. The strategic importance of government DNA funding to the forensic science market place is starkly obvious. Withdrawal of the funding could have a catastrophic effect, as it is most unlikely that forces could make up the shortfall. It is equally unlikely, given our assumptions about public expenditure constraints, that police spending on forensic services will continue to grow at a significant rate in the future. The size of the market may therefore remain relatively stable, although the mechanisms within it, and the services we seek, will change.

9. ACPO has come, admittedly somewhat belatedly, to the conclusion that the police service must become a much more intelligent customer, procuring forensic services in a strategic and structured manner. We now intend moving rapidly to competitive tendering, probably based on a series of framework agreements with providers in order to minimise bureaucracy. We will encourage collaboration between forces, leading to contracts for bulk purchase of services where possible, generating economies of scale and the potential for discounting. This, we believe, will generate more confidence amongst existing and prospective providers over customer loyalty and service volumes, encouraging them to invest in the forensic market. We hope it will also encourage investment in new techniques and technology as competitiveness increases.

10. There are dangers in this approach. A rapid shift of market share from the FSS might lead to a drain of experienced reporting staff from the FSS to competitors. Competition might increase the willingness of existing and new providers to "cut corners" in order to reduce costs to secure business. Providers might reduce the availability of some of the more specialised and costly services, which are rarely used but vital when needed, or might decline to provide services in remote parts of the country. None of these phenomena will be beneficial to the criminal justice system. A destabilised and rapidly failing FSS, currently widely regarded as the leading forensic provider in the world, and with up to 90% of market share at present, is potentially a disaster, which we would prefer not to contemplate.

11. ACPO therefore considers that an essential part of an orderly transition to a competitive market place will be the existence of some form of regulatory apparatus, which acts firstly, to control the dynamics of the market place, and secondly, to ensure that the scientific and technical standards adopted by existing and new providers are appropriate. The ACPO procurement strategy will, we believe, go some way to deliver the first, but we consider that the second is the responsibility of government.

12. We have been closely involved throughout the McFarland Review and subsequent discussions, and have stated the following objectives throughout:

— We seek to ensure that the widest possible range of forensic processes remains available to customers, ensuring, in the interests of justice, that highly specialised services, even if loss-making, are not withdrawn for commercial reasons.

— There must be guaranteed continuous access for the police service, to a comprehensive range of forensic services, whatever the vagaries of the market place.

— There must be a guarantee that sufficient volume of services will always remain available to meet forces' minimum needs.

— The quality and integrity of forensic processes must not, in any circumstances, be compromised in the interests of commercial competitiveness. ACPO has a central, but not the primary role, in ensuring the maintenance of these standards.

— A situation where providers are able to "hold the police service to ransom", exerting upward pressure on costs in an unregulated way, is not acceptable.

13. Looking to the future, the ACPO Forensic Strategy can be broadly described in a few words. "More, better, faster, cheaper, but with integrity". We believe that there is potential to increase forensic intervention in many more crimes; that there is a need to improve forensic techniques in order to recover more forensic evidence; that we should drive ourselves and providers to deliver results in shorter timescales; that better procurement practices will reduce costs; but that above all, we must never compromise on quality standards. Providers will need to understand this and position themselves to deliver services accordingly.

14. Turning to the FSS itself, it is clear to us that the organisation will need to move rapidly to a position where it can compete on professional sales and marketing terms with potentially aggressive competitors. The FSS has to become more customer focussed. Experience so far suggests that this transition has been slow, resulting in work being lost, and whilst a degree of downsizing might even be desirable, a rapid spiral of decline must not be allowed to develop. It is desirable, in our view, that the FSS has access to the same market freedoms that other competitors enjoy, if it is to be able to modernise, re-capitalise, and increase its speed of decision-making. The alternatives are to suppress the development of the market place to protect the FSS, or to allow the FSS to wither slowly away under public sector constraints.

The quality of forensic science education and training and the supply of skilled personnel in forensic science

15. The ACPO Forensic Science Training Portfolio was set up in 2000 following the publication of Her Majesty's Inspectorate of Constabulary's Thematic Inspection Report "*Under the Microscope*". HMIC highlighted the lack of a holistic training strategy within the police service, particularly drawing attention to the need for awareness training amongst operational officers, and for improved strategic provision of specialist training for forensic practitioners within the service. Since the report, much progress has been made, and the previously fragmented position has been resolved to some extent by the absorption of the Durham Scientific Support Training Centre into Centrex. However, this has not resolved other fundamental problems.

16. The Chairman of the ACPO portfolio group is now also Chairman of SEMTA, the Sector Skills Council for Science, Engineering and Manufacturing Technologies, bringing considerable synergy to the developing scene. SEMTA has recently carried out two pieces of work which set out a comprehensive picture of the forensic science training situation; an Occupational Mapping exercise, and a report "*Forensic Science: Implications for Higher Education 2004*". We are aware that SEMTA has submitted evidence to the Committee, and agree with the conclusions SEMTA has reached and the recommendations it has made. It is clear that for various reasons, degree courses and other higher education opportunities are of widely differing standards and content, often hybrid in order to attract a wide range of students, often unsuited to the needs of employers, and sometimes encouraging unrealistic employment expectations amongst students. Some courses of similar content and standard are marketed under very different titles. The supply of courses is considerably larger than the number of employment opportunities available. We support the view that there needs to be a single agreed set of national occupational standards covering all aspects of forensic science, around which degree and other courses can be constructed, providing in due course a better match between training for occupational skills, and employment opportunities.

17. Police scientific support is not wholly reliant upon educational attainment, and whilst forces report no difficulties in recruiting staff with degree level qualifications, practical performance in the field is paramount. Given the practical nature of some techniques there may be scope for a more vocationally based approach to recruitment and training, coupled with a clearer career progression structure. In any event there is a need for practitioners to achieve professional competence rather than simply gain qualifications. Police forces are now implementing more robust performance management for scientific support staff. Together with ACPO's support for independent accreditation of police scientific support staff by the Council for the Registration of Forensic Practitioners (CRFP) this will have the effect of driving up standards and encouraging lifelong learning.

18. Technological developments in the future will potentially increase the range of forensic processes carried out by police staff, suggesting a need to develop a culture of greater flexibility, rather than discrete specialisms. This in turn will have an impact on recruitment and the provision of training.

The levels of investment in forensic science R&D

19. There is significant scope to increase investment in forensic science R&D, although the size of the potential market perhaps acts as a disincentive at present. We have already alluded to the possibility of reduced market opportunities for providers should future technical developments deliver the means for police staff to carry out a wider range of analytical work in-house. The forensic field is one in which any major technological or scientific breakthrough, particularly if it involves miniaturisation or portability,

could result in short-term gain, but long-term loss of commercial opportunities for providers. To some extent, therefore, although increased competition may generate increased investment in R&D, a conflict of interest exists amongst providers.

20. A major weakness until recently was the lack of an overarching Home Office/Police Science and Technology Strategy. This has now been rectified, with ACPO playing a key role in developing the strategy. Central to the debate around investment is the question of what police capabilities will be needed to combat current and emerging threats. The Strategy contains an extensive list, which we endorse. Co-ordination and information sharing will now be key to delivery. It is important that government investment, often necessarily limited, is made in a way that develops those police capabilities most effectively and avoids duplication of effort. As part of this process, there needs to be a wide ranging debate with providers and a robust environmental scanning process, to identify emerging technologies, threats and opportunities.

The use of novel forensic technologies by the FSS and the criminal justice system

21. The forensic business is changing. Firstly, the pace of investigations is more rapid as police forces drive up performance and improve our success rates against persistent and prolific offenders. We need forensic results in hours, not weeks.

22. Secondly, the development of digital technology has allowed the creation of forensic databases such as the National DNA Database (NDNAD) and the National Automated Fingerprint Identification System (NAFIS). This has opened up possibilities for the use of forensic intelligence, to drive investigations, as opposed to the more traditional use of forensic evidence to support prosecutions. Forensic intelligence will become vital to intelligence led-policing operations, as we increase our understanding of criminality and are better able to identify links and patterns of offending, or sources of commodities.

23. A significant issue, which will need to be resolved, is the Custodianship of such data. Currently, there are signs that the FSS, and other providers, see the holding of such data as a means of generating business opportunities. ACPO will resist this. We consider that the bulk of data derived from forensic testing on behalf of agencies in the Criminal Justice System should be regarded as public property, under the control of the public authorities. We cannot support a situation in which the police service has to pay for access to its own data.

24. Thirdly, the development of new technology, for example, hand-held devices based on "lab-on-a-chip" technology, linked directly to forensic databases, will allow us to move more forensic analytical processes back "in-house", as the need for laboratory based services decreases. We are anxious to speed up identification of suspects through real-time custody-based DNA analysis, for example, and are currently testing digital transmission of fingerprints from crime scenes. This trend may reduce commercial opportunities for providers. Alternatively, it may drive providers towards improving value-adding interpretational services and increasing R&D investment to provide new technological solutions, instead of bulk analytical services.

25. Despite, historically, working closely in partnership with various providers to develop new techniques and technologies, the police service has been slow to see the potential cost implications arising from the ownership of Intellectual Property Rights. If this trend towards developing novel technologies does begin to occur, we will want to address these problems before we are faced with the costly restrictions of IPR licensing experienced with other forms of information technology. We believe there is a strong argument for government to retain ownership of IPR currently owned, under government auspices, by the FSS, or at least make provision during the PPP process, for it to be freely available to Criminal Justice agencies, although we recognise this will affect FSS' sale value.

The use of forensic science in criminal investigations and court proceedings and the extent to which shortcomings in forensic science have affected the administration of justice

26. The need to maintain public confidence in forensic science is not negotiable.

27. We have referred above to the vital importance of maintaining standards. Currently, the government relies for its professional advice on forensic matters, on the Chief Executive and other representatives of the FSS. If the FSS is to be perceived by competitors as operating on a "level playing field", and by the public as being truly objective, to continue this relationship would seem inappropriate. There is a need to create some other authoritative source of advice, either fully independent or directly linked to government, but representative of the wider forensic community, with no bias towards any specific provider.

28. External accreditation of both laboratories and individual personnel is important and necessary in this regard. The well-publicised miscarriages of justice in the 1970's did much to harm the reputation of forensic science but also provided the catalyst for the introduction of improved quality management systems which are subject to ongoing audit and accreditation by outside agencies (UKAS, BSI), and we welcome providers' willingness to submit their operations to such scrutiny. In support of this, ACPO policy is that force forensic personnel should be similarly accredited, through CRFP, and there is increasing take-up of this across the service.

29. The current situation is good and must be maintained. Continuity processes, safe handling, improved packaging, anti-contamination techniques and quality checking of results are now commonplace. Whilst it is not uncommon for a forensic expert to be challenged as part of the trial process, our experience suggests this almost always relates to the interpretation of scientific evidence rather than the accuracy. We are not aware that, other than infrequently, expert witnesses have been criticised recently by the judiciary for the quality of their work.

30. Current scientific processes are well-established, recognised as sound, and rarely challenged, but there is a need to ensure that new processes are subject to rigorous scrutiny before being deployed in court proceedings. There are also, inevitably, occasions when an individual scientist displays a lack of competency, or deploys novel theory, which on closer examination is not sustainable. We see the need for the Criminal Justice system to develop a consistent and clearly understood quality control and remedial process to cater for these eventualities.

November 2004

Annex A

THE ROLE OF ACPO

ACPO[13] is the professional association of the chief officers of the police forces of England, Wales and Northern Ireland. It performs a number of roles:

— It speaks for its members when appropriate. This includes the Service's relationship with the Home Office or to other bodies on issues where there is a common service interest. It does not seek to comment or discuss issues relating to single forces.

— It acts as professional advisor on policing matters to the Home Secretary.

— It formulates guidance for the service, eg to interpret new legislation.

— It co-ordinate the Service's response when it needs to act as a single force, in times of national emergency or when there is a major or catastrophic incident. Past examples of operations have included the fire officers' dispute and the RAF Fairford protests during the war in Iraq, both in 2003. It will also coordinate English, Welsh and Northern Irish mutual Aid to the Scottish Police for the G8 Summit next July.

In April 2003 Chris Fox, formerly chief constable of Northamptonshire, was appointed as the first full time President of the Association.

APPENDIX 9

Memorandum from Document Evidence Limited

EXECUTIVE SUMMARY

1. Document Evidence Ltd is one of the leading providers of forensic document examination in the UK.

2. As a supplier in a relatively small but nonetheless important niche area of forensic science, we consider it imperative that the operating constraints that apply to larger organisations should be such that they are unable to use any market share dominance to the detriment of smaller suppliers such as ourselves.

3. We are actively involved with the presentation of material on forensic document examination at a number of universities. Because of this, we have a perspective on both the value and potential problems such courses may have.

4. Contact with those in the process of fraud investigation, both within the prosecuting authorities and within the finance industry, allows us to form a view of the ways in which fraud investigation can be made more rigorous. We are independent of many of the influences that tend to lead to a polarisation of responsibility for fraud; the investigators want the institutions to take more responsibility and the institutions want more assistance from the investigators with the result that the burden falls between the two. We draw attention below to a number of measures that we believe could assist in bringing together some of the multi-faceted elements of fraud investigation and prosecution.

BRIEF HISTORY OF DOCUMENT EVIDENCE LIMITED

5. Document Evidence was established in 1992 by seven former senior scientists from the Documents Section of the Forensic Science Service (FSS) in Birmingham. In the years since its creation, it has increased its market share to the position where it is now one of, if not the, main providers of forensic document examination in the UK. More details about the company can be found on the website, www.docev.co.uk.

---

[13] NB: ACPO is not a staff association; the Chief Police Officers' Staff Association (CPOSA) performs that role.

Our customers include over half of the police forces of England and Wales, financial institutions, other prosecuting authorities, solicitors both in criminal defence and civil work, companies and members of the public.

6. Mr Mike Allen is currently Lead Assessor in the specialty of Questioned Documents for the Council for the Registration of Forensic Practitioners (CRFP) and is on the Executive Board of CRFP.

7. Mr Kim Hughes is an Assessor in the specialty of Questioned Documents for CRFP.

8. Dr David Baxendale is an examiner for the Diploma in Questioned Documents for the Forensic Science Society (FSSoc).

9. All of the senior experts within Document Evidence have examined thousands of cases and given evidence in court on many occasions, some of which include such high profile cases as the Omagh Bombing, the Birmingham Six and the trial of Dr Harold Shipman.

THE FORENSIC SCIENCE MARKET

10. Document Evidence was set up as a direct result of the opening up of forensic science to commercial competition following the change of status of the FSS to a Home Office agency in 1991.

11. Charging customers, the police in particular, changed some attitudes and values of forensic science; economic considerations could no longer be ignored, albeit they did not (and should not) be considered as over-riding the needs of justice.

12. Nonetheless, paying for forensic services has required the introduction of some, arguably overdue, realism to the process of determining which forensic evidence is going to be of assistance in a given enquiry.

13. Document Evidence has a track record that we feel gets the balance between money and justice right. The sense of public duty that rightly accompanies the profession of forensic science, together with the simple truism that satisfied customers stay loyal, ensure that we offer a service that is highly regarded and appreciated for its integrity and quality by our customers. We believe that it is possible to provide the commercial forensic service that we do in a way that is not inconsistent with the needs of justice.

14. Forensic science, of course, has a number of mainstream specialities, most of which are supplied by three main suppliers. They are the FSS, Forensic Alliance and the Laboratory of the Government Chemist (LGC). Of these, the FSS and LGC supply forensic document examination (alongside the other areas of forensic science) in competition with Document Evidence. An issue that has arisen from this situation is the "bundling together" of forensic services and the consequences of that on a niche supplier like Document Evidence. In other words, a supplier of several services could offer to a customer a "one stop shop" solution that might be regarded as attractive overall. But it might not take account of the quality of some of the individual services within the package. So a customer could, for pragmatic or financial reasons, chose such a package since splitting up their systems to cater for a larger number of small suppliers could be seen to be disadvantageous.

15. Worse still, a supplier of several services could, if so minded, offer an "economy of scale" with the effect of cutting the cost of individual services: use us for your DNA and drugs and we will do a deal on your questioned documents, so to speak.

16. Such practice, if it were to occur, and there is anecdotal evidence that some suppliers have done something similar, could put small suppliers such as Document Evidence at a significant and potentially commercially fatal disadvantage.

17. For this reason, it is essential that operating constraints are put upon major suppliers of forensic science so as to ensure that the competition with smaller suppliers is fair.

Forensic science education

18. There are now many forensic science courses at undergraduate level available in British universities, together with other post-graduate courses, the best established of which are at the university of Strathclyde and Kings College, London. Because forensic document examination is such a highly specialised area, a number of the universities have turned to Document Evidence to assist them with the delivery of educational material on their courses in this field. We are keen to assist, not least to ensure that the information and methods being taught in our area are appropriate.

19. Rightly, the forensic science community is expressing concern as to where the graduates from such courses are going to find employment. It would be clearly impossible for the large numbers of students now studying on such courses to all find jobs within mainstream forensic science or even within allied professions, such as scenes of crime work with the police.

20. The key elements that should be taken into account when evaluating such courses are the overall employability of the graduates, the quality of the scientific knowledge they receive, the quality of their non-scientific abilities (such as communication skills) and, perhaps most difficult to assess, what might those

students have studied had they not studied forensic science—would they have been "lost" to some other (non-scientific) discipline? In other words, there is perhaps a need to recognise that some courses and/or individual students will emerge well qualified for a career in mainstream forensic science by virtue of their academic ability, whereas others may be better suited to other careers some of which will also benefit from their general forensic training.

Fraud investigation

21. There is a lack of realisation of what forensic document examination can achieve, particularly in relation to major crime where drugs seizures and terrorism make the headlines, but where the hidden truth is that major crime requires financing and much of it is done for monetary gain. Fraud may be thought of as somehow victimless, but we believe this to be a serious mistake.

22. With our contacts at Document Evidence, including police fraud investigators, financial institutions and those working in entitlement assessment, it is becoming increasingly apparent that the investigation of fraud is under-resourced and is not being taken as seriously as it should. Over recent years, there has been a decline in the amount of casework in Questioned Documents being submitted by the police. This may in part be for want of their being better informed about the potential of forensic document examination; but it is also attributable, in part at least, to the demotion of fraud investigation as a result of the perceived importance of other types of crime. Nonetheless, there is marked variation in the extent of investigation of fraud from force to force.

23. The scale of fraud in the UK is being tracked by a number of organisations. Although the very large amounts of money are, it is argued, small in the overall scheme of things, the cost of investigating some of this crime is itself modest enough and it is our contention that for a relatively small investment in resources to combat fraud, the returns would potentially be significant. These could be not just the financial savings, but also the strangling of funding for other types of crime. The co-operation of the financial institutions in the investigation process is notoriously difficult to obtain, although there are exceptions and attitudes may be changing. As a generalisation, some banks seem less than enthusiastic about combating fraud. It is surely wrong that this attitude should go unchallenged. Put bluntly, what will the Bank of X have to say if it is revealed that a terrorist organisation has been laundering money through accounts held with it and this could have been detected by the adoption of some measures that might have prevented such a thing happening?

24. The investigation of fraud is further hampered because police resources (such as fingerprinting services) are not being prioritised as efficiently as they might be. This is a direct result of the absence of mechanisms for cross-force offences being routinely linked and from this there is a difficulty in determining which are the major and minor offences. It is our understanding that the decision as to which offences require the appropriate extra resources (because they are parts of major, systematic crimes) is a difficult one for the police to get right.

25. There are methods of assisting in the process of cross-linking cheque book offences on the basis of the writings on the cheques. We propose a national system for co-ordinating cheque fraud on the basis of both forensic and intelligence information in which the financial institutions and the prosecuting authorities can co-operate to ensure that everything is done to make cheque fraud as difficult as possible for those perpetrating it.

26. There is no compulsion in the UK for a suspect to give a handwriting sample upon request from a suitably authorised person, such as a police officer. In some countries, notably the US, it is generally compulsory to do so. It has come to our attention that a lot of suspects (often on the advice of their legal representatives) are refusing handwriting samples. This situation may make it impossible to investigate an offence if other samples of writing that can be attributed to that suspect are not available. Furthermore, the courts are not permitted to make inferences from the refusal of a suspect to give a handwriting sample.

27. We therefore propose that consideration be given to a change in the law that would compel an individual to give a handwriting sample unless they can demonstrate good reason why they cannot. In addition, should someone refuse a writing sample or give a demonstrably disguised sample, the court should be allowed to make an inference from this.

28. Many areas of entitlement require documentary proof of identity from an individual. Documentation is inevitably international in origin and the authorities should have some sort of basis upon which to make informed decisions as to the authenticity or otherwise of such documentation. Regrettably, as far as we are aware, no such resource exists. We are helping some organisations (in both the public and private sectors) by training their staff so as to give them some basic information about what kinds of features genuine and counterfeit documents might show, but we cannot provide specific information about particular documents—what should a birth certificate from country Z look like? We believe that staff that are making these decisions are concerned about their lack of awareness of these matters and the lack of a resource to give them document-specific information.

29. The creation of a searchable database of such information should, in our opinion, be a priority for organisations that need this kind of information to function properly.

SUMMARY

30. There are issues about which we as forensic document examiners are concerned. Finding the right forum to discuss these issues is often difficult or impossible. By making this submission to the Select Committee, we would like to not only highlight some of the problems but also to offer the assistance, expertise and enthusiasm of our staff to look for and implement solutions to them.

November 2004

APPENDIX 10

Memorandum from the Royal Society of Edinburgh (RSE)

1. In summary, the conversion of the Forensic Science Service (FSS) to a public private partnership may not have any effect on the provision of services to the criminal justice system, but it is likely to have an impact on the level of R&D undertaken by the FSS. There has been a large increase in undergraduate forensic courses, but these graduates are unlikely to be employed by the professional laboratories, both because of the limited opportunities and because such laboratories prefer employees with an in-depth knowledge of a science discipline and gain their forensic science through specialist post graduate training. Forensic psychology, however, is suffering acute shortages in qualified personnel and is struggling to meet the demands of the courts. The FSS need to develop, and be aware, of new technologies and further efforts need to be given to raising awareness of those concerned with the assurance of justice in the requirements of the forensic scientist and an appreciation of the delicate nature of the evidence at "scene of crime."

2. The specific areas of the call for evidence are now addressed below:

The likely impact of the Government plan to develop the Forensic Science Service as a public private partnership (PPP) on the competitiveness of the FSS and on the effective provision of forensic science services to the criminal justice system

3. In an adversarial system, such as the British justice system, it is important that both sides have access to equal levels of expertise. It is thus essential that there are independent scientists available who have the capacity to challenge evidence emanating from the FSS. Organisations, such as Forensic Alliance and the Laboratory of the Government Chemist (LGC) currently provide some equivalent services to the FSS and other companies could come into the marketplace. Therefore the conversion of FSS to PPP may not result in a major increase in competition or any significant change in provision of services to the criminal justice system. Nevertheless, there is a perception that any forensic service that is centrally controlled must work in favour of the prosecution. Specimens for scientific examination are collected by and for the police, and access to such specimens is unequal in practice. To this extent, conversion to PPP might provide an opportunity to rectify what is something of a monopoly situation.

4. At present the FSS has also to obey the Home Office procurement rules and advertise their intention to procure large orders for equipment and reagents in the *Official Journal of the European Community* (OJEC). This effectively announces their intentions to competitors and provides the competitors with a window on activities within the FSS. There is also currently insufficient freedom on adjusting pay and rewards, and due to Treasury set limits, and staff are being lost to competitors who are more flexible. In addition, competitors are not required to subscribe to central regulatory bodies such as International Organisation for Standards (ISO), however, the judicial system can bring attention to this and discredit second-rate competitors.

5. The effect PPP will have on the competitiveness of the FSS is unclear. Good management should be in place whether or not the FSS is a PPP. However, there will need to be transparency of quality provided (achieved by local quality assurance and routine inspections from a third party). There is, however, concern among FSS staff about the move over to PPP. Current staff have a public service ethos, with ethical concerns, and worry about their pension, conditions of work and job security. Uncertainty also surrounds who their partners will be, and what their long-term view for the service will be. Clearly the long-term existence of the FSS is important as there would not be sufficient provision in the marketplace if the FSS disappeared.

The quality of forensic science education and training and the supply of skilled personnel in forensic science

6. In terms of the supply of skilled personnel in forensic science, in recent years there have been a large number of courses at undergraduate level that include the word "forensic" in the title and there is current concern that this "explosion" in provision does not reflect the limited employment prospects in this area of activity. Teaching forensic science at undergraduate level can present a dilemma in the balancing of emphasis between basic science and forensic science. In general, forensic professionals prefer employees who have an in-depth knowledge of a science discipline and gain their forensic science through a balanced course or specialist post graduate training. The current expansion in undergraduate provision, however, will lead

to graduates who are unlikely to be employed by the professional laboratories, both because of the limited opportunities and because of the standard of their education. There may be merit in the Forensic Science Society providing guidance, accreditation and quality assessment to appropriate courses.

7. However, in the field of forensic psychology there is an acute problem with the training and a shortage of supply of suitably qualified personnel. Recent changes in the law, such as the introduction of Orders of Life Long Restriction in Scotland, and the introduction of Dangerous Severe Personality Disorder provisions in England and Wales, have greatly increased the demand for violence risk assessments. Current forensic psychologists are now unable to meet the demand of the courts and in some areas of Scotland there are no appropriate services available.

8. With regard to forensic training, the higher education sector can also play a valuable role in working with forensic scientists to ensure the standard of professionalism is maintained within the profession, through the development of joint continuing professional development programmes and close interaction with the relevant professional bodies and other relevant agencies such as the Council for Registration of Forensic Practitioners. In this context, it is important for credibility and of the professional standing of those who operate in the judicial system, to be subject to appropriate validation.

The levels of investment in forensic science R&D

9. Investment in R&D by the FSS is likely to fall if more emphasis is put on purely commercial issues, and R&D can be a significant drain on the resources of a commercial enterprise in the short term. Any fall in R&D investment could be detrimental, but this may only come to light in five years or more. In the past, the FSS could have been more commercially aware and more active in filing patents in certain areas. However, it should have been possible to introduce greater commercial awareness into the FSS within the existing structure and without conversion to PPP. Recently the Engineering and Physical Sciences Research Council has put resources into a research programme on crime prevention and detection. This is a welcome innovation and is making the UK academic community more aware of the possibility of applying their research to crime and terrorism issues. It is not, however, a substitute for R&D carried out at the sharp end by the FSS. It is important to maintain a close relationship between criminal investigation, awareness of current issues in the area, and research and development programs and this should remain a major remit within the FSS.

The use of novel forensic technologies by the FSS and criminal justice system

10. The FSS should develop new technologies, utilise them and license them to other users on a worldwide basis. The scientists at the FSS also have a responsibility to be aware of technologies developed elsewhere. The long-term financial viability of the PPP will depend upon adopting a strategic approach to R&D, so that highly novel forensic technologies are invented at the FSS. In this context, there is likely to be a gap of up to 10 years between research and application, so being able to take the long-term view about such research is vital.

11. Novel techniques may, however, require stringent quality assessment and the FSS should consider working in collaboration with those universities who are training their new recruits to ensure a rounded and secure approach.

The use of forensic science in criminal investigations and court proceedings and the extent to which shortcomings in forensic science have affected the administration of justice

12. Clearly close interactions should exist between Forensic R&D, applied forensic science and criminal investigation. Therefore the interaction between the police and the FSS should be close, both in terms of the "provider-user" relationship and in educating the police force in key forensic issues. This may be one of the major issues to deal with. Many investigations and court proceedings are detrimentally affected by a poor understanding by the police of the requirements of the forensic scientist, and a lack of appreciation of the delicate nature of the evidence at "scene of crime." It is important that commercial pressures at the FSS and the sensitive supplier-customer relationship do not have a negative effect on the role of the FSS in educating those concerned with the assurance of justice in the above issues. The education process could be carried out by different mechanisms but intuitively it would seem that organisations such as the Forensic Science Society, should be involved. If a significant commercial cost is involved in this training process, then bodies such as police authorities could be deterred from availing themselves of such services. Training should also continue to be developed within FSS to those who give evidence in court, so that their evidence can be properly understood by judges and juries.

November 2004

APPENDIX 11

Memorandum from the Biosciences Federation

SUMMARY

1. This response's principal points include:

(i) There is concern about the ability of the Forensic Science Service (FSS) to retain its independence as a public private partnership (PPP), although this would increase its commercial abilities (paragraphs 3 and 4).

(ii) Many forensic science courses have limited scientific credibility and recruits to the FSS tend to be graduates in analytical chemistry, biochemistry and molecular genetics. A partnership between forensic science organisations and university forensic science courses would help to ensure quality and value (paragraph 5).

(iii) There is a need for more co-ordinated, independent funding for forensic science R&D (paragraph 6).

(iv) Novel forensic technologies should be used by the FSS with caution; they should not overshadow proven existing approaches (paragraph 7).

(v) Any shortcomings in forensic science have partly arisen through poor training and quality assurance procedures and heavy workloads. In addition, in terms of the administration of justice, there are problems to consider when interfacing the two very different disciplines of science, which works on probabilities and risk, and law, which prefers hard facts and numbers (paragraph 8).

COMMENTS IN RESPONSE TO THE COMMITTEE'S SPECIFIC POINTS

The likely impact of the Government plan to develop the Forensic Science Service (FSS) as a public private partnership (PPP) on the competitiveness of the FSS and on the effective provision of forensic science services to the criminal justice system

2. There is concern about the ability of the FSS to retain its independence as a PPP. It is important in some cases for all individuals to have access to independent FSS material. In addition, while a PPP would help to ensure adequate funding for research within the FSS, the "commercialisation" that this would require may not be appropriate for a judicial service. For example, costly procedures may be denied on the basis of budgetary constraints and this would not necessarily best serve the investigative process or the justice system.

3. The FSS is currently not client or business orientated and turn-around times can be slow. Developing the FSS as a PPP would increase its commercial abilities, as it would have to provide a fast service at the proper market price. As a PPP, the FSS would have to be open and transparent with its pricing system, and may be able to better target the international market. However, applying full economic costing may increase the "price" to the criminal justice system and the demand for services may decrease. The Government is advised to study other PPPs, Agency Formations and Privatisations to ensure the process is effective and to avoid the many potential pitfalls.

The quality of forensic science education and training and the supply of skilled personnel in forensic science

4. Forensic science is one of the fastest growing areas of recruitment in higher education but many courses have limited scientific credibility. Skilled graduates are rarely emerging from existing courses and extensive on the job training is essential. A partnership between organisations such as the FSS and specific university courses, perhaps with accreditation through the Forensic Science Society, would ensure a tightening of quality and value. Currently, recruits to the FSS tend to be graduates in analytical chemistry, biochemistry and molecular genetics, followed by a Masters course, for example, at Kings College London. Many of these subjects and courses are in decline. The FSS should implement Continuing Professional Development to ensure skilled personnel at all levels.

The levels of investment in forensic science R&D

5. Whilst investment in R&D within the FSS and private companies, such as the Forensic Alliance, is reasonable, the Research Councils do not serve the discipline well. Therefore, independent funding of forensic science R&D is hard to obtain. However, the Research Councils are aware of this problem and EPSRC have had an overwhelming response to their "Think Crime" funding programme. This clearly displays a need for further funding sources of this nature. In particular, there is a need for funding aimed at the forensic science aspect of detection, as the Think Crime programme focused on prevention. A co-ordinated approach to the funding of forensic science is needed from the Research Councils and the FSS would be in a prime position to lead that approach.

The use of novel forensic technologies by the FSS and criminal justice system

6. The FSS should use novel forensic technologies with caution. Novel techniques have by their nature little history and may not stand up in court; they should not overshadow proven existing approaches. However, we support continued research into novel technologies, for example, modern genetic techniques, forensic entomology and spore/pollen analysis. Quality assurance is a key issue, however, and collaboration with universities where the specialists, as opposed to the generalists, are located would be the ideal mechanism to achieve this.

The use of forensic science in criminal investigations and court proceedings and the extent to which shortcomings in forensic science have affected the administration of justice

7. Any shortcomings in forensic science have arisen partly through poor training and quality assurance procedures, coupled with heavy workloads. The system is under a lot of pressure. In addition, in terms of the administration of justice, there are issues to consider when interfacing the two very different disciplines of science, which works on probabilities and risk, and law, which prefers hard facts and numbers. The problems involved were addressed at a recent policy seminar on science and crime organised jointly by the Institute of Biology, Royal Society of Chemistry and the Institute of Physics. It was reported that:

> *". . . scientific data obtained from a complex environment needs to be interpreted statistically, and in the context of other information".*

> *"Juries are not trained to evaluate probabilities or the quality of the scientific methodology."*

> *"Expert witnesses also need to understand the importance of presenting evidence to a jury in an intelligible way."*

> *". . . forensic scientists need to take more interest in the legal process . . . a multidisciplinary approach is necessary to set satisfactory standards in evaluating and communicating forensic evidence."*[14]

OPENNESS

8. The Biosciences Federation is pleased for this response to be publicly available and, with permission, will be placing a version on www.bsf.ac.uk. Should the Science and Technology Committee have any queries regarding this response then they should in the first instance address them to the Policy Co-ordinator, The Biosciences Federation, c/o 76 Portland Place, London W1B 1QW; email: info@bsf.ac.uk.

November 2004

Annex

MEMBER SOCIETIES OF THE BIOSCIENCES FEDERATION

Association for the Study of Animal Behaviour

Biochemical Society

British Association for Psychopharmacology

British Ecological Society

British Lichen Society

British Mycological Society

British Neuroscience Association

British Pharmacological Society

British Society of Animal Science

British Society for Cell Biology

British Society for Developmental Biology

British Society for Immunology

British Society for Medical Mycology

British Society for Neuroendocrinology

British Society for Proteome Research

British Toxicological Society

Experimental Psychology Society

Genetics Society

Heads of University Biological Sciences

Heads of University Centres for Biomedical Science

Institute of Biology

---

[14] *Science and Crime: Keeping one Step Ahead.* A policy seminar organised by the Institute of Biology, Royal Society of Chemistry and the Institute of Physics. 10 June 2004. Report available at: http://www.rsc.org/pdf/policy/science&crime.pdf.

Institute of Horticulture
Laboratory Animal Science Association
Linnean Society
Nutrition Society
Physiological Society
Royal Microscopical Society
Society for Applied Microbiology
Society for Endocrinology
Society for Experimental Biology
Society for General Microbiology
Society for Reproduction and Fertility
UK Environmental Mutagen Society

Additional Affiliated Societies represented by the Institute of Biology

Anatomical Society of Great Britain and Ireland
Association for Radiation Research
Association of Applied Biologists
Association of Clinical Embryologists
Association of Clinical Microbiologists
Association of Veterinary Teachers and Research Workers
British Association for Cancer Research
British Association for Lung Research
British Association for Tissue Banking
British Biophysical Society
British Crop Protection Council
British Grassland Society
British Inflammation Research Association
British Marine Life Study Society
British Microcirculation Society
British Phycological Society
British Society for Allergy Environmental and Nutritional Medicine
British Society for Medical Mycology
British Society for Parasitology
British Society for Plant Pathology
British Society for Research on Ageing
British Society of Animal Science
British Society of Soil Science
Fisheries Society of the British Isles
Freshwater Biological Association
Galton Institute
Institute of Trichologists
International Association for Plant Tissue Culture and Biotechnology
International Biodeterioration and Biodegradation Society
International Biometric Society
International Society for Applied Ethology
Marine Biological Association of the UK
Primate Society of Great Britain
PSI—Statisticians in the Pharmaceutical Industry
Royal Entomological Society
Royal Zoological Society of Scotland
Scottish Association for Marine Science
Society for Anaerobic Microbiology

Society for Low Temperature Biology
Society for the Study of Human Biology
Society of Academic and Research Surgery
Society of Cosmetic Scientists
Society of Pharmaceutical Medicine
UK Registry of Canine Behaviourists
Universities Federation for Animal Welfare

APPENDIX 12

Memorandum from GeneWatch UK

SUMMARY

This submission considers the management of the National DNA Database (NDNAD) in relation to the increasing commercialisation of DNA profiling; the need to balance crime detection, human rights and privacy; and the need to utilise new technologies effectively and ethically.

We highlight the need for:

— more independent, transparent and accountable governance of the NDNAD;

— destruction of individuals' DNA samples once an investigation is complete;

— an end to the practice of allowing genetic research without consent;

— independent assessment of the effectiveness of the NDNAD and the potential role of new technologies; and

— public debate about who should be included on the database and for how long.

INTRODUCTION

1. GeneWatch UK is a not-for-profit policy research group concerned with the science, ethics, policy and regulation of genetic technologies. GeneWatch works to promote environmental, ethical, social, human health and animal welfare considerations in decision-making about genetic technologies. Our aim is to ensure that genetics is used in the public interest.

2. During the past year, GeneWatch has been researching the human rights and privacy issues raised by the use of the National DNA Database (NDNAD). We will shortly be publishing a report: "*The Police National DNA Database: Balancing Crime Detection, Human Rights and Privacy*". Our submission therefore relates to the future status, governance and use of the NDNAD.

THE NATIONAL DNA DATABASE

3. The NDNAD is currently managed by the Forensic Science Service (FSS) for the Association of Police Chief Officers (ACPO). DNA profiling plays an important role in tackling crime and the police rightly have the powers to collect DNA samples during criminal investigations and use this evidence in court. However, there are important questions about the extent to which DNA samples and profiles should be kept indefinitely as part of the NDNAD.

4. On 4 April 2004, police powers relating to the collection and retention of DNA samples and data on the NDNAD were significantly extended. In England and Wales, the police are now allowed to take samples without consent from anyone who is arrested on suspicion of any recordable offence. This includes all but the most minor crimes. The new legislation also allows the police to keep DNA samples and profiles indefinitely, even if the person arrested is never charged. This means the database is the most extensive in the world, including more than two million individuals, and is projected to expand rapidly to include around five million people (about 10% of the population).

5. The NDNAD is a tool for criminal investigations but it is also an instrument of surveillance of the population included on it. DNA profiles can reveal family relationships (for example, non-paternity) and samples may contain personal information about some people's health. Concerns include:

— increasing threats to "genetic privacy" (revealing information which is not limited to an individual's identity);

— the creation of a permanent "list of suspects", which now includes anyone arrested for a recordable offence; and

— the potential to exacerbate discrimination in the criminal justice system.

6. GeneWatch UK recognises the benefits of the NDNAD but we also believe that its current operation does not strike an appropriate balance between the rights of the individual and the interests of the public. While there is no doubt that society does have an interest in the detection and prevention of crime, this cannot be used to justify every infringement of the individual's right to privacy and the loss of civil liberties.

7. When DNA profiling is used wisely it can bring major benefits to society by helping to convict serious criminals including murderers and rapists. However, GeneWatch believes that there are changes that could be made to the operation of the NDNAD which would protect people's rights and increase public confidence without compromising its role in tackling crime. The changes which fall within the remit of the Committee's current inquiry are outlined in more detail below.

GOVERNANCE

8. GeneWatch strongly supports the conclusion of the Review of the Forensic Science Service that the NDNAD's governance needs to be more independent, transparent and accountable and that the database itself must remain in public ownership. However, we think that, in addition to removing custodianship from the FSS, there is also a need to broaden membership of the NDNAD Board. There are serious weaknesses in the governance and oversight structures currently in place including:

— the lack of transparency around how decisions are made and whether these decisions are really being made the public interest;

— the lack of an independent oversight body to scrutinise uses of the database and provide guidance as to when controversial uses, such as familial searches (trying to find the relatives of a suspect), are appropriate;

— the potential for major conflicts of interest because of the triple role of the FSS—it is the main supplier of DNA profiles and an organisation carrying out forensic research as well as the custodian of the database, making decisions about how the NDNAD should be used.

9. As originally suggested by the Royal Commission in 1993 and since then by the House of Lords in 2001 and the Human Genetics Commission in 2002, the oversight mechanisms could be much improved by creating a new, independent advisory body that includes lay members. This body would need to oversee the entire operation of the NDNAD from sample collection through to the production and use of DNA profiles as well as deciding what uses of the database were appropriate. Such an independent body would provide the public with much more reassurance that the data and samples were being properly used and protected.

SAMPLE RETENTION AND RESEARCH USES

10. In addition to improving governance, GeneWatch believes that some practices adopted by the FSS to date in its management of the NDNAD should be discontinued. These practices are: (i) the permanent retention of DNA samples from individuals (rather than just the DNA profiles and associated data on the database) long after an investigation is complete; (ii) the use of the database for genetic research without consent.

11. DNA samples are currently retained indefinitely, linked to an individual's record on the NDNAD via a unique barcode reference number. The samples remain the property of the police force which collected them, but are stored by the laboratory which analysed them (either the FSS, or one of the other suppliers) for an annual fee. GeneWatch believes that DNA samples (except samples from the scene of a crime) should not be retained once an investigation is complete. This would remove concerns that samples could be used to reveal personal genetic information (such as health-related information) or be used for purposes other than identification (such as research into "criminal genes") without the individual's consent.

12. Suspects' samples need to be retained for a certain length of time so they can be analysed and the profiles can be checked. However, destroying the sample once an investigation is complete does not in any way restrict future searches for matches between DNA profiles. All the information that is needed is stored in the DNA profile held on the computer database. Physical samples do not need to be retained to prevent errors because a fresh sample must be taken anyway before DNA evidence can be used in court. Although it can be argued that samples may need to be re-analysed if the technology is updated, in reality upgrading the DNA profiling system used on the database would be costly and unnecessary and make the NDNAD incompatible with other databases internationally.

13. Research using the NDNAD can currently be conducted with the approval of the NDNAD Board, without any ethical oversight. Since 1995, five research proposals have been submitted to the Board for consideration. Of these two were approved, two were rejected and as of March 2004, one was still pending a decision. The two successful projects related to identifying suspects via their ethnic or family backgrounds and both were conducted by the FSS. Neither project sought the informed consent of participants.[1] It remains unclear whether or not the DNA samples linked to the database have been used in any research. However, the database itself has been used for at least one potentially controversial project: attempting to link DNA profiles with ethnicity.[2]

14. GeneWatch believes that neither the NDNAD nor the associated DNA samples should be used to conduct genetic research without consent. Research uses of the database itself (profiles and personal data) should be restricted to producing "quality control" statistics on the type of data that has been added and how the data is being used.

15. The right to consent or refuse to take part in research is an important right for individuals and for society. It is not necessary to use DNA samples or profiles taken without consent to do legitimate genetic research. Categories in the NDNAD such as "ethnic appearance" are meaningless for scientific purposes and the DNA profiles and samples will not be representative of either the general or the "criminal" population. Genetic research using the database is therefore likely to be misleading as well as controversial.

CONTRIBUTION OF NDNAD TO CRIMINAL JUSTICE

16. Like others, we are concerned that the legislative changes to date have been introduced too rapidly and in the absence of any meaningful public debate. We believe that further deliberation is needed to find out what the public would accept as a reasonable balance between protecting the right to privacy and protecting citizens from crime in terms of who is included on the database and for how long. There are no data available to evaluate whether crime detection will be improved by including DNA profiles from people who are arrested and not charged, or by continuing to hold data on people whose charges are later dropped or are found innocent.

17. Keeping records indefinitely raises concerns about civil liberties, particularly when offences are related to peaceful protest or political dissent. This practice also undermines the principle of rehabilitation. GeneWatch's current view is that record-keeping on the NDNAD should be brought more into line with that on the Police National Computer (PNC). PNC records for serious violent and sexual offences are kept indefinitely, but most other records are eventually removed. On the PNC, records from people who have been acquitted may be retained only in some specific circumstances (mainly related to sexual offences) and for fixed time periods.

18. GeneWatch believes an independent review of whose DNA profiles should be collected and retained on the NDNAD is urgently needed. Research on the use of the NDNAD database, its effectiveness and the justification for including innocent people, should be conducted to inform the debate. The questions that need to be addressed include:

— When should samples be destroyed?

— Whose profiles need to be on the database to ensure the most efficient prevention and detection of crime?

— Does the NDNAD reinforce existing inequalities in the criminal justice system?

— Is expanding the NDNAD the most cost-effective way of detecting and preventing crime when compared to other measures eg increasing the number of police officers?

— When should convicted criminals be allowed to reopen their case to seek exoneration via DNA profiling?

— Which databases should be linked together via the proposed National Identity Register?

— When should the police be allowed to access other DNA databases, set up for health or research purposes?

19. The Human Genetics Commission (HGC) is responsible for advising ministers on all developments in human genetics including their social, ethical, legal and economic implications. It has a clear remit to involve and consult the public and other stakeholders and should be encouraged to launch a public debate on this important topic.

20. DNA profiling is not foolproof and there are particular concerns about the difficulties in analysing samples from crime scenes, which may be degraded, contaminated or contain mixtures of more than one person's DNA. There has also been too little attention paid to the potential for DNA evidence to be used to investigate miscarriages of justice in Britain. In the US the "Innocence Project" has been set up exclusively for this purpose and has so far resulted in 141 post-conviction DNA exonerations, including the release of 13 prisoners from death row. A similar project in the UK could help increase public confidence that DNA profiling is being used to improve the criminal justice system.

UTILISATION OF NEW TECHNOLOGIES

21. The Short Tandem Repeats (STRs) currently analysed for forensic DNA profiling are located in non-coding sections of DNA. These are parts of the DNA that do not contain any instructions for making proteins or any other cell product. This means they are not part of genes and are not thought to be important in influencing biological differences such as health or appearance. Therefore, the DNA profiles themselves are thought to contain very limited amounts of genetic information.

22. However, two companies in the US, Applied Biosystems and Orchid Biosciences, have developed a DNA identification technique that does not rely on STRs but looks at different areas of the DNA called single nucleotide polymorphisms (SNPs). Most experts believe that for the foreseeable future SNP technology will only be useful for very specialist forensic applications. There does not appear to be any advantage to changing the DNA profiles kept in forensic databases to SNPs. Such a change would require all the millions of samples on databases worldwide to be re-analysed, which would be prohibitively expensive. The use of SNPs in a forensic database would also significantly increase privacy concerns. Although it seems unlikely that forensic DNA profiling will change radically in the future, the possibility of such changes is often used to justify the retention of samples and continued investment in SNP-based research.

23. Researchers are investigating links between SNPs and ethnicity; skin and hair colour; health; surnames; and behaviour. Some scientists believe that this information could generate a description of a suspect from a DNA sample alone, which could be potentially useful where no other intelligence information is available. However, it may be misguided to use predictive genetics to generate a description of a suspect because such predictions are generally poor. This could waste valuable police time by narrowing down searches in the wrong direction and perhaps implicating innocent people during the investigation. There is also a danger that this type of information is used selectively to reinforce existing prejudices: for example, about race or skin colour.

24. In April 2004, police reported for the first time that they had used DNA profiling in Britain to predict a suspect's origins.[3] DNA from a suspected serial rapist was said to contain "strands from America, Europe and sub-Saharan Africa", a combination claimed only to be found in the Caribbean. Based on this information, the police announced that they were looking for a suspect from the Caribbean and furthermore that over 200 police officers with Caribbean backgrounds were being asked to volunteer for DNA tests to help determine which island the suspect might have come from. However, DNA Print Genomics in Florida, the company that actually carried out the DNA analysis, later denied that the test could be used to predict Caribbean origin. The company explained that although broad ethnic ancestry can be determined from DNA, geneticists cannot say with any certainty that an individual comes from a specific country.[4]

25. It is important for the police to be seen to be using information wisely and accurately if they want to maintain public trust in DNA profiling. The merits of methods which attempt to predict the characteristics of individuals from DNA left at the scene of a crime should therefore be independently reviewed, taking account of both scientific and ethical concerns. There is a danger that attempts to predict physical appearance, or other characteristics, hinder rather than help investigations by providing misleading information.

COMMERCIALISATION

26. Other commentators are better placed to consider the impacts of the Government's decision to develop the FSS as a public private partnership (PPP) on the reliability of DNA evidence. However, the increasing commercialisation of DNA profiling raises a number of concerns from a privacy and rights perspective. In particular, the priorities of commercial companies may differ from the needs of the criminal justice system. Commercial priorities may include:

— permanent storage of DNA samples (for which suppliers are paid an annual fee);

— undertaking genetic research using the samples and/or database (which may lead to new commercial opportunities and patents); and

— expanding the use of new technologies such as SNP profiling, which may not offer any real advantage over STRs (see above).

All the above significantly increase privacy concerns whilst bringing marginal, if any, benefits in terms of tackling crime.

27. Increasing the number of companies acting as suppliers also increases the number of people with access to the samples, increasing the threats to privacy. Again, this concern is exacerbated by the decision to allow indefinite retention of the samples, throughout an individual's life.

28. The increasing commercialisation of DNA profile supply to the NDNAD therefore reinforces the need for:

— independent and transparent governance;

— a more thorough, independent and transparent assessment of the effectiveness of the NDNAD and the potential role of new technologies;

— destruction of individuals' DNA samples once an investigation is complete; and

— an end to the practice of allowing genetic research without consent.

29. It is also inappropriate for the Chief Executive of the FSS to continue to act as adviser to the Home Office on forensic science matters, because of the potential conflicts between commercial interests and the public interest.

November 2004

REFERENCES

[1] *Hansard.* 17 Mar 2004. House of Commons. Column 344W–346W.

[2] Lowe AL, Urquhart A, Foreman LA, Evett IW. Inferring ethnic origin by means of an STR profile. *Forensic Science International* 2001;**119**:17–22.

[3] Laville, S. Global DNA test narrows hunt for serial rapist. *The Guardian.* 28-4-2004.

[4] Adams, D. Can your DNA reveal where you're from? *The Guardian.* 6-5-2004.

APPENDIX 13

Memorandum from QinetiQ

INTRODUCTION

1. *QinetiQ's involvement in forensic science stems from disciplines, technologies and techniques developed in the first instance for the armed forces*

QinetiQ has itself recently been the subject of a PPP; we make no comment on the PPP proposed for the Forensic Science Service, beyond stating that the change in QinetiQ's own status has not affected its ability to offer a secure and innovative service in the field of forensic science or affected the mutual trust between QinetiQ and the public sector.

Our role as a provider of technologies and expertise in support of law enforcement and forensic investigation qualifies us to address some, but not all, of the questions raised by the Committee. Our comments are as follows:

2. *The use of forensic science in criminal investigations and court proceedings*

Technology applicable to the investigation of crime and the identifying and presentation of evidence is advancing rapidly. While in terms of human expertise the criminal can hope to stay one step ahead of better equipped police and intelligence services, it is harder (except possibly in the most advanced forms of computer crime) for an offender to cover their tracks as easily as in the past. DNA—one of the few fields of forensic science in which QinetiQ is not involved—is the best known example of this.

3. *What technologies exist that can be used in investigating crimes and as evidence against the perpetrators?*

Scientific research has generated, and will continue to generate, a vast array of technologies that can be harnessed to the fight against crime, both in terms of prevention and detection. The task of assessing which of these can make a significant contribution is a formidable one; in our view assessment of the potential of technologies is almost as important as the research itself.

While companies and universities throughout the UK and beyond are continually generating technologies that can make a difference to forensic science, QinetiQ from its own experience would single out the following:

(i) Digital Forensics, involving the use of advanced technologies to investigate computer systems—including forensic imaging and analysis of target systems and media so that the integrity of the original is maintained, and evidence is found in increasing volumes of data. This is proving valuable in investigating complex frauds, murder, drug trafficking, counterfeiting, paedophilia and pornography, internet/e-mail/mobile phone abuse and intellectual property issues.

(ii) Digital intelligence, involving the use of internet monitoring and intelligence gathering techniques to aid investigations into Internet crime. These techniques can also help identify potential criminal activities such as "phishing" web side scams; the capability, motivation and source of criminal activity; and activities leading up to a potential crime.

(iii) Advanced image and video enhancement and processing, going beyond the functionality of commercially available software to reduce blur, noise and defocus, and offset camera wobble. The same technologies assist data reconstruction, and digitising of video data without data loss.

(iv) Acoustic signal separation and recovery, improving the intelligibility of speech from telephone lines, video recordings or other sources. Through signal conditioning, analysis and extraction techniques, speech can be made more intelligible through the removal of noise or interference, tape discontinuities suggesting edits or insertions can be detected and particular recording equipment can be identified. It is also possible to identify characteristics of the recording environment like reverberations and background nose, so that the location of the recording can be narrowed-down or identified.

(v) Mathematical modelling of impact and explosive events. Different forms of science can be put together to explore the validity of different scenarios after an impact or explosion. The technology exists to "re-create" such incidents and feed in the relevant known facts and scientific properties. These techniques have been used to provide answers over the Lockerbie and Oklahoma City bombings and the blast that destroyed an ammonium nitrate plant in France.

(vi) Laser scanning and 3D computer modelling. Laser scanning is increasingly being used to record crime scene data in 3D. Accident investigators can draw their data from the scanner, and if necessary the accident or crime scene can later be reconstructed using data recorded by the scanner. This is of particular value in enabling a road to be reopened after an accident; now that all fatal Road Traffic Accidents are classified as crime scenes, the site can remain closed, causing severe congestion, if traditional recording methods are used.

3D computer models can be created from the scan data to create a reconstruction of events or show evidence in an easy-to-understand format and allow investigators to view detailed visual information from angles that a camera might not be able to capture. Real-time models can be used quickly to alter the view of an event to see it from any angle—an advantage to anyone trying to capture the "feel" of a crime scene. It is also useful in a court environment when the viewing perspective needs to be quickly altered, for instance to allow for a discrepancy in witness positions. It can thus place the jury in the murder environment.

The use of 3D visualisations to aid forensic analysis is developing fast, and is something particularly to watch.

4. *Are these technologies being used to their full potential in investigating crime?*

(a) One very important issue with new technologies in forensic science is the need for there to be a first adopter who will organise the procurement process in such a way that innovation is encouraged. Most public sector procurement in the field of law enforcement is highly fragmented, and often the reluctance of any one organisation to take the lead creates a situation where orders are placed piecemeal; the general inability of police forces to collaborate on procurement is a particular handicap.

In this climate, there is a strong disincentive to companies and organisations with ground-breaking technologies to develop them into product. This difficulty is evident right across government in almost every area of law enforcement and security, and it needs to be addressed at the centre.

In addition, it is essential that organisations which develop new forensic science technologies and support law enforcement agencies have a good knowledge of the criminal justice system that will allow investigations to benefit fully from using the technologies in the most effective way.

It is of particular importance that the philosophy and working methods set at the outset for the new Serious and Organised Crime Agency (SOCA) take full account of the technologies available. While SOCA's *raison d'etre* has to be the tackling of organised crime, it is vital that its establishment sets good practice in procurement and the use of technology for the rest of the law enforcement community, instead of becoming a further example of fragmentation.

(b) On specifics, there is a particular issue with automatic number plate reading (ANPR). Commercial systems are still at best 95% efficient, so such identifications are not sufficiently reliable to be used as evidence on their own. However, ANPR does act as a marker to find an image of a vehicle at a particular time and location in a database of recorded images. It can also be used as a trigger to alert the authorities to the presence of a suspect vehicle.

ANPR, supported by recorded images, could be used more widely to track suspect vehicles and to provide evidence of vehicle location in support of prosecutions. The success of prosecutions relies on the quality of the recorded image; prosecutions are assisted where the face of the driver is clearly seen. There may be potential in the future to add automatic face recognition, but this technology is not yet sufficiently far advanced.

In the area of computer and Internet related crime, the techniques being used by criminals are rapidly changing as the technology evolves and the skills of the criminals increase. Thus, law enforcement organisations need to work very closely with organisations that have up-to-date knowledge and practical experience of the relevant technology and techniques being used in order to deter, prevent, detect, investigate such crimes.

— QinetiQ is Europe's largest integrated R&D organisation, with nearly 10,000 employees throughout Britain, over 7,000 of them scientists. QinetiQ's involvement with forensic science derives from over 60 years of pioneering defence technologies as an arm of government. Now in the market under a PPP, QinetiQ is putting these technologies—and new ones—to work across a range of Government departments and public services and in the commercial world.

— Our work in supporting law enforcement covers digital investigation, digital forensics, image and video enhancement and processing, audio signal recovery, mathematical modelling of impact and explosive events, laser scanning and 3D computer modelling and human factors. We provide specialised equipment in support of operations, support to the intelligence gathering process and full traceability for presentation in court, backed where appropriate by Expert Witnesses.

November 2004

APPENDIX 14

Memorandum from The Royal Society of Chemistry

The Royal Society of Chemistry is a professional and learned scentific body comprising 47,000 members in the UK and around the world. Under its Royal Charter it has a duty "to serve the public interest" and it is in this spirit that the following evidence to the House of Commons Select Committee is submitted.

The Society does not itself take a formal view on any Government plan to develop the Forensic Science Service (FSS) as a public private partnership (PPP). However the Society regards it as important that the independence and integrity of the Forensic Science Service be maintained.

THE OPERATIONAL STRUCTURE OF FORENSIC SCIENCE

However, whatever financial structure is adopted, the Society is of the view that it is essential that "technique capacity" be retained. Short-term local trends in the nature and volume of crime should not be assumed to continue. For example, the reduction in gun crime in Northern Ireland following the Peace Process does not mean ballistics staff in Northern Ireland should be made redundant. Global patterns and trends evident elsewhere may begin to appear in the UK (eg gun crime shows signs of rising in parts of the UK) and the Society takes the view that a forward thinking business approach should be adopted. A more coherent and effective approach should provide an environment to allow full cost recovery, relative autonomy and opportunities for increased investment.

The Society takes the view that the flexibility to recruit, reward and develop staff in the forensic service and to secure investment in new technologies are the keys to the effective delivery of forensic science. This would enable the service delivery to be more responsive. The service could become more proactive in highlighting novel forensic means of tackling crime and applying proven technologies to volume crime (eg burglaries and car crime) which affects a greater number of ordinary people than does major crime (which in most cases inevitably attracts the resources needed). Currently the FSS is obliged to accept all incoming case work while other (private sector) providers can and do "cherry pick". By comparison this leaves the FSS vulnerable to criticism for taking longer or costing more for the more difficult work while being denied the commercial advantage of the high throughput routine work.

R&D

The FSS currently devotes some £14 million pa to Research and Development some of which is "blue-sky". This level of investment must be maintained if the UK is to retain its position as a leader in the forensic area. It is also very important for the FSS to maintain and develop relationships with academic researchers as it is from this synergy that the next generation of forensic science and scientists will emerge.

EDUCATION AND TRAINING

With regard to education and training, the best practical training ground for forensic scientists is in the FSS. Other (private sector) forensic science providers recognise this. While degree level qualifications in forensic science provide good context-based studies (eg case studies delivered by practising forensic scientists) they are not a substitute for good basic science qualifications. They are an indication of a strong interest in the area and can be helpful in general areas such as Quality Systems (ISO 17025), continuity of evidence, duty to the court of an expert witness etc. An element of forensic science within an undergraduate chemistry or biology degree, as an example of the application of chemistry or biology for the public good, can attract students into studying science based subjects, but it should not compromise the study and application of fundamental chemistry (particularly analytical science) and biology skills. The popularity of forensic science as a subject amongst the 15–18 age group has led to a rapid expansion of educational provision in this area. This interest has been generated mainly by the high exposure of "forensics" both in fictional television programmes and in books and in the news media. The effects of this rapid expansion on Forensic Science are still unclear but it can be expected to impact significantly both on recruitment to the Forensic Science Service and on FSS requirements for *in-situ* training.

EMPLOYMENT AND TRAINING

The Forensic Science Service was historically the main provider of forensic services within the UK and tended to recruit predominantly graduate or higher qualified staff with strong scientific backgrounds in Chemistry, Biology, Physics and Materials Science. However this pattern changed following the change of the FSS to agency status in 1991. Since then a raft of alternative provision has grown up outside the traditional FS service, including companies such as Forensic Alliance, together with a range of independent forensic consultancies and police force specific laboratories. Whilst many of the people employed within these laboratories are science graduates there is an increasing level of recruitment at the post-18 level. This has resulted in a growing demand for on-the-job training of many types. Some of this training is specific to a particular technique, which is provided either by instrument manufacturers or via specific consultancies, and some is more general as in the case of the Wetherby FSS laboratory which sends their technicians for part-time degree study in Chemistry.

UNDERGRADUATE EDUCATION

Undergraduate provision in this area has undergone an explosion over the last five years due entirely to the popularity of the subject. As a result the number of courses on offer which include "Forensic" in their title has risen from one (Strathclyde) to over 360 at 58 institutions. Of these approximately two thirds could be classed as non-scientific, linking Forensic studies with such diverse subjects as theology and tourism studies, and as such these courses are unlikely to provide appropriate training for the FSS.

Of the other third perhaps 20 could be classified as being predominantly Chemistry-based and of these only five or six have a specific emphasis on analysis. The emphasis of these courses is on harnessing the scientific enthusiasm of the students engendered by their interest in Forensic Science and to provide the necessary Chemistry and Analytical Science to produce employable graduates. It is likely, therefore, that these will provide the forensic science services with an alternative source of highly, and appropriately trained, graduates in the near future. The evidence for this comes from those institutions who offer a four year sandwich course, such as Huddersfield, where competitive placements were obtained in 2002–03 at the following places: HFL (Horse Racing Forensic Laboratories), the Regional Toxicology Laboratory in Birmingham, US Universities undertaking research for the FBI and GlaxoSmithKline.

The remainder of the forensic courses are generally found in institutions at which the Chemistry provision at degree level has been discontinued but where there is still a strong Biological or Biomedical provision. Generally speaking these courses focus predominantly on the biological and crime scene aspects of forensic science. It is likely that these courses will also provide suitable graduates in specific niche areas. However, this is a rapidly changing situation.

One major concern amongst providers in this area has been to ensure the validity of their provision. The starting point for many institutions has been the appointment of staff with direct experience of Forensic Science which, coupled with the good uptake of their sandwich students, would suggest that a small number of these 360 courses are providing "a relevant hard science forensic course" suitable for the Forensic Science Service and its competitors. The relevance of the 360 courses will in the future be more transparent as the accreditation process of the Forensic Science Society gets underway. Meanwhile those courses containing significant Chemistry coverage have already obtained recognition from the Royal Society of Chemistry.

16–18 EDUCATION

The interest in forensic science has now filtered down to the post GCSE level with a number of colleges offering courses in Forensic Science. It is probable that this will provide a continuing supply of students onto degree courses in the medium term and provide graduates with significant Forensic experience.

November 2004

APPENDIX 15

Memorandum from Ian W Parkinson

I am an employee of the Forensic Science Service and a member of the Prospect Union, but I must make absolutely clear I am writing in a purely private and personal capacity and the views expressed are my own and not those of either the FSS or Prospect.

KEY STRENGTHS OF THE FSS

— The FSS is, and is seen to be, working for the interests of justice and the public good.

— The expertise of staff in

— assessing the needs and examination strategy of individual cases;

— the quality of examination and analysis;

— evaluating, interpreting the scientific evidence; and

— presenting the scientific evidence to courts.

— The visible and demonstrative integrity and reliability of the evidence provided.

— Optimising the forensic input into investigations, which needs building of good working relationships with the police.

— Extending the capability of forensic science.

— The Home Office can steer the strategy of the FSS to support aims and goals of the Government.

ADVANTAGES OF TRADING FUND

— The accountability of the FSS to the public, Home Secretary (plus the Treasury and PAC) will be maintained.

— The FSS scientist, maintains the public sector ethos and as a public servant is clearly (and is understood in court) to be balanced and impartial.

— The ability of the Home Office to give strategic direction and to ensure the FSS supports Government aims will be preserved.

— The advice to, training of, and discussions with, the police relate to operational needs and are (and can be clearly seen as) free from considerations of the financial worth or costs of the work.

— The FSS can be seen not to be motivated to exploit a virtual monopoly position.

— Ensure the continued provision of a close to comprehensive range of services, including low return and little used (but nonetheless vital) services.

— R & D effort can be directed towards operational improvements and extending capability.

— The FSS's provider of last resort obligation would not be compromised.

— The FSS can maintain custodianship of national databases, eg The National DNA Database.

— Quality system and procedures are governed by considerations of best practice.

— There is no risk of the FSS failing.

— Free to focus all resources on core work; supporting law enforcement within England and Wales.

— International links (eg FBI and the European Forum (ENFSI) not jeopardised.

— Crown exemptions facilitate holding of normally restricted collections (prohibited weapons, drugs).

DISADVANTAGES OF PPP

Becoming a PPP is essentially shift of priority from a service operated in a businesslike way over to a business which makes its money by providing a service.

— The control and direction of the FSS would have a greatly increased emphasis on commercial reasons, rather than operational need.

— There would be no provider of last resort.

— Uncertainty for customers of continuity of services, as subject to changes in marketplace conditions.

— The Home Office would have a reduced influence (and could lose) strategic direction of the FSS to support Government aims.

— Public sector ethos would be eroded.

— Safeguards are needed to ensure the public interest is protected, which are of unknown reliability.

— There would be pressure to give training to police only where it suited commercial interests.

— Case advice etc also affected and given with a view to costs and financial worth.

— The perception of the police that the advice is affected by commercial considerations (whether true or not)would be an inevitable barrier.

— The range of services would be more likely to be reduced to those which are the most efficient earnings generators, with those expensive or rarely used being run down or withdrawn.

— Shareholders will demand a return putting upwards pressure on prices. Also not everyone is comfortable with tax payers money going to inflate the already excessive profits of big business investors.

— Pressure to cut corners, reducing quality would be increased as cost drivers become more emphasised.

— There is a risk to the perception of integrity and impartiality in court—privately employed scientists are perceived as more likely to represent a vested interest that a balanced opinion.

— Risks exploitation of virtual monopoly market position.

— Lower levels of R&D likely.

— R&D would be likely to be directed at developments which enhanced commercial interests rather than operational improvements.

— Increased likelihood of diversion of scarce skilled staff from core work to other markets to maximise earnings.

— Staff training and development—time and resource intensive in forensic science—likely to be reduced in emphasis and be to the minimum required:

  — Costs and time considerations.

  — Increasing rewards for staff as skill base increases.

  — Increased attractiveness as a competitor headhunt target.

— Increased/induced costs to Government for staffing:

  — National databases.

  — Regulators, and support staff.

  — Policy units.

— Home Office would have to pay full economic cost for projects.

— The Government would not be able to transfer risk, the FSS could not be allowed to fail.

— International links compromised, reducing influence of UK on these bodies and their policies.

— FSS itself marginalised from Home Office and CJS policy making.

— Commercially sensitive information less likely to be provided.

— Risk of the perception that business elements may influence policy in directions favouring their interests.

— Security clearance is an issue.

— IPR more likely to be kept within FSS for commercial reasons.

— Works against disclosure of material in cases between suppliers.

POSITIONING

I regard forensic science is naturally positioned in Government law enforcement, and is so positioned in all countries as far as I am aware. It is a core element of the evidence gathering function of the police within the CJS. I would suggest this view is shared by most police and FSS staff generally and the public.

The relationship with the police is one which needs to be handled with care, as there has to be a balance between supporting investigations and providing independent and impartial evidence, which may ultimately support the defence case. This relationship is, I contend, easier and more comfortable for a forensic scientist in the public sector.

EFFECTIVENESS AND VFM

The integration of the forensic evidence is generally considered to be a key element of optimising the effectiveness. A competitive market with different aspects done by various suppliers makes balkanisation more likely.

The current situation is that the police filter submissions (and information provided) select exhibits to be examined and control examinations. This leads to a risk that these decisions are made without consultation with the supplier, and may be not the best approach to the forensic evidence. This is already a problem, and a PPP is almost certain to exacerbate this situation, because of the suspicion of a profit driver colouring training and case advice.

It is quite clear that from a police perspective effectiveness is often judged by the actual outcome of the trial, which is a dangerous measure of VFM. It can lead to pressure to exaggerate scientific evidence to gain marketing edge. It is also clearly dependent on the non-forensic aspects of the case, and a lack of actual scientific evidence found does not mean that the examination was pointless.

MANAGEMENT, STAFF AND "BUSINESS" ISSUES

It is generally accepted that the FSS has acted in a businesslike way, with the only real issue being timeliness. This latter point is a symptom of a massive growth in volume and expansion of resource has taken place as rapidly as possible, constrained by the available capacity of the existing staff to train and develop staff, when this has to be balanced against the need to meet the targets for their own casework.

The bureaucracy is clearly something which should be minimised whatever form the FSS is in and much of this is internal to the FSS. Some is imposed by the CJS. I am not in a position to judge from an employee perspective other PPP organisations. I am sure this information could be obtained, but I would be surprised if staff of such organisations found massive improvements in this. The bureaucracy of recruitment did not prevent the FSS from nearly doubling in size (1,500 to 2,800) between 1997–98 and 2001–02.

There are three aspects to the current Trading Fund arrangements which are issues which in my view would benefit from greater control passing to the FSS:

— Procurement is a big problem and OJEC procedures are a real burden. I would say this was a key factor amongst those relatively few staff (predominantly managers I suspect) who favour PPP.

— The senior managers of the FSS do need to have the freedom to manage, with only a strategic steer from the Home Office.

— Improved access to capital for equipment investment.

COMPETITION

The impact of competition for some areas of work would be to make them effectively not viable on economic grounds, and these would reduce in a downward spiral of volume and disappear as expertise withered. These areas of expertise would then not be available for the occasional but serious case when they could have made a real difference.

Some insight into product range could be obtained from bench marking against analogous private education or health areas. It does seem likely that the approach of private schools and health care would be very different to SEN or long term expensive chronic care.

MCFARLAND REPORT

The report of Sir Robert McFarland which formed the basis of the decision caused me a number of concerns, and does not appear to me to be balanced. Some particular issues raised which I should like to point out are:

— The prerequisites for fair competition in the forensic science marketplace do not exist.

— The police are unable to predict demand levels.

— It is not possible to predict whether prices would fall or not if FSS were to be made into a PPP.

— Claims that the public sector ethos is of no value.

— Indicates that in order for a competitive market to function, the way the CPS and police operate together would have to be changed. There is no realistic possibility of this happening (and it is not consistent with later developments).

— There is a balance of advantages and disadvantages between the FSS and other suppliers for the FSS as a trading fund.

— Full privatisation should be considered in the future.

— Loss of staff due to uncertainty likely.

— Non-UK work should increase by nearly 10 fold (£3.8 million to £34 million).

— No evidence of:

— A "cost cushion".

— Any conflict of interest between the FSS as a supplier and as advisor or custodian.

— Given a monopoly purchaser investors may be unwilling to become involved.

CURRENT SITUATION

The uncertainty of the threat of becoming a PPP is already affecting staff career choices and the relationship with the police. Forensic Alliance are (at the time of writing) expanding and recruiting, and this timing is I suspect not a co-incidence.

CONCLUSIONS

The likely impact of a PPP is in my view to:

— Reduce effectiveness of forensic evidence because:

— The relationship with the police and influence via training and advice would be damaged.

— The independence and impartiality could be at risk, and the perception of this.

— Downward pressure on quality.

— Make the reduction of the range of services available more likely, by the loss of uneconomic services.

— Staff training and investment in R & D likely to be reduced.

— Investment in R & D directed to commercial imperatives rather than extending capability.

— Novel technologies less likely as the FSS as a PPP would probably be doing less and would not be likely to share technology with non-UK organisations. Any innovations from the FSS, IPR would be more likely to be kept in house.

November 2004

APPENDIX 16

Memorandum from the Engineering and Physical Sciences Research Council (EPSRC)

INTRODUCTION

1. EPSRC have produced this evidence in response to a specific invitation to do so by the Committee. When the terms of the Inquiry were published in July 2004, EPSRC felt that it could not address the specific issues raised by the Committee. Nevertheless, EPSRC welcomes the opportunity to provide information on the activities it is supporting in the area of forensic science, and it hopes that the information will assist the Committee in its Inquiry.

EPSRC SUPPORT FOR CRIME RESEARCH

2. Despite improvements in several important areas, crime and terrorism continue to pose threats on a global scale. A dynamic approach is needed to stay ahead of such developments, and innovative cutting edge technology has an important role to play. The deployment of such technology will help to keep ahead of the criminals. In doing so, care has to be taken to ensure that the new technology itself is not used by criminals to exploit their unlawful objectives. It is important therefore that scientists and criminologists work together to meet future challenges.

3. EPSRC is actively encouraging the engineering and science research base to develop the next generation of technologies for preventing and detecting crime. EPSRC is specifically asking scientists and engineers to think about how their discipline can help combat crime and improve security. The Crime Detection and Prevention Technologies (CPDT) programme with its strap-line "Think Crime" is raising awareness in the science community of how science can contribute to reducing crime. Researchers are encouraged to use their expertise to develop technologies which assist in the detection of crime, boost the security of people and property, products and information, and create environments which reduce opportunities for criminal acts. Incorporating crime prevention as essential design criteria for new products and process could also provide business opportunities, and give the UK a technological lead. The CPDT programme aims to support research into technologies that will improve the safety of our urban environments, help stamp out fraud and identity theft, and aid forensic science in crime detection.

4. The EPSRC Crime Prevention and Detection Technologies programme was launched with the "Think Crime" workshop in November 2002. The workshop was attended by over 300 participants from many different disciplines and was addressed by key figures in the crime prevention field from academia, industry, the police, and government bodies.

5. Under the CPDT programme, EPSRC is funding (as at November 2004) 34 research projects, including speculative feasibility studies and four networks that involve consortia of researchers thus promoting communication between academic and user communities with an interest in generating new research ideas. The emphasis is on improving crime prevention and detection though the use of novel, cutting-edge technologies in the engineering and physical sciences. Multidisciplinary approaches are expected to be a particular prominent feature of the approach to finding novel solutions to tackling crime. In recognition of the importance of ensuring that the technology is developed in a wider context such as its use in the criminal justice system and of any ethical considerations, EPSRC has broadened the remit to include technology aspects of the life and social sciences.

6. Crucially EPSRC makes it a requirement in the CPDT programme that there must be collaborative involvement between the researchers and at least one user organisation so that ultimately the research outputs have the potential for being taken up and used in the fight against crime and terrorism. Collaborators are in the private sector—manufacturers and service providers—or the public sector such as the police, government departments or other agencies. However, only high quality research proposals as judged by peer review with significant user involvement are supported. Close contact is maintained particularly with the Home Office, which has welcomed the CPDT programme. The Home Office is advising EPSRC on technological areas of focus (see Annex 1) and on the initial selection of research projects for further consideration.

7. During 2003–05 the EPSRC plans to invest £13 million in the CPDT programme. £6 million has already been invested. In addition, EPSRC will support meritorious projects which have a potential relevance to crime reduction through other funding routes.

8. In view of the important technology contributions that university researchers can make to fighting crime, the EPSRC would like to continue to support its crime programme beyond 2005. A decision will be dependent on the allocation of resources to EPSRC following the outcome of the Government's 2004 spending review.

EPSRC SUPPORT FOR FORENSIC SCIENCE

9. "Forensic" may be defined "loosely, of or pertaining to sciences or scientists connected to legal investigations" (Chambers English Dictionary, 1998). The scope is therefore very wide. In the EPSRC remit it could include research into digital forensics, but in view of the scope of the Committee's inquiry the submission focuses mainly on chemical and biological forensics, and the analytical tools and methodologies for detecting substances that can be used to identify substances or persons in crime investigations.

10. EPSRC's investment in chemical forensic science has increased due to the launch of the CPDT programme in 2002. In 2003–04 EPSRC awarded grants totalling over £2 million. In the forensic science sector there are three collaborating partners in several research projects that EPSRC are funding: the Forensic Science Service, Forensic Alliance Ltd and the Forensic Science Agency of Northern Ireland. Their financial contributions are estimated at over £100k.

Organisation	Projects	Organisation contribution £k	EPSRC grants £k
Forensic Alliance Ltd	3	28	248
Forensic Science Service	10	115	1,270
Forensic Science Agency of Northern Ireland	1	1	61

11. Projects in forensic science have applications to property crime (including fraud), serious crime, drug investigation and chemical warfare agents. Examples of the range of forensic science projects supported by the EPSRC are given in Annex 2.

12. In the latest call for new research proposals published in November 2004, EPSRC is giving particular encouragement to the submission of research proposals with new research ideas in forensic science, in particular to:

— Novel techniques for forensic measurements. Despite recent advances in forensics there are still significant measurements that cannot be determined with the quantitative accuracy required for investigation and conviction. Novel biologically-based technologies may have the potential to offer significant advances in this area. Non-invasive/non-destructive technologies would be particularly welcomed.

— Novel detection techniques—Illicit drugs, explosives and metal items (such as weapons) continue to play a major part in crime. At the scene of crime, location of such items, as well as biological samples is a practical consideration. Although some techniques for detection are in operational use and others are under development, there are limitations. Smaller, faster, multi-agent or more sensitive techniques are sought.

13. In addition to research projects, EPSRC is currently supporting nine postgraduate PhD research studentships training on various aspects of forensic science. Some are associated with the research projects listed in Annex 2, supported as a result of the Crime Technologies initiative.

30 November 2004

Annex 1

TECHNOLOGICAL AREAS OF FOCUS BY EPSRC

These areas are reviewed by EPSRC and in consultation with the Home Office. However, EPSRC does not preclude the support of imaginative and exciting research projects in other areas.

— crime prevention or reduction, especially of street theft, car crime and domestic violence;

— the novel application of technologies developed within specialist areas, such as materials and physics-based technologies;

— designing out crime, particularly: the use of materials resistant to explosives and vandalism; and retail supply chain shrinkage;

— novel techniques for forensic measurements such as biological-based technologies;

— systems integration;

— data extraction from surveillance images;

— person/situation identification from audio signals;

— the built environment;

— information management;

— biometrics, specifically for person identification from database;

— novel detection techniques;

— electronic crime; and

— tagging and tracking.

Annex 2

EXAMPLES OF FORENSIC SCIENCE RESEARCH PROJECTS SUPPORTED BY THE EPSRC

The following represents examples of the research projects that EPSRC has supported and is supporting:

— A group at the University of Strathclyde led by Professor Ewen Smith has been at the forefront of transforming surfaced enhanced Raman spectroscopy from a research instrument into a powerful analytical tool in forensic science. The power of the technique lies in its sensitivity. Under the right circumstances single molecules of material can be detected. This technique provides a new approach to forensic analysis and it has been targeted at the detection of ultra-trace amounts of explosives, drugs and DNA. A close collaborative partnership has been formed with the Police Scientific Development Branch.

— DNA analysis is vital to genetics studies, drug treatment regimes, and medical diagnostics. Professor Tom Brown's group at the University of Southampton is working on novel methods to replicate DNA samples for easier analysis. The objective is to improve the reliability, scope and utility of DNA analysis in forensic science to spot unique genetic fingerprints in a sample. Existing technology for detecting so-called short tandem repeats (STMs) and single nucleotide polymorphisms (SNPs) will be improved.

— Chromatography combined with mass spectrometry and nuclear magnetic resonance imaging techniques is being used to study how the chemicals that make up a fingerprint change with time. These investigations by Dr Sue Jickells at King's College London in collaboration with the Forensic Science Service will link fingerprint chemistry with the right technique so that forensic investigators can obtain the best image of a fingerprint for matching purposes. The research is also exploring the possibility of obtaining lifestyle information from fingerprints that might lead the police to a suspect more quickly.

— Finding new, quick and easy forensic methods for assessing suspect materials is the aim of research being carried out by Professor David Russell and his group at the University of East Anglia. They are investigating how they can coat metal nanoparticles just 16 nanometres in diameter—1/5000th of the thickness of a human hair—with a chemical that "recognises biological substances and produces a colour change of a test solution from red to blue. This colour change could potentially enable the quantitative measurement of suspect substances at scenes of crime activity.

— No reliable method of determining age at death is available for forensic scientists, especially if the individual in question died between the ages of 30 and 60. Dr Peter Zioupos at Cranfield University, in partnership with Forensic Alliance Ltd, the Forensic Science Service, University of Melbourne and CSM Instruments SA, are looking at bone structure and material properties as they relate to age. The key goals are to refine bone measurements to provide more accurate estimates of age, the validation of the method on bone stored under different conditions, and the assembly of a portfolio of results to support the use of the methodology in criminal cases. The project will also promote the method to forensic investigators and establish a service and accreditation system for provision of the method.

— Emerging technologies such as protein arrays, competitive displacement arrays (CDA), and peptidomics are methods that have the potential capability of application in forensic science, crime detection and biometrics. Dr Mikhail Soloviev at Royal Holloway, University of London, in collaboration with the Forensic Science Service and Celltech Ltd, is exploring the potential of the technology for fast and accurate analysis of samples containing proteins from crime scenes. Also being explored is self contained tests for biometric applications for the identification of individuals and tissue samples as a substitute for DNA-based analysis when genetic material is not available. The same technology could also lead to more accurate "time-of-death" estimates in suspected murder cases.

— Colour change devices capable of identifying and quantifying a range of chemical warfare agents are being developed by Dr Simon Aldridge at Cardiff University in association with Piezoptic Ltd. The aim of the research is to produce monitors and alarms for the public domain, forensic science kits for scene of crime identification of chemical weapons, and personal meters to quantify exposure to chemical weapons. The detectors rely on sensor molecules that change colour when exposed to specific chemical warfare agents. The scientific challenge is to design in the required specificity.

December 2004

APPENDIX 17

Memorandum from the Forensic Science Service

INTRODUCTION

1. The Forensic Science Service (FSS) welcomes the opportunity to contribute to the Science and Technology Committee inquiry into the implications of the decision to develop the FSS as a public private partnership (PPP).

2. This submission sets out the Service's views principally on the first of the points listed in the call for evidence. FSS evidence already forms part of the Home Office submission. Subsequent to that submission, the Committee invited the FSS to prepare a written submission to assist the Committee in its questioning during the oral evidence session on 15 December.

EXECUTIVE SUMMARY

3. The FSS welcomed the decision to move to PPP via a Government-owned Company. Trading Fund status was showing signs of having run its course because market competition was not only growing but maturing, signified by advances in technology and customers' pursuit of best value procurement. More freedoms than Trading Fund could offer were needed.

4. The FSS has lived with competition and its risks and consequences for some time. Indeed the acquisition of Next Steps Agency status in 1991 foreshadowed this.

5. Over the next few years the success of forensic science in the fight against crime will depend on how strategic market issues are managed. The development of an efficient freely competitive market will be key. The development of such market conditions will require greater transparency, the establishment of proper contracting arrangements, a commitment to a level playing field, and arrangements to ensure the FSS is not disadvantaged if it were to accept an obligation to be the supplier of last resort as the major current incumbent in the market place.

6. If these conditions are not in place there will be a serious risk to the interests of the Criminal Justice System.

7. The disadvantage which the FSS faces has become more pointed in the post decision phase. It needs to be able to operate in a culture of fast change and flexible response and in order to do this requires greater commercial and private sector style freedom.

8. Highly trained staff are now leaving the FSS to join competitors. The continuance of this would make the Criminal Justice System vulnerable given that those competitors at present lack the infrastructure and critical mass to offer the total 24 hour, 365 day service which is singularly the hallmark of the FSS.

9. There has now been identified a clear need to adopt an approach to the FSS change of status which supports an orderly transition to a competitive market and which addresses the wider public policy issues.

OUR PERSPECTIVE ON PPP

10. The Home Office memorandum of evidence rehearses comprehensively the history and rationale leading to the McFarland Review of the FSS and the subsequent decision by Ministers that the FSS should become a Government-owned company (GovCo) as a precursor to development into a private sector classified PPP.

11. Arguments concerning the emergence of a more competitive market and the risks to the FSS's ability to compete effectively in this new world are now familiar to all and were acknowledged by the FSS some time ago when our place in the market became open to challenge. Indeed, this was the fulfilment of a philosophy going as far back as the transformation of the FSS into a Next Steps Agency in 1991 with a mission to grow the forensic market in the knowledge that competition would emerge and intensify.

12. Advances in DNA science and its use in the creation of database technology, all pioneered by the FSS, were championed in the knowledge that these developments would revolutionise and transform the national and global markets for forensic science and research and its applications. We have therefore lived with a

degree of competition for some time and have seen this intensify more recently. We have also lived with some of the consequences of growth in competition, such as the loss of FSS trained personnel to other suppliers. Until recently, the FSS was the sole source of trained forensic scientists in England and Wales. Training costs can run to £100k per individual.

13. The FSS welcomed the decision to move to PPP for all the reasons the McFarland review acknowledged that a change of status was essential to our continued viability. Although Trading Fund Status had equipped us to meet the challenges of a changing market through the greater use of commercial freedoms, it was becoming clear that as the market matured, the FSS would struggle to maintain its position. It was not simply the emergence of more and larger competition which marked the maturing market but, more importantly, advances in technology and the exercise of freedom of choice by customers encouraged by the pursuit of best value procurement policies. McFarland came at a time when these developments were beginning to become evident and needed to be addressed. The major issue for the FSS is not therefore the likely impact of transformation, but the need to bring this about as soon as possible, given that a freely competitive market is developing rapidly.

THE MARKET IN TRANSITION

14. Over the next few years, the ability of forensic science to remain key to reducing and solving crime will depend largely on the management of strategic market issues. That there is potential for the market to continue to grow as a result of technological innovation and customer choice is not in question. The FSS accepts that there is no longer a natural monopoly in the provision of forensic science, as has been the case in the past. A freely competitive market has the potential to combine a diverse supply side and an efficient demand side based on informed and rational purchasing polices. Such conditions would stimulate efficiency and further innovations.

15. Sir Robert McFarland recognised the need to develop a workable solution for the National DNA Database. In our opinion there are however other features which will develop if the market is to be freely competitive. These involve issues of greater transparency in price and demand, particularly in the acceptance of the link between the value and volume of services and the price customers are prepared to pay. In addition there should be the establishment of proper contracting between buyers and sellers, reliably informed by rational decision making about customers' intentions.

16. For these conditions to be valid, we believe there needs to be a commitment to a level playing field for all competitors in order to encourage efficient competition and efficient competitors, and to ensure there is no disadvantage to players already in the market. There needs to be therefore, among other things, a proper basis for contracting which provides the best balance between the standardisation of terms and the possibility for innovation. There should moreover be a willingness to pay for such innovation and to provide a return on research and development investment in line with the value it creates. During the transition to an efficient market, the issue of consistent quality standards will need to be addressed. Further, if the FSS is to accept an obligation of the supplier of last resort, as the market develops, so as to protect continuity of supply and not jeopardise the interests of the Criminal Justice System, there will need to be arrangements to ensure the FSS is not disadvantaged itself by that obligation.

17. The disadvantage which the FSS faced because of its inability to deploy the commercial freedoms enjoyed by its competitors and which were highlighted in McFarland has become more obvious in the post decision phase. Without private sector freedom in areas such as investment, procurement, reward strategy and commercial joint ventures, the FSS will become seriously disadvantaged in a rapidly changing market geared to a private sector modus operandi and a culture of fast change and flexible response. There is a danger that the FSS will be seen as the place to train and then move on, as the market for forensic scientists develops in parallel with the supply market.

18. In areas such as staff losses to other suppliers, the concerns for the FSS as a business are understandable. The wider concern for the Criminal Justice System surrounds the movement of personnel from an established organisation providing a 24 hour service, 365 days a year to other suppliers, who for the moment lack the infrastructure and critical mass needed to offer the total service approach. This would leave the Criminal Justice System with the worst of both worlds. The uncertainty which the decision to move to PPP has created is given as the biggest single reason for trained scientists now leaving the FSS. In a truly competitive market such movement of personnel would represent a healthy consequence of market forces. In a transitional phase to a truly competitive market it could represent a risk to customers, stakeholders, and the existing market.

19. It is vital therefore that a level playing field is facilitated as a matter of some urgency. There is a clear need to emphasise an approach which supports an orderly transition to a competitive market and addresses the wider public policy issues. At the same time the aim should be to transition the FSS in such a way that meets the needs of all stakeholders, balancing the needs of each and recognising the tension between some of the different objectives which need to be achieved.

December 2004

APPENDIX 18

Memorandum from the Forensic Science Society

1. The Forensic Science Society

The Forensic Science Society (FSSoc) is an international learned and professional body with members in over 60 countries. The FSSoc publishes a peer reviewed Journal *(Science & Justice)*, awards qualifications, arranges scientific conferences in the UK and abroad and is engaged in setting standards and accreditation in the forensic sciences. Most of its members are UK scientists but there is a significant minority of other forensic professionals involved such as police officers and crime scene investigators. The Society has about 2,500 members most of whom are forensic practitioners.

2. Recent Developments with the FSSoc

2.1 *Internal developments*

Following a strategic review carried out in 2003 The Forensic Science Society was formally launched as a professional body in November this year. The move towards professional status was strongly supported by the membership, many of whom consider this to be a timely development. Key partners in the sector, for example, the Council for Registration of Forensic Practitioners (CRFP) also supported this development.

The Society is now undergoing a programme of extensive change to move it from a traditional learned society to a modern professional body. The most important of these changes is the membership reclassification. This is will award post-nominals for member (MFSSoc) and fellow (FFSSoc) in a manner analogous to other professional bodies such as the Royal Society of Chemistry and the Institute of Biology. Alterations to the constitution of the Society have been agreed and implemented and the new membership grades are currently in the pilot stage. Professional membership will be open to practitioners, support staff (such as managers) and academics. Professional membership will be linked to a Continual Professional Development (CPD) program and CRFP registration where this is relevant.

2.2 *External Developments and activities*

The Society has a growing portfolio of external activities some examples of which include:

— Submission of a memorandum to the Home Affairs Select Committee inquiry on the Criminal Cases Review Commission.

— A presentation to the Parliamentary and Scientific Committee—Science in the Fight Against Crime.

— Our program of accreditation of university forensic science courses.

— Our role in the Forensic Science Sector Strategy group in representing small employers.

It is the agreed intention of the Society and CRFP that they will work as close partners in representation, development and regulation of forensic science practitioners. We believe that the separation of responsibilities of representation and regulation are critical to the maintenance of public confidence in forensic practitioners and forensic science generally.

3. Issues Before the Select Committee

3.1 *Privatisation of the Forensic Science Service*

It is the case that a significant private market in forensic science is already in existence in England and Wales. The Forensic Science Society as a professional body will be in a position to support and develop standards in forensic science irrespective of whether this is provided from a private or public organisation. The mechanisms by which we consider this could be achieved include:

— Professional membership of individual scientists and practitioners.

— A structured and credible CPD program.

— Provision of qualifications.

— Accreditation of university forensic science courses.

— Linkages between employment needs and educational provision.

— Convening specialist meetings and conferences.

3.2 *Education in forensic science*

The Society is increasingly concerned with the huge growth in educational courses in forensic science. This situation appears to have been driven mainly by HE institutions and has little connection with the needs of employers or the employment prospects in forensic science. The recent Science Engineering Manufacturing and Technology Alliance report evidences this issue.[15] It is ironic that during a period when there is so much "education" in forensic science that lack of knowledge is still a key feature in delivering the potential of forensic science to the criminal justice system.[16][17][18]

The Society has developed an accreditation programme for university forensic science courses and this is in an advanced state. Twenty-four universities are engaged in this programme for specific courses that they deliver. It is the intention of the Society to continue and expand this programme in partnership with other organisations that have a common interest in setting standards such as other professional bodies and the sector skills organisations.

3.3 *Research and development*

Forensic science as an interdisciplinary activity is not well served by the normal funding processes via the UK research councils. However, a welcome development is the current Engineering and Physical Sciences Research Council (EPSRC) "think crime" initiative. Similar initiatives by other UK research councils are likely to be beneficial in the development of collaborative research networks and valuable research in forensic science. The FSSoc would be in a good position to advise EPSRC and similar bodies on research priorities.

4. CONCLUSIONS

The Forensic Science Society is the largest and most diverse body of forensic science practitioners in the UK. It is the intention of the FSSoc to work with key organisations in the sector, to provide a coherent source of advice and knowledge to support the establishment of standards, working practices and policies that enable a more effective contribution to the criminal justice system from forensic science.

December 2004

APPENDIX 19

Supplementary evidence from the Home Office

DEVELOPMENT OF FSS AS GOVCO

Q1. *How will development of the FSS as GovCo impact on the procurement procedures used by the FSS and the ability of the FSS to access additional funding?*

A1. As a GovCo the FSS will remain subject to public procurement regulations for the purchase of goods and services over a certain threshold, but will no longer be subject to additional Home Office rules that operate at lower thresholds.

We are working with the company to create a capital structure and generate a business plan that will enable it to finance its own activities from earned revenue. In the event that GovCo requires additional funding, we will seek to provide these in a way which maximises value for money.

Q2. *What is the planned timetable for the development of the FSS as a GovCo?*

A2. The aim is for GovCo to come into operation on 1 July 2005. This target is ambitious given the size and complexity of task, which includes obtaining certain approvals, contract or lease transfers and certifications from the entities outside Home Office or FSS control.

Q3. *Will staff in FSS GovCo still need to be security cleared and have the police been consulted about this?*

A3. The proportion of FSS staff to be security cleared will be a matter for the GovCo Board who will take customer requirements into account. They will, no doubt, have regard to general practice by companies providing services to the Home Office and police forces.

---

[15] *Forensic Science: Implications for Higher Education 2004*, SEMTA.

[16] Association of Chief Police Officers, *Using forensic science effectively*, 1996.

[17] Her Majesty's Inspector of Constabulary (2000), *Under the microscope: a thematic inspection of scientific and technical support*, London, Home Office.

[18] Her Majesty's Inspector of Constabulary (2000), *Under the microscope refocused: a revisit to the investigative use of DNA and fingerprints*, London, Home Office.

Q4. *What is the estimated cost of developing the FSS as a GovCo?*

A4. The overall transformation transaction costs of the transformation process, including that of Home Office staff, is estimated to be between £3 million–£4 million. The final cost will depend on the time required and the final status of the FSS.

Q5. *What effect is development of the FSS as a GovCo expected to have on its investment in R&D and on what evidence is this prediction based?*

A5. The FSS in determining its R&D strategy will have regard to the future needs of the business and its clients, and in this respect will have regard to appropriate comparable levels of R&D investment by competitors.

Q6. *What will happen to the IPR currently held by the FSS when it becomes a GovCo? What would happen to the IPR if the FSS was developed as a PPP?*

A6. At present, IPR is held by the Crown. FSS Management, the Police and police authorities will be consulted about the principles that which IPR should be transferred to FSS GovCo. The objectives are to ensure an appropriate balance between public policy objectives, VFM for the Police and the successful development of GovCo.

Q7. *Does the Home Office intend to make any changes to the way that it obtains independent advice on forensic science once the FSS has become a GovCo, for example by establishing a forensic science advisory council or equivalent body?*

A7. The Home Office's main vehicle for planning and co-ordinating the use of forensic science is the Forensic Integration Strategy. This is being developed in partnership with ACPO and the APA under the aegis of the Police Science and Technology Strategy. In addition to Departmental scientific and ITC staff, this draws on contributions from representatives of the Office of Science and Technology and Royal Academy of Engineering. In addition, the relevant ACPO chaired bodies have access to advice also from forensic specialists from all three providers, the Human Genetics Commission and can obtain additional scientific advice from universities and other bodies if required. These groups are reflected in the Forensic Integration Strategy governance structure. The NDNAD Custodian will function from within the Home Office on transition to GovCo and will continue to have direct contact with all market providers.

Q8. *Is there a possibility that the FSS will remain as a GovCo in the long term? What other possible structures, aside from PPP, are being considered for the FSS in the long term?*

A8. The Government intends that FSS GovCo should be a success. It could remain as such in the longer term, but it is likely to need to be a transitional structure, in order to access to private sector capital and skills through partnering in order to meet its full potential.

The Government will continue to consult all stakeholders, including the TUs, about how the FSS can best continue to met the needs of its clients, including access to development capital required to keep pace with scientific and technological advances.

Q9. *What assessments has the Home Office undertaken of the Independent Publicly Owned Corporation (IPOC) model for the FSS developed by Prospect and PCS trade unions? Would this structure be able to meet the stated requirements for the FSS in the future and, if not, why not?*

A9. This model was discussed with the TUs and HO financial advisers at a workshop held in July. Home Office officials suggested that there was common ground about issues such as the need to access development capital and broaden the FSS revenue base. There was greater divergence of views, however, about the significance of the consequences for the FSS of a competitive market and the risks that would affect the pricing and availability of development capital.

FURTHER DEVELOPMENT OF FSS GOVCO AS A PPP

Q10. *The statement issued on 11 January 2005 stated that "timing of the next stage will depend upon agreement with key stakeholders". Who are these key stakeholders and could development of the FSS as a PPP occur without consensus between them?*

A10. Key stakeholders include the FSS, ACPO, APA, and the TUs representing FSS staff. The views of all stakeholders will be taken into account when determining next steps, but the main focus will be on the interests of the business, the cost, development and availability of forensic science for the police and how to maximise its potential impact on the CJS in reducing crime.

Q11. *What criteria will be used to determine when or if the GovCo should be developed into a PPP?*

A11. Any future move will be determined against comprehensive tests that take account of the possible benefits of private sector participation, likely changes in the forensic science market, benefits to business, realisable value to the government and access to private sector capital.

Q12. *What criteria will be used to select the private sector partner(s) for a PPP and will any types of business be excluded? What is the fall back position if there is not enough interest amongst potential private sector partners?*

A12. Such criteria would only be developed if a decision has been made to secure private sector participation.

Q13. What research has the Home Office undertaken into how development of the FSS as a PPP would affect public confidence in the CJS?

A13. Maintaining the integrity of forensic science is critical irrespective of whether the supplier is public or private sector owned. As the market develops, the police will expect to see adequate arrangements in place to ensure quality. That is central to the procurement strategy currently being developed by ACPO, the APA and the Home Office.

Q14. *What precautions would the Home Office take to ensure that the FSS succeeded in the face of potentially aggressive opposition? Would the FSS be the supplier of last resort?*

A14. The principal action to ensure that the FSS will reach its full potential is to provide the necessary freedoms, powers and recourse to allow FSS to prosper in an increasingly competitive market place. In the event of actions by competitors of an anti-competitive nature, the Home Office would look to the application of Competition law to protect its interests in the FSS and the wider forensic market.

The development of a more competitive supply market is expected in due course to reduce the risk of a discontinuous supply. In the transitional stage commitments will be placed on the FSS to provide services to forces as a supplier of last resort, but subject to value for money considerations and appropriate remuneration to reflect the costs of providing such services. Police forces will also consider steps that can be taken to reduce the risk of such supply and the costs if so doing.

Q15. *What steps would the Home Office take to ensure that the development of the FSS as a PPP would not impair data sharing between different suppliers in a way that was detrimental to the CJS?*

A15. In keeping with its public service ethos, part of the contractual arrangement between FSS GovCo and its customers will be an obligation to share data with other suppliers. The ACPO, APA and Home Office procurement strategy will need to address the extent to which similar obligations should be placed on other forensic providers.

GENERAL

Q16. *What measures will be used to ensure that the forensic services market has the capacity to respond to a significant increase in demand, for example in the case of a terrorist incident or natural disaster?*

A16. Chief Officers of Police will be able to redirect or re-prioritise work from forensic suppliers to meet emergency needs under the Gold Command arrangements being used at present to co-ordinate the UK forensic response to the Tsunami.

Q17. *Is the Home Office intending to implement any measures to prevent the exclusive development or licensing of a widely-adopted new technology by a particular supplier from stifling competition?*

A17. The ACPO, APA and Home Office procurement strategy will reflect the extent to which technical and other standards for forensic work are needed in the form of output specifications in order to maximise the benefits of multiple sources of supply.

February 2005

APPENDIX 20

Supplementary memorandum from the Home Office

NATIONAL DNA DATABASE

1. This is a brief summary providing an overview of the policy and planning development of the project to separate the National DNA Database (NDNAD) from the FSS over 2004. The details remain subject to approval by Home Office Ministers.

2. The McFarland Review of the FSS made some specific recommendations for the NDNAD:

2.1 Independence of database governance—including integrity, accountability and maintenance of public and user confidence;

2.2 Custodian oversight of DNA sample storage;

2.3 Governance arrangements put on a formal legal basis;

2.4 Strategic development of the "Super Custodian" concept.

3. We have developed the plans with point 1—independence and transparency—as fundamental to all policy development. We propose:

3.1 The Custodian and support team will form the core of a regionally (Birmingham) based Home Office delivery unit. The Custodian will report directly to a tripartite governance board which sets policy and strategy. This board will have permanent lay representation, performed at least initially by the Human Genetics Commission. The board itself, through its membership, will be accountable to the Home Secretary, ACPO and APA.

3.2 DNA service providers are currently "accredited" and continually assessed to ensure quality standards in the provision of DNA profiles to the database. Non-FSS suppliers are particularly sensitive to the current arrangements and have reported both to McFarland (during the FSS review) and the Home Office, that this gives the FSS unfair oversight of their processes and development. We propose that this quality and standards system be considered "oversight" of the forensic market and thus handled within the HO delivery unit.

3.3 The NDNAD routine activity—receiving DNA profiles, reporting matches and relevant information arising, and maintenance of the IT system—are relatively generic database activities. For the purposes of continuity of service to the police and minimum impact on the FSS at transition to GovCo it is proposed that these continue to be provided by the FSS, but under a formal contract stipulating responsibility and accountability, to the Custodian. This contract will be competed after three years in order to ensure efficiency and VfM of service.

3.4 The Home Office DNA Expansion Programme has funded NDNAD IT and process improvements over the last four years. Work is underway to develop a more integrated and sustainable development programme on separation from the FSS. This will also be treated on a contractual basis to ensure delivery to time and budget.

4. Oversight of the original DNA samples, especially from suspects (rather than crime scenes) remains one of the most sensitive issues to the wider public. At present there is no plan to change the current arrangements where suppliers store the samples received from their police customers. This policy is subject to regular review by the NDNAD Board.

5. The recommendation that governance arrangements be put on a formal legal basis was the reason for considering a Company Limited by Guarantee (CLG) structure—also recommended by McFarland. This has proved to be unsuitable for legal reasons but the relationships, responsibilities and accountabilities of the tripartite board members will be more formally and clearly defined in the tripartite board constitution than is present under the Memorandum of Understanding between the FSS and ACPO.

6. The current arrangements will establish the Custodian oversight of the NDNAD. Work is underway to link this role to the ACPO forensic procurement and pathology oversight requirements with the intention of "adding" Custodian functions to the HO delivery unit incrementally as policy and practical arrangements are developed. Other forensic databases (such as footmarks and drug profiling) will be treated through establishment and oversight of common standards, without requiring control of the databases or services themselves. The priorities for developing this work will be driven operationally via ACPO-led forensic sub-groups working with the Home Office under the Government's Forensic Integration Strategy.[19]

December 2004

---

[19] The Home Office Strategic Plan 2004–08: Confident Communities in a Secure Britain (p73) "By March 2008; through the Forensic Integration Strategy we will ensure that the police optimise their use of forensic science, extending our global lead on the use of DNA to all forms of forensic intelligence. The strategy will bring about changes in operational management and workforce practice as well as exploiting IT and scientific developments, in order to raise the level of detections."

APPENDIX 21

Memorandum from the Bar Council of England and Wales and the Criminal Bar Association

1. The Bar Council are grateful for the opportunity to consider the important questions raised by the Committee. The questions in which the Committee appear to be interested suggest a broad remit. They cover management issues related to the FSS, as well as the education, skills and experience of professionals, whether as witnesses or professional lawyers and judges. It appears to us that the focus is almost exclusively on the criminal justice system, although many of the observations in the paper will also bear on civil justice.

THE ADVERSARIAL SYSTEM

2. We detect from some questions asked at oral hearing that there may be some concern amongst members of the Committee about the adversarial system itself. We may have misread this. It does however seem to be us to be important enough to address. This concern has been heightened recently by the comments of the Home Secretary on 8 February in evidence to the Home Affairs Select Committee in the context of terrorist cases when he said:

> "... speaking entirely personally and privately (sic), as we are here, I am not an absolute fan of the adversarial system of British justice by comparison with some of the other systems that we have. I would be prepared in due course to look at some other system that could work in certain areas to move in this area. As you would know better than I from your own experience, any change in that area is absolutely enormous and would require a massive, massive shift and very wide consultation, so it is not something that can deal with the situation at this moment, but I would be prepared to look at that in the round."

3. It is relevant to provide this counter to that view. The opposing view, which we suggest is one held by many with real experience of our courts, has been expressed by one of the most experienced of expert forensic psychologists who regularly gives evidence in courts in this country. In an address to the Criminal Bar Association by Dr Gilsi Gudjonsson of the Institute of Psychiatry of the Maudsley Hospital had some trenchant comments on a some other systems of justice.

In his paper, "Expert Psychological Evidence in Britain and Abroad" he *concludes that "testifying abroad has highlighted the unique merits of the present legal system in England and Wales, at least as far as the evaluation of disputed confession evidence is concerned. My view is that other countries can learn a great deal from the English system. During the last 15 years or so the police and the courts have shown an unprecedented willingness and ability to learn from previous mistakes and have instigated various improvements in order to reduce the risk of a miscarriage of justice. In fact I would go so far as to suggest that England is leading the world in its protection of 'Persons at risk' during police interviews and confinement, that acceptance of their wrongful convictions can be occasioned by false confessions, and the systematic training of police officers in sound interviewing techniques".*

4. Because of this dichotomy of view about the system we have, it may assist to have some understanding of its history and development. The evolution of the system has shown itself to be adaptable to the needs of a technological age. Where it has been of value, it has accommodated many changes that owe more to the judge-led continental system, without sacrificing its essential justification. It may also be important to the Committee to understand how continuing education has now become a requirement for practice for all barristers.

5. Every nation has its own legal system, but the system in the United Kingdom is one of the oldest and for better or worse has provided the model for many. Some countries, eg Italy, are considering embracing the adversarial system after experimenting with the inquisitorial or civil system for some time. The comparative merits of the two basic systems (although there are many variants), or a combination of both, are becoming better understood. No preference for the continental system can be expressed without a thorough understanding of its problems. This is however outside the remit of the Select Committee, and this paper does not address this question.

A SHORT HISTORY

6. The proper administration of justice is the key to the correct system, not simply cost and expediency.

7. Professional lawyering began in England during the 13th Century when the first centralised court system was established in London. Criminal trials for serious offences came eventually to be heard by Judges of the High Court travelling round the country "on Assize". Prisoners were brought before them, the case presented by a prosecutor with little or no opportunity for proper representation for the accused, and justice was sometimes as speedy as it was harsh. A true adversarial process did not exist then. The prosecution had the task of proof, and the defendant was afforded little opportunity to defend himself in terms we would understand today.

8. It was not until the end of the 17th Century that, as a result of public criticism about the work of attorneys, anything was done about seeing that a system of formal education for lawyers existed, rather than the somewhat haphazard instruction that took place at dinner in the Inns of Court in London and through the efforts of some of the senior pleaders known as Serjeants-at-law, who were the fore-runners of the modern title of Queen's Counsel. In 1729, the attorneys were required to undergo five years training before being admitted to practice, rather longer than is required nowadays. The middle of the 19th century saw a further formalisation of legal training. The subject is unlikely to be of great interest to you, except perhaps to appreciate that the greatest strides in the development of any justice system are made when formalised education improves the abilities of the lawyers to use the tools that they are supposed to understand.

9. The view has been expressed that the common law of England and the civil law of Europe were never wholly distinct systems[2], and the civil law has had a significant influence on the development of English law. The two can be seen historically as "*component parts of the same cultural context*". Some of the ways civil law shaped the development of the common law include that of canon law, derived from Roman (civil) law, which was exercised by the ecclesiastical courts in England. A number of English Universities continued to teach the civil law as an intellectual discipline, and Oxford and Cambridge both retained professorships in Civil Law.

RECENT DEVELOPMENTS

10. In modern times, adversarialism has sought the discovery of truth through the contention of counsel. When and if each party was represented, each put his own case in the best possible light; then in theory at least, the court would have the benefit of the fullest investigation and interpretation of the facts in reaching its verdict. It is no longer the case, as it was perhaps 200 years ago, that it was the rules of evidence, and the prejudice of the court and legislators against the prisoner, and often the unequal abilities of counsel, that determined events. Much in terms of educational advance has changed that, Parliament, in the Criminal Justice Act 2003 has also recently addressed other perceived imbalances in the system. The modern system has evolved into a practical, and sophisticated means of establishing clarity about essential facts. Whilst this is not a cause for complacency, as improvements will always continue to be made, there is no sound justification for such a procedural change in a society that has led the world in its openness about its failings. Inquisitorial systems have not always seemed so open.

11. These recent legislative changes are themselves a recognition of the benefits of importing a broader, internationally based approach to the way we receive evidence. In this country, we now routinely agree significant areas of evidence by way of formal admissions; witnesses whose statements of evidence are not broadly challenged, are now routinely read by consent. Schedules of evidence, agreed chronologies, graphs and charts are deployed in the presentation of evidence. In the last three to four years, IT based technology has entered the courts enabling the benefits of visual dissemination of evidence to become almost a commonplace in many courts. As more IT is installed, so more courts will benefit from these advances. The only limitation so far has been in funding, particularly in the civil courts. Rules of court have provided for advance notification of the defence and the matters likely to be in issue in any criminal trial. In April the Criminal Procedure Rules drafted under the 2003 Act will take effect. These provide for advance disclosure of the details a defence case, the witnesses to be called, and why they are needed, as well as a whole raft of new trial management procedures that owe more to the continental system than our own tradition. The Civil Procedure Rules have streamlined the civil justice system, and whatever criticisms there may be, lawyers have responded to the challenge. It is the great merit of the adversarial system that it can accommodate these changes without sacrificing that tension which enables the truth to be exposed.

EXPERT EVIDENCE

12. In few areas is that tension more important than in the field of expert evidence. If experts are not subject to proper scrutiny and challenge as to the views they express, then the dangers that we have seen in recent well publicised cases will become commonplace. Literature which deals with court proceedings over the last hundred years has exposed a number of self-styled experts whose lofty self opinion, has led them to garner a respect well beyond their ability. Before the recent examples from which confidence in our system continues to suffer (eg the cases of Sally Clark and Angela Cannings), we recall Alan Clift and the Preece case, Frank Scuse and the Birmingham Six, Ron Outteridge and the Stephan Cishko affair. The Confait Inquiry was largely responsible for the bringing into being of the CPS as an independent prosecution body. Much has been learnt from these cases, and it is to the credit of our system that these mistakes are exposed. It is of course of equal concern that they were not exposed in a more timely fashion.

13. The Statute passed by the United Nations that created the International Criminal Courts in the Hague (ICTY) and Arusha (ICTR) upholds the adversarial system as its model. The Hague has proved to be a melting pot where the advantages of differing systems have been brought to bear within the court's rules of procedure, and the best aspects of the continental system have married within an adversarial framework. The adversarial system is one that has never ceased to evolve, and improves as time and experience force change upon the process. English barristers have regularly attended The Hague. They have trained lawyers

from the many nationalities that form the cadre of defence and prosecution advocates at these courts in the art of advocacy, and the adversarial system, which was alien to many. They have more recently extended this to the tribunals in Arusha.

14. In the adversarial process, the rights that the state possesses to insist on legally admissible evidence being received is often a qualified right, and the defence are there to see that where it is qualified, the right to adduce it at all is subject to legal scrutiny. The judge is positively assisted by the lawyers in his task.

15. The way in which that task is performed by well-trained and experienced advocates is what has given adversarial advocacy its modern reputation. This has come to mean in England and Wales, an expectation that the advocate will be able to tackle difficult examinations and cross examinations involving technical questions and matters of sometimes quite abstruse expertise. If an adversary has integrity, both in terms of preparation, an understanding of his or her role, and possesses the disciplines needed the do the job well, then the system shows itself to be worth the value so many nations have placed upon it. We believe our system and the Bar have earned that accolade, but are far from complacent in seeing that our knowledge and skill base does not stagnate. That is the strength of an independent Bar whose members are in competition with each other as professionals.

16.1 *The training currently offered to the Bar*

16.2 This training is not delivered to everyone, is not mandatory, and depends largely on the professionalism of the advocate. Many gain their primary experience "on the job". Contrary to the impression that may have been given by the evidence by Mr Graham Cooke to the Committee on 31 January 2005, we believe the Bar is generally well skilled in this area. Whilst very experienced, Mr Cooke did not represent the Bar Council as the record states. Mr Cooke is a statistician by training. The anecdotes he gives, and the opinion he has formed, is not justified by experience of the work of most barristers, who rise well to the challenge of scientific evidence. In chambers where advocacy forms a large part of their professional life, the culture produces an ideal forum where experience and views as to how best to tackle such evidence can be discussed.

16.3 It is true that sometimes barristers have to pick up cases at short notice. In cases where scientific evidence is to be challenged, such an advocate will have the benefit of the reports from both parties, which have to be served in advance, so he/she is not "flying blind" when he/she seeks to cross-examine.

16.4 In criminal cases, wherever possible, barristers try to see their own expert in conference. Sometimes this is done at Court, but often, and ideally, in chambers before the trial date. There is no payment for this in the graduated fee structure, which militates actively against proper preparation of such evidence. Barristers however take a pride in performing to the best of their ability and representing their client (Crown or defendant) properly and prepare themselves nonetheless.

16.5 There is of course work done to teach advocates their craft, including training in dealing with experts.

(a) Advocacy skills generally

Advocacy has for some years been part of the syllabus for all students training for the Bar. It is also a compulsory part of the programme of training for new practitioners. It is taught not only in the educational institutions validated by the Bar Council, but also in the Inns of Court themselves. Such training naturally includes witness preparation. Each of the Inns delivers regular and carefully organised training programmes in advocacy skills. All students will of course be taught the special status of an expert witness in being able to express an opinion, and the duty the court has to satisfy itself that any such person is in fact a true expert. They also receive lectures from experts about particular scientific subjects, and in some areas medical expertise, particularly those who study professional negligence. The syllabuses however vary between these institutions who compete with each other. Generally student and new practitioners would not be likely to receive focussed training on how to handle experts until they have been in practice for three years, save through the training offered by their pupillage chambers and the Specialist Bar Associations (see below). That is because the primary focus is rightly on essential basic skills—getting the basics firmly implanted.

(b) *Advocacy skills and expert witnesses*

Training is now part of the Bar's culture. All members of the Bar, however experienced, are now expected to receive a minimum period of 12 hours continuing education each year in order to acquire an annual practising certificate. Most do more than that anyway.

— The Inns of Court provide training on the handling of experts on their advanced courses, but not for those in the first three years of practice, who will be receiving training in the more basic advocacy skills. Courses include weekend training sessions. The advanced courses runs by the Inns of Court include training on expert witnesses. The trainers are barristers, QCs, judges and some solicitors. The training involves an understanding of the skills necessary to prepare for the examination and cross-examination of an expert, how to conduct a meaningful conference with an expert witness, and how to ensure that you are prepared to test the methodology and experience of the expert you are required to cross-examine. The method of teaching is modelled on, and adapted from the method pioneered by the Australian, Professor Hampel, the first Professor of Advocacy Studies ever to be appointed. He is an honorary member of the writer's chambers, and has lectured there, and in the Inner Temple very recently specifically on expert evidence.

— The South East Circuit has for the last 16 years been running an advocacy training week every Summer at Keble College, Oxford. This is mainly for pupils and young barristers and teaching is conducted to very high standard. Expert witnesses in the field of accountancy and medical specialisms have always volunteered their services as witnesses for the students to examine and cross-examine. This is something that is taken very seriously. Other circuits offer similar training.

— Barristers' chambers, offer regular training to pupils and tenants alike. It is often obligatory for pupils. This training can usually be expected to cover the skills required to examine experts, although this is left to chambers to decide. The writer's own chambers, for example, do provide continuous training programme which includes the examination of experts. Training occurs once or twice a week in one area or another. It includes, of course, the whole gamut of new legislation, advocacy skills and other special skills required by a professional barrister. Such organisation within the major sets of chambers is now the rule rather than the exception, but has of course to focus on a much wider area than just expert evidence.

(c) *Training by Specialist Bar Associations*

Training in the field of expert evidence is also carried out by Bar Associations. For example, the Criminal Bar Association (CBA) represents approximately 3,000 members of the Bar, and has, of its own initiative, taken on the responsibilities for training its members in the widest possible field of expertise that barristers might sensibly require. The CBA also runs a regular lecture on advocacy as a supplement to the training barristers and students will have received elsewhere. The CBA features a section on the necessary skills for dealing with experts in its advanced advocacy course run annually at Jesus College.

The CBA is also planning to cover the subject in a "Children as witnesses/victims" conference later this year. Professor David Ormerod is also to lecture members of the association on expert evidence and novel forms of identification in April. A lecture was delivered at the Central Criminal Court for all members of the CBA, and any others who wished to attend (including judges) by Angela Gallop on "*Forensic Science in the detection of Crime*". This dealt with access to advice by those charged with defending clients and access to test results obtained by the prosecution. It also covered the whole new landscape developing in the accreditation of expert witness and how we should approach their evidence.

All lectures conducted by the CBA are now videoed and made available to barristers and the circuits around the country on request, either as self-standing training aids or as adjuncts to their own training programmes. This month, the CBA are training 1000 CBA members on the provisions of the Criminal Justice Act 2003, including section 35 of the CJA 2003 which deals with the notification of the names of expert witnesses instructed by the defence. Once that is done, expert evidence will continue be high on the agenda.

17. The likely impact of the Government Plan to develop the FSS as a PPP on the competitiveness of the FSS, and on the effective provision of forensic science services to the Criminal Justice System

17.1 The publicly funded Bar has always been a good example of how well, and how economically, a PPP can work. The high overheads costs of the Legal Services Commission and the CPS, by way of example, have shown the value of using outside legal expertise. Whilst we do not understand why there should be particular concern about a PPP, we are nonetheless concerned that a future model for the FSS may tend to centralise scientific specialism on the grounds of economic expediency. DNA evidence, for example, has, in many investigations, become the first and only port of call in the detection of crime, in much the same way as fingerprint evidence was once regarded as the most important area of forensic endeavour in the field of criminal detection. The major advances in analysis (eg, Low Copy Number DNA profiling and the FSS SGM Plus system and further developments) make such evidence more reliable and its reach more extensive. The faith placed in such evidence is not without good reason, but it hides the danger.

17.2 How such a public/private partnership would work in practice will would depend on how well such an endeavour is supported, not only in the rigour of its academic and practical application, but also in the breadth of the expertise that it offers to the criminal justice system, prosecution and defence alike. This means that a cash starved service could produce a second-rate outcome. Such a service should not become overly bureaucratic but should always retain a breadth of scientific imagination so that a healthy culture of genuine scientific endeavour is created rather than a simply a supply line for standard criminal justice needs.

17.3 We note that sometimes private enterprise can achieve speedier turn-around times than public bodies. This is part of the enterprise culture. It is often the delay in obtaining forensic results that delays a trial with its concomitant costs (eg, of a prisoner in custody) and sometimes means a trial has to go ahead without such evidence. Provided quality standards can be maintained, a PPP might prove to be the environment where efficiency will best survive.

17.4 We echo the sentiments of Dr Angela Gallop that " . . . *following the FSS creation as a Government agency in 1991, as time went by, concerns started to be expressed both from within the profession and from the police about the way in which the core of the profession was developing. In particular, the scientists were concerned about the effect a pile-em-high, sell-em-cheap philosophy—useful for a quick turnround of large numbers of the relatively simple sorts of cases, was having on their ability to solve more complex crimes, and the possible exposure of any personal shortcomings in such high profile cases. There was widespread talk of de-skilling with the emphasis increasingly placed on just five areas of endeavour—the five Ds as they were calle— Documents, Drugs, DNA, Doc Martens (shoeprints) and Digits (fingerprints). DNA in particular was represented as the panacea for all ills at the expense of effort in other areas."*

17.5 In 1996 the FSS amalgamated with the Metropolitan Police Laboratory to form a national agency. In order to guard against the dangers of over centralisation of forensic services, we see merit in the government encouraging the use of other agencies which would provide forensic services both in competition with and to complement existing services. For the latter group, a government grant might encourage the maintenance of the broadest possible range of forensic skills available to the criminal justice sector in much the same way as existing regional adjunct offices of the FSS are said to provide a comprehensive and competitive service. We consider there is an increasing need for specialist forensic units in the detection of crime (eg, for sexual investigations, organised crime, terrorism, high value fraud and fire investigations, car crime and burglary). This is an area where PPP might work well.

18.1 The Quality of forensic Science Education and training and the supply of skilled personnel in forensic science

18.2 The training received by the Bar has already been addressed. So far as the experts themselves are concerned, we do not feel able to comment constructively on the present position, but repeat the cautions expressed in paragraph 17 about avoiding a narrowing of the skills base for ephemeral and economic reasons.

18.3 What is required from any expert is a high degree of competence, clarity in explanation, without ambiguity. The witness should also be independent from the party calling him or her.

18.4 The cases of *R* v *Doheny, R* v *Adams* [1997] 1 Cr App R 369, CA[21] provide good illustrations of the need for scientific rigour in the analysis of scientific findings. These cases highlighted the paradoxical position of expert evidence in the field of DNA analysis. The Court laid down three principles. First, the scientist should adduce the evidence of DNA comparisons together with calculations of the random occurrence ratio. Secondly, the Crown should serve on the defence sufficient details of how the calculations were carried out so as to allow the basis of those calculations to be scrutinised. Thirdly, on request, the forensic science service should make available to a defence expert the databases upon which the calculations were based. In giving these guidelines the Court of Appeal also highlighted the singular importance of not allowing experts to step beyond their area of expertise. In this regard we suggest it is the duty of both advocates and the judge to see that this does not occur.

18.5 Both *Clark* 11.4.3 (2003) EWCA 1020 and the *Cannings* 19/1/04 (2004) EWCA Crim 01 (above) contain important statements and principles, which have significance beyond the discrete topic of criminal responsibility for infant death. I do not set these out although the Committee will no doubt have considered these vital cases which will inform their work. The cases raised concern about:

(i)   The responsibilities of a pathologist;

(ii)   Disclosure of medical records;

(iii) The role of experts in the adversarial system;

(iv)   The approach to statistical evidence, and the dangers of statistical evidence "by implication";

(v)   The presentation of expert opinion evidence, and the dangers of dogma;

(vi)   The Court of Appeal's approach to fresh expert evidence.

19.1 *The Level of Investment in Forensic Science R & D*

19.2 We do not have ready access to the information that would enable us to answer this question fully, but we would make the following observations that bear upon it.

(i)   expert evidence and forensic science evidence has become an increasingly vital component of most serious criminal investigations and trials. It is accordingly vital to maintain data bases and a general knowledge pool.[22]

---

[21]   See too *R* v *Adams* (No. 2)[1998] 1 Cr App R 377, CA and *Pringle* v R, *unreported, January 27, 2003, PC [2003] UKPC 17*

[22]   See too *R* v *B 23.10.02, in which the House of Lords ruled that a DNA sample, albeit retained in a database without consent or lawful justification was still admissible at a subsequent trial on another matter.*

(ii) Such evidence has made an immense contribution not only to securing the conviction of the guilty, but also in casting doubt on inferences that might otherwise be drawn from factual observation and other circumstantial evidence.

(iii) Such evidence has increasingly shown itself capable of supporting arguments that individuals have been wrongly convicted (see Criminal Cases Review Commission case files[23]).

(iv) The nature of the evidence is such that it can sometimes be conclusive of guilt or innocence, and thus has the potential for saving unnecessary and protracted trials.

(v) As the field of scientific knowledge expands the potential for cost saving both for investigations and trials seems clear.

(vi) There are always likely to be spin-off benefits when scientific knowledge is expanded.

(vii) The Crown Prosecution Service have found their liaison with the FSS to be essential in providing independent evidence to underpin the integrity of the decisions they make both to prosecute and to discontinue cases.

20.1 *The Use of novel forensic technologies by the FSS and Criminal Justice System*

20.2 It is not clear what the Committee may have in mind, but we consider that courts are generally astute to see that new areas of expertise are carefully scrutinised and are not just "cod science". No expert should overstep the line which separates his province from that of the jury. In the case of *Bonython* (1984) 38 S A S R 45, the South Australian Supreme Court decided[24] that a judge should determine two questions "*the first is whether the subject matter of the opinion falls within the class of subjects upon which expert testimony is permissible. This may be divided into two parts (a) whether the subject matter of the opinion is such that a person without instruction or experience in the area would be able to form a sound judgment on the matter without the assistance of witnesses possessing special knowledge and experience in the area; and (b) whether the subject matter of the opinion forms part of a body of knowledge which is sufficiently recognised to render his opinion of value in resolving the issues before the court*". This second question would only be likely to cause difficulties in the area envisaged by the Committee's question. In this area the true status of the witness is sometimes difficult to challenge. We therefore welcome the establishment of the Council for the Registration of Forensic Practitioners (CRFP) launched in October 2000. They publish a register of competent practitioners, and ensure periodic revalidation and appropriate discipline. The Committee will know that it is a non-profit making company limited by guarantee, independent of the Government but which was subsidised, initially, by grant from the Home Office until it was able to become financially self-sufficient.

21.1 *The Use of forensic Science in criminal investigations and proceedings and the extent to which shortcomings in forensic science have affected the administration of justice*

21.2 The latter question would require a survey to avoid the dangers of the kind of anecdotes that the Committee heard when receiving oral evidence on 31 January 2003.

21.3 We believe the wider question is best approached by a recognition of the increasingly recognised value of forensic science which we have already addressed.

22.1 *Training of Judges in the understanding and presentation of expert evidence*

22.2 In a civil case, this question is obviously of importance. In criminal cases (save for those tried by District Judges and magistrates) the assessment of the evidence is made by the jury. It is nonetheless important that the judge monitors the standard of explanation by the expert to ensure clarity, independence of mind, and lack of ambiguity. This is a usual role for a judge and one which their experience generally equips them well to perform. It is not of course the judge's task to present the evidence, nor to suggest how it should be presented.

22.3 We consider that IT has a valuable role to play in the presentation of such evidence. More courts are being equipped with video presentation facilities. The same facilities (eg at the Central Criminal Court) can also cope with document viewing, interactive charts and PowerPoint presentations that are computer based. They have the ability to receive evidence from overseas at a fraction of the previous cost now that section 51 of the Criminal Justice Act 2003 has extended the ability to use live link evidence beyond the realm of cases involving children and serious fraud. Such a change is essential in any modern system of justice, and offers the opportunity for both prosecution and defence to have access to the wider range of expertise that

---

[23] See for example CCRC cases *R* v *Derek Bentley* 30.7.98 (new psychological evidence on mental state), *R* v *Brown* 13.11.02 (linguistic evidence supporting D's assertion that his written confession was not in his language, non-disclosure of fibre evidence indicative of another suspect) *R* v *Sally Clark* 28.1.03 (new bacteriological evidence providing alternative explanation for baby death), R, Dudley, Maynard and others 31.7.02 (expert evidence questioning the timing of police interviews), *R* v *Reginald F* 14.2.02 (new expert evidence challenging trial expert), *R* v *Michael Frost 26.3.03 (new psychiatric evidence—one of several such cases), Nicholls 12.6.98 (new Pathological evidence), O'Docherty (Expert evidence of new auditory techniques), Ottoo 9.11.00 new DNA evidence supporting D's account).*

[24] Adopted in *Luttrell* (2004) 1Cr App R 12.

might lie beyond our shores. We would be concerned if the funding that was allowed to assist the presentation of such evidence in this way were to be such as effectively to prevent witnesses preparing such visual aids or using live link facilities. Experience shows that all of us, not just juries, are assisted in our understanding by visual images in a televisual age.

23.1 *Whether the defence gets as good a service as the prosecution in terms of access to, and presentation of forensic evidence*

23.2 The answer is that they can get as good a service, but they sometimes have to push harder and overcome more bureaucratic hurdles. Sometimes delay, bureaucracy and financial limits prevent the defence from doing so. At the investigatory stage, the prosecution/police can initiate forensic investigation because their experts are either themselves civilians with the police service, or used to reacting to police requests (pathologists, police surgeons, handwriting experts etc). They are also carried along by the imperatives of speedy investigation and the custody time limits that limit the time they can hold their suspect in custody. This galvanises the process.

23.3 One concern at the investigatory stage is that the defence rarely, if at all, have access to the first hand evidence. Their experts will depend on the results found by the prosecution. It is likely to be the Scene of Crimes Officer or the police officers at the scene who gather the material evidence. The way the evidence is gathered and the dangers of contamination may lie at the root of the reliability of the scientific conclusions. This is particularly true in cases where microscopic evidence is involved (eg fibres).

23.4 Once a person is charged, it may take some time before he or she is able to get access to the forensic evidence in written form and even longer to organise a regime whereby his own expert can have access to original material. The initial spur to action is now lost in the dying momentum of the process. In practice there are often difficulties in obtaining the fullest disclosure of the note and workings of experts relied on by the prosecution, or access to their database, if any.

23.5 The defence face other avoidable bureaucratic pressures. The Legal Services Commission often requires counsel's written advice before it will allow the necessary expenditure to instruct an expert for the defence. Prior authority is invariably necessary at a time when time might be of the essence. The fee often has to be agreed before it is known how much work will need doing and what the costs involved in presenting the case in court might be. This kind of negotiation causes delay and is not something that the prosecution, routinely at any rate, seem to suffer from. Whilst there must be limits on expenditure, there is not a level playing field in this area in all cases.

23.6 Once in court, there should not be any reason why any presentation tools should be different as between prosecution and defence. Only financial limitations give rise to occasional imbalance. Whilst a solicitor may take a risk that he or she will be granted ex post facto authority for expenditure on an expert, solicitors in the public sector work on very tight margins and would often be unwilling to take the risk. This can be a barrier to justice.

24.1 *Use of Single Experts*

24.2 In the criminal justice system, and we believe in some areas of civil justice, this would a dangerous route to go down. It would inevitably lead to an increase in miscarriages of justice. Some of the cases referred to above where too much credence was placed on experts who have since been discredited provide a sound enough reason why such a proposal would be dangerous. We echo the note of caution struck in a quotation from Angela Gallop's paper. She said "*For me, the only way to ensure safe Science in our adversarial system is for the evidence put up by one side to be properly and thoroughly tested by the other.*"

24.3 On the other hand we do applaud a culture of openness between experts, and a code of best practice. We are inclined to agree with Judge Thorpe in his evidence before the Committee that if experts speak to each other and compare notes, calculations and workings, or even perhaps run experiments together, then the area of dispute will be diminished; costs will be lowered, and perhaps only one expert will be necessary after all. This is commonplace under the Civil Procedure Rules in civil cases.

24.4 Although anecdotes are never a test of very much, the writer recently had a case where the defence solicitor refused to allow his expert in computer technology to see the prosecution expert in order to examine his findings and to run a test programme together, which might have demonstrated that she was wrong. The defence expert wrote to the prosecution expert apologising, but making clear that she could not disobey those who instructed her. This in our view is the wrong approach and demonstrates a wrong relationship between expert and instructing client. The expert should never be shackled in the work he/she does. If this happens, independence is lost. Under the Civil Procedure Rules the court could have intervened to insist on a meeting with the defence expert being subject to a debarring order if she did not comply.

25.1 Need for training of expert witnesses in the legal process and presentation of forensic evidence

25.2 This would be a welcome development which accreditation organisations, eg CRFP, or other professionals might usefully develop. For many scientists, court rooms are strange places and however well skilled in their laboratories and hospitals they may be wholly unskilled in presentation. It is for this reason we view with alarm the government's failure to fund a system of payment that allows conferences with expert witnesses as a matter of course.

25.3 A government grant for training experts in presentational skills and the legal process would be justified in terms of the value it would give to the system. This of course would need to be generalised training and not case specific training which might fall into the forbidden area of witness coaching.

26.1 *Need for Scrutiny of the Quality of the forensic evidence presented in court.*

26.2 As has been pointed out, scrutiny takes place because the adversarial system provides for the independent challenge of the prosecution view. This is an important safeguard. The second line of protection is the defence advocate who can be expected to intervene to prevent improper evidence or unsupported assertion. A third line is the judge who is expected to do the same. In our view these safeguards in practice have proved sufficient, albeit no system is perfect.

27.1 *Processes used to establish the validity of novel forensic techniques, and the basis on which they can be interpreted (prior to presentation of evidence derived from these techniques in court)*

27.2 A judge is already required to be satisfied that an expert is genuinely an expert in the terms that the law defines it (see above). This can be done in any case either of his/her own motion, or by the opposing party raising the issue. If this happens, the matter can be dealt with by the judge hearing evidence from the expert, and cross-examination from the opposing party in order to establish the justification for being allowed to give opinion evidence. Often it will be apparent from the papers that the individual is or is not an expert.

27.3 Pre-trial procedures (and the new Criminal Procedure Rules—currently in draft form) are expected to provide for the early identification of these issues so that the time of witnesses, juries and others is not wasted unnecessarily.

28.1 *Use of Judges with special expertise in highly technical cases (with or without juries)*

28.2 We do not see that a case has been made for this. It is the task of a judge (in cases where he/she is the fact finder) to see that he/she understands the evidence, and to ask questions and seek help where he/she does not. Judges will all have some considerable experience in the fields they are likely to encounter by the time they become judges. Direct training in these specialisms, however, would open them to the criticism that they might be substituting their un-examinable views for the views of the expert before them. This would detract from the concept of open justice.

28.3 Judges who try cases before juries are highly experienced in summarising the effect of scientific evidence to juries and reminding the juries that cases are not tried by experts but by themselves. This is absolutely right. If a judge gets it wrong then the Court of Appeal is able to scrutinise any errors made.

29.1 *Treatment of risk and probability in court*

29.2 *This was discussed by the Court of Appeal in R. v Doheny and Adams* [1997] 1 Cr.App.R. 369, CA. We do not feel we can usefully add to this analysis and the observations made by the court about what judges need to take in account when scrutinising the admissibility of expert opinion evidence based on assessment of risk and probability.

30.1 *The Training of Judges in the field of Expert Evidence*[25]

30.2 This is delivered by the Judicial Studies Board, which is funded by the Government. Within the restraints placed upon it by a limited budget, it provides training materials to the judiciary and runs courses in specialist areas (eg, Serious Sexual Offences for judges authorised to try such cases and for all judges in the new Criminal Justice Act 2003) All circuit judges and Recorders also receive formal residential training over a four day period every three years (continuation seminars) and annually on a one day session run by the Circuits. This Presiding Judges of the circuits have a role in identifying the issues needing special attention at the circuit seminars. The Serious Sexual Offences seminars touch on relevant areas of expert evidence.

---

[25] The writer is a member of the Criminal Committee of the Judicial Studies Board.

30.3 The criminal continuation seminars will always include some input from an expert. This may be in the field of medical, including psychiatric, science, or in advances in scientific detection (eg DNA, or assessing risk and dangerousness in offenders with mental illness and personality disorder). These often deal with the forensic scientist's approach. Some have also dealt with the way scientists prepare their reports and are able to cater for the interests of both prosecution and defence.

30.4 Both Circuit and continuation seminars will provide material for the judges and recorders on new case law. This will cover any important case law in the field of expert evidence. The Judicial Studies Board has also produced a specimen direction to juries on how to approach expert evidence.

30.5 There is no discrete training for judges in the preparation, examination or cross-examination of experts. This of course is not really the judge's role, but the role of counsel or the parties. There are also concerns about judicial release time for unnecessary training in view of the backlog that too much time away from court would cause.

31.1 *Mechanisms for scientists and lawyers to discuss ways to improve mutual understanding.*

31.2 It will be appreciated from the above that there are frequent opportunities, in conference, at seminars, and at lectures for members of the Bar and the judiciary to meet with professionals in other fields. Often, such experts are invited to dine with the judges at the Inns of Court. It is an entirely natural exchange. It is felt that we all have a stake in improving mutual understanding, and welcome any opportunity to do so.

February 2004

APPENDIX 22

Supplementary Evidence from the Crown Prosecution Service

RESPONSE TO GRAHAM COOKE'S SUBMISSION TO THE HOUSE OF COMMONS SCIENCE AND TECHNOLOGY SELECT COMMITTEE

1. The purpose of this document is to provide further clarity on the prosecution approach to the presentation of DNA evidence in light of the Court of Appeal decision in *R v Doheny and Adams,* and why the current approach adopted by the prosecution is consistent with this decision.

2. The full transcript of the decision in *Doheny and Adams* is attached. The relevant points are highlighted. The Prosecutors Fallacy is committed where the prosecution equate a statistical probability with the likelihood of guilt based on the statistical probability. As stated in *Doheny,* the prosecution are entitled to present evidence of the probability and the likelihood of a match.

3. The current wording used by the prosecution is:

The DNA profile obtained from the sample provided by [suspect's name] has been found to match the profile obtained from the crime scene exhibit listed above.

A statement that considers the relevance of the above result given the issues outlined in Appendix 1 can be requested by contacting the Confirmation Reporting Team

Annex 1

Any assessment of the weight of evidence associated with this DNA match will depend on the issues that will be in dispute in this case. If, for example, the source of the DNA is an issue, then it will be necessary to consider the probability of a match between two different individuals. This probability depends on how closely the two individuals are related:

— The probability that two unrelated people would have matching full DNA profiles is of the order one in a billion.

— The probability that two full siblings would share the same profile, on the other hand, is of the order one in 10,000.

— A pair of identical twins will almost certainly share the same profile.

It follows that a match between two profiles should not, by itself, be taken as conclusive evidence that the profiles relate to the same person.

If there are close relatives of the suspect who might themselves be considered alternative sources for the DNA then the most satisfactory course is always to take samples from them for DNA analysis and comparison.

If, on the other hand, the issue is not about the source of the DNA but is more concerned with alleged activities and how the DNA was deposited, then factors other than the match probability need to be considered before an evaluation can be offered.

Any explanations offered by the defendant are an essential element in a robust evaluation of the weight of evidence. These should be conveyed to the reporting scientist as soon as is practical to enable the scientist to provide an evaluation.

It is also essential that the scientific findings relating to the DNA be viewed within the context of any other evidence in the case, such as geography, opportunity and alibi.

4. The above wording does not fall foul of *Doheny and Adams*. At no stage does the wording suggest that the probability of a match equates to the probability of guilt. In fact the wording makes very clear that a matching profile is not conclusive evidence that they relate to the same person and that it must be viewed in the context of other evidence.

5. Graham Cooke has been asked on a number of occasions to explain how the current wording falls foul of the prosecutors fallacy but he has failed to provide any explanation other than the perception that in his opinion the lay public will be mislead by this form of wording. We dispute this and have suggested that the public be consulted in a scientific poll to assess the validity of this claim.

6. There are therefore two issues that Mr Cooke appears to be conflating. The first is whether the current wording falls foul of the *Doheny and Adams* decision. The answer to this, as explained above, is that it does not and thus the prosecution approach is consistent with the above decision.

7. The second question is whether the wording, whilst not falling foul of the prosecutor's fallacy is misleading to the jury and thus likely to lead them to prejudge the issue of guilt. This cannot be defined as the prosecutors fallacy as, stating the very obvious, they are not prosecutors. We are keen, however, to avoid any statement of statistical probability being read as an automatic conclusion of guilt. The wording used with the warnings given we believe achieves this protection.

8. In summary, the current wording used is consistent with Doheny and Adams and we remain convinced that the current wording is not misleading as there is a clear explanation of what the statistic does and does not mean; that it does not equate to guilt and must be considered in the context of all the other evidence. We are happy to consider any specific and detailed explanation which would suggest that this is not true. We would also consider that a survey of the public might assist in clarifying this issue. Equally we remain content for the court to be the final arbiter.

February 2005

APPENDIX 23

Supplementary Evidence from Professor Sir Alec Jeffreys

Many thanks for your letter of 14 February and the further questions.

Concerning Q 389 (numbers of markers), my reasons for recommending an increase from the current 10 markers are as follows:

(a) 10 markers give a chance of a match between two unrelated people of, on average, 1 in 10,000,000,000,000. While this is extremely low, the current size of the DNA database coupled with very large numbers of speculative searches means that even extremely rare chance matches will arise. This possibility is admitted in the DNA database annual report.

(b) The chance of a fluke match will be increased in those people who carry common markers, to whom the 1 in 10,000,000,000,000 figure does not apply. It will also be increased substantially in close relatives; for example, siblings will have a roughly one in 250,000 chance of matching over 10 markers.

(c) In Q 579, Dr Fereday asserts that "the database is used as an intelligence tool and those ten markers are adequate at present". I disagree. The same 10 markers are also used to "verify" a match obtained from the database before proceeding to prosecution. They are thus being used twice over, first to trawl for a suspect and then for prosecution. This approach fails the basic criterion of scientific reproducibility and would not trap instances of chance matches.

(d) The consequences of even one false match leading to a conviction that was subsequently overturned could be severe for the DNA database and its public acceptability.

(e) My suggestion for increasing the number of markers to 16 reflects my views on the numbers needed to trap instances of false matches. An additional six markers would guarantee, with better than 99.9% certainty, that any such false match would be detected in a given case. Three additional markers may be adequate for unrelated people but not for siblings, who would have at least a 2% chance of matching over three markers. An additional 10 markers would be an overkill.

(f) Trapping false matches does not require the DNA database itself to use say 16 markers. Instead, it would be reasonable for the database to remain with 10 markers and for the additional six markers to be used, following the identification of a suspect, to verify or disprove the authenticity of the match.

(g) Increasing the number of markers would also increase the power of familial searching by reducing the number of potential relatives identified in a database trawl. The statistics of this is complex, and I do not know how many additional markers would be needed to refine such investigations, but suspect that 6 may be close to the lower limit needed. This application would of course require that the full panel of markers be used in the DNA database.

Turning to other questions from the 9 February evidence session:

Q 568. The response from Caroline Flint does not answer my comment about the (lack of) evidence for suspect populations being enriched in future criminal behaviour. It may be "useful to have those DNA samples because they do sometimes have an effect in a criminal case", but the same would be true if people were pulled in off the street at random for databasing. Likewise, the following comment from Mr Wilson that "600 fairly serious crimes have been solved because we have retained DNA from people who are not proceeded with" is I am sure true but does not address the issue of whether similar results would have been obtained if the database had been expanded with random individuals and not cleared suspects.

Q 569. Dr Harris notes that familial searching will "raise issues of paternity and establish non-paternity with your kids and their relatives". The reply from Caroline Flint does not acknowledge the fact that if DNA information becomes available from a family group, then any non-kinship will be revealed. It is not clear to me whether the Human Genetics Commission has considered such disclosures and how the police would handle such sensitive information.

Qs 579, 582–585. Dr Harris seems to imply that I suggested that physical characteristics could be determine from current DNA profiles and that the ability to do this would increase if the number of markers were increased. This is incorrect? even a 16-marker system would be extremely unlikely to yield any information whatsoever on physical characteristics. Other than identity and kinship, the only other information discernible is ethnic origin, and this only weakly so.

Further note:

The human genome contains thousands of these markers, so there is no limitation to the numbers of markers available. The number 16 is not set in stone nor am I totally wedded to it; however, my feeling is that 16 is about right, though 14–15 might be adequate.

February 2005

APPENDIX 24

Supplementary Evidence from the Crown Prosecution Service

Responses to further questions following the evidence session on 31 January 2005

1. Karen Squibb-Williams said that the points being made by other witnesses needed "to be seen in the context of the criminal justice reforms that are going on because in many cases many of these points have already been taken". It would be helpful to have information on which of these points are being addressed by the criminal justice reforms and when the changes are likely to come into effect. (Q 450)

The reforms I have in mind and the issues that give rise to them are;

Criminal Case Management Framework (part of the Effective Trial Management Programme, Office of Criminal Justice Reform, DCA), launched July 2004. This sets out in detail the case progression responsibilities for all parties in the CJS, following new, robust case management principles. The focus of these reforms is the requirement that both parties actively identify issues in the case as early as possible. Compliance should reduce delays and wasted costs of lengthy reports/evidence where that part of the case is not in issue (that is a rape case where the issue is consent, there should be no need for full forensic analysis of the semen to establish identity). In particular the defence responsibility to identify the issues is outlined in paragraph 3.2 of the CCMF. Efficient application of the case management principles should reduce the need for expert evidence, both on paper and orally. Where a scientist does have to give oral evidence the issues should by then be very clear.

The Criminal Procedure Rules 2005 (CPR) give "teeth" to the CCMF case management principles and processes. When implemented in April 2005 it is anticipated that the judiciary will be far more involved in robust case management than hitherto. Section Three of the new CPR sets out the case management responsibilities of both the defence and prosecution. The judiciary are expected to consider this in making their decisions. The CPR Committee have considered the role of the expert analogous to the Civil Procedure of using a single expert in a case. In summary I understand (anecdotally) this has been rejected in favour of retaining judicial discretion.

A number of the reforms contained in the Criminal Justice Act 2003 are expected to be implemented in April 2005;

ss32–40 deal with the disclosure obligations of both parties, but importantly limit the scope for the defence to serve " fishing" case statements, or in some cases, no case statement at all; the new provisions stipulate that the defence must provide meaningful case statements wherein the issues in the case are set out.

ss 114–127 deal with the change in law making certain types of hearsay (in particular laboratory. Technicians/scientists) admissible subject to appropriate notification procedures; in addition a new obligation is imposed upon the defence to serve the prosecution with the name and address of any expert they instruct with a view to providing expert evidence for the defence case, whether ultimately replied upon or not. (See answer to Q3 below.)

The CJA 2003 amended s37(7) of PACE 1986 and moved the power to charge from the police to the Crown Prosecution Service in all but minor and some uncontested cases. The implementation of this significant change should be completed by Spring 2006. At present some 14 CPS Areas (of 42) and police forces have Statutory Charging in place. The key impact of the change is to "frontload" the process of case building, that is the Duty Prosecutor and Investigating Officer discuss the evidence in the case before the CPS decide the charges; it may be that further evidence is needed, or that even where there is sufficient evidence; it may not be in the public interest to proceed, then no charge will be laid. This early strategic partnership working centres on identifying the issues prior to charge and focusing case building on that, rather than wholesale production of "evidence" that is not in issue between the parties.

2. Nimesh Jani commented on the shortage of pathologists available to the prosecution: "In terms of the experts available to the prosecution, in the whole country we have probably about 35–40 people we can approach". What are the reasons for this shortage as you understand them and what, if anything, needs to be done to rectify the situation? (Q 455)

The reason for the shortage is that the pathologists are required to fulfil the criteria of their own professional body as well as that of the Home Office Pathologist Advisory Board Code of Conduct (Revised 2004). Pathologists can make more money with less stringent requirements working for the defence and therefore there is little incentive for them to register with the HO Advisory Board. When acting for the prosecution the HO set the scales of payment; it is believed that there is no equivalent structure for the defence.

3. Nimesh Jani said that "Under the current rules the only obligation on the defence to disclose an expert witness is where they use his evidence" but indicated that this was going to change. How will the new rules modify the duty of the defence to disclose expert witnesses and expert evidence? (Q 460)

Please see answer to Q1 above; CJA 2003, section 35 introduces the new obligation on the defence. This will be implemented in April 2005. It's effect is to add a new s6D to the CPIA 1996, subsection I, as follows:

> "If the accused instructs a person with a view to his providing any expert opinion for possible use as evidence at the trial of the accused, he must give to the court and the prosecutor a notice specifying the person's name and address."

4. Karen Squibb-Williams told us of the need for "absolute independence and integrity in the auditing of [CRFP] registration". What steps would be required to ensure this? (Q 470)

In every area of public life scrutiny and accountability are paramount ingredients. In the wake of recent experience, cf Cannings, Shipman, numerous inquiries into public disasters etc., ensuring appropriate checks and balances exist is fundamental. Internal processes should not be used as a panacea. To protect the public interest and ensure that public confidence is preserved, CRFP must demonstrably be subject to a robust accountability process.

It may assist to consider other models, eg Police Authorities—the use of an external "lay" body authorised to investigate complaints; Professional regulatory bodies such as the Bar Council give the "veto" of any disposal decision to external lay members who assist the Professional Conduct Committee. Despite many years of comparable (to the Law Society) success, in the latter example the recent Clementi Review has in fact concluded that this system now needs to be overhauled in favour of an external body overseeing the professional conduct of members of the Bar.

At this stage, despite being publicly funded via the Home Office, I understand that CRFP is a private company and as such is accountable to nobody, other than market forces. This final point represents my understanding and is not necessarily the view of the wider CPS community.

5. What training do expert witnesses appearing for the prosecution currently receive in the legal process and presentation of evidence in court?

Nothing is mandatory, but training is generally available to all expert witness—to illustrate, see the material I faxed across to the Committee two weeks ago. However, care must be exercised not to transgress the principle very recently upheld in the Court of Appeal, which stated, "That training or coaching witnesses in criminal proceedings, whether for prosecution or defence, was not permitted.

However, that principle did not prohibit pre-trial arrangements to familiarise witnesses with the layout of the court, the likely sequence of events when giving evidence and a balanced appraisal of the different responsibilities of the various participants, provided that there was no discussion about proposed or intended evidence." (*R* v *Momodou, R* v *Limani,* 2 Feb 2005, CA (Crim Div), TLR 9 Feb 05).

Any training that is provided has to be balanced, explain that the expert is expected to be clear, objective and honest; project voice; anticipate strong cross examination and to remain impartial as the first duty is to the Court.

6. Karen Squibb-Williams stated that "with the criminal justice reforms . . . you are not going to need the same kind of witness box skills as you might have needed in the past". What are the reasons for this? (Q 471)

Please refer to the answer give at Q1 above; these reforms are designed to narrow the issues in each case and weed out some of the need to call experts at trial; both parties are expected to identify what elements of the Crown's case are;

— agreed/non-contentious (s9, CJA 1988);

— admitted (s10, CJA 1988), or;

— in issue.

It is this last category that will generally result in calling live evidence so that the defence can challenge the Crown's expert through cross examination. From this, it is clear that robust case management (including the judiciary via the new Plea and Case Management Hearings, from 1 April 2005) will help to reduce any opportunistic (and expensive to the public purse) defence strategies (ie; ambush defences .)

7. What percentage of prosecutions involve expert witnesses? In what percentage of these cases does the expert appear in court (as opposed to just producing a written report)? How is this likely to change as a result of the criminal justice reforms?

We are unable to identify meaningful statistics to provide an answer. In addition see responses to Q1,3 and 6 above.

8. Nimesh Jani told us: "pleas and directions hearings are not happening or are not as effective as they should be to ensure that the issues are narrowed down quickly, I do not think, with due respect, that judges have the teeth they need". What are the reasons for the problems as they stand and what action would be required to improve the situation? (Q 483)

The action is manifested in the reforms outlined in Q1 and the anticipated consequences of those reforms outlined in Q6.

The "teeth" are being provided in particular by the expectation that the judiciary take a much more robust approach to case management (old PDH, new PCM) from April. Please see the Criminal Case Management Framework for the details. This "sea change"" will inevitably take some time to show results, but combined with a robust approach from the prosecution to wasted costs applications are expected to be effective. What is meant by this is that where it becomes clear that in all the circumstances of a particular case the defence have not complied with the CCMF case progression requirements, a prosecution application for wasted costs on the grounds of, for example, a failure to provide a defence case statement at any stage; would be significantly strengthened and more likely to succeed. As the defence acclimatise to the reforms, their practise will most likely reflect the changes.

9. Nimesh Jani made reference to "a disclosure project". What is the disclosure project and how will it impact on the topics under discussion? (Q 491)

The aims of the CPS Disclosure Project are to raise experts' awareness of the importance of disclosure and their role in the process.

It also aims to develop policy and guidance on the handling of disclosure, where the competence or credibility of an expert has been questioned.

In particular it will:

— Develop practical mechanisms to enable experts to inform the prosecution of material which might undermine the prosecution case or assist the defence, or which may affect the credibility or competence of the expert;

— Clarify their legal and professional obligations;

— Provide guidance to prosecutors on how to handle the different types of material which may require disclosure, for example, unsubstantiated allegations, disciplinary proceedings or findings, adverse judicial comments or general taint;

— Define the contents of a generic disclosure package, to disclose issues of competence or credibility to the defence;

— Provide guidance on reviewing current and past prosecutions where credibility or performance are in issue;

— Draft and agree a protocol between the prosecuting authorities, professional bodies and ACPO to govern the revelation of material.

10. When asked what forums exist for discussions between judges and scientists, Karen Squibb-Williams said: "There is work that is going on which joins up exactly those groups of people". It would be helpful to have information about this work. (Q 514)

— I do not have an exhaustive knowledge of this, but through my work as CPS lead for Forensic Science policy issues I am aware that the Office for Criminal Justice Reform has been extensively involved in discussions with the judiciary (led by Lord Justice Thomas, resident Judge for the RCJ).

— Any training provided to the judiciary is the preserve of the Judicial Studies Board; this is in order to maintain the integrity and independence of the judiciary. However, wherever possible opportunities have been seized upon to provide general awareness "training" on specific issues. For example LJ Thomas has taken a personal interest in the development of the Prosecution Team DNA Guidance. In addition the Forensic Science Service have given a number of comprehensive presentations (via the JSB) on the role of the Forensic Scientist in court.

— In general, the work of the CCMF (within the Effective Trial Management Programme) and the Criminal Procedure Rules Committee appears to have engaged with the judiciary and other relevant partners in a more collaborative manner than previous years.

11. Would the CPS support the development of a group of barristers and solicitors with specialist technical expertise, for example in statistics, or digital or DNA evidence? If not, why not?

— Evidence (eg digital and DNA) is now no longer limited to serious crime, but is used throughout the criminal law, including volume crimes, eg theft, burglary, TWOC, fraud—ATM and parking meters. Therefore the topics are no longer a discrete area of specialist knowledge, but are now widespread elements of criminal prosecutions. To support the creation of a narrow group of specialists would be counter productive to the need for the widespread knowledge and skills of all prosecutors—it could risk giving the appearance that an understanding of this area of evidence is an optional specialism, whereas in fact everybody involved should have a good understanding of the issues and then go on to conduct the applicable specialist research on a case by case basis.

— In addition to on-going and regular production of national guidance and bulletins, the CPS now has such a developed national communications structure that all prosecutors can be advised of material developments in the law or policy within a matter of hours if necessary. There is also a well established network of IT "bulletin boards" whereby prosecutors can ask a question and gain access to an answer from another prosecutor anywhere in the country on any topic—this represents a significant opportunity to harvest the skills and experience of all CPS lawyers nationally (an online knowledge bank).

— The support of the CPS to the future development of a specialist group would depend on the terms of reference of any such group—ie to identify key areas for development; but not simply to dictate or use as a pressure group against contentious policies.

12. What specific training do CPS lawyers receive in the understanding and presentation of forensic evidence? Is any of this training mandatory?

— CPS lawyers do not receive any mandatory training on the subject.

— All Chief Crown Prosecutors received a brief awareness raising session (of the new Prosecution Team DNA Guidance) at the national Senior Managers Conference in October 2004.

— All lawyers have a duty to comply with their professional obligations under the "Continuing Professional Development" (CPD) on-going training requirements of their professional governing body; the Code of Conduct for the Bar also imposes a professional duty upon barristers to maintain an up to date knowledge of the law/legal developments, as well as the duty to refuse a brief if they do not have sufficient expertise to act in the case.

— See response to Q11 above regarding the extensive use of IT. In addition the CPS IT system provides access to a very wide range of information and legal research.

Finally, Karen Squibb-Williams offered to submit some training materials. The Committee would be very happy to receive these, preferably in electronic form. (Q 529)

— Already sent via email.

February 2005

APPENDIX 25

Supplementary Evidence from the Forensic Science Service

Responses to further questions following the evidence session on 15 December 2005

1. *How many staff have left the FSS since the McFarland Review commenced (please give the staff position and destination where possible)? How does this compare with staff turnover in previous years? How many of the staff who have left have cited uncertainty or concern about PPP as their main reason for leaving?*

In 2002 209 staff left the FSS representing turnover of 6.7%. 91 of these were scientific staff.

In 2003 410 staff left the FSS representing turnover of 13.2%. 168 of these were scientific staff.

In 2004 287 staff left the FSS representing turnover of 9.8%. 138 of these were scientific staff.

2002 had an unusually low turnover. In previous years it had averaged 9 or 10%. The figures for 2003–04 include downsizing.

It is not possible to give details of leavers' destinations. We have a whole catalogue of reasons for leaving. What we can say is that over the past three years 66 people gave "other employment" as the reason for leaving; 12 said they were transferring to other Government departments; and nine said they were going to work in a private sector forensic lab.

2. *What were the results of the latest survey of staff attitudes towards the development of the FSS as a PPP? Did the survey address attitudes towards the development of the FSS as a Government-owned company? (Q 130)*

Please see attached (Annex A) Re: PPP. The survey did not address GovCo. A further survey which will address GovCo is planned for April 2005.

3. *What percentage of Reporting Officers have been trained from scratch by the FSS? How many Reporting Officers has the FSS recruited from overseas?*

At least 99% of our Reporting Officers have been trained from scratch. We have recruited a handful from Scotland. We have none from overseas to some extent because of constraints imposed by Civil Service rules on nationality.

4. *What percentage of FSS scientific staff are agency staff? Please give figures for the last five years.*

Figures are only available for the last three years when a new HR operational management system went live.

Currently 3.2% of scientific staff are agency. In the 2004 calendar year it was 5.4%. In 2003 it was 5.4%. In 2002 it was 4.3%.

5. *What percentage of its revenue does the FSS spend on scientific or technological R&D? Please give as detailed figures as possible for the last five years.*

The FSS has spent the following on specific Scientific Research over the last five years:

2003–2004	£2.6 million 2 % turnover
2002–2003	£3.4 million 2 % turnover
2001–2002	£3.7 million 3 % turnover
2000–2001	£3.2 million 3 % turnover
1999–2000	£3.2 million 4 % turnover

In addition to the research effort the FSS invests in other development activities such as new products and services, automation, IS strategy development, operational excellence and organisational development. Together with the scientific effort these activities represent an investment of 14% of turnover this year to date and 12% for 2003–2004.

6. *How many R&D collaborations has the FSS conducted with partners in academia or in industry in the past five years? How many of these involved international partnerships?*

The FSS recognises that collaboration is a necessary and effective means of conducting R&D in an environment of applied science. Academic and industrial partnerships complement the FSS strength in adapting novel technologies for the often unique and specialised forensic application. Such relationships are essential for effective horizon scanning, international standardisation, technology transfer and commercialisation.

The process of entering into collaboration begins with future scanning activity within R&D and exchange of confidentiality agreements with external bodies whose scientific/technological activity is of interest. This facilitates free discussion and exploration of potential for both parties. As a measure of the extent of this activity, FSS R&D has entered into at least 108 such agreements in the last five years. Some of these have led to R&D collaborations, others to commercial contracts, some have not been pursued and others are still pending. Any detail about these exchanges remains confidential under the terms of the agreements.

Technical discussions have led to formal R&D collaborations in at least 11 cases in the last five years. Of these collaborations, two have involved international partnerships. This number reflects true collaborative activity. It does not include cases where the FSS has commissioned R&D at specialist laboratories, has been commissioned by an external party to execute specific research, or tested "fitness for purpose" of commercially available software or technology; neither does it include participation in national or international networks. These latter functions however are relevant and are a significant part of the FSS's connectivity with the wider national and international scientific/industrial communities.

Over and above the collaborations referred to previously, the FSS has had extensive involvement with the Engineering and Physical Sciences Research Council, under the umbrella of the Office of Science and Technology. This Research Council launched a programme promoting "Technologies for Crime Prevention and Detection" in 2003. Academics are encouraged to bid for funds to focus their technology of interest on counter-crime applications. In order to be eligible for funding the academic team must engage with an "end user"". The FSS is supplying consultancy, guidance and technical support to nine such projects funded in calls one and two, and has offered to support 20 projects in calls three and four, the results of which are still pending.

7. *What changes will the FSS make to the availability and charging basis for training for the police and other customers once the FSS becomes a GovCo?*

The Customer Training and Development Service (CTDS) within the FSS has undergone development over the last year and more changes are planned over the next 12 months.

The development plan will increase the number of training courses and seminars available to police customers and others in the Criminal Justice System.

These training courses will cover a wider range of forensic subjects and more courses and seminars will be available.

The design and content of all training courses has been tailored to complement specific roles within the police service.

In addition to the delivery of training courses the CTDS is currently developing distant learning packages which are more suitable to the wider CJS such as the CPS where abstraction is an issue. A series of fact sheets are also being developed for the judiciary and magistrates to keep them up to date on new forensic techniques and applications.

From April the CTDS will be moving away from a block charge per course on a daily or half daily basis to a charge per attendee for most of its courses with a discount available for high users. This will bring the CTDS in line with other training organisations such as Centrex.

The CTDS will continue to provide some training at no charge and seek external funding from sources such as the Home Office to sponsor the production and supply of training packages and courses.

8. The Home Office told us in oral evidence that the FSS has already had to undergo "major restructuring" and make "major reductions" to remain competitive. What has this entailed? (Q 21)

The environment in which we work is changing rapidly. For example, the Metropolitan Police Service (MPS) has adopted a policy of multi-sourcing their forensic science provision. As a result we lost some MPS business to other providers, although we remain their main provider. Furthermore the expansion in the use of forensic science that we have seen in recent years is likely to slow down. There is, however a growing understanding that "forensics" starts at the scene and ends potentially in the courtroom. This understanding leads to the conclusion that their should be ownership and integration along the supply chain: from pathologists, to blood pattern interpretation, to the finding and interpretation of fingerprints, the matching of DNA profiles, the discovery and probity of trace evidence etc. How much more effective could all of this be if it were managed as an end to end process that moves through the investigative phase to the evidential phase?

We restructured the FSS so that we could respond to and turn all of these factors and others to our advantage. In 2003 we had an opportunity to balance capacity and demand, and use that capacity to drive turn round times down in a way that was truly customer friendly.

Part of this restructuring process required us to look closely at our costs. Cost cutting initiatives needed to be undertaken to make us more efficient, to provide us with a firm base from which to shape the organisation for the future. Regrettably, we could see no way of avoiding the reduction of the size of our workforce.

No organisation resorts to redundancy without very careful consideration. Our clear objective was to position the business to enable it to develop and prosper in a competitive environment.

In all 141 staff lost their jobs. Only seven of these were on a compulsory basis.

9. *Aside from development as a GovCo and possibly as a PPP, what steps does the FSS intend to take in future to improve its competitiveness?*

The FSS has a rigorous cost management plan in process and has been able to demonstrate significant efficiency improvements, and year on year has been able to pass on these efficiency improvements to customers through lower prices. This is planned to continue. Our Agency target is to limit price increases to only 75% of the Average Earnings Index each year. These we have achieved, and have indeed limited increase to below RPI. For example our price increase from 1 April 2004, now represents a composite increase of only approximately 1%. In some product areas, such as DNA, we have been able to pass on significant price reductions following our automation strategy.

The FSS also has a challenging process improvement plan in place to drive improvements in the timeliness of our services. This is planned to continue. For example, in 2003–04 we were able to demonstrate a significant improvement in our timeliness, only just falling below our very challenging Agency target. This improvement has continued in 2004–05 and we are able to demonstrate further improvements in timeliness against our 2003–04 performance. This improvement process will continue.

To be able to provide improved timeliness at lower real prices, and be able to implement new products and services will improve FSS competitiveness. This is linked to our Agency target to invest in development activities.

10. *Does the FSS routinely conduct customer satisfaction surveys? If yes, please provide results; if no, why not?*

The FSS most certainly does undertake customer satisfaction surveys, (Annex B). The main effort is put into an annual "transaction" survey seeking customers views on how the FSS has met customer's expectations on each case. The results are then analysed by lab, customer, etc.

In addition to the above we also undertake more specific assessments on individual FSS products and services as required. We also have plans in this year's work to undertake 121 customer satisfaction interviews with key stakeholders within police forces piloting this work with scientific support managers in the NW forces associated with Chorley

11. *What input has the FSS had into the Forensic Science Society's forensic science degree course accreditation scheme? Will the FSS preferentially recruit graduates of accredited courses?*

The Forensic Science Society set up a committee comprising the FSS, Forensic Alliance, the Scottish laboratories and the police, together with representatives of the academic sector and others to consider what a course in forensic science should comprise.

The employers' unanimous view was that the type of undergraduate degree courses available at the time in "forensic science" were not appropriate. However, given that there did not seem to be anything to prevent the mushrooming of these courses, it was felt that there was a duty on employers to offer guidance on the relevant areas of forensic science and crime scene examination that a course with "forensic science" in the title ought to cover.

The Forensic Science Society then chose to construct a scheme whereby HE providers could apply to have their courses assessed for compliance against the criteria referred to above. We are not aware that any HE providers have yet come all the way through the assessment process but there have been over a dozen applications and some may be close to compliance. The FSS has not been involved in the assessment/ accreditation process—the assessors being mainly academics. Not all HE providers are interested—two of the leading HE providers, APU Cambridge and University of Central Lancashire, do not intend to apply, preferring it seems to rely on the reputation of their courses. Other providers may well see recognition as complying with the FS Society standards as giving them a marketing edge.

The FSS criterion for recruiting scientists at trainee Reporting Officer level remains a good science degree (chemistry, biochemistry, genetics etc). Any "forensic science" qualification should be at Masters level. It follows that applicants from FS Society accredited courses would be unlikely to be given any preference.

12. *How many FSS staff contribute to university science or forensic science degree courses by lecturing or providing laboratory-based training?*

The major input of lecturing is in the King's College, London MSc Forensic Science course. This was something originally undertaken in a purely private capacity by staff of the MPFSL. Post merger we tried to put this on a more formal footing nationally and agreed that we would allow staff to do this in "FSS time". There are probably about half a dozen or more staff lecturing on the course who have retired from the FSS over the last year or two and around a dozen still employed by the FSS who contribute to the course. In addition the FSS takes a couple of students a year on placement.

In terms of the rest of the country, we do not have any hard data but would expect it to be minimal, based around local contacts.

13. *What percentage of FSS work comprises services provided for the defence?*

The following details the proportion of defence cases undertaken by the FSS over the last couple of years

	2003/04	*2004/05 (to 31/01/05)*
Total number of cases submitted	134,461	111,883
Total number of defence cases	149	133
Percentage of defence casework	0.11%	0.12%

14. *Does the FSS currently provide any services that none of its competitors provide?*

To our knowledge we appear to have uniqueness in the following areas:

— Low copy number DNA.

— Intelligence services. Pendulum list searching (a DNA process for identifying matches from 2 person mixed samples).

— Familial testing.

— Firearms intelligence.

— Specialist training activities.

— Managed services in violent crime and sexual offences.

— Specialist fingerprint services using powerful enhancement techniques.

15. *What measures, if any, should the Home Office or police take to ensure that the FSS retains less cost effective techniques in its catalogue?*

The key to retaining "less cost effectiveness techniques" is to ensure that these products and services are appropriately costed and priced to ensure that in providing these services the FSS is not financially compromised. This could also be achieved directly, or indirectly, through the provision of a grant or subsidy by the Home Office (or other customers) via a specific contract to maintain an operational capability which would otherwise be uneconomic to provide.

16. *Does the FSS currently provide forensic services to other countries? Are there any barriers to the development of a global market in forensic services?*

The Forensic Science Service provide forensic services to some other countries which can range from "test" work, such as highly specialised DNA, to expert witness evidence in court work. Barriers exist within this global market as judicial systems attempt to create their own capability and retain funding within their system. Many countries do not have an understanding of the investment needed and therefore resources are often inadequate.

Barriers exist within the Forensic Science Service as procurement rules do not allow the agility necessary to capture technologies in a speedy fashion. The Forensic science Service can overcome some of these barriers by its quality and world-renowned expertise in certain technologies.

February 2005

Annex A

STAFF SURVEY—FEEDBACK REPORT INTO FSS BECOMING A PUBLIC PRIVATE PARTNERSHIP

SUMMARY

This survey was carried out (calendar quarter one, 2004) for the Executive Board following a pilot last year (quarter four, 2003). The questions differ from those in the pilot survey, so as to take greater account of staff views, to get a clearer idea of the issues and concerns, and to evaluate specific communication channels set up following the pilot survey.

In this survey, we have asked staff to consider statements which best describe their views towards FSS becoming a PPP. Then choose from a 10-point scale in accordance with current FSS practice, with 10 being the highest score indicating strong agreement, and 1 being the lowest score indicating strong disagreement.

Since the pilot survey three important communications events have taken place. The Executive Board gave its quarterly presentations to staff, Bill Bunce, HR Director of NPL, visited FSS sites and the first issue of the FSS PPP Update was published. All three of these gave staff the opportunity to learn more about PPP and to raise any concerns or issues.

KEY FINDINGS

There was an acceptable response of 36% compared to 40% for the first survey. The survey looked at three key areas:

1. Comparison, where possible, with the previous survey in relation to staff views on PPP and issues/areas of concern.

2. Feedback on communications in general.

3. Feedback on specific communications—eg site visits by Bill Bunce and executive board quarterly presentations and the FSS update.

From the results it was clear that the communications strategy and site visits are giving staff a good understanding as to the reason for the proposed move to PPP (although not necessarily agreeing with the move).

For communications in general, there was broadly similar score for level of understanding of information from the executive board and local management.

All three specifics of communications—Bill Bunce, board presentations and PPP update gained a similar average score.

In the first survey 20% of the staff had said they didn't have enough information on the move to PPP to form an opinion on the change. However, in this survey the question asking whether staff supported the move to a PPP did not give this option as a choice. Using the 1–10 scoring system, (assuming 6 and above is favourable view/support and 5 and below is unfavourable to some degree) the reply to this question showed a swing of 18% of those with a favourable view of PPP from 7% (in the pilot survey) to 25%. There was also a swing of 11% of those with an unfavourable view of PPP from 64% (in the pilot survey) to 75%.

Key issues for staff included a desire for more information to help staff understand about the PPP, the perceived loss of public service ethos, concern about possible changes to working conditions (including pensions) and overall impact on the FSS within the Criminal Justice System. A full summary of staff comments is attached as appendix D. They have been grouped onto the following categories; general issues with regards to a lack of understanding of a PPP, a loss of civil service ethos, a change in the stability of the FSS and a change in working conditions.

DETAILED FINDINGS ON THE QUESTIONS ASKED

— The average score was 6.3 when respondents were asked if they understood the reasons behind the move to a PPP (Q1) (even though they might not support them). This question was not asked in the pilot survey

— When respondents were asked if they consider the prospect of PPP an opportunity or a threat to organisation (Q2), average score was 4.1. When asked whether the prospect of PPP was an opportunity or threat to them personally, a similar average score of 4.2 was obtained. This question was not asked in the pilot survey

— When asked if they support the move to a PPP (Q4) the average score was 3.5. Although we cannot directly compare with pilot:

— 75% of respondents in this survey gave a score of 5 and below for this question—which suggests they have an unfavourable view to some degree. This compares with 64% of respondents in the pilot survey indicating that they did not support or had an unfavourable view towards the move to a PPP.

—24% of respondents gave a score of 6 and above when asked if they support the move to a PPP for this question—which suggests they have a favourable view to some degree. This is compared to 7% of respondents in the previous survey indicating that they had supported or had a favourable view towards the move to a PPP.

Note: for all three of these questions—Q2, Q3 and Q4, the score that attracted by far the most responses was 1—that is the lowest possible score. This suggests a significant number of people who are very strongly against the move to a PPP.

— When asked about communications, average scores were broadly similar for these three questions; I believe I am receiving sufficient info about the move to a PPP (average 5.1), I understand the info I receive from exec board (average 5.7), I understand the info I receive from local management (average 5.3).

— On evaluating specific communications, when asked how useful staff found the FSS bulletin (Q13), section on PPP at quarterly exec board seminar in December (Q14) and site visits by Bill Bunce (Q17) average score was similar for all three—5.2, 5.0, and 5.5.

— There were no significant differences between staff of different grades, business areas, age or length of service.

— Responses were also analysed from two operational sites and Trident court the only site to show any significant difference in score from the national figure was Trident Court, where the average score was significantly higher.

Results of actions from previous survey

The following actions were recommended after reviewing the results of the last survey:

— address our communication plans in this area urgently to ensure that we provide staff with sufficient information to form an opinion.

This has been taken on board and more communication has been conducted.

— establish some time-related targets for the positive and negative views from staff so that we can work towards achieving these through our combined efforts measured by future employee surveys.

This is an ongoing action and is being measured through this and future surveys.

— separate out personal from organisational issues in future communications.

This action has been completed through the redesign of the survey that focuses on both personal and organisational issues.

PROPOSED ACTIONS

Actions will be agreed by the PPP steering group once the results have been reviewed. Suggested actions are:

— Repeat survey in this format every three months to allow direct comparison of results.

— Design communications to specifically address concerns.

— Continue to use wide range of communications—eg bulletins, visits etc as all have got broadly similar feedback.

Appendix A

RESPONSES TO SECTION "MOVING TO A PPP"

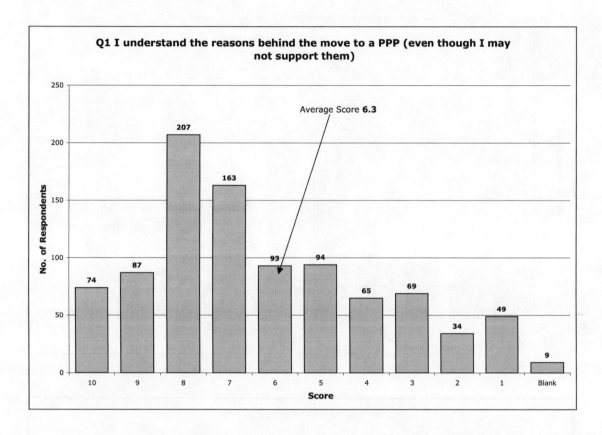

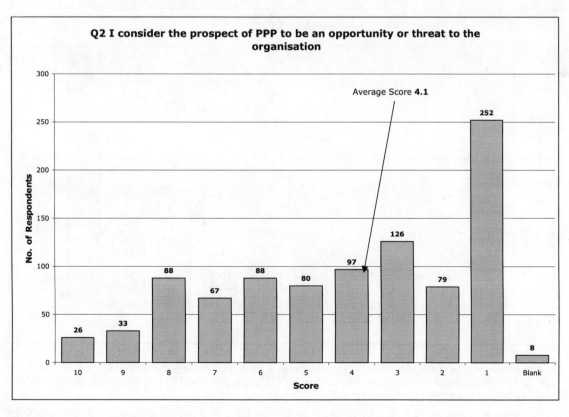

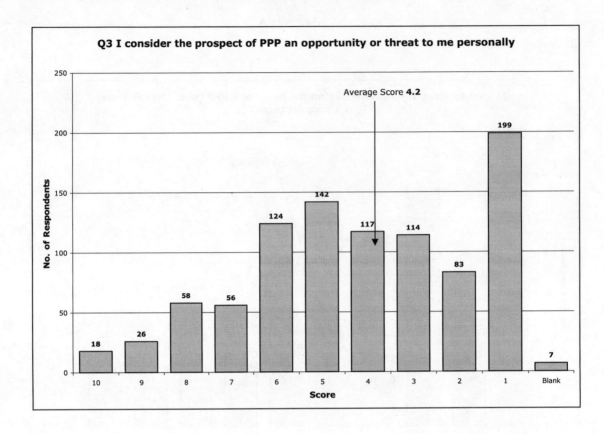

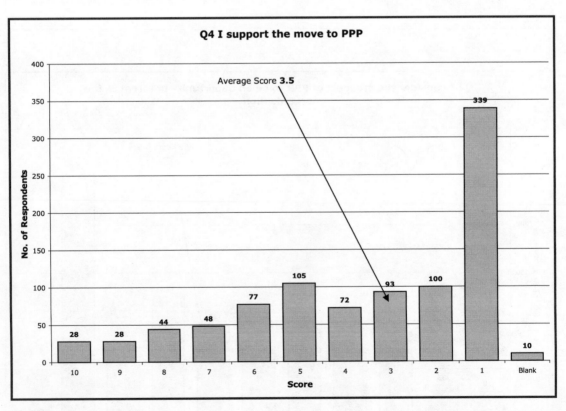

The above graphs show staff views on the move to a PPP. There is a significant difference between the number of respondents that support the move to a PPP [average score 3.5] and those that understand the reasons behind the move [average score 6.3].

Respondents indicated that their views towards the move to a PPP are the same whether looked at from a personal and organisational perspective.

Responses to "Communications""

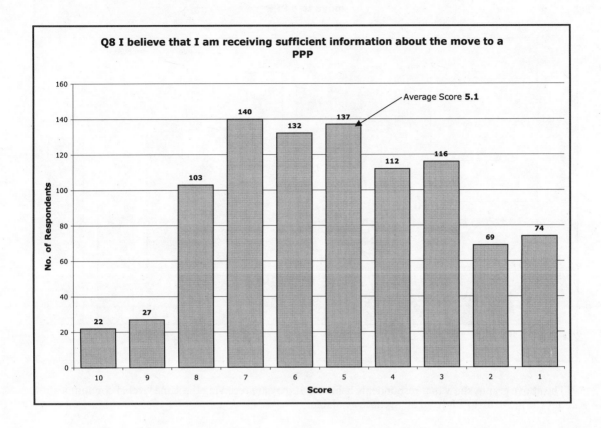

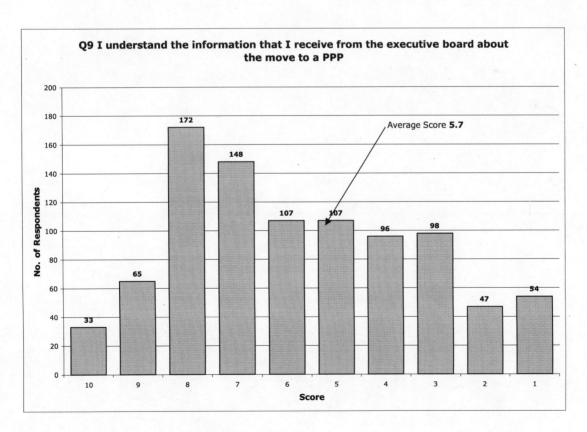

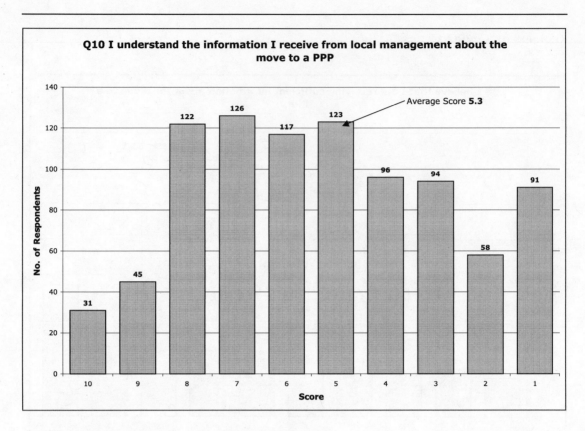

Q10 I understand the information I receive from local management about the move to a PPP

The above graphs show that respondents believe that they are receiving the same level of communication about the move to a PPP from all avenues available.

APPENDIX B

RESPONSES TO "EVALUATING SPECIFIC COMMUNICATIONS"

Q12 *Did you read the PPP update bulletin recently emailed to all staff?*

Yes	884
No	43
Blamk	17

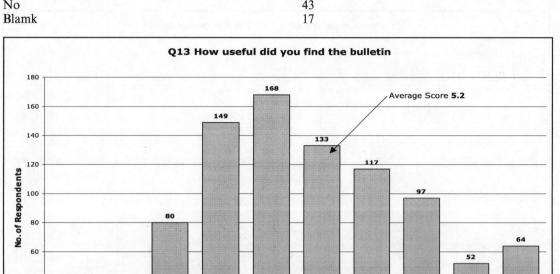

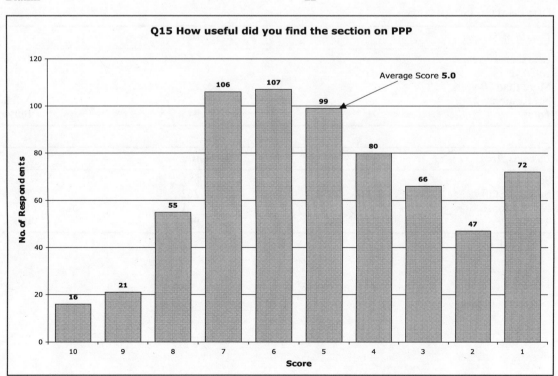

Q14 *Did you attend the quarterly seminar in December*

Yes	617
No	305
Blamk	22

Q17 *Did you attend the site visits by Bill Bunce?*

Yes	225
No	698
Blank	21

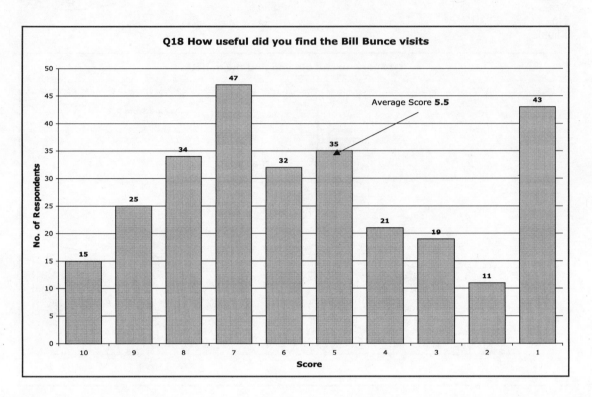

APPENDIX C

DEMOGRAPHIC INFORMATION

Length of Service	Responses	%
Less than 10 years	666	70.6%
10-20 years	125	13.2%
More than 20 years	127	13.5%
No Response	26	2.8
Total	**944**	**100%**

Business Area	Responses	%
Scientific	681	72.1%
Support Staff	262	27.8%
No Response	1	0.1%
Total	**944**	**100%**

Q21 Site	Responses
Chepstow	90
Chorley	76
Doranda Way	3
Huntingdon	104
London	274
NFU	8
Oldbury	5
Priory House	138
Trident Court	144
Wetherby	102
Blank	0
Total	**944**

APPENDIX D

Summary of Written Comments

The following is a summary of the written comments of FSS staff from the recent PPP Survey. Views and opinions, although varied, fall into distinct categories.

PPP

A considerable number of staff are still unsure about the basic history, idea and principles of the PPP scheme. What is it? How does it work?

Staff are questioning why we need to change. What are the reasons for proposing PPP? Is it the only option open to the FSS? What are the plus points on a corporate level?

Many comments revolved around financial subjects. Will a PPP be "profit-driven"? Will product prices increase? Will this have knock-on effects on quality, reputation or ethos?

What is the future for a PPP? Where does it lead? Is it just a stepping stone toward 100% privatisation?

What will happen to the management structure? Will it just be a large overhead ("Fat Cat Syndrome") or will the "private sector" bring effective and efficient management?

Civil Service Ethos:

Many members of staff are extremely proud to work for the Civil Service, in particular the FSS. The general view is that the FSS is a "service as opposed to a business" and should remain so.

Staff are concerned that casework objectivity will be lost and the battle between "profitable science and effective science" will result in the latter losing. The question of the moral issues was also raised. Is it right to "make a profit from rape, murder and paedophilia"?

Staff see the FSS as an unbiased and impartial service which provides the CJS and police forces with a quality of product which is unsurpassed. If the FSS became a PPP would the opinion of the CJS and the police change with regard to the FSS and would the quality of product suffer as a result.

FSS

Staff know the FSS is a world-leader and are afraid that the international prestige the service has will be put in jeopardy under PPP.

How will the relationship with the CJS be affected? What will make the FSS stand out from the crowd of "private sector" competitors? Will juries have a different opinion of the FSS under PPP?

The FSS can draw on information from a range of sources—CJS, Police, ACPO, and MPs. Will this all be lost under PPP?

The FSS's impartiality is important to staff. Will public opinion, customer confidence in the service and the reputation be sacrificed for profit?

Staff are concerned that experienced staff will be lost and there be a lack of investment into Research and Development.

WORKING CONDITIONS:

Staff are concerned that they will be adversely affected by the move to PPP. The main concern is that pensions will change considerably. The term "broadly comparable" has been used but staff wish to know what this means exactly. Will terms and conditions change? If they do, how will they change? Will pay reflect the change in pension schemes? These comments took up the majority of the written part of the survey.

Some comments highlighted that this is a great time to "shake up" the pay/benefit/pension situation.

Staff enjoy the "perks" of being civil servants. The benefits, pension and flexi-time are all valuable and staff wish to know if they will disappear under PPP. Will staff be "treated better" and "will the quality of managers improve"?

COMMUNICATIONS:

There are mixed opinions on the information that is being released regarding PPP. The majority believe there is too much "positive spin" on the information. They require "facts" as opposed to "speculation". "Why are the board biased?" "What is the truth?"

INFORMATION REQUIRED:

— What is PPP? How does it work?
— How has PPP come about? Why has the "Government pulled out"?
— Time-scales. Where are we now? Where are we going?
— Details of PPP meetings/discussions.
— Who are the potential buyers? Visits possible?
— What is the "Flip-Side"? What are the negative points of PPP? Visits from people for whom PPP wasn't a success? Are there contingency plans if it goes wrong?
— Management proposals ensuring that a structure is in place that can survive in the private sector.
— PPP alternatives and why they are not being pursued.
— Results of the survey.

Annex B

National Generic Customer Satisfaction Survey Results 2004

SUMMARY

The 2004 customer satisfaction survey was carried out over a period of three months at all sites except London. A survey was sent to the OIC in all instances in which a statement was produced. A total of 3,804 surveys were returned as a result of this exercise which shows a very good response rate when benchmarked against previous surveys.

RESULTS

NATIONAL RESULTS

Satisfaction Index

The satisfaction index for this survey is 90.9. A score at this level (ie 90–94.9) is classed as very good when benchmarked against other organisations. The overall national satisfaction index for 2002–03 was 87.7 which shows a +3.2% difference over the past 12 months.

Areas for Improvements and Gap Analysis

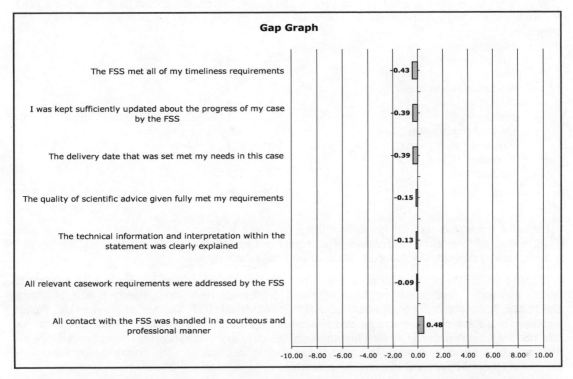

The above graph shows the Areas for Improvement (AFIs), which identify where FSS resources need to be directed, these are identified from the larger negative gaps. In this survey the significant AFIs are:

— The FSS met all my timeliness requirements [–0.4]

— The delivery date that was set met my needs in this case [–0.3]

— I was kept sufficiently updated about the progress of my case [–0.3]

The above chart shows that there are six negative gaps and although these need to be addressed (which is also highlighted in the comments section) these gaps are very small in comparison to previous external surveys conducted by the FSS. The possible range for these gaps is from +10 to –10. These negative and positive gaps are the same at all sites.

The area in which customers' expectations have been exceeded in terms of the importance to them as identified from the larger positive gaps is:

All contact with the FSS was handled in a courteous and professional manner [+0.5]

APPENDIX 26

Memorandum from the Department of Forensic and Investigative Science, University of Central Lancashire

The University is well aware of the current debate concerning forensic science degrees, and has been engaged in this debate since it opened its own provision in this area in September 2000. Our Department of Forensic and Investigative Science is now the largest in the UK, with 31 academic staff (half of these being forensic and policing professionals recruited from outside academia) and 750 students at undergraduate and masters/PhD levels. We offer education in forensic science, chemistry, biology, anthropology and policing. Approximately one third of students are engaged with policing, rather than forensic science. We are well placed to provide a perspective from the HE sector for the current debate. I have listed below my opinions regarding the most common issues relevant to the debate, and would be pleased to provide further information on any of these is this would be of value.

Employability. It is clear that not all graduates can gain employment in Forensic Science. This is usual for most degree programmes, as only a small percentage of graduates, even from accredited courses such as Biomedical Science, take up a career in their specialist field. Applicants (and their parents) are made well aware of the difficulty of gaining employment in forensic science at visit days to the Department during their application process, and also in writing through publicity material and our website. It is essential that this information is provided prior to entry.

Employment of graduates of our forensic science course has been excellent. Our first graduating cohort of 98 students was tracked in detail, and we have had 85 responses from this cohort (an 87% response rate). No student contacted is unemployed or not in full time study. The main areas of employment for this cohort are:

Forensic posts	10
Armed services	3
Police	9
Scientific laboratories	11
Education	13
Further study	15 (includes 8 in forensic fields)
General employment	20
Part time employment	3
Travelling	2
No response	13
Total	**98**

I attach a spreadsheet with the full information as evidence of the above table. I am aware of a similar, if not better, achievement from forensic departments in England that I rate as providing high quality courses, such as those at APU, Lincoln, Staffordshire and Glamorgan.

We have found that our graduates are able to pursue careers outside forensic science, both in scientific laboratories and in those areas of employment related to forensic investigations, such as Policing, Customs and Excise, Insurance and Fraud industries, NHS Counterfraud, BTP, the Armed Services etc. We are targeting these areas of employment for current students. Since a third of our current students are enrolled on a BSc degree in Police and Criminal Investigation, designed to prepare them for a career with the Police, we expect the Police to be our single largest employer in the future, and it is worth noting that currently some 100 of our students have enrolled as special constables.

As the SEMTA report evidences, FS courses have been successful in attracting students, particularly women, into science departments, at a time when applications for chemistry, biology and physics departments have been in steady decline. Entry requirements are high (ours is 280 points, including chemistry/biology) and since we are not reliant on the clearing process to meet target, we can maintain this level of entry qualification. This is a significant advantage to us arising from the national popularity of forensic science, as it permits us to maintain a good level of entry qualifications on the part of our students.

COURSE CONTENT

There is clearly great variation in the content and quality of forensic science degree programmes, and this is a great cause for concern. In the opinion of most Heads of Forensic departments, there is a need for (i) a QAA benchmark in Forensic Science and (ii) a robust accreditation scheme with high academic standards, preferably based on National Occupational Standards. There is also a need for universities to ensure that course content includes a significant proportion of pure and applied science (particularly in the areas of chemistry and molecular biology, mathematics/statistics and practical/laboratory experience/skills). In my opinion, while forensic education, in the form of scenes of crime training, expert witness training and the law, is valuable as it develops a wider range of communication and critical thinking skills than is associated with students on more traditional science courses, it should not detract from the science within these courses, particularly chemistry and molecular biology. The advantage of combining these elements in the right proportions is that forensic aspects enhance the learning process in science modules, as it provides students with the opportunity to apply the underpinning science to examples and cases, by which they are highly motivated.

FORENSIC SCIENCE AND CHEMISTRY

The study of Chemistry has been identified by the FSS and large private sector FS companies as the single most important academic area for their needs, and yet chemistry departments and courses in the UK have been steadily declining in number. This is a grave national concern for large numbers of other employers as well. In our case, although our chemistry department was closed in the 1990s, we have been able to retain research and education in chemistry within our department: without the forensic science course, this would not have been possible, and we would have lost this area completely. Indeed, we have expanded chemistry provision to support forensic science, and are now able to re-open BSc (Hons) Chemistry in 2006–07. We have also been successful in increasing research and consultancy in this area. It is worth considering what would have happened to other Chemistry departments in the UK without the emergence of Forensic Science courses.

EMPLOYER COMMENTS AND ACCREDITATION

Consultation with forensic employers has been positive and fruitful (though more cautious of late, since the SEMTA report). Employers have provided input into our degrees at their design and review stages, and act as external examiners to ensure standards and content are appropriate for their needs. Their feedback on graduates employed recently has been very positive. It is important that employers are able to distinguish between those courses that are fit for their purpose and those that are of more dubious value, and a national accreditation system is essential to achieve this. The Forensic Science Society has developed such a scheme, but Heads are generally critical of this for the following reasons. Firstly, the scheme is very expensive compared with other professional body accreditation schemes. Firm prices are hard to obtain, but will be between £5,000 and £7,000. Secondly, it does not consider National Occupational Standards, despite these being enshrined in many courses. Thirdly, many Heads, including myself, believe that the scheme is not robust enough to distinguish between those courses that are worthy of accreditation and those that offer Forensic Science education on the cheap. The danger is that the scheme will not result in the raising of standards or reducing the national number of students in this area, but will instead serve as a lucrative income stream for the FSSoc.

Despite these reservations, Heads agree about the need for accreditation and, given that the FSSoc offers the only such scheme on the horizon, will sign up for it. I hope that concerns such as those outlined above can be addressed during the implementation and initial review of the scheme.

CONCLUSION

A useful analogy for Forensic Science education is that of Biomedical Science. In the 1980s, when biology departments first began to experience recruitment difficulties, many opened courses in Biomedical Science, since many biologists found this attractive as a career pathway because of its relevance to medicine. Today, these courses recruit high numbers of students and there is a rigorous accreditation scheme, operated by the Institute of Biomedical Science (IBMS). The IBMS also sets a professional code of conduct for its employees and students, and oversees state registration for entry to the profession. This requires successful graduation from an accredited course and a year of subsequent in house training (often arranged in partnership with an HEI). Academic standards are high and employers are satisfied with the quality of graduates. However, only a minority of students graduating form these courses pursue this career due to the limited job market in this area.

It is my belief that a similar situation is required for Forensic science courses: we need a robust accreditation system which can distinguish between good and poor courses, a QAA benchmark, and good lines of communication and input with prospective employers, and an accredited career route for high quality graduates to enter the profession for subsequent training.

February 2005

APPENDIX 27

Memorandum from Dr Robert Keith Bramley, Custodian of the National DNA Database

Dr Bramley was a forensic scientist with the Forensic Science Service (FSS) for over 34 years. From 1970–1985 he specialised in the field of criminalistics and the provision of a wide range of analytical services. He also examined scenes of crime and gave evidence in court as an expert witness. From 1985–1993 he held various senior management posts and in 1993 he was appointed Regional Operations Manager, overseeing the output of all casework services from the Birmingham laboratory. In 1995, he took on the additional responsibility for the establishment and management of the first laboratory for analysis of samples for the newly created National DNA Database.

In 1996, Dr Bramley was appointed Chief Scientist of the FSS, and in this role was instrumental in the development of standards and quality assurance in forensic science, both in the UK and internationally.

From 1997 he also acted as Custodian of the National DNA Database under a Memorandum of Understanding with the Association of Chief Police Officers. The Custodian has a regulatory position for setting standards and monitoring performance against these for all laboratories in the UK, both public and private sector, who provide DNA analysis services for the National DNA Database.

Dr Bramley retired from his position as Chief Scientist at the end of September 2004 but has continued in his role as Custodian on a part-time basis in order to help facilitate the smooth transition of the Custodianship arrangements from the FSS to the Home Office.

1. INTRODUCTION

1.1 This memorandum is in response to a request from the Select Committee for written evidence regarding the Custodianship of the National DNA Database. It describes the development of the current arrangements for oversight and governance of the Database and how these will change, in the short, medium and longer terms, as result of the changing status of the FSS.

2. ARRANGEMENTS FOR OVERSIGHT AND GOVERNANCE OF THE NATIONAL DNA DATABASE: 1995–2004

2.1 Following implementation of the Criminal Justice and Public Order Act 1994, the Home Office issued a circular, HOC 16/95, giving advice on the operation and use of a National DNA Database for England and Wales. This formed the basis on which the National DNA Database was eventually established and went into use in April 1995.

2.2 Initially, the Association of Chief Police Officers (ACPO) and the FSS shared oversight of the operation of the Database through joint chairmanship of a User Board. At that time the FSS was appointed as the sole supplier of DNA profiles for the Database and as Custodian of the Database for the next five years under a Memorandum of Understanding with ACPO. The Custodian role at that time was intimately associated with that of the FSS as a supplier and was largely concerned with the loading of DNA profiles to the Database, the provision to the police of reports of matching profiles and the quality management of the Database.

2.3 The User Board evolved over time into the National DNA Database Board, which had a more strategic role in relation to the Database. This Board was chaired by the ACPO portfolio holder for forensic science and the Board membership included representatives of the police forces in England and Wales, the Association of Chief Police Officers (Scotland), the Home Office, and the FSS as both supplier and Custodian.

2.4 From 1997, other organisations sought approval as suppliers of DNA profiles to the Database, alongside the FSS, and a competitive environment developed for the provision of DNA profiling services. In order to ensure a level playing field and confidentiality of any commercially sensitive information provided by suppliers to the Custodian, the role of Custodian became vested in the Chief Scientist of the FSS, and "Chinese walls"" were erected between the Custodian and the FSS as a supplier.

2.5 The Chief Scientist as Custodian became accountable to the National DNA Database Board for ensuring that all prospective suppliers could provide reliable, compatible DNA profiles for the Database, for recommending to the Board their approval as suppliers and for the on-going monitoring of their standard of performance on behalf of the Board, as well as the efficient and effective provision of the Database services specified by the Board, maintaining the integrity of the data held on the Database and ensuring the highest possible standards in the management of the Database.

2.6 Suppliers seeking approval to provide DNA profiles for the Database had to satisfactorily complete proficiency tests provided by the Custodian; gain accreditation through the United Kingdom Accreditation Service (UKAS) to the international quality standard for testing laboratories, ISO 17025, for their DNA analysis work; and demonstrate that they have adopted the internationally recognised protocols for quality assurance in DNA analysis, as issued by the DNA Working Group of the European Network of Forensic Science Institutes, by providing the Custodian with current copies of their relevant laboratory procedures for assessment. In addition, they had to agree to UKAS sharing with the Custodian the findings from their annual surveillance visits to Suppliers' laboratories; on-going performance monitoring through an annual programme of blind and declared proficiency tests provided by the Custodian, blind duplication of a proportion of all their analyses; integrity checking by the Custodian of the DNA profiles they submit for addition to the Database; and the implementation of any corrective or improvement actions specified by the Custodian.

2.7 A Suppliers Group was established, under the chairmanship of the Custodian, as a forum for the Suppliers to get together to advise the Board, through the Custodian, on scientific and technical standards and potential scientific developments of a strategic nature. A DNA Operations Group, chaired by an Assistant Chief Constable, was also established to deal with the more detailed practical considerations related to implementation of Board policy, particularly in relation to the police service.

2.8 The Memorandum of Understanding giving Custodianship of the National DNA Database to the Chief Scientist of the FSS was renewed in 2000 and again in 2003.

3. CONCERNS ABOUT THE OVERSIGHT AND GOVERNANCE ARRANGEMENTS

3.1 The House of Lords' Select Committee on Science and Technology (March 2001), in its report "Human Genetic Databases: challenges and opportunities", recommended that the Government should establish an independent body, including lay members, to oversee the workings of the National DNA Database, to put beyond doubt that individuals' data are being properly used and protected.

3.2 The Human Genetics Commission (May 2002), in its report "Inside Information: balancing interests in the use of personal genetic data", acknowledged the high level of public acceptance of the need to collect and store DNA material that would enable offenders to be identified. But it also emphasised the importance of retaining public trust and raised a number of ethical issues about the storage of samples. It identified a number of concerns about future research and made proposals for an independent body with lay membership to oversee the National DNA Database, and a separate national ethical committee to approve all research projects involving the use of DNA samples.

3.3 The National DNA Database is, in simple terms, an operational policing tool, and the Board felt it was essential to maintain police involvement in oversight and use of the Database to provide police intelligence for the detection of crime. The Board therefore responded to these concerns by inviting the Human Genetics Commission to nominate one of their Commissioners to sit on the Board. The role of the Commissioner was primarily to advise on ethical issues and matters of wider public interest relating to the management and operation of the Database and the use of the DNA samples and data for research purposes. This proved successful and more recently led to discussions being initiated with the Central Office for Research Ethics Committees (COREC) to seek their support in ethical oversight of the research proposals.

4. THE MCFARLAND REVIEW

4.1 Meanwhile, in July 2002, Robert McFarland was asked by the Home Office to undertake a review of the FSS in relation to its organisational structure and performance. In March 2003, McFarland recommended that the FSS be transformed into a private sector classified public private partnership.

4.2 McFarland was also asked to consider, in the context of the recommendations of the reports from the House of Lords' Select Committee on Science and Technology and the Human Genetics Commission, and any future organisational changes for the FSS, the need for independent oversight of the National DNA Database and the role of the Chief Scientist of the FSS as Custodian of the Database.

4.3 McFarland recognised that the present arrangements for Custodianship and management of the National DNA Database had been successful and found no evidence to suggest that they were being abused. Nevertheless, he recommended a variety of different structures for the governance and oversight of the National DNA Database and that the Custodianship of the Database should be removed from the FSS. He also proposed that accountability for the storage and access to CJ samples, currently held on behalf of police forces by suppliers, should pass to the Custodian, and he supported the concept put forward by the Human Genetics Commission for a national ethics committee. McFarland emphasised, however, that no change should jeopardise the robustness and integrity of the system developed by the FSS and ACPO.

4.4 In July 2003, the Home Secretary announced his decision to accept the recommendations of the McFarland review that the FSS should begin the transition towards a change of status. The Home Secretary also agreed that, whatever happened to the change of status of the FSS, the overall management and Custodianship of the Database, including the scientific advisory, accreditation and monitoring services, should be separated from the FSS and retained within the public sector, controlled by the Home Office, ACPO and the Association of Police Authorities (APA).

4.5 The programme of work to give effect to revised management arrangements for the Database and the repositioning of the Custodian role is being led by the Science Policy Unit of the Home Office with support from consultants and the Custodian. The strategic goal, within three to seven years, linked to IMPACT Programme timeframe, is for independent governance and oversight of the National DNA Database wholly within the public sector, with Database operations and development run under competitive contract(s) and fully connected to the National Intelligence System developed though the IMPACT programme in response to Bichard.

5. SHORT TERM PROPOSALS

5.1 The proposals for the immediate way forward are still being developed, but the following is a summary of current plans and progress agreed with the Chairman of the National DNA Database Board.

5.2 A reconstituted National DNA Database Board and revised terms of reference are currently being established. The next Board meeting, on 3 March 2005, will be the last to be held under the current arrangements. Subsequent Board meetings will continue to be chaired the ACPO portfolio holder for forensic science, now Chief Constable Tony Lake. The Board members will be Mr Tim Wilson, representing the Home Office, ACC Stuart Hyde representing ACPO, and a nominee, yet to be decided, from the Association of Police Authorities. The lay representative nominated by the Human Genetics Commission, and the Custodian will be permanent invitees. There will be no representation of Suppliers on the Board, although they and other parties may be invited to Board meetings where appropriate. The discussions with COREC to provide ethical oversight of research proposals will continue.

5.3 The Board will also continue to be supported by the Suppliers Group, under the chairmanship of the Custodian, and the DNA Operations Group chaired by the ACPO representative on the Board, ACC Hyde. The terms of reference for these two bodies are in the process of being redrafted.

5.4 A Home Office based team will be formed to support the Custodian. It is proposed that this team will be responsible for setting the scientific, quality and performance standards for Suppliers to the National DNA Database, and the management of contracts for the delivery of services from the National DNA Database, development of the Database and the provision of DNA sampling kits. It is also proposed that the accreditation and performance monitoring of Suppliers would best be carried out from within the Home Office based Custodian team. The Custodian team will therefore be enhanced by a number of DNA specialists to carry out accreditation and performance monitoring and data integrity checking, and to make recommendations for improvement and corrective actions where appropriate, and by several ex-police officers with experience of police practices and the Police National Computer, to assist with data reconciliation issues.

5.5 The contract for delivery of services from the Database will cover the provision of all accommodation, staff, hardware and software applications required to manage, maintain and deliver the specified operational services and management information, and will be let initially to the FSS for 3-5 years.

5.6 The separate contract (or contracts) for development of the National DNA Database will be based on the work being carried out by PA Consultants to establish a "User Requirement" for the National DNA Database and a review by PA of the extent to which the existing IT hardware and software are able to meet this requirement.

6. Medium to Long Term Proposals

6.1 By the end of the initial contract periods, it is envisaged that there will be physical separation of the National DNA Database from FSS premises and the FSS IT network, and co-location of the Home Office based Custodian group with the facilities for the provision of database operational services in new accommodation in the Birmingham area.

7. Development of the Custodian role

7.1 Experience to date has suggested that the National DNA Database Custodian role may be used as a model for the oversight and quality management of other databases (eg NAFIS, shoemarks, firearms, drugs) and there is a concept of a "super-Custodian" to oversee and develop the standards by which these databases are operated and interrelate.

7.2 Another proposal has been to develop the Custodian into a regulator for the provision of the wider range of forensic science services, to ensure that quality and performance standards are set and maintained in what will be increasingly a commercial marketplace.

7.3 It is envisaged that either of these two issues will come to fruition in 2007–08, under the Forensic Integration Strategy, when ACPO and the Home Office will have put in place arrangements to ensure that maximum value can be extracted from all types of forensic data accountable to the police within a structure that will ensure that UK use of forensic intelligence and evidence remains at the global cutting edge.

February 2005

APPENDIX 28

Memorandum from the Human Genetics Commission

In June 2001, the Human Genetics Commission (HGC) visited the Forensic Science Service to learn about the organisation and management of sampling, profiling and the National DNA Database. In May 2002, the Commission published their report Inside Information—Balancing interests in the use of personal genetic data, which contained the following recommendation:

> "We recommend that, at the very least, the Home Office and ACPO establish an independent body, which would include lay membership, to have oversight over the work of the National DNA Database custodian and the profile suppliers."

Further, it recommended that: "In the short term the Home Office and FSS introduce an independent research ethics committee, to approve such research."

Following publication of the HGC report, the National DNA Database Board invited the HGC to put forward one of their members to sit on the Board and this arrangement has continued since that time.

You indicated that the Science and Technology Committee was particularly interested in the HGC's view of the current custodianship arrangements for the database and what changes, if any, need to be made.

I can confirm that the HGC stands by the recommendations contained in "Inside Information" and continues to make the case for the establishment of an independent body to oversee the work of the custodian of the database, which would include lay membership. As the Science and Technology Committee heard at the hearing, work is underway to separate the roles of the custodian of the National DNA Database from that of Forensic Science Service and the Commission views this an ideal time for it's recommendations to be taken forward.

Currently, there is no ethics structure that properly assesses the research proposals which are submitted to the National DNA Database Board. The presence of an HGC member on the Board does not provide for adequate consideration on the ethical issues involved in research proposals.

The HGC are also concerned about the nature of research proposals, specifically around what constitutes "research". As the respondents to the Committee correctly said in their evidence, the number of external applications submitted to the Board to use National DNA Database samples are few. However, requests to carry out internal development, for example to develop familial testing, are more frequent. This kind of work could be regarded as research and previously went ahead without ethical review. Project proposals of this kind are now discussed at the Board but, again, they are discussed in the absence of formal ethical oversight.

Finally, it is worth noting that the HGC member currently sitting on the National DNA Database Board, Dr Stephen Bain, has professional experience of designing and working with large DNA databases and he also sits on an multi-research ethics committee. However, not all HGC members have this level of experience or knowledge of the moral and legal issues involved. That is why the Commission has continued to request that there be lay involvement on the National DNA Database Board and that a system of formal ethical oversight be established. Furthermore, it is important that these measures are not dependent upon the continued existence of the HGC.

February 2005

APPENDIX 29

Supplementary Evidence from Forensic Science Alliance

Attached are some additional observations about the questions put to us in the oral evidence session on 12 January 2005 which we hope will be of assistance to the Committee during its current deliberations.

Our central message here is that there can be no doubt that private forensic science in the form of Forensic Alliance and the LGC, has been a very good thing for both quality standards and service delivery in the profession. In particular, Forensic Alliance has demonstrated time and again how imaginative new approaches—some drawing in science and technology from the wider scientific community, can be remarkably effective in solving intractable complex cases. LGC has demonstrated how proper focus on process and delivery can dramatically improve speed and cost of laboratory based analyses. All of this has forced the traditional supplier—the FSS, to sharpen up its act across the board and in a way that would never have happened had things been left the way they were.

So long as the market is properly regulated, the playing field for suppliers is made level, and the Government receives sound, balanced advice from suppliers, full privatisation of the market should be positively welcomed as providing by far the best route to innovative, timely, safe and cost effective forensic science provision for the future.

We remain very keen for the Committee to see private forensic science at first hand and, to this extent, should be delighted to welcome any Committee members who are interested to our Culham laboratory just outside Oxford.

ADDITIONAL POINTS FOR CONSIDERATION BY THE SCIENCE AND TECHNOLOGY COMMITTEE ARISING FROM THE ORAL EVIDENCE SESSION ON 12 JANUARY 2005

Q224

The Forensic Science Service and Forensic Alliance offer a broadly similar range of services to police forces. Both offer a comprehensive forensic science service covering all offences against people and property along with toxicology and drugs analysis. Forensic Alliance offers several additional services traditionally on the periphery of forensic science, and access to greater analytical power through links with scientists and instrumentation in the wider scientific community.

Q225

The other main service provider is the LGC; they offer a range of laboratory-based forensic testing services but do not provide the sort of comprehensive scientific investigation services required for serious crime including, for example, examination of murder and other complex scenes of crime and reporting at court as expert witnesses on all forensic aspects of a complex case in the context of specific case circumstances.

Q227

Competition between the three major players in the market is increasingly a combination of bidding for work by competitive tender and those bids being judged by respective police forces. Judgement is based on past experience of one or more supplier and reputation of those suppliers in terms of delivering value measured by a combination of turn round times, price and quality. Forensic Alliance is particularly happy to be judged on its reputation.

The experience of Forensic Alliance is that the police are increasingly shaping the market themselves and driving significant price cuts and reduction in turn round times, leaving the supplier to look for imaginative ways to maintain and improve quality. There is some concern that there is currently insufficient understanding by police about quality what it is and how it might best be measured.

Q228

The increased sophistication adopted by police forces in specifying the requirement for forensic services has sharpened their approach to getting suppliers to deliver improved value. In some cases forces have decided to source some of their work "in-house", providing further impetus for suppliers to examine carefully the standards and the speed of each service they provide.

The Forensic Science Service is in a very similar position to other suppliers and the keener, more competitive market place will impact on them whatever their status. It is for debate as to whether or not a "GovCo" or a PPP will improve the overall service level offered by the Forensic Science Service. In the end, it should be the quality of the science and service delivery that matters most.

Q231

A totally independent regulator is needed for the market:

Definitely for;

— Acting as custodian of DNA, firearms and other national forensic databases.

— Overseeing the accreditation process for forensic scientists.

— Overseeing the accreditation process for laboratories.

— Regulating and standardising the tendering process to ensure a consistent, regular flow of tenders from police forces.

— Providing an independent person/body to balance the requirements of the Home Office, the Association of Chief Police Officers, other users of forensic science and the forensic science providers.

— Acting as ombudsman for forensic science as a whole and providing an independent focus of complaints from police, the Crown Prosecution Service, suppliers, the judiciary and for barristers.

— Receiving advice from suppliers and others and passing on a distilled and neutral version of that advice to government. This might best be achieved via some sort of advisory panel including the main forensic science suppliers.

But not for;

— Controlling the economic aspects (eg prices) of the market

— Apportioning work to suppliers

It is completely wrong for the Forensic Science Service to have any controlling role in the market as they cannot be impartial. Government needs to be advised by a neutral panel helping to optimise the forensic services available to police and making sure that the Crown Prosecution Service has timely responses of the right quality available to it, as well as maintaining the databases in good order, with equal access rights for all accredited suppliers.

Q232

It would seem that several forces in police regions are to join together in asking suppliers to tender for all or part the of forensic science work in their region. Whilst this would increase the buying power of those forces and help to ensure a standard charge for specific aspects of the work, it might not drive down prices overall some of them will inevitably be at rock bottom. Rather, such arrangements might inspire more imaginative side benefits, for example, in connection with collection and delivery arrangements, police training and so on. Naturally, separate Service Level Agreements would be needed for each force as long as the forces do different things in different ways.

Q233

It may then be possible and right for the forces that have used their joint buying power to split the award of tenders to take best advantage of the relative skills of the suppliers, eg allowing niche suppliers to win specialist areas of the total work and, frankly, to play one of the three major suppliers off against at least one of the other two and generate improvements in standards of service from all suppliers.

Forces would have the ability to switch some of their work between suppliers to take advantage of good performance by one supplier in a particular area, on particular crime types, or at a particular time whereas they would not have first-hand ability to judge the performance of all suppliers if they had worked with only one.

Q234

There should be complete equality of data sharing in respect of databases owned by the police and operated on their behalf currently by the Forensic Science Service but hopefully soon under the auspices of an industry regulator.

Specific case data also needs sometimes to be shared when more than supplier is working on the same case. Currently this tends to present few problems at an operational level although it would be helpful to have some guidelines drawn up for clarity, and to ensure that as the market becomes more complex, common cause always prevails.

Other data that needs to be shared relates to reliable summaries of the history of the volumes of each crime type by force so that each supplier knows the volume and type of business for which it is tendering.

Q235

Intellectual property rights can impede the progress of tendering and award of contracts, particularly in cases where some police forces word their tenders so that they try to claim all intellectual property rights for work done by the supplier, using skills built up over a number of years, when all the police have contributed is a request for the work to be done!

It is possible that progress on a case may be impeded while the police and suppliers debate intellectual property surrounding some of the work, but only some general contractual terms can be agreed before the specific intellectual property issues emerge from a case.

Q236

A Regulator should be tasked with devising a proper framework involving the (nationally owned) forensic databases under a neutral Custodian, using an advisory panel including, but not limited to, the major suppliers and direct government funding for research and development.

Q237

Information sharing of crime statistics and national database data should not be a problem if properly managed by a Custodian and Regulator.

Q238

In terms of the value of work for the year to 31 March 2004, Forensic Alliance provided services to the police and similar regulatory services totalling some 50percent more than the LGC.

Q239

Furthermore, with the Forensic Science Service, Forensic Alliance is the only other full service provider of forensic services to police, so we would certainly assert that Forensic Alliance is the UK's leading private sector supplier of forensic services.

Q240

As a full service provider, Forensic Alliance has never cherry picked the services it offers. Right from the start, the Company has offered a "one-stop-shop" for police with the vast majority of services provided in-house. Having said that, and to ensure that the police obtain the broadest possible assistance from science and technology, external experts been brought in to help with particular aspects of specific cases. As a result, we have built up relationships with a number of suppliers of specialist services in the wider scientific community which has enriched the scope of traditional forensic science.

The key principle here is that we do not turn work away just because it is too difficult or not profitable or we do not do it ourselves. We consider that we have a duty of care to our customers and aim to ensure that they are well served. On a number of occasions police have been directed to us from other suppliers because they do not provide a specific service but they know we will one way or another. We are very proud of our reputation here.

Q241

The Forensic Science Service no longer has any obligation to pick up all the work that the other suppliers cannot or choose not to provide. They should not be entitled to any "compensation" for having to provide excess capacity to enable them to take work from other suppliers. They are in no position now to pick up all the work done by Forensic Alliance and by LGC and do it to the same standards. They have only bid for high throughput routine work out of choice and have occasionally been seen to do so at prices that are not sustainable in the long term and way below prices that Forensic Alliance can offer whilst maintaining proper quality.

Forensic Alliance has never turned away work from a police force that it had promised to do and which had then to be picked up by the Forensic Science Service.

Q242

If the Forensic Science Service became a private company it would make no difference per se to its wish or ability to cherry pick.

Q243

Whilst Forensic Alliance has not cherry picked in the accepted use of that phrase, it certainly has directed its work to areas in which has chosen to specialise; a good example of that is in the more complicated murders in particular in "cold cases" where a fresh approach can solve crimes that had previously been unsolved and put on hold by the police. Specialising in areas of strength does not mean that more routine work is turned away.

Q247

I would tell the Higher Education Minister of my concern over the loss of any "pure" science courses and particularly the loss of chemistry courses. We are finding it hard to recruit good quality chemistry graduates but often still choose to try to employ such "pure" scientists in preference to products of pseudo forensic science degree courses. Many "forensic science" lecturers do not have quality experience, if any, in the forensic field and their techniques and equipment are often out of date.

Q248

Forensic Alliance has provided a large number of different training courses for police, some part of our standard package and others tailored to specific force needs. We have not seen provision of these courses as a way to make money, but rather as a chance to improve understanding about forensic science so that we get the right samples presented in the right way to capture the most intelligence and evidence for police if it is there to be found. These courses are an extension of our healthy working partnership with our customers.

Q255

Forensic Alliance has trained about 25% of its staff from scratch and augmented the training of many others. Currently, 9% of our staff are from overseas, although this figure is flexible depending on how "overseas"" is defined (eg is Eire overseas?) and whether you include administrative staff as well as scientists.

Q256

The forensic science market is different from the broadcasting market; if we ended up with the forensic equivalent of Big Brother, every criminal in the country would escape prosecution. Unfortunately, the quality of our work cannot always be judged by the results as our viewing figures are not easily determined. The Crown Prosecution Service are not able/willing to assess the degree to which the forensic evidence was crucial to a case being won and the police seem unable/unwilling to measure the extent to which prompt, high quality forensic work on a major investigation has saved them hundreds of thousands of pounds in police time.

Q257

The public sector ethos and the commitment to providing the police with a high quality forensic service is very much part of the Forensic Alliance approach and—to be fair—the other major players seem to try to take the same line. Only if the police themselves force suppliers to cut costs and turn round times to such an extent that quality must suffer is the aim of getting the best result likely to fray at the edges. To guard against this we need a much better understanding of what quality means in forensic terms, and the balance between quality, cost and timeliness. A Forensic Regulator and Advisory Panel will have important roles to play here.

February 2005

APPENDIX 30

Supplementary Evidence from the Association of Chief Police Officers of England, Wales and Northern Ireland

RESPONSE TO ADDITIONAL QUESTIONS:

1. ACPO has had no input into the Forensic Science Society's accreditation scheme. Although the Police Service is the biggest employer in the forensic science sector, graduate qualifications are not sought in respect of most of the roles, eg crime scene examiner or fingerprint officer. Basic literacy and numeracy combined with good inter-personal skills are valued and tested in the recruitment process. Job training is bespoke and is best delivered with a basic course of a few weeks duration followed by development in the workplace. There are no plans, therefore, for ACPO to give preferential treatment to graduates of accredited courses. The issue of matching learning provision to need reaches far wider than the Forensic Science Society, ACPO or any existing single body. There is a pressing need in our view in respect of forensic and all scientific disciplines) for a UK Sector Skills Council dedicated to science and mathematics.

2. ACPO, as a body, has no involvement in the establishment and delivery of university forensic science courses.

It is clear, however, that some universities are looking to the police to "badge" their product. Some institutions have arrangements with local forces, some of which assist universities with learning materials and the provision of expert speakers, but this is usually after they have decided to run such courses and have "sold" them to students. The Metropolitan Police Service has in the past worked closely with Kings College on the development of an MSc course, but this predates the current expansion in numbers of forensic science degree courses.

3. A number of bodies have such responsibility:

— The ACPO Forensic Science Sub-Committee (FSSC) is the authoritative body on behalf of ACPO for ensuring that national guidance and policy is maintained. The Sub-Committee encompasses a series of thematic portfolio groups and National Boards, and sponsors and maintains, for example, the DNA Good Practice Guide in conjunction with the National DNA Database Board.

— The National DNA Database Board, (NDNADB) chaired by the ACPO Forensic Science portfolio holder, has overall authority and responsibility for police practice and policy in relation to DNA matters, and issues policy directions and guidance in liaison with FSSC.

— The National Fingerprint Board (NFB), chaired by ACPO and set up in 2003 under the auspices of the FSSC, has overall authority and responsibility for police practice and policy in relation to Fingerprint matters, and is now beginning to issue policy directions and guidance.

— The Crime Scene Management Board, set up in 2004, chaired by ACPO, will have similar authority in relation to crime scene preservation and management.

— Various bodies outside ACPO also have a distinct role to play;

— Centrex, in liaison with the above Boards and FSSC, has responsibility for the overall design and accreditation of training to meet force requirements.

— The National Centre for Policing Excellence (NCPE) under the auspices of Centrex has authority under the Police Reform Act to issue Doctrine, Codes of Practice, and Guidance on policing matters. The FSSC has for some time been in negotiation with NCPE with a view to producing a Physical Evidence Doctrine which encompasses all matters forensic. The project is still in discussion and has yet to fully commence.

— The Police Standards Unit has a specific role to improve performance within the police service. FSSC has co-operated with PSU on a number of significant pieces of work, notably arising from the DNA Expansion Programme, which have been designed to improve processes around the country. Over the last two years FSSC, through Derbyshire Constabulary, has also been working closely with PSU to produce and roll out to the police service a diagnostic tool for the improvement of forensic processes and timeliness, using proven commercially available simulation software.

— Phases 1 and 2 of a 3-phase programme have been completed and the resulting tool, known as "SWIM", the "Scientific Work Improvement Model", has recently been made available to all forces. Early results are encouraging. Phase 3 is due for completion in Spring 2005.

— HM Inspectorate of Constabulary has a further and distinct role in ensuring through its Thematic, Baseline and BCU inspection programmes that forces are using forensic science effectively, applying the most up-to-date techniques and processes, and their thematic Inspection Reports, "Under the Microscope" and "Under the Microscope Revisited" have formed the basis for much of the FSSC's strategic approach and thinking during the last three years.

— It is anticipated that the newly-proposed National Policing Improvement Agency (NPIA) will take on responsibility for ensuring that nationally agreed good practice on some policing issues is implemented in all forces.

— Clearly despite recent improvements, and some rationalisation by the FSSC, this is still a somewhat confused picture with agencies having overlapping responsibilities. The forensic science field encompasses a wide range of disciplines which have not always in the past related closely to each other. Further rationalisation is needed. As an example, prior to 2003, ACPO responsibility for fingerprint policy was shared between three groups,

— the National Fingerprint Conference (the Fingerprint Experts' conference),

— the Non-numerical Standard Working Group (a group set up to review the 16-points of comparison evidential standard which was formerly used to decide whether fingerprint evidence could be used in court), and

— the IDENT1 Board (The national project board overseeing the implementation of the replacement Automated Fingerprint Identification System, known as IDENT1).

This led to uncertainty over leadership, an unclear strategy, and confusion over where authority lay. The creation of the NFB has clarified the situation, focused the work and enabled rapid progress to be made.

ACPO has sought to be inclusive in its approach to the various bodies, engaging them in our thinking and becoming engaged in projects suggested by them. Relationships are generally good and co-operative, and much progress has been made. However, we believe there will be a need in future to rationalise the roles of HMIC, PSU, NCPE and the NPIA, so that strategic direction is clear and controlled, and duplication and wasted effort is avoided.

4. The HMIC review "Under the Microscope" (2000) set out overall guidance in relation to the training of specialist and non-specialist staff (recommendations 14–16). The service has responded to the need to keep patrol officers updated. Material delivered to basic recruits has recently been revised. The effectiveness and consistency of delivery was audited by the Police Standards Unit in during 2003–04.

An interactive training package "Think Forensic" has been the cornerstone of awareness provision for officers outside the probationary period. The package is currently being re-written under the leadership of the Forensic Science Service. The scale of the problem should not be underestimated. With all the other training that police officers and staff need and the turnover we experience, we need novel and different means of raising awareness and increasing knowledge, which minimise time lost from front line policing duties.

5. We believe that the situation has improved significantly since "Under the Microscope" was published, but we are not complacent. FSSC has ensured that Regional Groups have an active programme of work and are supplied with current information as to national developments. It is true to say that, due to competing demands, it has sometimes proved difficult to achieve the required level of ACPO involvement at regional level, but each ACPO regional group does now have an ACPO Chair. We anticipate that the developing ACPO Forensic Procurement Strategy engender more regional collaboration and will thus raise the profile of forensic science at regional and force level.

6. In relation to police training in forensic science, we estimate the proportion of provision as follows:

Internal	> 90%
FSS	< 5%
Private Sector	< 5%

We tend to use forensic science providers on demand and have usually found that all forensic science providers are keen to provide training without too much emphasis on generating income.

7. There is no evidence of a current drift away from the two national training centres. The Metropolitan Police requirement easily justifies the Crime Academy resource. The Centrex facility at Harperley Hall, Durham is currently subject of a Gateway review to assess the viability of site acquisition. This proposal is founded upon existing success and future anticipated need. ACPO supports the retention of this facility. The maintenance of consistent and high standards across the service is crucial both to public confidence and inter-operability. In terms of training style, we are certainly moving away from extended formal training. However, this is not a reflection on the quality of the training but more a move to a competency based approach, and encouraging professional development. The days of sending someone on a 12-week course that sets them up for life are long gone. In future we will encourage training and development that improves performance and the contribution of forensic services.

8. It is difficult to respond with any degree of accuracy to this question. Many forces and individual members of staff have contacts and maintain liaison with academic establishments, individual academics, and private sector groups, and all these groups frequently seek police service support for their research. We anticipate, and hope, that the developing Home Office Police Science and Technology Strategy will address this issue in the future.

9. ACPO has played a full part in the development of the Home Office Police Science and Technology Strategy. The basis of this Strategy is a desire to identify current and future scientific and technological capabilities required by the police service, to enable the service to counter current and emerging criminal threats arising from the use of technological or other means, and to align research and development efforts towards delivering these, within the resources available. A full list of capabilities, endorsed by ACPO, can be found within the document. ACPO R&D Committee involves itself in decision-making by various awarding bodies and conducts regular surveys across the various ACPO Business Areas to identify new requirements. In my response to the uncorrected transcript of the Committee's hearing on 26 January, I indicated that on reflection I felt I had given an inaccurate response to a question on ACPO's relationship to the EPSRC. After carrying out further enquiries, I am now able to say that ACPO is indeed consulted by the EPSRC on research proposals relevant to policing, and provides a professional opinion to assist the Council in its deliberations when making awards. We feel, however, that there is much room for improvement in the deployment of research and development funding towards forensic science, and that the proper vehicle for this should be the Home Office Police Science and Technology Strategy Steering Group.

10. There is clearly an issue about accessing experts who are up to date in the rapidly moving areas of digital forensics. The cost and resource implications of computer and mobile telephone analysis, for example, are already significant and increasing rapidly, and need to be addressed. The provisions of the Police Reform Act which enable direct recruitment of specialist investigators will assist in this.

11. We would welcome an open system where professionals within the investigative process and criminal justice process; Senior Investigating Officers, Prosecutors, Counsel and Judges, or even members of the public, can report concerns to some central point. There would then need to be a process for validating the concerns in quick time, a mechanism for suspension from expert work if necessary, and a risk assessment as to current and previous cases. The CRFP could provide such a system, but it would need to be in partnership with law enforcement agencies, the legal profession and the judiciary, and would probably be most effective if CRFP registration was mandatory.

12. We were followed in the session on 26 January by a group of eminent forensic scientists, and Professor Black suggested during her evidence that there was often competition between defence and prosecution to secure the services of the best "expert witnesses". This observation, with which we agree, clearly demonstrates that some experts are perceived to have more credibility and are more persuasive than others. It is also true, of course, that some are more experienced, skilled and able than others. However, it is widely believed by police officers that whatever one expert says, it is usually possible to find another expert who will disagree and often present an equally plausible explanation for a particular piece of evidence. Commonly used forensic scientific techniques are generally accepted as sound science and any dispute around forensic evidence almost invariably centres on interpretation rather than the science itself. In an adversarial system it is critical to each side's success to exploit differences of interpretation or opinion, and quite proper that they do so. Unless we are to change this system totally, little can be done beyond ensuring that individual experts are independently assessed as competent and accredited as such by bodies such as the CRFP.

It may simply be a case of more rigorous use of the provisions for pre-trial review by Judges, in an attempt to limit areas of challenge to the minimum. Thereafter, ensuring that juries are clearly advised of the soundness of the scientific techniques themselves would be helpful in preserving the credibility of the science.

13. To a large extent we are at the mercy of the criminal justice system as we have no agreed method of getting new techniques validated. In the USA "Freye" and "Daubert" hearings are an interesting development in seeking to establish that forensic evidence is soundly based before it is used in active cases. The police service has hitherto relied upon the advice of the Chief Executive or Chief Scientist of the Forensic Science Service to provide advice as to the reliability of forensic techniques. Although this advice has proven to be consistently reliable, our view is that when the FSS moves into private sector classification and operates in a competitive market, for commercial reasons it will no longer be appropriate to seek or receive advice in this way, and there will be commercial sensitivities in any event. There will continue to be a need for government and the police service to have access to independent and unbiased advice from a body which has no commercial interest in any technique in question. We have suggested the creation of a "Forensic Regulator" to perform this important role, although we see the possibility that the NDNAD Custodian role, about to be separated from the FSS, could be extended to encompass this, given the appropriate level of resources. It is of critical importance that plausible "quack" techniques and individuals are weeded out of the system before their deployment results in miscarriages of justice.

14. There are opportunities for all forensic science providers to provide forensic intelligence. A more diverse and increased number of forensic science providers may increase the range of information available to police forces. However, it is important the production of forensic intelligence is driven by police requirements, that this data is managed by the police service and remains the property of the police service.

15. We have been undertaking work on forensic procurement for some time. We held a national seminar in October 2004, at which all forces attended and endorsed our proposed approach. As a result, the National Police Forensic Procurement Steering Group has recently been implemented. This group, chaired by ACPO, including Home Office and APA membership, is working to achieve a managed transition from the current procurement situation to the "post-FSS transition" market place. Forensic procurement within the police service is currently undertaken in a variety of ways, some of which are contractual, whilst others are simply based on an historical relationship with FSS, and are not legally enforceable. We intend in the first instance to encourage and enable forces receiving services from FSS to convert existing SLA-type arrangements into contractual relationships with the FSS, followed later by a structured, nationally organised schedule of tendering exercises. This will help stabilise the FSS as it transforms into a GovCo, it being critical, in our view, to ensure that the transition of the FSS does not result in a rapid uncontrolled decline in its market share, as this will present problems in terms of overall supply of services, and also potentially create a market for forensic scientists, rather than forensic science. It will also ensure that forces do not simply all rush to tender at the same time, thereby creating a huge drain on resources for the providers, fostering unhealthy competition between forces for priority treatment, and potentially discouraging smaller providers from bidding for work.

We have done, and continue to do, substantial work to identify and improve the specification of user requirements so that contract specification is improved, and we will create a procurement toolkit, with standard contract terms and conditions for use by forces, to ensure a uniform approach which underpins forensic quality standards. Our intention is, where possible, to specify a range of standard products and to procure through collaborative arrangements, probably based on ACPO regions, but where bulk automated services are concerned, for example, these will probably be procured in larger volumes through larger consortia.

16. The response to Question 15, above, deals with this to some extent. We believe that a properly controlled procurement process will go a considerable way towards controlling the trend in prices, and at least in the early days of the new market, price will be a key determinant of success for providers. We do not, at present, see the need to consider "capping" prices, as this might be seen as an incentive for providers to push up towards the cap, and thereby act as a "price umbrella", when the desire from ACPO is to push prices down. We do, however, believe that overall trends need to be carefully monitored, perhaps, as we have previously suggested, by the Custodian or Forensic Regulator, and reviewed when the market has been in operation for some time and experience of price trends has grown. It is unlikely, given the financial constraints in which the police service is operating, that substantial new money will be found to meet increased costs or volumes of forensic work. Significant increases in prices will therefore increase the pressure from forces for the development of hand-held technology such as Lab-on-a-chip, and encourage forces to in-source more work, ultimately resulting in less work being tendered to suppliers. It is therefore in suppliers' interests to focus on low-cost, high quality, timely service delivery.

March 2005

APPENDIX 31

Supplementary Evidence from the Home Office

Supplementary Questions posed by the Committee further to the Ministerial evidence session on 9 February.

1. *What has to happen for the FSS to become a GovCo on the target date (1 July 2005)? What precisely does the Home Office need to do during this period?*

The Home Office, working with FSS management and other stakeholders, needs to incorporate the new company and develop its constitution, addressing:

— Corporate governance for the new company.

— Staff transfer and pension arrangements.

— Business planning.

— Commercial strategy.

— Initial capitalisation, financing and performance targets.

— Contractual arrangements for the FS continued operational role in respect of NDNAD.

It must also revoke the Forensic Science Trading Fund Order 1998.

2. *Caroline Flint said in oral evidence: "GovCo gives an opportunity for the FSS to have far clearer and tighter contractual arrangements with their customers". Why is this the case and what specific changes can be expected in these contractual arrangements once the FSS becomes a GovCo? [Q 542]*

As an arms length Government owned company, subject to normal commercial principles, the FSS will have a separate legal personality to the Home Office and any other central government clients. This means that its work for central government will be subject to legally enforceable contracts with a proper level of remuneration for the service it provides.

As far as other clients are concerned, the FSS will move from a series of Service Level Agreements and Letters of Understanding to enforceable contracts, with a clear basis for remuneration in respect of the performance it achieves.

3. *What specific criteria will be used to evaluate whether GovCo has been a success and when will this evaluation be made?*

Typical measures for evaluating the success of a company of this type include:

— The stability of the business going forward.

— Growth in the value of the business.

— The company meeting its financial targets.

— Stability of supply of forensic services for CJS clients.

— We shall be developing specific targets for the FSS over the next few months as we settle the governance framework.

4. *Caroline Flint stated: "We will be setting conditions about any move to PPP that would involve that sort of private investment in the service". What sort of private investment is being referred to here? [Q 549]*

The potential for private sector investment could range from development capital to a partnership with a company that brings additional skills and expertise eg in logistics.

5. *To what extent is the success of the FSS as a GovCo or PPP dependent on increased demand for forensic services?*

The key criterion in this respect will be to provide the forensic science services and products that most effectively contribute to the detection and prevention of crime, in a way that optimises value for money.

6. *Caroline Flint said that discussions were taking place with ACPO and the APA to "come up with the best model" for a regulator. What models are being considered and when is a decision likely to be made about the form of regulation? [Q 561]*

See Annex A.

7. *Does the Home Office foresee an international market in forensic services whereby the FSS and the private sector suppliers in the UK compete with suppliers overseas for business in the UK and in other countries? Are there any barriers to the development of this global market?*

Under the Government Procurement Agreement to which the UK is a signatory, through its membership of the World Trade Organisation, the UK forensic science market, like that in other GPA countries, is open to organisations based in any of those countries.

The FSS has a record of providing forensic science services and assistance to a number of countries across the Globe.

In order to build on this the FSS will require development capital for business ventures as well as for research and development. In addition, it is likely to need business partners with local knowledge or a presence in target countries. Consideration will also need to be given to whether business risks from such overseas ventures need to be ring-fenced to limit the FSS's exposure in a way that such activities do not result in unacceptable risks to its UK forensic services and products.

8. *Des the Home Office guarantee that the funding for the DNA Expansion Programme will not be withdrawn in the foreseeable future?*

In Hazel Blears Statement on Provisional Police Funding (grant allocations for England and Wales 2004–05, *Hansard* 19 November 2003: Column 31WS), commitment was made under the National Policing Plan 04–07 to continue funding from the DNA Expansion Programme. In Dec 2004 the Ministerial Statement for Police Funding in 2005–06 (*Hansard* 2 Dec 2004: Column 53WS) noted ongoing support for the DNA Expansion Programme and its successor programme, the Forensic Integration Strategy (FIS). FIS is planned from April 2005 to March 2008 and is referred to in the National Policing Plan, the a Home Office Strategic Plan 2004–08 and the Police Reform White Paper.

9. *Is the Home Office satisfied with the current arrangements for the national firearms database? What improvements, if any, are planned for that database in the future?*

Yes. There are no immediate plans to alter the existing arrangements.

10. *What discussions has the Home Office had with colleagues at DfES regarding the quality of forensic science undergraduate courses?*

The Home Office has made no approach to colleagues, nor has that Department sought Home Office views on the quality of forensic science courses.

11. *Tim Wilson said in oral evidence: "We are also establishing a database to try and make sure we know where the research activity is going on". What information does this database contain, what is the purpose of the database and what stage of development is the database at? [Q 603]*

The Police Technology Database (PTD) is a tripartite initiative, backed by the Home Office, ACPO and APA as members of the Police S&T Strategy Group. It contains information about the science and technology initiatives being conducted by the 43 forces in England and Wales as well as data on crime and policing projects being carried out by the Home Office.

The main objective of the database is to provide a central information resource for forces. Hosted on the Criminal Justice Extranet (CJX) it allows all forces to have access and share information in a secure environment, providing an insight into developments across the service and assisting in the elimination of duplication.

Initial data collection has begun and we have detailed responses from 19 forces. In addition, it includes information on all Home Office policing related projects. Currently available as a demonstration system, forces will be able to input directly in the second phase of development.

12. *Apart from developing the database referred to in question 11 and the Police Science and Technology Strategy, what is the Home Office doing to accelerate the development of key forensic technologies?*

The Home Office has developed the Forensic Integration Strategy (FIS) to provide greater strategic support to the police service in its use of forensic science. FIS is a workstream of the Police Science and Technology Strategy. It addresses not only the use of new and existing technologies, but the managerial, procedural and working practice issues associated with maximising the value of government investment and efficiency in the CJS. Development of new forensic technologies, and enhancements to existing ones, will be supported through the same review and prioritisation processes adopted by the Police S&T Strategy.

13. *What discussions has the Home Office had with colleagues in other departments regarding the need for adequate training of lawyers and judges in the understanding and presentation of forensic evidence?*

There have been discussions between the FSS and CPS with regard to training for CPS lawyers. See A15.

14. *What mechanisms exist to enable expert witnesses (eg from the FSS) and the police to give feedback on the ability of lawyers and judges to handle forensic evidence?*

No formal mechanism exists, although from time to time scientists do report back on their courtroom experiences.

15. *What action has the Home Office taken to promote links between the FSS and the judiciary, Bar Council and Crown Prosecution Service?*

All judges are provided with training on forensic science at Criminal Continuation Seminars, including a session on developments in forensic science delivered by the FSS. The scope for further linkage via the Judicial Studies Board is currently being pursued by FSS.

There are no formal links with the Bar Council, although FSS publish a lawyers guide to DNA.

Work with the CPS has resulted in the development of a National Tripartite Protocol, agreed between CPS, ACPO and FSS which sets out how the forensic requirement is identified in each case, and how that is translated into the examination strategy and timeliness requirements. The Protocol supports current CJS reforms including statutory charging.

Work is overseen by a Tripartite Steering Group led by FSS, out of which is being developed a training package for CPS lawyers.

16. *Who should be responsible for training forensic scientists how to present evidence in court?*

Responsibility for all training should rest with the employer.

17. *Does the Home Office see the need for scrutiny of the presentation and use of forensic evidence on court? Who should have responsibility for this?*

The Prosecution Team DNA Guidance was published July 2004. This guidance also "launched" as national CPS policy staged reporting, although initially it is restricted to. cases involving DNA. In the mean time, but on an area basis, Crown Prosecutors are being encouraged to introduce staged reporting in other forensic areas, that is; fingerprints. The FSS are currently working closely with CPS conducting six pilots looking at staged reporting in cases involving drugs and other analysis.

Staged reporting means the Crown will rely on an abbreviated statement from the forensic science provider where the contents are not in issue; there will then be no further statement required from the scientist unless a not guilty plea is entered and issues identified by the parties [— in particular defence under para 3.2 of CCMF, the new CPR and ss33—40, CJA 2003,] when implemented in April 2005.

Only those latter cases will go on to involve full evidential statements from the scientists. [NB the implementation of s114 and s127 of CJA (hearsay) in April will also impact on this.]

Simultaneously the CPS Disclosure Project is looking very closely at the issue of expert evidence, not just that of forensic scientists. The Disclosure Project Team has held discussions with CRFP amongst others in the course of their work. This work is likely to hasten the establishment of an "industry" standard for giving oral evidence that is disseminated as good practice.

The HO welcomes and supports the above reforms being taken forward by the CPS and the way that this is likely to result in increased cohesion within the forensic provider community around improvements in effective and efficient presentation in court. Officials will continue to co-operate with colleagues in the CPS and the Department awaits with interest the emerging conclusions of the Disclosure Project.

EXPERT EVIDENCE

A number of issues related to the provision and use of expert evidence in court are already being addressed. The nature of expert evidence and its application within the Criminal Justice System means that this is not a single issue but a range of distinct but interrelated issued. In each case the organisation responsible would be that with most direct interest in the issue.

Issues already under consideration include:

— The rules of procedure which apply to the use of expert evidence in court are being addressed by the Criminal Procedures Rules Committee and a number of significant changes will be introduced in April 2005.

— The National Centre for Policing Excellence is developing guidance on the use of people with expertise.

— The Crown Prosecution Service has established a project to ensure disclosure requirements are clearly defined to, and met by, expert witnesses.

— The Home Office has programmes of work dealing with the provision of forensic pathology services and with the wider issue of expert witness quality.

A group created by the Office for Criminal Justice Reform ensures all parties are aware of other projects underway. This extends to work being taken forward outside the CJS. Including, for example:

— Work by the General Medical Council on guidance for medical experts.

— Work by the Chief Medical Officer on medical expert witnesses.

— Work in the family and civil court systems.

— The work of the Legal Services Commission.

— Projects undertaken by professional and learned bodies

18. *What input has the Science Policy Unit had into the development of training for judges and magistrates by the Judicial Studies Board?*

SPU provides no direct input. However, the Home Office is represented on the Magisterial and Criminal Committees of the Judicial Studies Board (JSB) to whom it alerts changes in legislation, flagging up any areas where it is considered there might be a training need. It is for JSB to decide how that training should be provided and by whom.

19. *How are the Home Office arrangements for forensic pathologists changing? In future, will the same standards currently applied to forensic scientists be applied to forensic pathologists (eg for training and peer review of reports)?*

New medical standards for training in forensic pathology have been introduced by the Royal College of Pathologists. These have been incorporated by the Home Office into new criteria for registration with the Home Office ("Home Office List"). In addition, new standards for training in aspects of the criminal justice system are being introduced by the Home Office and will apply to all new registrants. It is envisaged that these latter standards will be broadly comparable with those currently applied to forensic scientists.

Peer review of critical conclusions in forensic pathology reports is a fundamental part of the new quality system currently being introduced by the Home Office. It will reflect the code of practice (done with the mark up of transcripts for forensic pathologists) that has been sponsored by the Home Office and recently published in conjunction with the Royal College of Pathologists. Peer review will be facilitated and monitored by the new ITC system for forensic pathologists, which should go live in April 2005 as part of the CJX (Criminal Justice Extranet).

February 2005

Annex A

QUALITY REGULATION IN FORENSIC SCIENCE

Forensic science is one of the key resources of the Criminal Justice System. If this position is to be maintained, and the public confidence in the system maintained the quality of the information and evidence provided to the CJS must be of an acceptable quality.

What is an acceptable quality depends on a number of factors including the evidence type, the offence type and the purpose to which the information or evidence is to be put.

In a commercial market, quality is a matter properly dealt with as part of the purchasing decision. However, there is an issue with whether 43 separate police forces could efficiently set quality standards for the range of services provided by any supplier. It would also place a substantial burden on any supplier to have to tender for and then provide services to a large number of different quality standards.

The current market in forensic science within England and Wales is dominated by three suppliers. The Forensic Science Service (an executive agency of the Home Office) is by far the largest single provider. The other two organisations, LGC Ltd and Forensic Alliance Ltd, either have a history as part of the public sector or senior staff from that background. As a consequence there is what may be described as a public service ethos. There is a strong emphasis on the quality of the service provided to the CJS. This is, of course, entirely consistent with the reputational risks that would materialise for forensic science providers to the CJS were they not to maintain the professional standards and integrity of their services and, hence, is wholly aligned to their commercial interests.

The further commercialisation of the forensic science market, especially with untested new entrants, could, however, change this position.

It is therefore important that independent safeguards are put in place to ensure the quality of forensic science provided to the Criminal Justice System is of an acceptable quality. Moreover, this is a common objective for customers, those dependant on the results of commissioned work (eg other members of the CJS, individuals and the defence) and providers.

The model of regulation under consideration involves the creation of a single quality assurance regulator (building on the experiences of the Custodian of the National DNA Database) accrediting suppliers who wish to provide services to the police and, by arrangement, other entities within the CJS. The accreditation would be granted at the corporate level but the accreditation process would be based on appropriate quality standards applying to:

— The corporate body;

— The products and services provided; and

— The individuals responsible for the provision of service.

The standards in relation to the products/services and the individual practitioner would not be enforced directly by the regulator but via the corporate body. It would be a requirement of accreditation that the corporate body has processes in place which ensure the relevant standards are met in relation to products/services and individuals.

Clearly a single regulator would not, as an entity, be in a position to set and assess standards across the range of specialists fields employed. The Regulator would have to work in association with a range of individuals and organisations to set the standards. These would include for example:

— ACPO.

— Crown Prosecution Service.

— The main suppliers.

— The Forensic Science Society.

— The Council for the Regulation of Forensic Practitioners.

— Learned and Professional bodies in the appropriate fields.

— Academic institutions.

The bodies involved in any specific decision being based on the nature of the standards being set and the expertise required.

These standards would create a minimum standard. It would be open to police forces to require higher standards—perhaps for specific areas of work.

It is envisaged that with the exception of highly specialised services, some of which for instance may only be available from abroad, police forces would only procure services from those organisations which were accredited with the Regulator.

The creation of the position of regulator may also provide a focus for work to improve the provision of forensic science services to the Criminal Justice System. There could be opportunities to work with other parties in the CJS to ensure common understanding of the requirements placed on forensic scientists, to assist the development of best practice and to provide advice on the robustness of new or developing techniques. In doing so the enhanced quality could apply beyond the suppliers accredited.

The setting of standards and clarification of other requirements would stimulate and inform R&D.

SPU

February 2005

Annex B

FORENSIC INTEGRATION STRATEGY: PROGRESS REPORT

This paper outlines the current stage of thinking on the development of the Forensic Integration Strategy. As agreed at the last Police Science and Technology Strategy Group meeting, this paper provides an outline of the work streams and key development issues that the strategy seeks to address under the management of the DNA Expansion Programme Board which has agreed the content of this report.

1. INTEGRATION: A VISION OF FORENSIC EXCELLENCE

The strategic vision of the Forensic Integration Strategy agreed with ACPO is to ensure:

The optimal use of forensic science and technology to reduce crime, bring more offenders to justice and increase public confidence.

In addition to being a major driver for increasing detections and deterring offenders, it will be a catalyst for modernisation by enhancing professionalism, changing workforce practices and focusing management to maximise the impact of forensic work on intelligence led-policing. In order to achieve this aim, three key operational objectives can be clearly identified;

— Deliver more, faster, and better support and intelligence thus contributing to an increase in detections, while achieving substantial (real) savings in unit cost.

— Standardise and optimise the techniques and processes in a manner that results in benefits realised for the entire CJS.

— Support and learn from International colleagues to ensure that domestic investments in forensic capacity and capability gain added value from effective international co-operation, and represent or reflect international good practice.

2. CONTINUAL DEVELOPMENT

There has been a great deal of extremely successful work in developing the processes and scientific techniques that are currently employed by the police in the fight against crime.

While the foundations for success are in place—fingerprints, DNA, other physical evidence types, police processes and resources, forensic service providers—there is still substantial scope for improvement. A range of key issues and actions that need to be addressed through development of implementation plans for the strategy are being developed. These include:

— More usable physical evidence needs to be recovered.

— More offenders need to be identified and linked conclusively to their crimes.

— Diversity to reflect different operational requirements of "similar force" groupings must be balanced by standardisation of processes, and compliance with recognised effective practice.

— New technologies and expensive national developments need an invest-to-save approach, managed to get quick wins and reduce long-term costs (for example, providing wider access to Livescan terminals or contractualisation (eg the storage, retreival and logistical arrangements for forensic evidence/ DNA samples)). Some new developments (eg improved scene material recovery) will need increased investment before savings can be shown.

— Wider analysis of available information and collation of current research evidence should be co-ordinated to maximise the benefits of available resources, where resource and time savings could be made and extend process efficiencies through the entire Criminal Justice System. For example the average cost of the police investigation of a homicide is £11,000, but the aggregate CJS and societal cost is £1.1 million.

3. CO-ORDINATION OF WORKSTREAMS

The overall structure of the FIS is illustrated diagrammatically below:

From DNA Expansion Programme to Forensic Integration Strategy; Genesis and Development

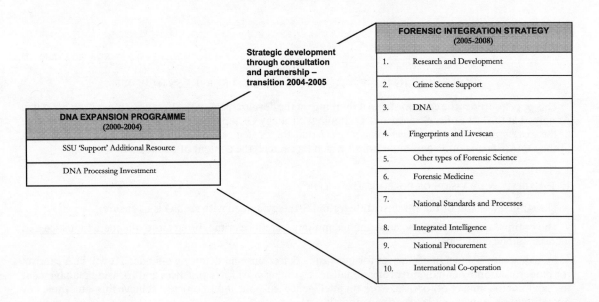

4. SMARTER WAYS OF WORKING

The approach being developed to taking this forward within SPU is to manage the transition from DNA Expansion to FIS within the CRCSG reorganisation staff profile (approximately a 30% reduction in staff numbers by 2006–07). In any case, even in different circumstances, a FIS Development Group would never have sufficient resources to take forward all of what needs to be done. Moreover, it is essential not to duplicate work already being taken forward by other organisations or groups. Thus, there is a significant role within FIS of ensuring effective communication and co-ordination of work already underway, or clearly the responsibility of the various stakeholders, in order to ensure a ground-up approach to the development of forensic science.

The principles for developing this smarter way of working will include:

(a) Communication and co-ordination to ensure the alignment of the work of different groups and organisations that have an interest in or will have an impact on FIS.

(b) Efficient stakeholder representation through the minimal use of additional Home Office boards:

(i) We are discussing with ACPO the merger of the DNA Expansion Programme Board and NDNAD Strategic Board to manage DNA delivery issues. This would, at a conservative estimate, save 36 person days a year at ACPO rank and grade 7 to SCS grades.

(ii) The opportunity also exists to merge the NDNAD Strategic Board's DNA Operations Group and the DNA Expansion Programme Board's Monitoring and Evaluation Group. This would in addition to significant manpower savings provide a means for ensuring that data analysis focuses on operational requirements in order to develop best practice.

(iii) Non-NDNAD work and overall co-ordination of FIS might be managed through the ACPO Forensics Committee.

(iv) Within the Home Office in internal Project Management Board would be responsible for risk and audit management, together with resource allocation management.

(c) Operationally driven programme management: the wider operational input from (b) as well as ensuring greater efficiency in the use of senior staff time and the avoidance of duplication, will ensure that the programme makes the best possible use of operational knowledge, experience and judgement.

5. Scope of Work and Prioritisation

Work is currently being undertaken to identify what is already being progressed by other groups and organisations; to identify priorities for continual FIS development, chiefly on the basis of operational need and where the lessons/skills of the DNA Expansion Programme are most likely to add value; and the key issues that need to be addressed within each workstream.

Two emerging priorities where there may be political or economic opportunities exist to deliver benefits from FIS are:

(a) Central pump-priming to ensure livescan availability in all custody suites by the end of 2005–06, thus maximising the benefits of the new fingerprint powers obtained by the CJA 2003, with long term gains in both cost and quality of fingerprint intelligence.

(b) The sharing of DNA intelligence data:

(i) initially via a pilot based on unsolved sexual offences using the Interpol DNA Database and I 24/7 secure network.

(ii) Followed by a technical study to evaluate the longer term efficiency and effectiveness of the use of search engines against different types of international databases for larger DNA intelligence pooling.

The first two projects are being undertaken jointly with ACPO and PITO; the second project is also being undertaken in co-operation with the European Commission, Europol, Interpol and a number of EU Member States.

FURTHER PROGRESS REPORT

Next Police Science and Technology Strategy Group: 4 October 2004

Next Expansion Programme Board: 17 December 2004

Next Police Science and Technology Strategy Group 6 December 2004

APPENDIX 32

Supplementary Evidence from Graham Cooke, Barrister

Comments on the Evidence Presented by the CPS

1. In the first place, I will set out the main issues as I see them. Some of the differences between the CPS and me may not, in fact, need to be resolved.

2. Doheny and Adams in Cases Where Identity is the Issue

2.1 Is the wording currently used in Court by scientists called by the prosecution loyal to the Doheny approach of "random occurrence ratio"?

(The CPS say it is. I say it is not, see Paragraph 4 below.)

2.2 Whether or not it is loyal, does the wording that the scientists use commit the Prosecutor's Fallacy in any of its forms?

(I agree with the CPS that it does not.)

2.3 Does such wording tend to mislead listeners into their committing any form of the Prosecutor's or other fallacy?

(I say it does. The CPS do not accept that, their reasoning being that there is no or no sufficient evidence to that effect.

2.4 Is there a better form of wording, less likely to mislead a listener?

(I say there is. The CPS do not have a view other than saying that the wording to be used in statements and in oral evidence in court is a matter for the "scientific community", not for the CPS. I say that this attitude ignores persuasive evidence to the contrary and, further, it is an abdication of their responsibility for bringing and carrying through properly presented prosecutions.

3. Main Issues

3.1 Of all the issues, it seems to me that two are most important:

(i) Is the wording used in Court loyal to the Court of Appeal guidance in *Doheny and Adams*?

(ii) Whether it is or not, can we find a way of presenting the DNA evidence in a way that is less likely to mislead?

3.2 Of these, the second is, in my view, by far the more important.

3.3 It was concern over this issue which was the driving force for forming the informal Group in March 2004.

4. The CPS Written Evidence of 21 February 2005

4.1 The CPS deal with the first issue by saying that the current wording used in Court does comply. A transcript of the judgment in *Doheny* has been provided with highlighted passages. The CPS does not identify any specific passage that supports their view.

4.2 I say that nowhere in that transcript is there any approval or hint of approval of a wording which begins or continues along the lines:

> "If the defendant was not the source of the crime stain and it was left by an unknown man unrelated to the defendant, then the probability of obtaining matching profiles is 1 in X."

4.3 All the focus in the judgment is along the lines of "1 in X of the population" followed by an estimate of how many people in the population might have the profile (see in particular, passages starting at the bottom of page 5).

4.4 I say that self-evidently the past (since *Doheny*) and present wording used in Court does not comply with *Doheny*.

4.5 The underlying point of the Doheny approach is to make an estimate of how many people in a population might have the same profile in other words "how big is the pool of people from whom the profile might have come".

4.6 One can test this proposition by taking a hypothetical example where the DNA profiles of all residents on a closed island have been recorded. Given a DNA profile from the scene of a crime, a search of the database would show the number of people in the "pool". The frequency of the profile would not be needed.

4.7 When we have not got a complete database, we need a "frequency" to estimate how many others might have the same profile and so be in the "pool". Using that, the jury can then go on to estimate the weight of the DNA evidence combining it, of course, with the other evidence.

4.8 The CPS does not, in my view, deal with the "misleading to a listener" issue at all. Although Mr Jani was present during the first two meetings of the Group, he did not dissociate himself from the consensus view.

4.9 At the meeting in July 2004, the minutes read:

> "Mr Jani offered to take the proposed wording to a standing group comprising representatives from the Forensic Science Service, the police, and other authorities, for its comment and to report back. The group met twice a year, the next meeting being held in September or October (2004)."

4.10 Sadly, we have not had any response from the CPS and we have no knowledge of what happened at the intended meeting. The CPS does not, even now, provide any reasoned response on this most important issue.

4.11 The following (see 4.12) attended the meeting of our group in March 2004, when the issue of finding an improved version (for the disputed ID case) was on the agenda and was thoroughly discussed. A consensus emerged that there was an acceptable alternative, namely:

> "The probability that an unknown person, unrelated to the defendant, would have the same profile as him is 1 in X."

4.12 Those attending in March 2004 were:

Judge Thorpe,

Dr Bob Bramley (Scientist, Deputy Director of FSS, Custodian of the DNA database and Council member of CRFP)

Dr Ian Evett (FSS, statistician)

Dr Angela Gallop (Scientist. Forensic Alliance and Council Member of CRFP)

Roy Green Scientist, Forensic Alliance

Matthew Greenhalgh, (Scientist Orchid Biosciences Europe Ltd)

Nimesh Jani, (CPS lawyer and member of CRFP Consultative Forum)

Dr Sue Pope (Scientist, FSS; lead assessor for human contact traces CRFP)

Dr James Walker (Scientist, Laboratory of the Government Chemist)

Ms Sue Woodruffe (Scientist Forensic Alliance)

Dr Kate Home CRFP office

Mark Fenhalls, barrister of 23 Essex Street chambers

Graham Cooke, barrister

4.13 I suggest that this is an impressive membership coming to an important consensus on a better way forward. In my view, the proposed new wording is not disloyal to the spirit of the *Doheny* judgment and is a very important step forward in finding a form of words which is less likely to produce mis-understandings amongst jurors, judges, journalists, police officers, magistrates and lawyers.

4.14 Let me repeat the old and new wordings:

(i) Old wording:

"If the (crime stain) came from a person other than the defendant and unrelated to him, then the probability of obtaining matching profiles is 1 in x (say a million)."

(ii) Proposed new wording:

"The probability that an unknown person, unrelated to the defendant, would have the same profile as him is 1 in x (say million)."

4.15 In the *Doheny* judgment, it is noteworthy that in the middle of page 4, there is a reference to "the frequency ratio of the blood group" and its inclusion in the calculation of the overall (DNA and blood) random occurrence ratio. (See also middle of Page 13).

5. OTHER ASPECTS OF THE CPS EVIDENCE OF 21 FEBRUARY.

5.1 I turn to the CPS written evidence of 21 February 2005. They and I are plainly at cross-purposes. There are some matters, particularly in Paragraphs 5 and 6, which I do not address. My silence does not mean I agree with what is said, just that the points do not need to be resolved at this stage.

5.2 In Paragraph 2, we find:

"The Prosecutor's Fallacy is committed where the prosecution equate a statistical probability with the likelihood of guilt based on the statistical probability."

5.3 Although this definition is not wholly wrong, the main mischief with the Fallacy is that the listener tends to invert the "statistic" by hearing "1 in a million" as "million to one on", the issue at that stage usually being "who is the source of a crime stain", not "is he guilty by dint of the DNA evidence alone?".

(See Paragraph 5.12 below. Some of the CPS arguments depend on the wrongful use of the word "guilt" in their definition.).

5.4 In Paragraph 3, they start by saying "The current wording used by the prosecution is:"

5.5 They go on to use "above wording" (Para.4) and "current wording" (Paragraphs 5 and 6) and leave the impression that Appendix 1 represents the wording used (past or present) in Court in a trial where identity is in dispute.

5.6 They are simply wrong (see Paragraph 4.14(i) above for the wording actually used in Court).

5.7 The wording in Appendix 1 has a restricted use. I criticise it but, for the moment, this disagreement does not matter when we consider the issues in Court when identity is in dispute.

5.8 A different point arises out of CPS paragraph 7, "This cannot be defined as the prosecutor's fallacy, as, stating the very obvious, they (presumably the scientific witnesses) are not prosecutors."

5.9 In the middle of page 5 of Doheny, "Such reasoning has been commended to juries by Prosecuting Counsel, by judges and sometimes by expert witnesses. It is fallacious and it has earned the title of 'The Prosecutor's Fallacy'".

5.10 I find it difficult to respond in reasonable fashion to such an obviously fallacious proposition from the CPS. Is the CPS really saying that if one of their witnesses commits a fallacy, they are absolved of any responsibility simply because the witness is not a "prosecutor" and because the fallacy has earned the name "Prosecutor's fallacy"?

5.11 The last point I make concerns the CPS reliance on the warning in their Appendix 1. It says:

> "It follows that a match between two profiles should not, by itself be taken as conclusive evidence that the profiles relate to the same person."

5.12 That is fine as far as it goes. But a more important health warning is needed to help the jury (and others) who might think that the scientist's evidence is saying that it is "1 in a million" chance of the defendant not being the source of the crime stain or, the other way up, it is a "million to one on" that he is the source.

5.13 I set out in the Appendix below three matters that the Committee might find helpful.

5.14 Finally, I must stress that although I gave oral evidence on behalf of the Bar Council, the content of this written Note of evidence is my responsibility alone.

APPENDIX

1. The Committee has a copy of the proceedings which includes edited copies of Ian Evett's talk and of my talk on 10 April 2003 to the joint FSS, CRFP and the Expert Witness Institute Conference (my underlining added):

  (i) at the bottom of Page 57 I said:—"When on earth are the FSS going to take on board the fact that they are using an expression, however much it is theoretically correct, that produces these disastrous misunderstandings?"

  (ii) in the middle of Page 58: "All those are "frequencies" but the FSS will not talk about frequencies. They will "bash" the judges in *Doheny and Adams* who came up with "random occurrence ratio". I was in that appeal and pressed them to use frequency. I know what they mean by it, they mean "frequency". Angela (Gallop), when she introduced the subject, used frequencies. You found them all perfectly understandable, and then you don't have to have any of this "match probability" stuff. To those suitably qualified, Ian (Evett) is right. If he was addressing a jury consisting of qualified forensic scientists, he's right."

3. R V PRINGLE PRIVY COUNCIL APPEAL NO. 17 OF 2002

The following appears in Paragraph 19:

> "Let it be assumed that the evidence about the random occurrence ratio is that one person in 50,000 has a DNA profile which matches that which was obtained from the crime scene. The fact that the defendant has that profile tells us that he is one of perhaps 50,000 people who share that characteristic."

March 2005

APPENDIX 33

Supplementary Evidence from the Home Office

Thank you for the opportunity to give evidence to the Committee on 9 February about forensic science and our proposals to transform the Forensic Science Service.

As I made clear in my statement to the House on 11 January, our intention is to transform the FSS into a Government owned company (GovCo), and for that company to be a success. GovCo will be given the opportunity to prove it can deliver, but we recognise that in future it may need access to private sector capital and expertise in order to meet its full potential. That is why we have not ruled out the prospect of private sector partnering if that is judged to be critical to the longer term needs of both the organisation and the wider criminal justice system.

I would again wish to emphasise that this does not represent a change in policy, but a clear commitment to ensuring that the FSS remains at the forefront of forensic science, not only in the UK but internationally.

During the course of the hearing my officials and I undertook to provide further information on a range of related subjects:

Q551

Tim Wilson drew attention to a reference published by the NAQ about the benefits if PFI; namely, a key conclusion reported by the Select Committee on Public Accounts in its thirty-fifth Report during the session 2003–04, that "PFI is delivering greater certainty on timing and on the cost to departments of their construction projects".

Q576

In response to Robert Key I can confirm that there is no reference to DNA in the Identity Cards Bill, nor was the matter raised during its passage through the House. In short, there is no provision in the Bill enabling a DNA sample to be required.

Q604

I have also noted the concern expressed by Professor Haswell (University of Hull) that potential advancements in forensic R&D may be fettered by a lack of communication between researchers and practitioners. This is clearly fundamental to the future success of the FSS and a matter that will be tackled when we agree the capital structure for GovCo.

Q632

I also undertook to explain why it was decided not to adopt the recommendations of the House of Lords Science and Technology Committee and the Human Genetics Commission to establish an independent body with lay membership to oversee the National DNA Database (NDNAD).

The NDNAD is, in simple terms, an operational policing tool, and the NDNAD Board felt it was essential to maintain police involvement in oversight and use of the Database to provide police intelligence for the detection of crime. The Board therefore responded to the recommendations by inviting the Human Genetics Commission to nominate one of their Commissioners to sit on the Board.

Formal oversight of the use of data from the NDNAD and the samples for use in research is undertaken by the Custodian and the NDNAD Board which now includes Dr Steve Baine, a Commissioner from the HGC. The chairman of the Board has also recently approached the Central Office for Research Ethics Committees in relation to their providing a further level of independent oversight in this area.

Q632

Finally, the NDNAD Custodian has provided the following information about research requests received since the database" inception in April 1995.

From	*Real*	*Agreed*
1. External research request from universities etc.	6	1
2. Police operational requests relating to specific investigations, including familial searching.	4	2
3. Requests to assist forensic providers for R&D papers, for future use in cases not specific investigations.	11	6
4. Database improvements	1	1

February 2005

Reports from the Science and Technology Committee since 2001

Session 2004-05

First Report	The Work of the Economic and Social Research Council *(Reply HC 401)*	HC 13
Second Report	Annual Report 2004	HC 199
Third Report	Office of Science and Technology: Scrutiny Report 2004 *(Reply HC 453)*	HC 8
Fourth Report	The Medical Research Council's Review of the Future of the National Institute for Medical Research *(Reply HC 454)*	HC 6
Fifth Report	Human Reproductive Technologies and the Law	HC 7
Sixth Report	The Work of Research Councils UK	HC 219

Session 2003-04

First Report	Annual Report 2003	HC 169
Second Report	Chief Executive of the Medical Research Council: Introductory Hearing *(Reply HC 629)*	HC 55
Third Report	The Work of the Biotechnology and Biological Sciences Research Council *(Reply HC 526)*	HC 6
Fourth Report	Office of Science and Technology: Scrutiny Report 2003 *(Reply HC 588)*	HC 316
Fifth Report	*Too Little too late?* Government Investment in Nanotechnology *(Reply HC 650)*	HC 56
Sixth Report	Within REACH: the EU's new chemicals strategy *(Reply HC 895)*	HC 172
Seventh Report	Director General for Higher Education: Introductory Hearing *(Reply HC 1015)*	HC 461
Eighth Report	The Work of the Council for the Central Laboratory of the Research Councils *(Reply HC 1199)*	HC 462
Ninth Report	Director General of the Research Councils: Introductory Hearing *(Reply HC 1059)*	HC 577
Tenth Report	Scientific Publications: Free for all?	HC 399
Eleventh Report	Research Assessment Exercise: a re-assessment *(Reply HC 34, 2004-05)*	HC 586
Twelfth Report	Government support for Beagle 2 *(Reply HC 301, 2004-05)*	HC 711
Thirteenth Report	The Use of Science in UK International Development Policy *(Reply HC 235, 2004-05)*	HC 133
Fourteenth Report	Responses to the Committee's Tenth Report, Session 2003-04, Scientific Publications: Free for all? *(Reply HC 249, 2004-05)*	HC 1200

Session 2002–03

Session 2001-02

Printed in the United Kingdom by The Stationery Office Limited
3/2005   994641   19585

ISBN 0-215-02338-2

9 780215 023384